1

Paul Dayton is the author of Correcting Our Financial Miseducation: Raising the Bar for the Average

Check out articles, media clips, news, and more, at www.PaulDayton.us

SOCIALISM:

The "Gift" That Keeps On *Taking*

Paul Dayton

2024

Dedicated to my mother and my father, who I love

A popular American parable that I've heard many times, in many variations, yet have never heard at all. It is a story which is always told slightly differently each time, and one that I seemed to find around on the radio, television, and in print, when I was younger, and find less and less as I age; with a seeming cessation during the present day:

The Land of Liberty, the United States of America

A penniless man -without any personal or professional contacts in the land- has landed fresh off of the boat from his former homeland, and finds himself in a big city. Without any of the paid to fail socialism of the 20th century, this man has to survive or face extinction. On Monday, the man goes down to the baker, and in what common language the two can muster, bargains a job as the baker's assistant in exchange for one loaf of bread each day. The man found shelter where he could that night, and helped himself to a single slice of the precious bread.

Having earned his bread on Monday, the same man humbles himself before the butcher in his neighborhood on Tuesday, and is able to bargain a job as the butcher's assistant in exchange for a pound of meat. That night, the man dared not touch that meat, instead nourishing himself on a single slice of the bread.

On Wednesday, the man goes to a busy area in his city with a makeshift table, set up with his meat and bread, and sold sandwiches; thus putting a few coins of the realm into the man's pocket. After selling out his product, the man used the coin to obtain very modest lodging in a place that many of the more well-to-do in the land wished outlawed -for no reason other than because the conditions seem revolting in their *own* eyes, but which outshine homelessness to those who are actually likely to be customers of such an establishment.

On Thursday, he's back at the bakery, and on his way, as he was now in this land of liberty; imbued with the liberty to pursue any opportunity to strike a bargain in an effort to enrich one's self. Earning his meals, and slowly acquiring currency, he may in the years to come elevate himself to great heights of business ownership and innovation, or may find himself right back in this same ramshackle dwelling. His fate was in his own hands, and on that day, for the first time in his life, he truly knew what it was to be a man.

Table of Contents

Introduction: Which Class Benefits?

"...yet experience hath shewn, that even under the best forms, those entrusted with power have, in time, and by slow operations, perverted it into tyranny; and it is believed that the most effectual means of preventing this would be, to illuminate, as far as is practicable, the minds of the people at large, and more specifically to give them knowledge of these facts, which history exhibiteth, that, possessed thereby of the experience of other ages and countries, they may be enabled to know ambition under all its shapes, and prompt to exert their natural powers to defeat its purposes..."

-Thomas Jefferson, 1778, A Bill for the More General Diffusion of Knowledge (1)

Central planning, whether labeled as communism, socialism, democratic wokernism, egalitarian fascism, or any other synonymous concoction denoting abrogation-of-choice-ism, makes economic conditions worse for the masses; this will be illustrated with ample evidence throughout the entirety of this volume. These reductions in material living conditions, remuneration, and health, often occur as quickly as 2-5 years after the implementation of so-called "helpful" controls by the state over the citizenry. This diminution in the liberty of the people, having given their freedom to choose over to the state, will often and perplexingly result in an immediate sensation of positivity among the very people who have not only lost freedoms vital to the determination of their fate, but who also are most likely to be harmed the most significantly by such legislation -that is, the least-moneyed class of the citizenry. Like a chronic smoker alleviating their nicotine withdrawal with another pack of cigarettes, this element clamors for its own demise and calls it "help"; bringing themselves closer to lung disease, cancers, and a variety of other maladies while also *forcing* the others who do not share these same poor and self defeating choices to suffer the same fate.

Socialist -this world will, throughout this text, be used interchangeably with those mentioned in the above paragraph, as well as with all of their brethren- policies, while affecting to be solutions, in fact simply create new problems which are usually worse than the conditions which had prevailed prior to their implementation. A politician, particularly one of the professional variety -seeking office at all costs of principal and decency, as the person holds office for a living and wants to avoid getting a real job; real job being defined as a position whose success or failure, and sustainability, depends upon actual commerce- seeing no further than the next election, can prey upon the ignorance of the electorate by passing "help" monikered legislation which in turn creates a positive reaction in the short term for the politician. This so-called redistributive legislation has one outcome which is factually the most likely, and that is a negative one for the very people who provide the politician with the positive feedback and votes. Such positive sways upon an alarmingly large proportion of the electorate are often simply generated by headlines that such legislation has been proposed during legislative session, or mentioned in a speech. In such cases, the central planner doesn't even have to go through the trouble of enacting odious "make work" jobs, or direct handouts, in order to seduce their prey. *It is the ambition of this book to elevate the populace to such a level that will render these outcomes uncommon*; outcomes which continue incentivising the office seeking politicians to revoke freedoms from the citizenry.

The "solution" itself creates a new problem in the near future, which the politician can then "solve" with another socialist measure, in turn providing said politician with short term positive headlines on which to run for election or re-election, before the new problem arises that is a direct consequence of the previous "solution", which then provides another opportunity for a socialist "solution", and the cycle perpetuates itself for as long as it takes to wholly decimate the prosperity and liberty of the people. The now familiar contemporary axiom "let no crisis go to waste" obviously lends itself to "let no election go by without a crisis". Several crises have been shown to have been orchestrated from within, and some will be featured in this book, such as the episode in France beginning 1789, Germany in the 1930s, and the New Deal period in the 1930s USA.

Like a firefighter arriving on the scene of a building ablaze and then "helping" by tampering with the wiring of all the buildings nearby, ensuring that they'll continue to be summoned as saviors in the near future and engage in similar dereliction of duty under the guise of philanthropy, while they have an eye only on the perpetuation of their job as saviors -at all costs to their character and decency- politicians are enticed by the allure of easy access to election day success to ensure that no election goes by without a crisis. ***The purpose of this volume is to do its part in curing the ignorance of the electorate*** which enables these politicians to prey upon them, and in-so-doing to victimize the rest of us. ***This book will take no sides on matters of opinion or view, but will rather focus upon the closed questions which are treated as though they were open questions.*** This book is written in the 21st century AD, a time which, through increased attention to record keeping and retention of said records during recent centuries, along with increased access to information during the past three centuries, abounds with ample evidence of the actual outcomes of the insultingly false promises of wokernists. ***Such a large faction behave as though such ideas have never been attempted before***, and that nobody kept any record of the outcome of these attempts; that mankind is perpetually doomed to a fate of clumsily groping in the dark for answers, awash in their voluntary ignorance; behaving as though nobody could possibly know which outcomes could be expected; ***as though it were simply a matter of ideology or belief, as opposed to a matter of fact.***

It will be shown by example after example of what happens to real people, in real life, with real money, that there is one class and one class of society only which benefits from central planning: the planners, themselves. The politicians win office, and revocation of choices from the citizenry with regards to their own lives is simply the fulfillment of a campaign promise. By concentrating the power to make day to day decisions of the many into the hands of the few -the politicians and bureaucrats- in the name of helping the many, the few -the politicians and bureaucrats- are taking a gamble that the damage being done to the country as a whole will be just slight enough to allow for enough expropriation from the citizenry so that a riot is not provoked. It is via this method that these politicians are able to live quite well indeed. If politicians were systematically forced to be private citizens with real jobs in the real economy immediately after a term served in office, and perpetual office holding were illegal, this outcome might be avoided. (see part VII, Term Limits Scheme)

Like so many others, I often find myself out shopping for books secondhand and at relatively low prices, and as I pick up a book that strikes me as though it may be intended for use as a textbook, I wonder to myself for which grade level the material was intended. While noting the copyright date on the book, I mostly examine the book in search of actual proof. The books that are filled with factual data on seemingly every page -such as graphs; data tables; discussion of the breadth of evidence, including evidence which seems to counter the hypothesis or to counter the remainder of the evidence- are books that I suspect to be intended for adults. That is, advanced high school courses, or for serious collegiates or professionals. Books that are 200 pages and which contain perhaps 20-30 pieces of evidence, mostly featuring names, dates, and locations, I presume to be aimed at children. That is, high schoolers, middle schoolers, and down. *Responsible adults with competent minds demand and examine evidence* before arriving at any conclusions, while **children are spoon fed stories with little to any substance** contained therein, and accept the message of the storyteller unconditionally. I advise others to adopt this approach, and to give priority to the material which seems to be prepared for consumption by grownups. When I examine many books on the shelves of bookstores, they are clearly aimed at children, as they are incredibly light on substance, while their stories are wholly disproven by the facts contained in adult material. Those who wish to be treated like adults should behave accordingly when it comes to matters that impact others.

There are three themes which the reader will notice run throughout all of history, and which will be recurrent throughout this book:

The Fallacy of the Lamp

One of the incredibly successful prevailing popular fictions apropos of socialism, though insultingly false, is what can be described as the fallacy of the lamp. This moniker draws from fables which tell of a person rubbing a magic lamp and having their wishes granted. *Many are suffering under the delusion* that all of the power will be concentrated into the hands of the few by decree, and *that all of this concentrated power will serve themselves, personally.* Their own myopia masquerading as charitability. The United States is a nation which in 2020 had a population of 330 million people, and the world in that same year had an estimated population of approximately 7 billion. *When hundreds of millions, or billions, of people each make their own individual, self-serving, wishes, they are bound to conflict with and to contradict each other ceaselessly.* The farmers wish for sun and rain, while petty burglars wish for darkness and dry conditions in order to provide cover for their movements. In the end, the concentration of power into the hands of the few by decree, a necessity of wokernism, only grants the wishes of those holding power in the government. All others have no rights other than to obey the whims and dictates of the bureaucrats, their wish for socialism having been granted, and now results in eternal privation of future wish granting; a classic example of another old fable, involving "a pact with the devil".

Chain the Beast, Unchain the Citizenry

The state or the government will be referred to, throughout this tome, as the Beast -the word will be capitalized throughout, to distinguish this use of the word from other uses. The state can be very powerful, indeed. A small, restricted, government which is kept in its proper place, can show tremendous strength once one of its shackles has been removed and it has been summoned into action. Such an exhibition can be tempting for the public and politicians alike. The temptation for politicians to become more powerful is self-explanatory, and will always be the case. *It is the public's clamor for further liberation of the Beast, that this book aims to quell.* Imagine an 8,000 pound gorilla with 3 limbs chained to a wall inside of a building, its free arm turning a crank which generates and stores electricity -such as the stationary bike at the power reservoir which have been available to tourists at the hydroelectric plant near Niagara Falls, NY, for example. The beast, with a single arm, produces more electricity in 4 hours than 1,000 strong humans, laboring for 12 hours a piece, can produce in a month. To many come the thought that "if we can get *this* out of it with one arm, imagine how beneficial it would be to us to free *all* of its limbs!". That such a practice is a mistake becomes clear once the 8,000 pound gorilla is wholly unchained, as *the roles of master and servant are inverted. The Beast no longer serves the people, the people serve the Beast*; and re-shackling the Beast is quite a tall order once its gotten access to weapons and culled allies with empty promises of power for themselves, revenge upon their enemies, satiation of jealousies over those who have done more with their lives, material remuneration, and threats regarding their fate if they refuse alliance. This book shows *the importance of speaking the language of evidence* in the face of lavish promises, laced with ambiguities regarding the plan to fulfill those promises, while all known evidence shows the promised outcomes to be wholly unlikely, given the inputs. Take the shackles off of the citizens, and place them back on to the Beast.

The Tightening, or Loosening, of the Beast's Grip Upon the Windpipe of the National Economy

A recurring theme of history, which will be illustrated factually throughout this text, is the phenomenon of what could be described as the Beast tightening or loosening its grip on the windpipe of the populace. This tightening or loosening is a reflection of what we today call taxation and regulation. The tighter that the Beast -the state- squeezes, the more that economic growth is restricted, and the less that money and prosperity make their way to the least-moneyed; the more relaxed the Beast's grip becomes, the more the economic activity flows freely, enabling growth and innovation, and providing the best outcomes to those who begin in the least-moneyed portion of the society.

Contemporary readers will be well advised to be wary of the word "believe" when used by politicians, or those outside of office who are proponents of one political issue or another. The term believe is frequently utilized by shysters during their platitudes in way in which a translation, or re-statement of their sentence for greater clarity, would reveal that the word as used to be short for "make-believe", a synonym for "pretend"; as opposed to I won't "believe" you until you prove it to me by speaking the language of evidence, and proving the statement to be true or untrue. This use of double entendre will also be referred to when warning of the historical use of the word "liberal" in a political context. As described in another book (2) the Intellectual Lower Class -or ILC- the problem class and voluntary underbelly of society, utilize deflector shield words in their cupidity to evade not only reality, but the *inclusion* of facts and evidence into any attempt to resolve important questions. One example of such behavior is the act of dismissing critical thought, attempting to pass into a state of vapid serenity by labeling facts as "beliefs", along with labeling unsubstantiated, or disproven, tee shirt slogans as "beliefs", utilizing equivocal language in an attempt to portray each as equal. Just as the word "beat" can mean to defeat someone in a game of checkers, or to physically thrash a person, such dissolute individuals might ask a man who engages in a family game night each week whether or not he ever beats his wife. A yes or no reply, without any inquiry at all into the details, leaves one in a position to arrive at two vastly different conclusions due to the usage of ill-defined terminology. Speaking the language of evidence -as a responsible adult living in an epoch succeeding the Enlightenment, an era of science over superstition, during an era of unprecedented access to evidence, in a time in which the compilation of evidence is at an all-time high, must do- is an outcome that the ILC avoid as though it would cause their arms to fall off. See more about the ILC in part IV.

Just as an elementary school teacher reiterates to their single digit aged pupils on a weekly basis, adults too *must comply with the evidence*. It doesn't matter if you don't like that the cow says moo, and that the horse says nay, your disapproval doesn't make it any less accurate; even if the basis for your objection or disapproval is mere embarrassment over not having stated the correct answer the first time asked. 2+2=4 whether one likes it or not. The four wooden blocks before you, no matter how many ways they may be arranged into groups of two, still make a total of four. *Anyone who attempts to persuade you into the conviction that obeying the evidence is harmful to you, is simply not your friend*, is not looking out for the best interest of your advancement towards fulfilling your potential as an individual, and *is thereby hindering your being a part of the strongest and most productive society possible*.

The necessary entity known as central government must be confined to its three legitimate purposes:

1   To establish and defend borders for the citizens
2   To provide an instrument for the mediation of disputes between citizens
3   To coin and regulate issuance of currency for the use of citizens

PART I

Populist, "Redistributive", Movements: the Autoimmune Disease of Political Strategies

"What we must go through to get back tiny handfuls of our own money."

–Magnitogorsk Mayor Mikhail Lysenko, late 1980s (1)

The trustbusters, New Dealers, Bolsheviks, Maoists, Jacobins, and others, have each actively sought, attacked, and often destroyed, productive and life giving parties or practices existing within a country -producers, entrepreneurs, hard workers, aggressive savers- while promoting and perpetuating self-defeating and life devouring practices -the demonization and suppression of successful people, thereby reducing or eliminating altogether the fruits of their success such as food, clothing, housing and building materials, technological developments, or medical advances. Also, since the populace are forbidden advancement and success, the emergence of achievers from all levels of wealth and age ceases. Like an autoimmune disease in humans, these "populist" types of movements impair and destroy prosperity, **attacking the good elements as though they were bad**, diminishing the whole of the nation while hurting most those who are the least-moneyed; all under the guise of helping the little guy! What's worse, this nefarious activity is compounded by, additionally, **defending elements which are tangibly harmful as though it were factually beneficial** to the masses.

Money stolen from those who have produced it -through investment, labor, or both- is indeed redistributed to someone who did not produce it. However, a great deal of it is redistributed to government bureaucrats, as opposed to the numbskulls who voted for or supported the concentration of power into the hands of the few by decree, known as socialism. Each of these latter two parties can lay an equal claim upon the stolen money, as each is 0% responsible for the productive behavior which produced said money, so that neither of these two had been wronged prior to this theft via taxation, and therefore cannot be wronged in the divvying up of the stolen booty. It seems prudent to point out the plain fact that the rubes who drew upon their own tremendous wealth of ignorance as to the historical consequences of the false promises of self anointed Robin Hoods, that the money stolen will not be handed to them; at least, not very much of it. And neither will the goods and services which are not produced by the people who used to make money producing them, end up in the hands of the vapid wokers of any given nation.

Take, for an example, John D. Rockefeller and his Standard Oil Company. Rockefeller had many partners and stakeholders -ranging from those holding significant chunks of stock, to those "regular folk" who might buy a few shares with some of their savings, as opposed to other uses- though he was always in a position of prominence and control. The Standard thrived throughout the second half of the nineteenth century in the United States. Rockefeller was joined in his entry into the business by dozens upon dozens of others who bought oil claims, who endeavored in refining, who sought fortune and an easier life than would be otherwise necessary for survival. Most lost their shirts in their ventures, some made decent livings, fewer struck it rich, but nobody equaled the zenith of the success achieved by John D. Rockefeller. At his peak, his Standard briefly controlled 90% of the world's supply of oil in the 1880s until new oil was discovered in Russia, as nature quashed his temporarily "monopolistic" position in oil; several decades prior to being tried by the trustbusters, by the way. His greatest level of wealth has been estimated in U.S. dollars as $815,647,796.89 in 1911. (2)

Standard Oil brought improved the heating and lighting of homes and businesses for an ever increasing proportion of Americans, and this due to the company's own innovations as they sought greater profits. Oil and gas were reduced in price for the consumer as their quality improved. *No government "energy program" can hold a candle to the results obtained by the Standard* in terms of: increasing access, reducing price, improving quality, increasing supply, and doing it all in a self-sustaining fashion, without any coercion or force used to achieve these outcomes. Government efforts, we know from the pages of this text, rely solely upon coercion and force while achieving few if any of the positive outcomes mentioned in the previous sentence. And yet, a group of *politicians teamed up to manufacture a "crisis"* of alleged exploitative capitalist monopolists. This was done to drum up populist fervor, attack the private property rights of a targeted extreme minority group, and to transform this act of thuggery -which also directly attacked a key energy and product manufacturer as well as distributor- into an act of politically profitable "nobility". This group was called the trustbusters. This is a case of the "auto-immune disease" in practice, attacking the productive citizens, as well as the mechanisms for producing and innovating necessities, as though they were bad.

To eliminate public charities such as socialized medicine; food stamps; cash prizes for failure to be productive, and/or for persistently irresponsible behavior, from which the person is paid to fail to become responsible because becoming responsible would revoke the payment; housing vouchers; or anything else, does not make it *illegal* to give to private charity, or to lend money to the state for use in its purposes through purchase of government bonds. It does however cease the forcing of people to have their money turned over to *sham charities, run by government bureaucrats*. With their staggering and often accelerating costs, commingled with the diminishing returns which pale to those returned by free citizens over extended periods, these types of government agencies are simply commerce hubs for the professional political class -masquerading as charities to benefit the public well-being. It is easy to subscribe to this bizarre religion which advocates methods proven undeniably to reduce the availability of goods and services when one is not among the beggars, and it is certainly not an unjust outcome for this same person to be the one who is left without the resources eliminated by the methods that they themselves advocated, knowing full well that the outcome will be to make less for everybody.

It is worth noting that the press in the United States have been earning a reputation of low esteem amongst thinking men for quite some time. Tocqueville wrote of the press after his visit during 1831-32: "So, generally, journalists in the United States have a lowly status, their education is rudimentary and the expression of their ideas is frequently coarse." He went on to say that "The spirit of the journalist in America consists in a crude, unvarnished, and unsubtle attack on the passions of his readers; he leaves principles aside to seize hold of men whom he pursues into their private lives exposing their weaknesses and defects." The foreigner continued by writing that "Above all, the result is that the personal opinions of journalists carry virtually no weight in the readers' eyes. What the latter look for in newspapers is knowledge of facts; only by altering or distorting these facts can a journalist gain some influence for his views." He concluded that, taken as a whole, "the periodical press nonetheless is the most powerful of social forces." (3) Many today have a decided lack of respect for much of the popular press, while one important difference two centuries later is the noted absence of facts and evidence contained in the works of the press when it comes to major issues, while another, perhaps more important factor, is that today nobody seems to *notice* that they are consuming intellectual empty calories, and that people *resist* a limitation of the discussion to the language of evidence.

Disguising Friends as Foes:
Trustbusting, and Other Assaults on the
Providers of the Necessities Life

"The whole aim of practical politics is to keep the populace alarmed (and hence clamorous to be led to safety) by menacing it with an endless series of hobgoblins, all of them imaginary." -H.L. Mencken, as printed in: Jack W. Germond & Jules Witcover, Whose Broad Stripes and Bright Stars?: The Trivial Pursuit of the Presidency 1988 (New York: Warner Books, 1989), un-numbered page preceding the acknowledgments

The benefits lavished upon the least-moneyed element of any society by free trade and the unequal accumulation of capital are manifest. This bounty which has created, enabled, and sustained, so many life-years for humans -in terms of extending lives, of imbuing those years with a higher quality of life, and of enabling so many more pregnancies to be born and enabling those who are born survive early childhood- is severely curtailed, and sometimes even turned to famine, by the interference of meddlers through the instrument of government. In a political and advertising campaign wholly removed from the reality illustrated by evidence, the precious givers of life and of luxury -businesses, especially businesses which have grown large via legitimately accumulated riches, derived from pleasing the customer- are fictionalized and reconfigured to represent evil monsters. The campaigners destroy the so-called monster, *slitting the throat of what in reality gives jobs, goods, food, and life*.

This chapter familiarizes the reader with a variety of instances in which intervention by government, done in the name of the common good and of uplifting those presently least-moneyed, celebrated as victories for the commoners, *in fact harmed the commoners most of all*. Antitrust legislation has been popular in the United States of America for a little over a century, as of this writing; there were even a group of politicians monikered as the "trustbusters" at one time, who attacked the ultimate provider of jobs, goods, services, and food. The New Dealers assaulted businesses during a time at which unemployment and food shortages were already a problem, thereby exacerbating both. *This autoimmune disease*, attacking what is good as though it were bad, *must be stamped out*. The cure is the examination of the hordes of evidence which exist. I encourage the reader to look beyond the handful of examples presented hereafter, and in particular to locate and to publicize any examples in which the practice of attacking free competition, attacking capital accumulation through the pleasing of customers and not through government monopolies, and attacking income inequality, have actually resulted in the creation of more and not of less, and actually resulted in the least-moneyed class being elevated. The record of history shows that outcomes of the variety which follow are par for the course; results of the variety mentioned in the prior sentence are remarkably scarce, if any exist at all.

One example of phantom private "monopolists" being attacked occurred in the USA during 1904. A Supreme Court decision declared Northern Securities to be a combination in restraint of trade [antitrust]. Northern Securities was a holding company founded by James J. Hill of the Great Northern rail line, as well as by J.P. Morgan of the Northern Pacific railroad. Established November 1901, the already steadily falling rates for customers continued their tumble into 1903. ***Though consumers were benefiting, and though no private monopoly existed, it was declared illegal.*** This decision set a legal precedent which was utilized as a device to assault the private property rights of American citizens, to increase costs for consumers, and to reduce jobs for workers in those future instances -just as it did in the Northern Securities case. (4) The power of the state over the individual had expanded, and was done under the auspice of protecting the individual.

Conflating "first place presently" with "monopoly" is a common tactic used by advertisers while they engage in their ruse. In the USA, beginning during the late 19th century and going on into the early 20th century, there was such an episode in the sugar business. The Sherman Antitrust Act was passed during 1890 -ostensibly to "protect" the populace from phantom private business monopolies which were to subject them to high prices, poor selection, shoddy quality, and prevent competitors from giving customers choice in the marketplace- was weaponized by the federal government, more specifically the Justice Department in particular, during the year 1893 as they brought suit against the American Sugar Refining Company as a result of their having acquired four other companies. At the moment of acquisition, this gave the company 98% of the present sugar refining market.

A verdict rendered in 1895 by the Supreme Court mercifully sided with the company; though it ***failed to declare the Sherman Act unconstitutional.*** Away from the company, unrestrained capitalism, and the desire for personal gain, were left to do their work. In short order people began deriving sugar from new sources, and through new methods; so that the property of the American Sugar Refining Company no longer comprised such a large proportion of the current sugar refining market. This occurred in absence of the use of occupational licensing; as well as without any regulation which granted a monopoly to the few, under the guise of saving the masses from the horrors of monopoly. Not surprisingly, the company's proportion of the market share declined steadily, from its colossal apex of 98% in 1893, to only 61% by 1905, and down to 25% by 1927. By 1920 a minimum of 105 plants specialized in beet sugar production, which was an important innovation vital to the rapid deflation of American Sugar's market share. (5)

YEAR	AMERICAN SUGAR REFINING COMPANY'S MARKET SHARE	RAW SUGAR WHOLESALE PRICES (cents)	REFINED SUGAR RETAIL PRICES (cents)	"MARK UP" (cents)
1880		9.602	9	(0.602)
1890		6.71	6.9	0.19
1893	98%			
1895		4.152	5.3	1.148
1900		5.32	6.1	0.78
1905	61%	5.256	6	0.744
1910		4.972	6	1.028
1927	25%			

SOURCE FOR CHART: D.T. Armentano. Ph. D., *Myths of Antitrust: Economic Theory and Legal Cases* (New Rochelle: Arlington House, 1972), p.57-58

Rockefeller, and the Standard Oil Company

The Standard Oil Company will receive its own brief section, before the forthcoming section delivers a menagerie of examples of the draping of friends of the people in the banner of foes by duplicitous shysters, as it was an American company which elevated the quality of life of so many not only in its home country, but all over the world; yet it is treated as though it were evil and shameful. *John D. Rockefeller, and the Standard Oil Company, did more to benefit the rank-and-file American than the New Dealers, the trustbusters, the Great Society backers, American liberals, and the 21st century wokers, all put together.* The environment of relatively unbridled pursuit of individual gain yielded an era of ruthless price-cutting, irrepressible innovation and the resultant cavalcade of new products for consumers, relentless pursuit of efficiency in operations, and the steady employment of legions of workers.

Rockefeller was a man of humble beginnings, with a flim-flam man for a father though he was frequently not around. John was an honest and decent man, who was a regular at church services wherever he lived, and was an ardent giver even when he had meager means. Conversely, William Avery Rockefeller, John D.'s father, in comparison with his tremendously scrupulous and thrifty wife:

"...was at every point different. A young man of powerful physique—nearly six feet tall, deep-chested, muscular—he had an abounding energy and a daring adventurousness. He loved gaiety, song, talk, and general sociability; his temperament was jovial, exuberant, ostentatious. Vibrant with health, full of the joy of life, and supremely self-confident, he took the center of every gathering, and made any circle merrier as soon as he appeared. But he also had stronger—and darker—traits. He did precisely as he pleased; his will brooked no opposition; he lacked moral scruple in certain relationships, and followed his impulses without proper thought of the consequences.

Although he owned farms first at Richford and later at Moravia, William Avery was no tiller of the soil. He was a trader, a businessman, and in a small way an entrepreneur. Thirty-four years old when the family removed to Moravia, he left the farm work chiefly to a hired hand. Legendary material, derived from neighbors, pictures him as sometimes going away on long mysterious trips, from which he returned with handsome horses, a spic-and-span wardrobe, and plenty of money. Perhaps at this time, and certainly at a later date, he peddled patent medicines and herbal remedies."

"For a time he advertised himself as 'Dr. William A. Rockefeller the Celebrated Cancer Specialist,' selling 'cancer treatments' and medicines; when he first appears in the Cleveland directory it is as an 'herbal doctor.' " (6)

The Rockefeller family frequently relocated: Moravia, NY; Oswego, NY; Richford, NY; Cleveland, OH. (7) John D. Rockefeller's first business venture was begun in Cleveland, Ohio, on March 18th, 1859. Rockefeller partnered with Maurice B. Clark to found a venture as middleman merchants; beginning with grains and hay, then venturing to minerals and pork during the American Civil War. Rockefeller's attention to detail, along with his high scruples, were later attested to by Clark: "He was methodical to an extreme, careful as to details, and exacting to a fraction. If there was a cent due us he wanted it. If there was a cent due a customer he wanted the customer to have it." (8)

Rockefeller's early income and charitable activity are informative. In Cleveland, Ohio, during the period spanning December of 1855 to April of 1856, Rockefeller's income was $95. As to giving, he spent $1 on pew rent while contributing an additional $5.88 to various charitable objects other than his church. The cumulative balance of these figures rivals his expenditures on clothing during the same period, which amounted to $9.09. Rockefeller biographer Allan Nevins: "This was a remarkable performance: on his meagre income, allowing himself almost nothing for amusements, and skimping on luncheons, he had approached the literal interpretation of the Biblical injunction respecting a tithe of a man's earnings." (9) When, in 1859, his church needed $2,000 to save its building, Rockefeller spearheaded the fundraising campaign. During that same year, Rockefeller himself gave charitable gifts totaling $72.22; a full tenth of his income in that year. Rockefeller gave to coloreds, as well as to whites, at least twice in the 3 year period 1859-1861 giving gifts to free blacks so that they might purchase their enslaved family or friends. As his income began to swell, so did his donations; John gave $671.86 in 1864, in 1865 more than $1,000. (10) During 1864 his firm -then Andrews, Clark & Co.- built a cooperage shop to save money on barrels. Rockefeller was seen, during times of need on the part of the shop, wheeling out loads of shavings, along with rolling barrels to their destination. (11)

During February of 1865, John and his partner Sam Andrews bought out their three partners, the malcontent Clark brothers. Their firm was now known as Rockefeller & Andrews. Concurrently, John left the shipping business venture in which he had been enjoined with Clark. Rockefeller would later remark: "I ever point to the day when I separated myself from them as the beginning of the success I have made in my life." (12) Later in 1865 (13), during a decade in which Nevins notes that "Any man with $10,000 could establish a small refinery, any one with $50,000 a large one." (14) Rockefeller took a $4,000 -drilling equipment cost about $200 (15)- plunge into a single Cleveland refinery; a speculative play if there ever was one. By 1868 a few faces had changed, joining Rockefeller as partners, but reducing costs through efficiency and economy were already paramount in Rockefeller's mind; and a little money was already rolling in as a reward. (16)

Historians Hidy and Hidy relay to us that, for aspiring oilmen during the 1860s, "Capital was not easily obtained for the new, risky enterprise". The teamsters monopoly in hauling barreled oil from the wells artificially increased prices, while reducing options, for consumers. (17) Possessed by the desire for immediate sales and profits, "oilmen yielded to no one in price cutting and bargaining." *This meant lower prices for those purchasing the products.* (18) The consumers benefited immensely from John D. Rockefeller's Christian training, which stressed upon the importance of thrift and austerity, as this propelled the man to incessantly pursue increases in efficiency. These many improvements, often minute in degree, were amplified over many hundreds of thousands or even millions of transactions, to provide better products at lower prices and in greater quantities to consumers, while also steadily employing legions directly and supplying work indirectly to those in the employ of businesses utilizing the Standard's products to maintain their operations.

Rockefeller's attention to detail, seeking optimum balance of costs and quality, was evident in the early 1870s at Long Island City. An assortment of machines readied the processed kerosene for sale and distribution in five gallon tin cans. The first machine dispensed the kerosene into the cans, a second apparatus cleaned lids onto the cans, and a third machine dropped solder onto the lids to fasten them to the cans. Rockefeller's inquiry as to the volume of the solder used for each can was met with a reply that 40 drops were used. John then asked that 38 drops be tested, and the result was that 6-7% of such cans leaked. From there, 39 drops per can was tested. 1,000 such canisters showed no leakage, and thereafter 39 drops of solder were used for every can so prepared by the Standard. (154)

Efficiency was pursued in an effort to *lower the price*, in order to *benefit the consumer*, so that *consumers would choose* Standard Oil products and *bring profits to Rockefeller and the other shareholders*. Glue for specific by products was monitored:

"As reports came in that cans containing Russian cased oil were defective, Standard Oil men gave even more attention than before to upholding the quality of their own. Every effort was made to send out oil in leak-proof cans."

"To prevent leakage of export oil the Cooperage Committee made detailed studies, encouraged plants to carry out experiments, and made repeated recommendations to affiliated companies. In 1885 it decided that except in unusual circumstances imported used barrels, known as "ship seconds", should not be employed for the export of Water White kerosene or deodorized naphtha. When the committee's studies two years later indicated that the extra cost of three-quarters of a cent per barrel for a second coat of glue was justified by the results, the members advised all Standard Oil interests shipping export oil to "double glue" their new barrels. Detailed rules as to the temperature and quality of glue to be used for each season were given; at least three days were recommended as the period between the application of the two coats. The committee advised the use of steel or extra-heavy iron chime hoops weighing twelve pounds per set on all barrels containing naphtha, and, on those for export, nine-pound rivets on chime hoops instead of the usual seven-pound. When the development of bulk marine transportation did away with the necessity for millions of barrels to make a return trip across the Atlantic each year to be repaired and refilled, the members of the Cooperage Committee sent one of their own experts to Europe to teach, as they expressed it, "our methods" of reconditioning "ship seconds". (19)

The *improvement of life for the least-moneyed faction of society* was a direct boon of the activities of profiteering capitalism, and of the Standard Oil Company. Prior to 1870, household illumination -via candles, or through whale oil lamps- had been a luxury of "the rich". During the 1870s, new innovation and efficiency would bring the cost of operating kerosene lamps down to $1 per hour. Burt Folsom, Jr., points out: "Working and reading became after dark activities new to most Americans in the 1870s. (20) The Lenoir gas engine was patented 1860 in France, 1863 in the USA. (21) Throughout the successive decades of the 1890s-1900s, one cylinder stationary combustion engines steadily began to populate *the workspaces of the average person, easing their lives and lessening the harshness* of the miles that people would put on their bodies by performing jobs such as "...pumping water, sawing wood, grinding meal, and other small jobs." (22)

YEAR	AUTO PLANTS	CAPITAL INVESTED	WAGE EARNERS
1900	57	$5.7 million	2,241
1905	121	$20.5 million	10,239

SOURCE FOR CHART: Allan Nevins, *John D. Rockefeller: a One-Volume Abridgement* (New York: Charles Scriber's Sons, 1959), p. 203

The Standard, and by extension the USA, uplifted the world through their desire to make profits for themselves:

"Since until the rise of the automobile export market was much more important to the Standard than the home consumption, Rockefeller and his associates paid assiduous attention to its development and defense. In the seventies the United States stood almost alone as a producer of oil for Western Europe and Asia, its exports of kerosene rising in that decade from 97,900,000 to 367,325,000 gallons. The early eighties witnessed the sudden and powerful entrance of Russia into the world market, while the nineties saw the oil fields of Burma and the Dutch East Indies becoming formidable competitors in certain areas. Nevertheless, American kerosene exports rose to 551,000,000 gallons in 1890, and to 740,000,000 in 1900. Rockefeller for some years stood alone, the one giant in the world's refining industry. Then lesser but important figures rose beside him—Alfred Nobel, Henri Deterding, Marcus Samuels. Only by keeping prices low and quality high did American manufacturers maintain their unquestioned supremacy, In doing this the Standard played the leading role, and to its enterprise, system, and shrewdness must be given credit for the maintenance of American primacy." (23)

Rockefeller's care for the workers has been described thusly: "The Standard's president not only selected men, but kept the keenest interest in their work and advancement. He made suggestions for shifts, keeping the welfare of the individual in mind as firmly as the welfare of the Company (he would have said that the two went hand in hand). He was no less concerned on occasion about humble workers." (24) As they say in the movies, "greed is good", as personal gain motivates private business to bring jobs, and luxurious new goods, to those who have not. A massive refinery was built in Whiting, Indiana, after high taxes and complaints from the locals about the smell of the Chicago plant drove the Standard's operation from that city. Jobs related to building the plant began in May of 1889, with jobs working at the constructed plant arriving in 1890. The refinery had 80 crude-oil stills and a refining capacity of 24,000 barrels of crude oil. By 1893 paraffin and candles began to be mass-produced by the plant, in 1900 a site devoted to lubricants was opened. The Whiting Works was the foremost supplier of refined oil products for the Midwest, Far West, the Northwest, and even supplied parts of the Orient. (25)

Innovation by private businesses increases the natural resources available to the people. Standard scientist, Dr. W.M. Burton, developed a method for cracking oil, significantly increasing the yield of gasoline. This was done at the Whiting, Indiana, works. (26) *The Standard uplifted the masses all over the globe*:

"The foreign trade of the Standard had many romantic aspects. Sampans poled by coolies carried "case-oil" far up the streams of China; oxcarts laden with it lumbered along the great North Road that Kim traveled in India; it lighted the compounds and palaces of the barbaric chieftains whom Sir Hugh Clifford has described in his books on Malaya. Joseph Conrad in his days under the red ensign doubtless watched many a boatful of Standard products unloading in the ports of Oceania. Our consul in Singapore in 1887 stated that the Standard, as yet unworried by foreign competition, transshipped oil for all the wide regions roundabout. It was sent to the east coast of Sumatra, to the Isthmus of Malacca, to British Burma, to Siam, to French Cochin-China, and to the greater part of Borneo. The consul described its distribution to numerous harbours and islands of the Dutch and British possessions by small steamers, Chinese junks, and Malay prahees. Tens of millions of gallons of kerosene were sent by 1890 to all parts of Latin America, being distributed from coastal cities to river towns, plantations, ranches, and mines." (27)

A once trendy fashion worn by celebrities during the 1990s, and those who blindly follow their lead, was the "save the whales" campaign. The petroleum industry, more than a century prior to its being fashionable in the USA, helped to "save the whales". The search for a better illuminating oil would result in a cessation of dependency upon whale oil and tallow candles for said purpose. During the 1850s kerosene -coal oil- producing outfits multiplied, and the hefty split of $1 per gallon between crude oil purchased, and kerosene sold to consumers, kept the plats coming and humming. The whales were spared, and *all consumers in both the U.S. and abroad had access to cheap means of lighting their houses and places of business.* U.S. production of crude oil in 1859 was 2,000 barrels, rising in 1869 to 4.8 million barrels, and by 1871 it was 5.2 million barrels. *Jobs were created and sustained due to free markets and the desire for personal gain* on both the part of the party offering the job as well as that of the job seeker. Though the losses were frequent, and often substantial, to the parties who bought oil claims and or refining outfits, the employees hired by them always got to keep all of their money. (28)

The oil industry, and pipelines -then largely owned and controlled by the Standard- improved the people's situation immensely during the early 1880s:

> "Once the pipe lines were placed, they gave little evidence of their existence; only the tanks and shacks, and engines at the pumping stations, and the "walkers" patrolling the lines day and night. The pipes were underground. Few Americans realized that even by 1882 some 14,000 miles of iron webbing lay beneath their soil, silently carrying the heavy fluid that would light the homes of their land, lubricate their machinery, and provide them with dozens of products from paints and vaseline to candles and chewing gum! Here was a transportation unit the length of four transcontinental railways, yet for the most part hidden from men's sight. It had grown to maturity in fifteen years, had revolutionized the carrying of oil, and was already taken as much for granted as the humble kerosene can which had suddenly become a household article around the world." (29)

The societal plague that is the ILC (see part IV) has always existed, and the supposed advancements in education have done nothing to quell its existence. Giving in to them, as opposed to curing them, has always been detrimental to the greater good, while beneficial only to the minority class of politicians who exploit these folks with their supposedly populist campaigns. The quartet of authors of *The American Petroleum Industry: The age of energy 1899-1959* observe: "Thus, while Standard Oil may *in fact not have been* the 'archetype of predatory monopoly,' public opinion certainly considered it so. There was little let-up in the journalistic and semi-scholarly outpouring of anti-Standard literature." (30) The false accusations of monopoly, or of harming the general public, or even of harming the others within the petroleum industry, stick with the Standard to this day. These unsubstantiated claims, levied at John Rockefeller's company, will be disproven in the forthcoming pages.

The fluctuation of prices prior to the Standard becoming a behemoth did nothing to aid those in the business to stay afloat. Crude oil prices ranged: in 1862 $0.10-2.25 per barrel, 1864 $4-$12.125, 1871 $3.825-4.825. (31) Obviously, the American Civil War was an important factor for the first two dates in the sequence. The plight of the oil producers was their own doing, due to overproduction. In June of 1870, oil was down to $0.70/barrel, but they kept on drilling anyway, doing nothing to increase scarcity in the already saturated market. (32) An outside factor contributing to the Standard's consolidation during the middle 1870s was the general business downturn following the Panic of 1873 (33). Nevins calls it "the long depression of 1873-77". (34) *During this period, the Standard expanded to preserve the quality of its products.* In 1873, *having grown weary of middlemen perverting the products of the Standard*, prior to retailing them to the public, Rockefeller expanded beyond a mere manufacturing operation. John picked up a 50% interest in Chess, Carley, & Company, largely because this firm was well engaged in the distribution of oil products. (35) Though the motivation may have been purely venal, the outcome was to protect the consumer from inferior quality products.

The Victim Politics Industry (see part V) was at work in the United States, even during the 19th century. Self-inflicted, behaviorally created and perpetuated, wounds were blamed on so-called oppression. During the 1877-79 period, though the Standard had a strong, well earned, position, it was not guilty of achieving it via nefarious means. Hundreds, and even thousands, of producers and refineries existed outside of the scope of the Standard. *These independents*, displeased by the daunting success achieved by the mighty Standard, *called a meeting* during November of 1877 and there suggested that they all pitch in -*also known as colluding to "act in combination"*- to build one or two of their own pipelines; lines which may be superior to the Standard's newly acquired network. Self-inflicted wounds caused by the poor discipline among these same independent producers caused prices to plummet, and belts to tighten. Record production ensued:

> 1877 13.5 million barrels
>
> 1878 15.3 million barrels
>
> 1879 nearly 20 million barrels

Rockefeller: "Had it not been for the interposition of the Standard Oil interests in building tankage, making pipe lines, and otherwise providing for this surplus of oil which came gushing from the earth these producers, many of whom had no working capital, would have seen their oil go into the ground." *Rockefeller justifiably mocked and ridiculed his critics among his rival oil men*: "We have disregarded all advice, and produced oil in excess of the means of storing and shipping it. We have not built storage of our own. How dare you refuse to take all we produce? Why do you not pay us the high prices of 1876, without regard to the fact that the glut has depressed every market?" The Standard rushed to build enough new tanks to store millions of barrels worth of oil, in addition to dropping everything to build hundreds of miles worth of new pipelines, to accommodate the irresponsible drilling of its competitors. (36)

By 1880, the Standard owned significant interests in 25 other refineries, and had bought 140 others outright. The Pennsylvania government scraped the barrel of their statute books in order to discover a law permitting them to tax the Standard on *all* of its stock holdings -even those outside Pennsylvania borders- and other states showed an interest in following the lead of Pennsylvania. This would effectively result in enormous tax liabilities for the Standard, and so *the greed of government forced private ingenuity*. The Standard dusted off the statute books themselves, and utilized an old common law device known as a trust -later, a holding company. Private individuals pooled their private property into a trust, and elected managers. The Standard Oil Trust functioned for 3 months in 1882, before being outlawed by the Ohio Supreme Court. In 1899 the same men did the same thing, as the Standard Oil of New Jersey holding company was formed. Small, failed, inefficient, firms were replaced with large, efficient works. ***Production and quality improved markedly as prices declined***. The Standard's market share in 1879: 88%; in 1895: 82%. While one company's proportion of the market was gargantuan, notice the reduction in prices for consumers, as prices of barreled refined oil per gallon fell steadily: 1880 9 ⅛ cents, 1885 8 ⅛ cents, 1890 7 ⅜ cents, 1897 5.91 cents, ***the lowest price ever***. Standard's refining cost per gallon was 0.29 cents. Standard also owned 17 refineries in Europe, hundreds of warehouses, and their own shipping equipment. (37) Insultingly false accusations against the Standard were made by writers of the future. One such writer, Joseph A. Schumpeter, writing during the mid-20th century, mentions the Standard specifically in a chapter entitled "Monopolistic Practices". Schumpeter remarks of the Standard: "...so that at any point in time they seem to be doing nothing but restricting their output and keeping prices high." (38) What nonsense!

"New York newspaper men are pretty well confirmed in the habit of parlor socialism. It is nothing but a form of mental laziness somehow translated into dreamy egotism. Writers of the parlor socialist type do not bother to seek the facts, and their small entourage does not want facts; it wants lazy ecstasy." –Colonel Robert McCormick, Publisher, Chicago Tribune, 1932 (39)

As we will see in the Supreme Court cases which follow, the language of evidence was subordinated to the language of unsubstantiated claims and of reciting the scriptures of the religion of collectivism and redistributionism. Hating anybody better than themselves calls for the downfall of the party being envied, per their dogma. There's an old saying that a retraction in the middle of the newspaper does little to undo the damage caused by the headline of a prior day, and the false accusations made against the Standard did colossal damage in the eyes of the general public, from whom populist politicians fetch for approval. During 1879 a variety of illegitimate claims secured headlines and inhabited the minds of many in the public, arousing scorn and mistrust of the Standard ***whereas the exposure of the accusers as liars ought to have brought this fate their own way***. One such false accuser was the widow of former Standard bookkeeper Fred Backus. Backus manufactured and marketed his own line of lubricants, with which the Standard did not compete during his lifetime which ended in 1874. Backus had known Rockefeller since their days teaching Sunday School during boyhood. Fred's widow claimed to have been victimized at the hands of the big, bad, Standard Oil Company, asserting that she had been preyed upon during a downcycle in the industry and that in 1878 the Standard had swooped in and pressured her into selling for a mere third of what the business was worth. Mrs. Backus claimed the enterprise to have had a value of $200,000 while accepting only $79,000 in exchange for it, while also alleging that her wish to retain a 15% stock ownership of the company was refused by the Standard.

The reality of the situation was that Mrs. Backus was revealed to have secretly valued the business and its holdings at only $150,000, and had in fact entertained an offer shy of that figure during 1876 which fell through because the purchasers couldn't get the money together. Rockefeller paid $79,000 for the works, good will, the oil on hand, and successorship. The remaining property of the company, which when placing a price tag for sale upon them, Mrs. Backus claimed to have a value of $60,000, Mrs. Backus was permitted to retain as it was excluded from the purchase agreement. The $79,000 paid, plus the $60,000 value Mrs. Backus put on the property which she kept, meant that she in fact walked away with cash and property totaling the amount of $139,000. Moreover, when Rockefeller recommended that the Backus widow hold on to some of the company's shares of stock, he was met by her statement of desire to wash her hands of the business entirely. *Her tissue of lies should have branded her as unsavory*, and the Standard as proper, but *the accusation stayed with many in the public* and unfairly tarnished the reputation of the Standard. What's more, this deceptive and untruthful woman passed away with a net worth of approximately $300,000. She had plenty of money, but was bankrupt in virtue. (40)

The practice of making false accusations designed to prey upon the emotions of the public, while illustrating a flagrant disregard of fidelity to the evidence, made the national stage as what would today be known as a "professional protester", and as a "tabloid scandal sheet peddler", called Henry Demarest Lloyd entered the fray. Lloyd, who knew nothing of economics yet lectured on political economy and wrote of big businesses and their operations, had been let go by a slew of "causes" such as the silver movement, the anti-Tammany revolt, the free-trade uprising, and the Liberal Republicans. Continuously in search of a cause -seemingly, any cause- Lloyd wanted to retain employment as a propagandist, holding a job at the Chicago *Tribune*, and so first attacked the rails in an 1880 piece read to the Chicago Literary Club called "A Cure for Vanderbiltism", and then the Standard in the 1881 article "The Story of a Great Monopoly" which was published in the *Atlantic Monthly*. (41) The *Atlantic* article was read nationwide and republished in England. Whether Lloyd's writing ignited a wildfire of illegitimate and counterfactual attacks upon the hand feeding the masses, or was merely the first article which touched upon a pre-existing condition of lunacy to gain such a widespread audience, a flood of similar fictions followed in its wake. (42)

The illegitimacy of the article was patently obvious to anybody who put its claims to any degree of scrutiny whatever. Lloyd attacked the Standard for the low price of oil in 1878, citing record production of 56,000 barrels per day; the economic illiterate was unable to realize that record supply should be expected to outrun demand and therefore to reduce prices. The writer noted a diminution in the amount of refineries in the Pittsburgh area, and *a priori* presumed that some evil competitors must have undermined and wronged those who went out of business. Much as we see the ill-informed presume the evaporation of American Indian (see part V, American Indians) nations to be unique, and to be evidentiary of some genocidal nation overtaking them -all the while nations all over the world for thousands of years have passed into extinction largely through their own mismanagement and poor conduct- Lloyd failed to account for the poor management of the now defunct refineries; *the marketplace yielding the most efficient suppliers and producers.*

Lloyd falsely reported the rate of profit of the Standard using childishly simplistic methods which ignored operating costs, plant depreciation and the necessary reinvestment in equipment, and other factors, and thusly plucked the figure 8.75 cents per gallon of kerosene more or less from the air and stated this to be the Standard's profit. Internal communications within the company reveal the actual rate to have been a fraction of a penny, in August 1883 at 0.413 cent. (43) A work of fiction, labeled today as 'investigative journalism', created the phantom of an evil behemoth injuring the industry and the public, while in reality the Standard may have been the best thing to ever happen to either. And of course *the recommendation was to have government bureaucrats displace those competent in the industry* as the decision makers for this vital company. (44)

COMPETITION DESTROYS MONOPOLY

Of course, competition destroys monopoly, while only central planning creates and perpetuates monopoly. *There have always been individuals who attempt to collude amongst themselves, and to exclude all others* from their activities, and there likely always will be such behavior. *Government bureaus simply codify into law their ability to do so*, while absence of regulation permits competition, as the desire to better one's position serves to break up the private schemes. During April of 1874, a cabal of oil producers engaged in a conspiracy to artificially increase scarcity, and therefore prices, by joining in concert to cease drilling for 90 days. Individual desire for gain among some motivated them to continue on with production. Not wanting to sit idly by while the others produced and sold oil, the agreement signed that month –stopping drilling at 130 sites– was annulled May 15th, and the conspiracy was quashed. (45) *The loose grip of the Beast, via light oversight and absent regulation, lowers prices and improves quality*: "The reduction in prices for sales through Meissner, Ackermann & Company was only one part of Standard Oil's adjustment of prices to meet competition in the foreign markets. As soon as sellers of American oil abroad had been forced to lower prices in order to compete with Russian kerosene, prices to exporters in the New York markets were reduced, just as similar pressures had pushed prices down in the domestic market during the early 1880's." (46)

The Standard orchestrated a rate fixing deal involving the PA, Erie, and NY Central rails, along with oil refiners, both large and small, in Cleveland, Baltimore, Pittsburgh, Philadelphia, and New York. Their pact was signed September 4, 1874. (155) This pact had broken up by September 4th of the following year, as *rails and refiners alike went behind each other's backs*, sought and obtained special rates immediately after the signing, along with access to more shipments for hauling, so that within a year's time a new agreement was deemed necessary to be struck, and under different terms than the first. (47) "Monopoly" is also cured by nature. Oil discovered in foreign countries reduced the proportion of world supply owned by the Standard. Writing in 1897, a producer within the Standard ranks: "Now that oil has been discovered in the Far East in profitable quantities," he wrote, "you must *forever* count on its being an important factor in this [Oriental] trade and the only question to consider is how best to meet it." (48)

The *universality of railroad rebates* deserves mention here, as some assert that the Standard was somehow wronging their competition with secret rebates obtained from the railroads. The Hepburn Committee in 1879 found *6,000 special rate contracts agreed to by the NY Central Railroad alone*, between January and August of 1879. The most attractive shippers regularly received 50-80% off of sticker price for their cargo. Nevertheless, the Hepburn Committee final report of January 22, 1880, labeled the Standard "a unique illustration of the possible outgrowth" of preferential rail rates and referred to "the colossal proportions to which monopoly can grow under the laws of this country". (49) The Standard, in fact, saved shippers money by providing the Standard's own facilities for loading and unloading: "several hundred thousand dollars a month" admits Matthew Josephson in his 1934 book *The Robber Barons*. This contributed to lower shipping rates than competitors could otherwise obtain. (50) On the subject of competition amongst the oil companies, we should point out that devoting one's energy to improving one's self -as opposed to bringing down those who one envies- is more likely to yield self-improvement. Unsuccessful legislation, aimed at their betters, was pursued by the flailing independents -instead of focusing on improving their **own** conduct- in Pennsylvania. Public indignation towards the Standard began to swell, nonetheless. (51)

Deregulation and free markets protect the consumer. Samuel Downer, in association with Joshua Merrill and the Atwood brothers, is credited with having "had probably done more than any other refiner to set high standards of quality and to introduce new techniques" in plats located in Corry, PA, as well as in Boston and

Portland. Ruthless competition to please the consumer and to win his trade motivated this, as it *was done entirely in absence of legislation requiring him to do so*. (52)

COMBINATION AND TERMS OF TAKEOVER

Some urban legends exist which assert that the Standard was a peculiar case of coalition through diversification or absorption. Business combinations were common, and neither unique to the Standard nor to the oil business. During the 1850s and 1860s, The Ocean Oil Company was a corporation of assorted shareholders designed to diversify the risk of the investors. The Columbia Oil Company had a variety of shareholders -including noted steel man Andrew Carnegie. William Barns Dall was both a producer and a refiner of oil. Jacob Jay Vandergrift was a part of minimally half of a dozen producing outfits. W.H. Abbott was involved in both purchase and refinement of crude oil, along with pipeline construction. (53)

Far from being predatory in its quest for firms to take over -the firms were always mis-managed, and frequently ardent in their desire to be bought out- and lightyears from offering paltry sums to the distressed outfits, the Standard in fact preferred to keep the best pieces of whatever firms were acquired; including in particular, the employees. The prior owner or owners were often sought to remain on as a manager, using the Standard's methods of operation, and offering whatever talents such men may possess to benefit the company as a whole.

Approached during summer 1873, with the agreement reached dated April 20, 1874, the Erie Railroad sent representatives to Rockefeller in an effort to persuade him to send more of his oil freight business their way. The Erie offered to match the rates on refined oil offered by the New York Central Railroad, but the Standard objected to the hidden costs which the Erie pushed on the customers at their Weehawken, NJ, oil transfer plant. Hard up for the commerce of such a customer, and desperate in their desire to keep this pricey oil transfer yard from harming further their bottom line, they suggested that the Standard take over the yard on the condition that the Standard paid a lease on the yard and entered into the shipping agreement for refined oil. (54)

Examples of generous terms upon takeover can be found in these mergers, agreed to during October of 1874 prior to being dealt with at the shareholder's meeting of March 10, 1875:

#1- Pratt & Co. bought 3,125 shares of Standard Oil Company stock at $265 each, for a total cost of $828,125. Paid $250,000 cash, then used their works and material as "payment" for the remaining balance. ***To sweeten the deal for the incomers***, the Standard approved $1,000,000 in new stock issued, in addition to the $2.5 million already in existence; the Standard stated that these new shares would receive dividends of $115 per share, just as those holding previously existing shares would be paid. The $359,375 dividend check on the new shares issued *covered the cash payment* of Pratt and Co., ***plus*** put $109,375 into their cash supply, ***and*** the Standard paid the outfit $578,125 for their properties.

#2- William G. Warden, Phi; Charles Lockhart, R.J. Waring, William Frew, Pitt; Charles Pratt, H.H. Rogers, NY. This group bought 6,250 shares of Standard stock at $265 each, for a total cost of $1,656,250. They paid $400,000 cash, then put up their property to account for the remaining balance due. The dividend of $718,750 *covered their $400,000 "payment"*, while *enriching their cash supply* by $318,750 beyond that. Additionally, the group was paid $1,256,250 for their property. (55)

Rockefeller wanted the talent, and the good workers, at these companies as much as, if not more than, their locations or machinery. Rockefeller didn't need their methods, as those of the Standard were superior, but rather he wanted to combine the good workers and their talent with his superior and ever-evolving system, and in so doing to make for a better company; as opposed to wanting to quash them so that they might die starving in the gutter, as he greedily hoarded all of the money for himself.

Generous terms upon takeover were again evident when the Pennsylvania railroad, and the Empire Transportation Company, were in dire straits during 1877. Riotous strikers, unmolested by law enforcement, wreaked havoc upon the property of these concerns. Short of funds, their stock in a dismal state, Rockefeller and the Standard rescued their shareholders, bond holders, and employees. Rockefeller went all over New York city, as well as Cleveland, rounding up every cent that he could raise from the financial houses. $3.4 million was paid out. John did not quibble about the price paid, as the vast earning power to be had from such an acquisition was not worth losing over a few percentage points on the initial deal. Those running the two aforementioned companies had their figurative bacon saved. (56)

STANDARD'S MARKET SHARE

Claims of monopoly, and that the Standard *harmed the general public* during the brief period in which it held a massive proportion of the market, *will lilt before the evidence on both counts*. These assertions are such flagrant fiction that when reacting one seemingly must choose between outrage due to insult, or hilarity due to the absurdity. In addition to the facts preceding on these matters, a few more will be cataloged here. Keep in mind that the Standard was ordered broken up by the Supreme Court in the year 1911.

CAPACITY FOR THE REFINING OF CRUDE OIL POSSESSED BY STANDARD OIL

1880	1899	1906	1911
90-95%	82%	70%	64%

SOURCE FOR CHART: Harold F. Williamson, Ralph L. Andreano, Arnold R. Daum, Gilbert C. Klose, *The American Petroleum Industry: The age of energy 1899-1959* (Evanston: Northwest University Press, 1963), p. 7

Writing in 1963 regarding the Standard's market share:

"Recent studies of the evolution of the industry's structure have tended to diminish the weight attached to the Standard's own efforts to restrict competition during this period, and to suggest that by 1911 external events and autonomous market forces had already significantly affected both the structure of the industry and the Standard's marketing position.

More specifically, the pattern of change during these years involved the interaction of five mutually dependent forces: (1) the episodic nature of crude oil supplies; (2) the variations in the quality of crudes; (3) the changing composition of consumer demand for petroleum products; (4) the set of dynamic market forces generated by the "flush field mechanism,"; and (5) certain managerial failures on the part of the Standard to move quickly into new and developing areas and markets." (57)

Of note to those who conflate possession of first place presently with monopoly, and who assert that the interference of government is a necessity in the prevention of the company's iron rule over the general public, Henrietta M. Larsen in her writing entitled "The Rise of Big Business in the Oil Industry", noted that the large and rapid expansion required to rise to first place both exhausts and handcuffs such an entity; stifling its continued rate of expansion, as well as affording competitors an opportunity to make up ground. "As for entering upon the manufacture and sale of new products, its whole system was occupied with its traditional products lines. Standard was suffering from the fate that has normally overtaken pioneers in industrial development, that of being tied by earlier investments and operations." (58)

In 1873, the Standard refined 34% of the total industry's output, with a 20% earnings upon capitalization. (59) In November of 1877, Henry Flagler estimated the Standard to, after a merger freshly completed that month, control fully 5/6ths of the pipelines then in use. (60) April 10th, 1878, Flagler estimates the cumulative refining interests in existence in the U.S. at that time to be valued at $36 million. Author Allan Nevins estimates that the Standard, including leasing quotas among small independent refineries, "probably controlled $33,000,000 of this great investment." Rockefeller, on January 5, 1878, estimated that a $200,000 plant being discussed amounted to just under 1/150th of the total Standard holdings, excepting leased interests. (61)

During the 1880s, the Standard lost ground in Austria-Hungary. The entrance of Russian crude -high in kerosene output- along with treachery -Galician oil companies were selling poor quality products in containers labeled "Standard Oil Co., Long Island City, Refined Standard Petroleum"- contributed to the decimation of USA oil product sales in the country. During 1882 the USA sold 571,400 barrels of its kerosene in Austria-Hungary; 1890 zero barrels; 1891 some 16,700; 1892 zero barrels. (62)

The market share of the Standard in 1870 was 4%, by 1880 it was 80%; the number of independent refiners in 1870 had been 250, in 1880 whittled down to 100. *The national price of refined kerosene declined steadily in nominal dollars*: 1869 $.30, 1874 $.11, 1885 $.08. During this period, Standard reduced their production cost per gallon from a level of $.03 in 1870, to 0.452 cents in 1885. Occurring partway through this series of years, resumption of the redemption of currency for gold on the part of the Treasury occurred in 1879, bringing about some deflation of the currency from its puffed up wartime levels, and the accompanying reduction in money prices, causing all prices to be reduced during the middle and late eighties, after having dropped some during the middle seventies. (63)

Prices of oil products in particular were also lowered by the cessation of demand caused by the culmination of the American Civil War in 1864, leaving a glut of production which well oversupplied the market during the immediate term. Businessmen from nearly all lines of work struggled, or faced ruination, in great quantities during this period, and oil refiners were no exception. The Standard -through its persistent attention to increasing quality, and reducing costs through efficiency- bought out failed, former competitors, often at the eager behest of the party being acquired. The good people at the newly purchased refineries were retained by the Standard, the others let go or replaced, and the Standard applied their own methods of efficient operation to the existing works. The quality of refined oil available improved markedly during this period of declining prices; *Standard had high quality products at low prices*, besting competitors on both fronts, while *benefiting the public*. (64).

Healthy competitors were plentiful. For instance, in 1888 the Tidewater Pipeline Company formed the Tidewater Oil Company. Performing numerable functions -such as: exporting, producing, refining, and transporting- the Tidewater operation controlled approximately 10% of the nation's petroleum business. (65)

DISSOLUTION OF STANDARD, AND FINAL THOUGHTS

Nonetheless, the autoimmune disease of populist, redistributive, envy satiating, political movements saw fit to "solve" a non-existent problem; to "slay" a phantom dragon, one that was really there to save the people. There was never a monopoly, certainly never a menace to the public, and this became increasingly evident during the many years preceding the so-called trustbusting action. A market shift from kerosene, to gas and electricity -which was advantageous to the Standard- nonetheless cut deeply into the dominance of the Standard's position. In the year 1899 kerosene accounted for 58% of all refined petroleum products, but by 1914 a mere 25%. Fuel oil had an inverse change during the same timespan, comprising just 15% of the same array of products in 1899, but a whopping 48% by 1914. During the year 1908, there were minimally 125 independent refining outfits in the U.S.; in 1911 there were 147 or more.

The explosive growth of the industry -competing freely- was too dynamic to be controlled or orchestrated by any single company; even less so any detached and disinterested, bureaucratic body, centrally planning from mission HQ. Nonetheless, trustbusting and satiating the jealousy of the average person's professional betters, were fashionable among media scandal sheets and tabloid stories of the day. Ida Tarbell's famous series of articles in *McClure's* -Tarbell's brother was treasurer of one of Standard's competitors, Pure Oil Company, by the way- were just a drop in the bucket. Newspapers, *Life, Collier's, Harper's*, and books, ***all attempted to cash in on the counterfactual populist furor***. Such a state of affairs beckoned for political opportunism; to attack the private property rights of all citizens, while showcasing the immediately evident heavy legal costs and personal strain placed upon the attacked minority group as though it were a victory for the people of the nation, so done because it may round up a few votes among the "mob mentality" crowd; and this done unto to innocent victims. In the wake of antitrust suits filed against the Standard in 10 different states during the period 1904-1906, a federal charge was brought against the Standard on November 15, 1906. (66) The company was ordered by the Supreme Court to be broken up in 1911.

The abhorrent Supreme Court ruling of 1911 did not alter the practice of competing for custom by lowering prices which had amply existed prior. The period 1910-1919 was no different from any of the four decades preceding it on this score. Unknown or untested companies used tactics such as initially undercutting their better competitors, as well as the tactic of extending credit to the retailers -easing the cash troubles of retailers- in an effort to enrich themselves by lowering prices for the general public. (67) Political persecution was not halted by the headlines garnered by the 1911 case, the aversion to evidence remained in tact as well, when in 1915 the Federal Trade Commission complained that the Standard companies were *refusing to cut prices* in markets in which more than one operation within the Standard's umbrella might reach, because doing so would make their operation less profitable. With one hand of government contradicting what the other hand is doing, the populist legislation attacking, and eventually dismantling the once mighty Standard, *condemned price cutting* as predatory. (68) My, how immensely beneficial to the consumer!

It is important to point out the glaring U.S. judicial hypocrisy involved, and how incredibly counterproductive -achieving the outcome precisely anterior to its stated objective- the Sherman Antitrust Act truly is. *Oppressing good minority groups, in an attempt to satisfy poorly behaved majority groups, is behavior beneficial to one class, and one class only -professional politicians.* Whether called *gilds* during centuries past, or labor unions today, such outfits when given authority to prevent production from occurring during strikes, including authority to prevent others in the labor pool from working the jobs at which the striking workers are turning up their noses during work stoppages, are actual monopolies; while legitimate and lasting business monopolies never exist in real life, with real people, and real money, in absence of government regulation enabling them to do so. The Supreme Court decision in May of 1911 was one which could only have been politically motivated, as the facts regarding the impact upon the public and upon the oil industry, were *forbidden from consideration* by the Court. Justice White wrote in his opinion that a body is guilty if the group's actions are "...of such a character as to give rise to the inference or presumption that they had been entered into or done with the intent to do wrong to the general public and to limit the rights of individuals, thus restraining the free flow of commerce and tending to bring about the ends, such as the enhancements of prices, which were considered to be against the public policy." *The Court never actually substantiated that the Standard wronged the public.* How could they, when the evidence dictates precisely the opposite conclusion? (69) While the Standard was decidedly not guilty of the above quoted behavior, labor unions, with legal backing, are all actually guilty of this, yet this plain truth seems to be so rarely discussed; particularly in the halls of the Congress. (see also: part I, Government Makes Monopoly in Jobs, page# 72)

We notice, also, that the description of Justice White fits precisely the actual consequences of government enabled monopolies unleashed in the name of protecting the public from monopoly! The Interstate Commerce Commission of the late 19th century through present day, the AAA of the New Deal through present day -though struck down twice by the Supreme Court and reinstated by the tyrannical New Dealers, the third piece of legislation remaining after the court-packing scheme had been undertaken- the National Health Service in Britain, Canadian monopolized medicine (70), all come to mind as classic examples of: combinations in restraint of trade, entered into with the intent to harm the general public, that limit the rights of the individual, that increase prices without increasing quality or availability, and which restrain the free flow of commerce. *Only government makes monopoly.*

Less than 20 years after the Supreme Court heinously broke up the Standard Oil Company, in 1928 the Federal Trade Commission (FTC) implored *cooperation* among the oil producers -the very cooperation which Rockefeller had sought and achieved through the construction of the mighty Standard- in an effort to harness supply levels, and to improve production methods. The American Bar Association, in addition to recommending cooperation, in that same year suggested *immunity* for the oil producers with regards to the antitrust laws. (71)

John D. Rockefeller's immense fortune, even by his own account, was an accident of history. He behaved well in his business practices, but it was not through unparalleled ingenuity, nor via dishonesty and cheating, that his wealth swelled so handsomely. If he had been a printer, or a grocer, or entered some other variety of business, he likely would have done well. Being in the oil business when he was, with the rise of the combustion engine occurring concurrently, the rise of industrial equipment in need of various lubricants occurring concurrently, and finally the rise of automobiles approximately three decades after the combination really began to hum in the 1870s, all made a perhaps above-average bookkeeper and shop owner into a tycoon attaining heights unrivaled by any man at any time prior in history. As Allen Nevins tells us:

> "It was the world that spread upon petroleum. For twenty years after Drake's discovery man saw little in oil but a means in banishing night. The invention began to make it an instrument of power and speed: the gas engine, the automobile, the Diesel motor, and the airplane rendered it the propulsive force of civilization. The search for it spread over all continents, until new fields had been opened in every clime. Great Powers came to depend upon it, guarding their pipes and tankers fiercely as their food supply. As it thus rose to world-wide puissance, the Standard Oil Company rose with it to a strength and wealth of which its heads had never dreamed, and Rockefeller's fortune became perhaps the greatest the world had yet seen. The powerful and efficient organization Rockefeller and his partners had created was by 1883 one of the most dynamic organizations in the world and its expansion in the next decade was continuous." (72)

The importance of the Standard to the history of the United States, to its excellence and prosperity:

"These new resources became available at the very time that the flow of Pennsylvania oil began to decline; at the very time, moreover, that invention demanded great supplies of gasoline and lubricants, and that the United States needed cheap oil to meet Russian competition. Sunset was descending upon the Regions, so long a fountain of gold. Although West Virginia produced vigorously in the eighteen nineties, had the United States depended solely on the Appalachian pools the price of crude would have shot upward, new industries built on the gasoline engine would have been retarded, and Russia and the Dutch East Indies would have captured the world market." (73)

John D. Rockefeller's giving has already been touched upon, and will be illustrated briefly once again, as it was both immense and perpetual.

"In 1865, as we have noted, Rockefeller's gifts went above a thousand; they were $1012.35, to be exact. Then in 1866 he gave a total of $1320.43. In 1867, evidently a poor business year, the sum fell to about $660.14; but in 1868 by way of better amends he gave a total of $3675.39; and in 1869, doing still better, a total of $5489.62. Once more, we may emphasize the fact that he had not waited to grow rich before he began giving. It is to be noted that save for one year, his gifts constantly grew larger, and that by the later sixties he was giving some considerable lump sums—$558.42 to Denison University, for example. In his early giving, as later in life, he freely crossed lines of creed, nationality, and color." (74)

Rockefeller's giving by 1887 amounted to over $250,000 donated; 1891 topped $500,000; 1892 $1.35 million. "Hardly a Baptist college in the land failed to get assistance...", said Nevins. Some colleges receiving grants from Rockefeller included Brown, and Vassar, along with Adelbert College in Cleveland.

Some of his rules for giving:

1- He generally did not pay off debts, or contribute to current expenses; endowments were his favorite method.

2- In 1892 resigned positions on boards and such, as he did not wish to feel compelled to give to unworthy recipients, merely due to such association.

3- He liked to give to trustworthy organizations, such as the Baptist Education Society, rather than investigate every church or school who solicited him for funds.

4- Never give alone. If their cause is worthy and their intentions noble, then why won't anybody else give to them?

5- Don't give to lost cause organizations. There must be some reason to expect that the gift will be used judiciously.

Rockefeller preferred to donate anonymously. (75)

Private charity, from Rockefeller as well as from all over the nation during a time of -in comparison to the conditions prevailing since the advent of the New Deal- hardly any taxation or regulation, *expanded the university supply in the USA*. In 1880 the USA had two colleges of note: Johns Hopkins, and Harvard. By 1905 the picture changed drastically. In 1891 Stanford opened, in 1892 the University of Chicago, 1894 brought Clark University. "The universities had shot up suddenly to maturity. Such swift and far-reaching innovations as distinguishing new universities like Chicago and Leland Stanford, and old universities Columbia and Harvard, were possible by munificent gifts." (76) John D. Rockefeller, and the Standard Oil Company, did more to benefit the lowest citizens, enabling many to rise above that station, than any government bureau ever has. The Standard Oil Company is one of the most prominent achievements in American history, and its destruction by government a clear example of so-called populist, redistributive movements, being evidentiary of an autoimmune disease within politics.

OTHER EXAMPLES, A POTPOURRI

While masquerading as a party which holds the best interests of the general public as its paramount priority, and while affecting to uplift the masses, most populist, redistributive, political movements deliver precisely the opposite outcomes. To paraphrase Peter Bauer: Socialism reduces adult aged people to the status of children, perpetually. Adults manage incomes, whereas children are allotted pocket money. This is not only a redistribution of income and of wealth, but also of responsibility. The adult responsibilities are abrogated by the state. (77)

False Alarms and Phantom Monsters
(See also: Part VI, Myth of
Colonial "Rape", page# 378)

In the USA, the Sherman Act of 1890 was passed as a result of *actual* fear of *phantom* private monopolists. The post American Civil War period of 1865-1897 featured "declining prices year after year" during "a wonderful era for the consumer and a frightful age for the producer", or so wrote historian Joseph W. McGuire during the mid-twentieth century. The same man mysteriously concluded that the reduction of competing firms was a legitimate warning sign of "collusion", as opposed to simply an elimination of the weakest and least efficient outfits. (78) *As the market maximized efficiency* through the self-regulation of prices, supply, and demand, the rubes asserted that central planning and heavy handed government regulation were the paths to increased efficiency and consumer protection. *Consumers were not in danger from private monopolists, but fear of that straw-man has been used to propel a monopoly from Washington, in industry after industry, ever since.* The declining prices for, and expanding supply of goods for, consumers during the period was something that government needed to shield them from, evidently.

Conflating being in first place today with the presence of a monopoly existing in perpetuity is a common tactic of the populist practitioners of victim politics;

impugning those who have much simply because they are prospering as opposed to starving, as though they were guilty of a crime or had stolen the money from some person, or peoples, or land.

Circa 1970, a group of college students at Cambridge, in England, put out a brief pamphlet about supposed moral obligations of the West to then undeveloped countries. The students illustrated their ignorance finely as they humiliated themselves by asserting that: "We took the rubber from Malaya, the tea from India, raw materials from all over the world and gave almost nothing in return." (79) As we fact check this unsubstantiated claim, we discover quite quickly that rubber had been absent in Southeast Asia until the British imported rubber seeds to the area from the Amazon jungle, which then germinated into the rubber industry. A century later, during the time concurrent with the Cambridge pamphlet, a substantial proportion of the rubber plants in the area were Asian owned. These Asians who had known only poverty and existence in a desolate region beforehand, now had jobs and some even owned businesses, *thanks to the work of the West in creating this industry for them*. Whether the Asians in the area would have chosen to become entrepreneurs or not, the benefits to the rest of the world would have been transferred just as well, as people all over the planet lived better because of the access to rubber made possible by the planting of this industry in Southeast Asia by the British. How do you suppose automobiles with wooden tires would have progressed in comparison? Or how about bicycles? The ILC (see part IV) see prosperity exist, ask no questions about how it got there or who put it there, and merely pretend that those who benefit from the existence of this prosperity are harmed by it.

Continuing our fact check, we note that the British also imported the tea industry to India. A similar paragraph could be written about it as the preceding paragraph about the rubber in Southeast Asia. I'll save the reader the redundancy, and point out that *the West made these markets out of nothing, and are cast as villains by the socialists in return*. Envy is one hell of a drug, yes? (80) (for more on colonization see part VI, Myth of Colonial "Rape")

Political myths contrary to the actual evidence are quashed by comparison to said evidence. The "West" in fact brings new industries, technology, and culture, to backwards nations; enriching the backwards countries, and bringing commerce -the medicine which treats and cures poverty and materially backwards conditions. Lies asserting the contrary are contained in an article penned by Cyril Connolly, and published in the *Sunday Times*, London, 23 February 1969:

> "It is a wonder that the white man is not more thoroughly detested than he is....In our dealings with every single country, greed, masked by hypocrisy, led to unscrupulous coercion of the native inhabitants....Cruelty, greed and arrogance...characterized what can be summed up in one word, exploitation...." (81)

This is true as well of a July 1976 piece written by Ronald J. Sider in *Christianity Today*. Sider asserts that: "It would be wrong to suggest that 210 million Americans bear sole responsibility for all the hunger and injustice in today's world. All the rich developed countries are directly involved... we are participants in a system that dooms even more people to agony and death than the slave system did." (82) It comes as no surprise that a religious periodical, whose publisher's entire industry is dependent upon guilting and frightening people into turning over their money in the name of charity, is interested in attempting to pull on their reader's heartstrings, but *this method of chicanery is hardly restricted to to any church*. The religion being peddled by politicians that pushes all facts and evidence aside, in favor of edicts and unsubstantiated claims labeled as "truth", conjured up by the speakers and/or their scriptwriters, is much the same and it continues as of this writing.

Would it come as a surprise to any reader if the preceding two quotes in major publications had occurred during any decade thereafter? Or by politicians seeking a high office in the United States during that time span? I highly doubt it, if they're in the practice of speaking the language of evidence. *The same lies are told and accepted year after year, and generation after generation, in spite of the mounting evidence disproving these fictions*. It's easy to fault the purveyors, who are undoubtedly behaving in an incredibly sleazy, duplicitous, and evil fashion when they put forth these falsehoods. However, faulting the audience seems more appropriate, along with seeming like the best path to improving this situation.

No matter how many laws anybody passes, predators and evil people will always exist in this world. That people will be power hungry; venal; amoral; ruthless in their vigorous pursuit for, or retention of, power; will never change. *The first obvious solution is to restrict the power and size of government bodies*, so that even operating at full capacity in the hands of those who seek to be tyrants, they cannot come anywhere near enslaving the populace. *The second obvious solution is to speak of evidence* and to therefore eradicate the political profitability of the lie for the power seeker, whoring themselves for votes. This unsavory character will still say or do anything, for no other reason than because they think it will positively impact their power position in the world, even if it's the truth! *Make it politically profitable to obey the evidence, and the office seekers will have their speechwriters give them platforms and speeches which do so*.

In Africa, the so-called "exploitation" at the hands of the West during the 19th and 20th centuries was the key link to the greater economic well-being that the Africans have experienced. The "oppressors" of the Western cultures converted the empty and undeveloped regions of Africa into productive areas, with some newly created well-off Africans as conspicuous proof of the benefit to the colonized. Nonetheless, *African politicians were alerted to the political profitability of, and the immense power and riches to be gotten via, the use of victim politics*. Redistributionism is merely a massive bureaucracy, ostensibly a public charity, which pays much of the money it takes in to itself. The agencies employ many people and pay generously, as well as giving the ruler justification for exercising greater control over the populace -increasing taxes, stifling commerce through monopolies, in some cases instituting a perpetual military state- in the name of helping "the masses".

In 1975, then President of Tanzania, Julius Nyerere, made the following unsubstantiated claim during an official visit to London "If the rich nations of the world go on getting richer and richer at the expense of the poor, the poor of the world must demand a change...." A simple fact check reveals quite readily that upon initiation of a permanent contact with the West during the 19th century, this area was sparsely populated, while those few who were there frequently encountered Arab slavers. The same old story has the same old ending, as the improvement in development and of material quality of life experienced by the area and its inhabitants, are directly linked to the so-called "oppression" of the West. (83)

Dr. Kwame Nkrumah, the inaugural President of Ghana upon its independence from Britain during the mid-twentieth century, also used nonsensical and fictitious statements in an effort to exploit their political profitability. Ghana, an area which was able to develop an upper class of wealthy individuals largely due to cocoa exports to the West, nonetheless asserted that Western capitalism was "a world system of financial enslavement and colonial oppression and exploitation of a vast majority of the population of the earth by a handful of so-called civilized nations". (84) Do you suppose that either of these fellows returned the wealth that their country had accumulated to the Western nations who were solely responsible for its creation? You know, because it was so oppressive? Precisely the opposite was the case.

COMPANIES ASSAILED

The companies, instruments formed and owned by people, corporations through which are provided jobs, goods, services, and a better life for everyone, are frequently targeted by charlatans as doing harm to the general public so that these same shysters can implement a government monopoly -which will *actually* harm the general public- in its stead. The politician, rather than being assigned blame and condemned, is instead usually assigned credit and praised, by the very same general public who are being harmed by such behavior. Having already covered the Standard Oil Company, the next section brings forth a handful of other companies which benefited the public more than any government program ever has, yet were assailed by the populists.

AMERICAN SUGAR

Conflating "first place presently" with "perpetual monopoly" was evident in the USA during the late 19th century, and into the early 20th century, in the case of the American Sugar Refining Company. The Sherman Antitrust Act was passed in 1890 -ostensibly to "protect" the populace from phantom private business monopolies which were to subject them to high prices, poor selection, and shoddy quality, while also preventing competitors from giving customers choice in the marketplace. This Act was utilized in 1893 by the federal government, in particular the Justice Department, as they brought suit against the American Sugar Refining Company in the wake of the company's having acquired four other refining concerns. At the moment of acquisition, this gave the company 98% of the present sugar refining market.

A verdict rendered in 1895 by the Supreme Court mercifully sided with the company; though it failed to declare the Sherman Act unconstitutional. Unrestrained capitalism and the desire for personal gain were left to do their work, and as people derived sugar from new sources, and through new methods -without occupational licensing, or regulation which granted monopolies to the few in the name of helping the masses- the company's market share fell steadily. From that 98% proportion in 1893, to 61% by 1905, and then to 25% in 1927. By 1920, a minimum of 105 plants specialized in beet sugar production; a new technological development which expanded the market in ways that the stroke of a pen on a statute book never has. (85)

The following chart contains data compiled by D.T. Armentano, Ph.D. Armentano provides a theoretical price difference, which differs arithmetically from the prices he lists as wholesale and as retail. I presume this alternative difference is due to some formulaic transmission of the raw data which goes unexplained; however, it could also simply be due to computational errors. The minute discrepancies between the difference listed for a few of the years chronicled, and the difference when calculated from the raw data provided, does nothing to alter the picture of steadily declining prices for consumers with margins of mere fractions of a penny in almost every year.

YEAR	Wholesale Sugar Prices	ASRC Prices	Theoretical Difference, Per Armentano
1880	$0.0962	$0.09	
1882			$0.01437
1890	$0.06171	$0.069	$0.0072
1895	$0.04152	$0.053	$0.00882
1899			$0.005
1900	$0.0532	$0.061	
1905	$0.0526	$0.06	$0.00978
1910	$0.04972	$0.06	$0.00784

SOURCE FOR CHART: D.T. Armentano. Ph. D., *Myths of Antitrust: Economic Theory and Legal Cases* (New Rochelle: Arlington House, 1972), p. 57-58

U.S. STEEL

U.S. Steel -The United States Steel Company- was formed in 1901 as a coalition of eleven formerly separate companies. The enjoinment, at the moment of its inception, accounted for 44% of total output of steel products in the USA. (86) *For a decade the company manufactured quality products, provided employment to thousands, featured declining prices for consumers during that span*, and was attacked by purveyors of victim politics, as the populists brought the company before the Supreme Court in an attempt to destroy this beautiful machine. The attackers asserted that during the period 1901-1911 U.S. Steel had monopolized the steel market, as well as that the company had unreasonably restrained trade within the industry, each of which are blatantly fallacious.

U.S. STEEL'S SHARE OF OUTPUT IN THE USA

1901-1911

Product	1901	1911
Pig iron	43%	45%
Finished rolled product	50.1%	46%
Steel ingot production	66%	54%
Wire nails	67%	55%

Source for chart: D.T. Armentano. Ph. D., *Myths of Antitrust: Economic Theory and Legal Cases* **(New Rochelle: Arlington House, 1972), p. 103**

During 1911, U.S. Steel Produced only 22% of all wire products -netting, fencing, etc..- and a mere 30% of all structural steel. (88)

PERCENTAGE INCREASE OF PRODUCTION FOR

U.S. STEEL AND ITS COMPETITORS, 1901-1911

Bethlehem Steel	3,779.7%
Inland	1,495.9%
Labelle	463.4%
Jones and Laughlin	206.7%
U.S. Steel	40%

Source for chart: D.T. Armentano. Ph. D., *Myths of Antitrust: Economic Theory and Legal Cases* **(New Rochelle: Arlington House, 1972), p. 104**

INDUSTRY-WIDE STEEL PRICE DECLINE

1901-1911

Product	1901 Price	1911 Price
Wire nails	$51	$36
Steel bars	$33	$25
Steel beams	$36	$27
Billets	$27	$24

Source for chart: D.T. Armentano. Ph. D., *Myths of Antitrust: Economic Theory and Legal Cases* **(New Rochelle: Arlington House, 1972), p. 105**

The decline of the sale prices for products offered to the public by U.S. Steel, while the *prices incurred by the company in order to manufacture the metal rose*, is illustrated in the following:

DECLINE IN PRICES OF U.S. STEEL PRODUCTS, INCREASE IN SHIPPING COSTS AND WAGES PAID 1904-1912

U.S. Steel's Products	Price Change (%)
Domestically Sold Fabricated Products	–19%
ALL Other Products	–11%
U.S. Steel's Costs	
Freight on coke and limestone	+10%
Wages	+25%

Source for chart: D.T. Armentano. Ph. D., *Myths of Antitrust: Economic Theory and Legal Cases* (New Rochelle: Arlington House, 1972), p. 105

In an alarmingly close decision of 4-3, in 1920 the Supreme Court refused to break up the company, having actually consulted the pertinent evidence, and subsequently obeying the conclusions dictated by said evidence. Benefits to consumers continued unmolested; unlike the Standard Oil and the American Tobacco cases. (88)

AMERICAN TOBACCO COMPANY

The American Tobacco Company was formed as a result of a merger of the five leading cigarette producers and sellers, this occurring during January of 1890. At its inception, the outfit made 90% of domestic cigarette sales, but just 74% by 1907. (89) American Tobacco underwent a second merger in 1904, this combining 20 other large concerns to form the new American Tobacco Company -that is, the second incarnation under the same name. This was a separate entity. A famous contemporary example would be the new General Motors, formed after the socialist bailouts of the George W. Bush administration. Nevertheless, competitors were *abundant*. In 1910 there were several hundred independent cigarette manufacturers in the USA. Thousands of firms competed with each other in the overall tobacco market -cigarettes, snuff, cigars, chew, etc..- and American Tobacco was among their number. The cost of entry into the business was low, and mechanization made for inexpensive production of the also inexpensive raw materials; opening the door to upward professional mobility to any who would take on the risk, including tobacco workers. As the Standard Oil Company had before it, American Tobacco bought out competitors at generous prices, according to buyer and seller alike. (90)

American Tobacco exclusively employed free workers, thereby escaping the grasp of greedy monopolists from the Tobacco Workers' Labor Union. This increased the number of workers employed; affording them the opportunity to advance their position on the career ladder, improving from the position of unemployed to that of employed, and eventually graduating from employee to that of business owner; improved productivity afforded the public more goods to buy, at lower prices; and saved the company money. *Every class won*. (91) The only excluded element was that of the greedy monopolists in the union, who themselves sought to restrain trade via systematic exclusion of all those who were outside of their little club.

A glimpse at prices offered to the public by American Tobacco show *a near doubling of the cost for the company's raw material*, leaf tobacco, while the price offered to the public of only one of their major products rose at a similar rate. *The company's major products*, aside from plug tobacco, *held steady in pricing or reduced in price*, during the period 1895-1907:

American Tobacco Prices 1895, 1902, 1907

PRODUCT	1895	1902	1907
Cigarettes (per 1,000, no tax)	$2.77	$2.29	$2.20
Fine cut (per lb, no tax)	$0.27	$0.33	$0.30
Smoking tobacco (per lb, no tax)	$0.25	$0.267	$0.301
Plug Tobacco (per lb, no tax)	$0.155	$0.277	$0.304
Little cigars (per 1,000 no tax)	$4.60	$4.37	$3.60
Price of leaf tobacco (raw material)	$0.06		$0.105

Source for chart: D.T. Armentano. Ph. D., *Myths of Antitrust: Economic Theory and Legal Cases* (New Rochelle: Arlington House, 1972), p. 94

The American Tobacco "monopoly" was dismantled, in spite of prevailing evidence of thriving competition and positive outcomes for consumers. In 1908, American Tobacco Company had 3 of 4 circuit court judges rule that their company was in violation of the Sherman Act as in restraint of trade. *3 of the 4 circuit judges noted the economic benefits to the public caused by the company's conduct* that they were declaring to be illegal. The one dissenting judge simply stated that any two companies, who exist to any extent in two or more states of the union, are in restraint of trade as the law is written; *referring to the Sherman Act as a "drastic statute"* in their opinion submitted to the court. The circuit court judge who voted to convict, but noted the public benefit the company had committed, derided the law in his opinion when submitted. Judge Noyes posed questions, the answers to which exposed the perversity of the law. Noyes concluded his thought by stating "But these are all legislative, and not judicial, questions." (92)

In the 1911 Supreme Court case *no* attention was given to the important statistics -prices, competition, etc... Nonetheless, the company was deemed to have committed "wrongful acts" which were a "danger" to "individual liberty and the public well-being." The company was ordered to be deconstructed at the pleasure of the circuit court. (93)

On the subject of tobacco, potential monopoly, and the level of government interference in -known alternatively as regulation of- commerce, a case of the loose hand of the Beast preventing monopoly from occurring during the mid-17th century in the New World, is worth considering. Tobacco was the staple cash crop of the privately funded and operated colonies of Virginia and Maryland (see part VI, Grip Tightens, Masses Suffer Monopoly; also part VI, Colonial America; for more). By mid-century, tobacco was even being utilized as a means of settling debts with the government. As with all products, overproduction could flood the marketplace with supply thereby reducing nominal returns. These diminutions could bring some farmers below profitability; even with the increased units sold at the lower price. Virginia men at least once thought of acting in concert as planters to limit production, but Maryland farmers would never cooperate. *Diffuse authority prevented this cognition of monopoly from being manifested.* (94) Only state action creates monopolies.

ALUMINUM COMPANY OF AMERICA

	Output of Aluminum USA (LBS Per Day)	Price to Consumers of Aluminum Ingot (US Dollars Per LB)
1887		$5
1889	50	$3
1892	1,000	
1897	8,000	
1899		$0.50
1910		$0.38
1937		$0.22
1941		$0.15

Source for chart: D.T. Armentano. Ph. D., *Myths of Antitrust: Economic Theory and Legal Cases* (New Rochelle: Arlington House, 1972), p. 108-109

Alcoa grew the aluminum industry exponentially, through a combination of ingenious patented invention, tremendous industriousness, and hard work. Nonetheless, the government attacked Alcoa because politicians do their campaigning on the headlines purchased by these kinds of prosecutions -and *the purpose of this book is to drastically reduce the proportion of the public upon whom such tactics are effective*. Even though a 1925 Federal Trade Commission (FTC) case accusing ALCOA of monopolistic malfeasance was decided in ALCOA's favor -mopping the floor with the absurd charges- the New Dealers in 1937 brought an antitrust case against ALCOA -along with a rash of others such as Andrew Mellon (95), and Sam Insull (96). Decided in 1941, with *a dismissal of all* 140 of the government's charges, the District Court Judge quoted the from the FTC case:

1. The record also shows that respondent [Alcoa] never attempted to monopolize the scrap market; that it is impossible to do so, the scrap market being so scattered and diversified and in such great available quantities that one concern, no matter how large its purchases, could never corner the said market.

2. Respondent has no monopoly on bauxite [the ore of aluminum]; there being sufficient supplies of bauxite in the world, exclusive of respondent's holdings, available for many generations to come.

3. Respondent has no monopoly on water power; its holdings now being only a small per cent of available water power in the world.

4. The respondent does not now nor has it ever attempted to control or dominate the policy of the Aluminium Goods Manufacturing Company.

5. Respondent has never attempted to control and does not now control the market for foreign aluminum in the United States.

6. That foreign aluminum is imported into the United States and competes with respondent in the sale of virgin aluminum ingots.

7. There is no arbitrary or direct differential between the purchase price of scrap aluminum and the selling price of virgin aluminum. The purchase price of scrap depends upon the law of supply and demand.

8. That respondent has never had a monopoly of the sand castings industry of- the United States. (97)

The government couldn't appeal to Roosevelt's now-packed Supreme Court (98) due to the conflict that existed, arising from the fact that four of the justices had been prosecutors of Alcoa during their tenures at the Justice Department. ***The New Deal Congress voted to have a court act in place of the Supreme Court***, the Circuit Court of Appeals. It was in this court that ***they found a judge who created a rigged game*** when he disqualified aluminum derived from secondary ingot from inclusion, for the purposes of the case, in the same market with virgin ingot; even though he himself confesses that the two compete ***nearly interchangeably*** in the market! The appeals judge sneered at the factual evidence, claiming that Alcoa's 10% Return on Investment -ROI- was immaterial: "...the whole issue is irrelevant anyway, for it is no excuse for "monopolizing" a market that the monopoly has not been used to extract from the consumer more than a 'fair' profit. The Act has wider purposes." (99).

Mercifully, the verdict did not involve any consequences for Alcoa, other than forevermore carrying the classification of a "convicted monopoly". This would likely be a troubling characteristic to possess, particularly having already suffered nearly a decade of the ***New Deal's fascistic assault*** on the nation's producers of goods and the providers of jobs -known alternatively as corporations- as ***the central planners relentlessly thrusted their tentacles in every direction***, squeezing tightly around every industry, and reaching into every citizen's pocket, ***as their gang sought monopolization*** of every facet of industry. The monicker was like a bullseye, perpetually taunting the innocent convicts, until the next time that politicians might desire some headlines and take another shot at Alcoa. Both sides still hungry for a clean victory, they petitioned to re-open the case in 1948. Alcoa got a pat on the back, and the label of "monopoly" was removed. The court did, however, order that shareholders in Alcoa, as well as Aluminum ltd., choose: one, or the other, or none in 1951. (100)

GOVERNMENT MAKES MONOPOLY IN BUSINESS

(see also: part VI, Grip Tightens,

Masses Suffer Monopoly, page# 350)

"Just as the human spirit is abused by restrictions on the exchange of ideas, so the welfare of peoples is restrained by chains which are imposed on production and the exchange of material goods. Only when they establish among themselves general, free, unrestricted commerce, will the nations of earth reach the highest level of physical well-being." -Petition presented to the German Diet of the Confederation by the Commercial and Industrial Union on April 20, 1819 (101)

Departing from the false accusations against the business enterprises which outshine any jobs program, energy programs, or production program, put forth by central planners, we now turn to **the only realm in which actual and lasting monopolies exist; that in which they are created and perpetuated by government**. Government made monopoly can be found in Africa during the period 1937-1975. During 1937, cocoa producers on the Gold Coast, and those firms which were their largest customers, each separately attempted to collude in an effort to impact prices. A government commission recommended that a government body interfere with the price of cocoa -standing between the producers in Africa, and their customers. WWII broke out, and wartime policy involved the British government purchasing as much as was produced in the area. This wartime bureau was soon replaced by another, claiming to protect the interests of producers, the West African Produce Control Board (WAPCB). From 1947-1950 the WAPCB gave up its monopoly in purchasing cocoa, passing it down to a variety of local monopolistic boards, with Nigeria in particular receiving a 1954 update of 3 bureaus to dictate terms within various regions of its country.

"The boards had by law the sole right to export produce, and thus they held monopolies. They also held by law the sole right to buy for export the produce under their control." The author, Frederick Pedler, continued: "As a corollary of their monopoly rights, the boards had the power to fix the prices which were paid to the producers." (102) These government entities, erected under the guise of benefitting the producers, dictated prices and the market in which a producer may attempt to sell his wares, to these very same producers; harming the very people that they affected to be assisting. These boards also hoarded capital and used it to further exercise influence over the people. Price fixing of groundnuts destabilized incomes for producers, while also preventing purchasers from enjoying low prices during times of high supply.

This meddling, in addition to export duties and other interference, *harmed the producers immensely* -the very people the boards claimed to be helping when they had been established! This government interference likely cost cocoa producers in Ghana 40% of their would-be incomes during the 1947-61 period; 25% for Nigerian producers. High taxes were imposed upon these producers, to compound the offense of the bureaus. Moreover, the hoarding of capital by these government boards kept it out of the hands of the cocoa producers, preventing them from putting it to use any number of ways. "These factors affected the kind of society which took shape in Africa, restricting the growth of a prosperous peasantry and of a property-owning middle class. (103)

The aforementioned (in the False Alarms and Phantom Monsters section, page# 52) learned behavior of the creation of monopoly through central planning, acquired from the politicians of their European colonizers, was illustrated in Dahomey, Africa, during the mid-20th century:

"The trading companies were the same ones as took the lead in industrial development in Nigeria, Ghana, and Ivory Coast, and they came under pressure from the government to do the same in Dahomey. It seemed impossible to identify any activity which offered hope of success. The companies were accused of preserving a capitalist monopoly, though the loss-making competition which existed in Dahomey was a curious situation to describe as 'monopoly'. *It was the government which formed a real monopoly* by inviting the three principal merchant houses (1962) to join with it in setting up a 'mined company' (that is, in French parlance, a partnership between the government and the private sector) for the purpose of handling imports of certain staple commodities. It was known as SODACI, in which the government had two-thirds of the equity, and the commercial partners shared the other third." (104)

Evidence showing that government makes monopoly, while private enterprise never does, can be found in Greece during the 4th century BC. Gold and silver mines located in Greece, or in one of their colonies as was more common, were property of the Greek government. Mines were leased to private individuals. The lists of lease grantees/purchasers, and the list of those prominent in civic affairs, overlapped mightily. (105) In England during the 1st quarter of the 17th century, monopolies pervaded as the central planning enacted by the monarchy mirrored what would later be called socialism/communism. (106)

As is so often the case with regulators, their "help" just hurts. In Southern Rhodesia, pre-WWII official regulation of maize production sought to give the maize-milling industry help by forbidding foreign competition, thereby granting a domestic monopoly to the existing producers. This, of course, led to higher maize prices -*due to the monopoly which government instituted and perpetuated*- which throttled the production and profitability of products incorporating, or derived from, maize. Such products as glucose, starch, and cornflour, were impacted by the socialist, centrally planned monopoly. *All of the citizens, in all classes*: business owners, their employees; along with indirectly involved elements such as transporters, re-sellers, and bakers, in both the owner and laborer classes, *suffered as a result of this "help"*. (107)

We see the fallacy of the lamp in action during late medieval Europe, as *state action to prevent private monopoly in fact codified a monopoly*. Equality of liberty was sacrificed for "equality" of outcome, as the general interest was trumped by the special interest. The merchant towns, originating during the 11th century, of course did not cultivate their own food, as trade between the town and country was necessary to provide for each party. Unfortunately for all parties involved, the town government often regulated such trade with an enormously heavy hand. The important variable (see part VII, Key Variable), while set to self-regulation -AOL- as the people were enabled to rise from paupers to merchants and establish these beautiful towns (see part VI, Social Mobility), this was set to the POS setting within the town, as central planning became involved. In a stated attempt to "protect" small consumers from high prices, regulation held back the small sellers such as peasant farmers, and local bakers or butchers.

Stiff regulations in restraint of trade -such as forcing peasants or tradesmen to sell directly to the town burgess, which enabled dictation to the seller of the price; monitoring purchase of supplies along with sale of finished products; along with the prevention of stockpiling of supplies for a rainy day- were easily thrust upon locals, but impossible to force onto large shippers -wholesalers- who could walk away with their shiploads of goods if their price was not met. (108) The various restrictions and controls instituted in the name of "eliminating middleman mark-ups" of prices, along with protecting the consumer from a supplier's monopoly *in fact created a middle man monopoly amongst the burgesses*. (109)

MAGNITOGORSK, RUSSIA, STEEL PLANT

The Marxist revolutions and regimes in Russia which nearly spanned the duration of the 20th century, gave us many illustrations of the inferiority of central planning, the harm done to the masses, the suppression of the rights of the presently least-moneyed, while cloaked in a banner declaring itself a "dictatorship of the proletariat". The incomparable Stephen Kotkin, in his tremendous book *Steeltown, USSR*, provides an illuminating account of this failure of central planning, from which I have taken but a few tidbits to relay to the reader within this section. The Magnitogorsk Steel Works were founded 1929 in an effort to build the world's largest and most advanced iron and steel plant. 1932 produces pig iron, 1933 produces steel.

200,000 townspeople live in barracks, tents, and mud huts. A notable scarcity of running water or a sewage system, along with an absence of street lights and paved roads, existed. By 1939 the Magnitogorsk Works produced 10% of the USSR's steel, after being desolate 10 years prior. This site produced 50% of steel used for tanks during the Second World War.

From these beginnings, we advance to the early 1960s, when over 50% of townspeople were still living in the 1930s barracks. During the 1980s the plant produced 16 million tons of steel per year -equal to the national output of Great Britain- making it the largest steel complex on earth. Yet, the locals in this redistributive "dictatorship of the proletariat" were finding a perpetual scarcity of food and clothing for themselves. (110) The juxtaposition between the "plenty" produced by the mill, and the "poverty" of the workers and inhabitants of the town nearby -such contrasts occurring in situations in which the regulatory environment was loose enough to dictate the conclusion that there was more to go around for everyone, and that people had the utmost opportunity to improve their standing on the financial ladder, were utilized in an effort to cast unjust aspersions onto such instances; a disparity which was then, and is still now, promised by the proponents of setting the important variable to the Proponents Of Slavery (see part VII) -POS- setting to *cease from existing*- is striking. Central planning perpetually inflicts the very pain that it claims to eradicate.

During the late 1980s, over 85% of the plant's production was mandated by central planners to be kept away from the inhabitants of Magnitogorsk. The sewing factory, as well as the shoe factory, in town exported 98% of production out of town while the locals were in need of all of the above. ***This failure to fulfill the promises that those who perform labor will be entitled to the lion's share of the products produced***, if all private property rights are concentrated into the hands of the few by decree, is similar to the experience of Chinese peasants involved in grain production during Mao's era, only to have the grain kept from them upon harvest, imposing a scarcity of food among the workers laboring to produce the grain. Magnitogorskis travel 1,500 km to Belarus in order to buy shoes made in Magnitogorsk. They then return another 1,500 km to sell the shoes to the citizens of Magnitogorsk. (111)

American John Scott arrived in 1932, bedazzled by the promises made by the socialists. Scott worked diligently for these same communists until 1937, when Stalin and his cohorts were perpetrating The Terror of 1937-38, making innocent people disappear -many of whom were known by Scott. It took 4 years of back and forth with the ruling overlords of the socialist state for his wife to secure her exit papers, prior to their departure in 1941. *Scott spent the rest of his life speaking of the importance of standing up to socialism* in all instances and all parts of the world in which it might occur, having learned first hand that *the word does not match the deed.* (112)

The stagnation, even regression, of conditions, and the lack of innovation which are a few of the trademarks of socialism, grow more flagrant with the passage of time. By 1987 the Japanese auto-focus camera, the Japanese laptop, and ziplock bags, were all entirely foreign to the native population. (113) The poor performance from workers who are living in a society obsessed with so-called equality, compared with those who are "oppressed" by the opportunity to gain or to lose -although they were badly hampered by union monopolists enabled by government- was evident when in approximately 1990 the Magnitogorsk Works with its 60,000 workers produced 16 million tons of steel; mostly of poor quality. In the USA a plant in Gary, Indiana, produced 8 million tons of steel with just 7,000 workers. Both plants operated concurrently. (114)

In 1987 in Russia, as well as in the late 1970s in China, government officials were incredibly concerned with information control, for the purposes of suppressing the truth about the realities of central planning and its results, compared with the superior approach of free trade. Stephen Kotkin in Russia, and Fox Butterfield in China, each report similar experiences as writers who were known foreigners. (115)

GOVERNMENT MAKES MONOPOLY IN JOBS
(See also: part III, Labor Monopolies,
Castes, Wage Controls)

Job Creators' Union: A coalition of the few, whose enduring existence is made possible *only* by government decree, whose aims are to deny opportunity for entrance and advancement to all others, to limit supply for all others, and to artificially increase prices imposed unto all others.

Job Holders' Monopoly: A coalition of the few, whose enduring existence is made possible *only* by government decree, whose aims are to deny opportunity for entrance and advancement to all others, to limit supply for all others, and to artificially increase prices imposed unto all others.

Whether labeled as *gilds*, trade associations, labor unions, or anything else, such organizations seek to exclude outsiders from accessing jobs, and even intentionally suppress the amount of jobs created -preferring that new jobs not exist at all, rather than to exist under terms that do not match their liking; even if those outside of their group were to work the jobs! By switching the familiar terms of "monopoly", which has traditionally been affixed to businesses; with the term "union", which has traditionally been affixed to those employed by another's business; the uniformity of the behavior becomes unmistakable, and for a person to consider such behavior on the part of one such group to be evil or to be desirous, that same person must reach a similar verdict pertaining the other group, or else admit prejudice in their judgment. If the person in question sincerely seeks equality of liberty for all citizens, then that person must desire the legal and practical eradication of such groups no matter which side of the employee/employer coin the group may be formed.

The reader may find themselves confronted by parties telling half-truths, attempting to dupe the reader into supporting or even *demanding* that monopolies be given immense legal permissions to violate the private property rights of all those outside of the monopoly; stating that employees who are granted entry into a union monopoly under the previously mentioned conditions of inequality of property rights, obtain higher wages or payment packages than those who are excluded from the union monopoly, but are in a similar line of work. Such tactics are appallingly insulting to anybody who subjects this statement to even the slightest amount of scrutiny. When a group, let's say it comprises 0.5% of the labor pool, is selected -referred to colloquially today as "privileged"- by government so that it has peculiar legal license to *exclude* the remainder of the labor pool from competing with them for jobs, that such a group will succeed in extracting greater compensation than those who are on the outside looking in, *is not a surprising outcome*. Conversely, *an outcome that I find fascinating* is that a monopoly which excludes 99.5% of the labor pool from these jobs is considered beneficial to the workers *as a class*! To conclude from this that to pack everybody together into one massive labor union will bring forth the utmost prosperity to the workers as a faction is to make a grave mistake. (see part II, Germany; also part II, China; also part III, "Worker's Paradise"; also part VI, Karl Marx Stuff)

A trade union monopoly is a situation in which its members have the terms of their employment dictated to them by the few who are heading the group, and doing the negotiating on behalf of the members. This dictation is tolerated by the members for a variety of reasons, not least of which is that the member feels that they are receiving more money than they would be in absence of their government enforced monopoly position. As we see in Germany, France, China, and Russia (see note in prior paragraph), when everybody is thrown into one massive pot of "collective bargaining" what results is in fact "collective slavery". *Now that the freedom to choose has been revoked, what had been the dictation tolerated in the small trade union scenario, in which members perceived themselves as gaining an undue advantage of some variety over those who were on the outside looking in*, and in which the members are in fact free to choose to leave that employer to pursue their objectives in a multitude of alternative ways -no matter how much they pretend that they are victims, forced to work for one particular employer, absent any actual alternatives- *becomes intolerable dictation from the few in charge*, as they are now *in fact* without any alternatives, *with all jobs and prices in all industries and occupations controlled by central planners.*

A smattering of examples of what some authors or politicians describe as "strong labor", or as ample "workers' rights", will follow and the illustrations of their negative impact upon the worker as a class, as well as of the myopic and destructive genuine motivations of advocates of such groups, will be unambiguous. More on this Faustian predicament can be found in part III.

During the middle of the 19th century in Germany, there occurred something of a revolution -some might refer to it as simply severe domestic tumult- during which new houses of legislature were formed and attempted to promulgate their own laws. Much like the situation in France half of a century prior (see part II), the complaining employees got their hands on the car keys after incessant and violent demands to drive someone else's car, and like immature teenagers proved that they didn't know what to do with the car once they got their hands on it. *Simply decreeing prosperity*, a worker's paradise, or high wages, *does not mean that such can or will occur*, in an enduring fashion, as a result of any such decrees.

"Monopoly" and "union" are synonymous terms in practice, harmful to all aspects of a society when enabled by government, and this was certainly evident in Germany during 1848. In the name of helping "the worker" as a class, the trade monopolists sought a legally codified, unearned -certainly unearned by the merit of their abilities in their stated trade, but we could say that it had been earned by the merit of their abilities in political influence- advantage which:

> violated the rights of their customer -employer- to negotiate a price freely for that which they intend to buy;
>
> violated the right to negotiate his price for all aspiring workers who were excluded by the legal monopoly -often being denied opportunity to attempt to gain a job at all;
>
> and which imposed a higher nominal cost upon the end consumer of the product to be manufactured.

From June 11th to the 14th, printers appealed to the provisional congress for less freedom to purchase print related machinery for current and aspiring entrepreneurs; this would also impinge the market for the sale of the machinery manufacturer's ware, negatively impacting *all* workers involved in that enterprise from owner, to laborer, to janitor, to those mining and transporting the metal to the shop to be made into machine parts, and then finally the printing press. The printers also demanded artificially high wages to be extracted from the citizens who owned the company employing them, and that this be done through the strong-arming of the state. During the 20th to the 25th of July, tailors appealed to the congress for elimination of *all* jobs in shops selling ready-made clothes, also seeking an artificial suppression of jobs involving manufacturing with a needle -this, intended to increase scarcity for employers. Others followed suit. The carpenters of Bremen referred to the guild system as "a priceless asset." (116)

Violence, terror, and tyranny, pervaded this episode in Germany, as the rioting animals made less for everybody, in order to appease the greedy few. Viersen weavers terrorized their way into a pact with their superior in the business community, Friedrich Diergardt. As soon as these animals were out of sight, Diergardt simply ordered a reduction in the quantity of production -known synonymously as output- of his business, making less for everybody. Then he skipped town to wait out the storm. On March 31st, Elberfeld weavers forced a pact restricting production. All this effort to increase prices and scarcity, done while people throughout Germany were cash-strapped. (117) These people could hardly be said to have the best interests of the masses at heart. They were clearly self-serving and myopic.

Union monopolists, the teamsters, were displeased by the competition which had been brought by locomotives and steamships against transport shipping via horse and wagon, during the most recent 20 years. On April 5th, they vandalized the Taunus Railroad, adjacent Kastel in Nassau. The savages uprooted rail ties and wrecked the station house. This, after many ungranted petitions for government sanction of their desired monopoly over transport. Everybody suffered. (118)

The special interest was shown to outweigh the general interest for guild cabal members, as sailing boatsmen stood in the way of industrial progress in a variety of ways. Why should they stand in the way of industrial progress? It is industrial progress and the creation of new competition -each person *themselves* permitted an equal chance at both success and failure- which persuades sellers to seek to please the customer by delivering better quality and prices, and in turn uplifts the masses. The impact of increasing the volume of goods sold, as well of services sold; while reducing the price to consumers, provides an immediate and momentous impact that open competition and low government intrusion can be expected to deliver. Such industrial progress, designed to positively impact the ability to trade, and also intended to be utilized by those who are planning and conducting business affairs, both creates and sustains jobs. This occurs both directly by employing those necessary to operate the steamship, as well as those who load and unload the cargo; while also indirectly, via those employed at the positions in other businesses and industries, who work the hours that are sustained by this increase in commerce. Industrial progress, and competition therein, have also shown a strong tendency to yield an increase in access to markets -be they the job market, or business ownership, or perhaps a specific type of job, or business- to aspiring entrants, while simultaneously yielding a reduction in the operating costs for all financial concerns, including private households. This assists with, and often provides a genesis for, mobility up and down the ladder of the financial classes.

These selfish sailors, along with their like-minded confederates who sought monopoly in their own professions, used cannons and muskets against the steamships traveling the Rhine, between the Mainz and Cologne, during late March and early April. Their terrorism was rewarded, as an agreement was struck to: cease the production of new vessels, lessen the quantity of ports patronized, and to remove coal barges from the vessels utilized in the transport of manufactured products. (119) Less for everybody -including the rioters and their families- bringing about an immediate and temporary increase in wages for those in the cabal, was all that the short-sighted and myopic vandals had in mind. One of many cases in which *the special interest outweighs the general interest, in the name of "uplifting the masses"*.

Truly a sick ruse, but the undeniable efficacy is what causes its frequent invocation by shysters as they attempt to *convince the people that their shackles are in fact their liberation*. Such an outcome is an alarming indictment of any society to which it justly applies.

On April 27th, 1853, Otto von Bismark remarked while in Frankfurt, Germany: "Here corporate associations, ...serve rather as the arena for petty political and personal squabbles and as a device for the successful exploitation of the public and the exclusion of competition." Bismarck also noted high prices, poor selection, and low quality of goods; in addition to poor service and a slovenly workforce, and work ethic. (120)

A few years later, another instance of monopolists looking out for themselves, at the expense of *all* others occurred in Germany from 1860-64. Guilds of handicraftsmen petitioned the government, advocating a banning of department stores, along with restrictive legislation providing restriction or prevention of the right to buy and sell stock, banks, machines, and many additional items, on the open market. In fact, openly encouraging a blanket, all encompassing, industrial code thoroughly invading every nook and cranny of the economy possible. (121)

Nearly a century later, during 1933 in Germany, an episode that will be repeated later (part II) within the context of the succession of *actions delivered by people claiming that they will act in the best interest of the masses once the masses have forfeited their freedom to choose*. In what serves as a fine example of the Beast unchained, transforming from servant to master, National Socialism delivered the elimination of choice for the worker, or labor, as a faction. This took place just 3 months after seizing the helm of government, with power now heavily concentrated into the hands of the few by decree, and with immense centralization of authority and planning. Adolph Hitler declared the standard Socialist European workers' holiday of May Day to be a national holiday, proclaiming May Day 1933 to be the "Day of National Labor". Prior to the festivities, Hitler spoke to a group of labor union delegates in the Chancellery in the Wilhelmstrasse, reassuring them of his commitment to the unions. In his speech to the six figure crowd at the gala in the airfield, he proclaimed: "Honor work and respect the worker". The following morning, May 2nd, 1933, S.S. and S.A.

men occupied trade union offices nationwide, and arrested the leaders so that they could be beaten and taken away to the camps. All workers: employees, management, employers, and the self employed, were now placed into a single, centrally planned and controlled, union called the Labor Front. State ownership of business means ownership of collective bargaining rights, along with private property rights. The People, through the mechanism of the State, owned -and controlled- everything; *which of course, in practice, meant that the handful of people in government positions at the time owned and controlled everything.*

Workers were chained to their assigned job at their assigned workplace; similar to Maoist China, and precisely what Frank Roosevelt had in mind with NIRA and the NRA in the USA during the 1930s (122). Workers were given papers without which they could never be hired by any employer -again like China would institute a few decades later. The finality of the job placement by the state was legislatively enshrined in 1938, though it had already been law in practice for some years prior. (123)

Elsewhere, and several centuries prior, in late Medieval Europe, the towns -created a century or more into the past by private traders who themselves rose from nothing, without regulations tying their competitors' hands behind their back, and who freed all those who came to their towns from the perpetual servitude of feudal "equality" (see part VI, Social Mobility)- were now overtaken and ruled by what would be termed "unions" in the West from the 19th century to present day. A labor union seeks a monopoly for its own members, to the detriment of *all* others, who are excluded from the opportunity to work the job by the union members themselves.

"However divergent their professional interests might be, all industrial groups were united in their determination to enforce the utmost monopoly which each enjoyed and to crush all scope for individual initiative and all possibility of competition." ..."The great aim of workers in export industries was to raise wages, that of those engaged in supplying the local market to raise, or at least stabilise, prices. Their vision was bounded by their town walls, and all were convinced that their prosperity could be secured by the simple expedient of shutting out all competition from outside." "…for each group the notion of the common good gave way before that of its own interests." (124)

If one wished to sell his wares in the town, then his shop must be within the walls of said town. (125) In Northern Belgium -Flanders- during the 14th century, armed bands routinely raided the neighborhood, burgling or irreparably damaging, looms and fulling vats of those outside of the "union". (126) The love of monopoly, and disdain for equality of liberty, as well as disdain for "the worker" as a class, were on full display in a suit filed in 1373 against the municipality known as Ypres, in Flanders. The workers on the outside of the monopoly sought "the natural right of each man to gain his livelihood", while the monopolists controlling Ypres claimed an "urban right" to forbid competition. (127) Like Mao in China two centuries later, care was taken to reduce the locals who had become large scale merchants, independent men who created wealth and facilitated commerce, to mere shop heads under the restrictive system. *The great men simply left the local town beneath them, and carried on with wholesaling abroad so that foreigners might enjoy goods, jobs, and prosperity.* (128)

By mid-century, workers had already begun to flee the "paradise" for England and Florence, but the destruction of the industry was too far along to be saved -when in 1435 freedom of trade and of contract was granted to wholesalers of cloth in Brussels- from the harm of the union monopoly. (129) During the second half of the 14th century in Flanders, towns began to be freed from the restrictive yoke of regulated monopoly in cloth. Clearing the way for the capitalism of the 15th and 16th centuries, "liberty now replaced privilege in the sphere of manufacture; this young rural industry was quite clearly a capitalist industry, and in it the rigid municipal regulation was replaced by a more elastic system, in which the employee enjoyed complete freedom to enter into a contract and to fix his wages with an employer." (130)

TAXATION

A recurring fiction in the literature of the purveyors of class envy, of victim politics or the politics of hate, and of theft through redistributionism, is that those who have more do not have more because they have made better choices, but rather that they have more because those who have less are not given adequate license to pick their pocket via the mechanism of the state. Some versions of this in the USA have been the cries of "soak the rich" from Frank Roosevelt's New Dealers, and the demand from the so-called American liberals of the Barack Obama era that the class already paying by far the most tax dollars must "pay their fair share".

We know in practice that there is no limit to the taking, no stated amount which has been illustrated to deliver prosperity to those financially beneath the parties being victimized by such a hold up; *their only concerns involve the punishment of their betters, and perceiving themselves as getting something for nothing* when the ill-gotten loot goes into their own pockets. Although instances of taxation are peppered throughout this volume, forthcoming are a smattering of examples of the impact of taxation upon productivity, which illustrate which class does or does not benefit from heavier or lighter taxation. The consequences delivered by certain tax policies, in contrast to the promised consequences, are also discussed. Additionally, a few examples of taxes in quite ancient civilizations are included because I thought they might be of interest to the reader.

The following data table illustrates quite clearly that high taxation on labor and on consumption discourages work. Many consider the working definition of "slavery" as having been achieved when one is permitted fewer than half of their earnings by their master. 6 of these 10 countries were above the 50% mark in the realm of labor and consumption tax as of 2015. Note that the only two countries to show an *increase in effort working their jobs* were the two countries in which these combined *taxes were least*: Canada and the United States of America.

Labor, and Consumption, Taxes: 1950-2015

Country	2015 Combined Taxes	Increase (%) of Tax Rate on Labor Income and Consumption Tax	(%) Change in Hours of Market Work per Adult
Austria	63.1%	36.7%	-36
Belgium	58.2%	31%	-34
Canada	38.7%	19.5%	+8
France	64.8%	26.1%	-38
Germany	55.8%	26.5%	-40
Italy	61.5%	36.6%	-29
Netherlands	58.1%	27.9%	-21
Spain	47.4%	31.9%	-13
UK	42.7%	17.8%	-22
USA	28.7%	11.6%	+4

Source for chart: Lee E. Ohanian, "The Effect of Economic Freedom on Labor Market Efficiency and Performance", Hoover Institution Prosperity Project, p. 6+7

Communists are merely thieves without the guts to do their own robbing; "equality" tactics utilizing redistribution *bring equality of poverty* to the populace. Taxation in pre-Hellenistic Athens during the 4th century BC certainly did not aid in the uplifting of the masses, as so-called "wealthy" Athenians were taxed, and taxed, until they themselves became one rainy day away from ruin. *The rest would just keep on taking and taking*, occasionally upping the ante, almost *like one would extort an enemy into destitution for spite*. Failure to comply would result in being punished "just as much as if they had caught you stealing their own property." (131) The "you are cheating us by not paying your 'fair share'" crowd show signs that such people have not evolved beyond this character defect for thousands of years, unfortunately.

Taxes in Athens: 4th cent BC:

Taxes on metics –citizens of a different city, presently residing in
Athens:

For simply residing in the city

On their trade, particularly in the Agora.

2% tax on all goods –both imports and exports– passed through their seaport
hub of trade, Peiraleus. (132)

Taxes on citizens:

Taxed on their property –horses

Use of public weights and measures

Tax on property –slaves (133)

Another form of taxation utilized during the ancient civilizations of Greece and
Rome has been described by Edward Channing: "The Greeks and Romans were
hard-money men; their language has no word for bank notes or currency; with them
there was no stock market, no brokers' board, no negotiable scrip of kingdom or
commonwealth. Public expenses were borne by direct taxes, or by loans from rich
citizens, soon to be cancelled, and never funded." (134) Of course these so-called
loans, taken by the government from the citizens, and never repaid, are nothing more
than a tax adorned with a different wig.

The impact of taxation upon productivity was evident in Russia during the
years spanning 1860-1900 when a 4.5 fold increase of *indirect* taxes occurred.
Attempts by the state to spend treasury funds in an attempt to contrive a marked
domestic demand for domestic-produced goods –keynesianism– caused an artificial
increase of domestic prices in the amount of 20-25%; thus harming their own citizens
–the consumers– broadly, ***as the special interest prevailed over the general interest***. (135)
This is like feeding a cat its own leg, an unsustainable survival strategy.

In 19th century Japan, 40% of agricultural products were taxed away into the hands of the 270 territorial lords, called *daimyo*. The 60% of the crop which remained after the tax collector was through, was strained in the effort to deliver subsistence to the population. Under such tight regulation and taxation, the delicate ratio of food to population -scarcity- was habitually perilous. The *daimyo* also paid out to the shogun, who was the hereditary leader or king. (136)

Between WWI and WWII, although there were several state monopolies in existence -thereby immediately taxing the populace- outside of those, particular industries and endeavors were generally treated equally by the tax code. That is, that subsidies were sparse as were rapacious tax rates enacted to satiate the envy that one financial class possesses of another. The tax system "sought to minimize the deterrents to large-scale capital accumulation and business enterprise." (137) Interest on national bonds was tax free. After 1926, some class preference was shown to owners of very small farms, and other varieties of businesses possessing an adequately puny stature, as they were exempted from paying taxes on their business profits, in addition to being exempted from the land tax. (138) Corporate profits were taxed within the range of 5-10%. Overall taxation during the years between the World Wars consumed in the range of 10-15% of the national income. (139) Times were far more prosperous for the Japanese during the 1920s and 1930s, than during the 19th century when taxation and regulation were far heavier.

During the mid-18th century in Japan, *heavy taxation from the top level of government*, rolled downhill -as they say- and *was passed along through each financial class until it reached the lowest*: "From 1750 on the Shogunate was in almost constant financial difficulty. It sought escape by heavier taxes, borrowing, and disorderly debasements of the currency." William W. Lockwood goes on to say that "The traditional institutions of Japanese feudalism were progressively undermined at the foundations by the slow growth of a commercial economy, and the rise of a new and ambitious class of merchants and townspeople.

"As in Europe, the old self-contained barter economy, and the rigid pattern of class relations associated with it, gradually crumbled under these mercantile influences. The *samurai*, a *rentier* caste, became progressively impoverished and indebted to the merchants (*chonin*) as their rice stipends proved inadequate to meeting increasing money requirements. Attempts to extract larger revenues from the peasants only intensified the difficulties of the latter, who likewise found themselves exposed to the insecurity of a growing money economy. Currency debasement and crop variations brought wide fluctuations in the price of rice, the one crop that was the precarious base of the economy." (140)

The phrase familiar to the ears of contemporary readers in the USA, "roads and bridges", has been waved as the justification to tax, while the money collected goes on to be spent elsewhere, for hundreds of years and all over the world; even during the Middle Ages in Europe, and during the 9th century in particular. The remains of the Roman roads had disintegrated, but the tolls were still collected along the way, *and* new taxes were levied ostensibly to pay for the roads -this tax known as the *teloneum,* or market toll. The *tonlieu* -the first toll- during the Middle Ages simply impeded commerce, and "Not a single farthing of it was set aside for road-mending or for the rebuilding of bridges." (141) The developing towns successfully repealed many of these odious obstacles to the flow of goods, and to the legitimate earning of money. Some towns were able to arrange for their merchants to be specially exempt from such legalized piracy. But progress in repealing such harmful action did not equate to a complete success. At the close of the 1400s, 35 such taxes were noted around the Elbe, 64 on the Rhine, and a whopping 77 on the Lower Austrian patch of the Danube. (142) Yet, the state of disrepair remained perpetual in absence of privately funded efforts, undertaken by private building concerns; private construction which created what was perhaps the first suspension bridge across the Saint-Gothard pass. During the year 1332 in France, the people of Ghent, frustrated in their efforts to ship to Paris, privately rebuilt the road from Senlis. (143)

As a matter of mere trivia to satisfy the curiosity of some, for a millennium and a half in ancient Egypt, nearly all meat, along with all "surplus" agricultural products -"surplus" deemed to be above the centrally dictated "necessity" level- were taxed by the tax collectors on behalf of the massive bureaucracy overseeing their 40 districts.

Additionally, peasant farmers were taxed through conscription of their labor on government projects -amounting to a 100% income tax on their labor. Egypt was without a standing army until the second half of the second millennium BC, roughly 1,500 years after their civilization began. (144) This rate of taxation prevailed during the Old Kingdom period -3100 through 2200 BC- as well. (145)

When it comes to prices and excise taxes, someone's always got to pay. In India during 1878, taxes on salt were higher in southern India, while lower in northern India. Salt was sold "by the pinch" as opposed to in bundles or by weight -portions entirely unregulated by government- and so the merchants simply altered their pinch size accordingly, *as they passed the cost of the high taxation along to the customer*. (146) The central planners could dictate a price per unit sold, but were unable to control the size of each unit. The reduction in quantity found here is far preferable to the reduction in quality witnessed in the case of price regulation on the bakers of bread in 18th century England (part III, Wage Controls), which included the mixing of undesirable elements into the bread. Whenever government dictates low prices in an attempt to curry favor with a particular special interest group, that very same group incurs the cost through either an increase in scarcity of the good or service in question, a decrease in quality, or a decrease in portion.

In the late 1980s in the USSR, there was a 100% corporate income tax levied on the Magnitogorsk Works. This, after being placed on a "self-financing" policy by the central planners. This "self-financing" only applied to capital improvements, repairs, maintenance, etc.. It simply meant that the plant, which was still made up of 1930s technology, after more than two decades of pleas for upgrades and renovation, was on their own to keep their facility in working order, or to update its condition. (147) If someone approached the reader and took away 100% of their earnings each month, then told the reader that they were on their own to finance their wardrobe, one can easily foresee the outcome awaiting one who is in need of clothing but is without money. In 1989 Ivan Romazan, director of Magnitogorsk Works relayed that "more than one-half of all fundamental equipment has been in use for more than thirty years." In 1987 Iurii Levin, deputy director for economic affairs: "The factory", speaking of Magnitogorsk, "has the largest assemblage of obsolete equipment in the country." (148)

When government offers its help, it's often best to respond by stating that your help just hurts. In Germany, during the 1st quarter of the 19th century, a blessing for its people was hampered by government's affectation of assistance. The market's introduction of the steamship improved transportation of goods, and of passengers, alike. The various municipalities were eager to tax the new mode of improving the lives of the people. The assorted governments reached their grubby little paws into the pockets of the people, claiming that more taxes would improve the safety of the waterways; however, *they just pocketed the money.* This, of course, hurt the steam operators; their employees; and the consumers who may have received cheaper goods or fares from this innovative technology, as prices were raised and the waterways were increasingly eschewed in favor of the less regulated railroads. (149)

ENVIRONMENTALISM

"Environmentalism", "conservationism", the "Green New Deal", and other labels have been affixed to movements which claim to be in the best interests of the masses, using the health of the planet earth as a device to cloak the true desires of politicians to horde power and treasure for themselves, and of their supporters to satiate their envy of their betters in life through dictation of their behavior, picking their pocket for the enrichment of the jealous, while also satisfying the overwhelming zeal of the envious to engage in destruction while affecting to be constructive. Private solutions again show themselves to be both adequate and advantageous, while government often leaves a result more damaging than would otherwise have been the case if government had abstained from any involvement whatever. The level of pollutants on the planet, or access to natural resources, are no different from other areas of human activity, including energy sources such as oil or electricity, of steel, of food, of clothing, spices, homes, or any other area of private enterprise in which government places its grubby and ineffectual paws only to yield inferior or sometimes lethal results.

In England, during the 18th century, soil conservation was undertaken. *Private initiative brought clauses into leases* which introduced measures designed to dissuade tenant farmers from engaging in practices which would be more likely to exhaust the soil, while also encouraging good crop rotations. The land was undoubtedly a long term asset of the landlords, the value of which is impacted significantly by the arability of the land, while perhaps appearing a short term commitment of the tenants who may be tempted to "burn out" the soil -in search of high volume, short term, yields; colloquially "to beat it like a rented mule"- and then to move on to a new lease renting a different plot. *Nothing other than the desire to preserve the value of the landlord's asset, while recognizing the incentives presented to their tenants* -accompanied by a healthy respect for the latter's position- *caused these measures to appear in private contracts.* No state intervention whatever was involved. (150)

Private interests also improved aggregate agricultural output for the masses. *The desire of the landlords to increase the value of their capital* -in this case land- by improving the crop yield so as to entice higher rent payments by tenant farmers, caused the building of walls -called "enclosures"-; installation of drains; digging of irrigation ditches; the construction of sturdy farmhouses complete with avenues of trees, as well as barns. *Private funds* tore down old shanty cottages that would attract vagrants. (151)

Private interests reforested England during this time. As the number one military power in the world turned to the era of naval primacy in military branches, during a century of almost constant English warfare -Wars of William and Anne, also 1739-48, War of American Independence 1770s, William III- many trees were cut down in order to build the ships necessitated by such conditions. Trees were also cut to create enclosures for agriculture, which improved the national crop yields. Originated by a desire to acquire long term gains from the trees planted, desire to protect their assets and liberty with trees for future ships to use in the military or as commercial trading or fishing vessels, or simply from a desire to enjoy the tree lined scenery at their homes, T.S. Ashton tells us that "It was the great landlords, on enclosed estates, who did most for the preservation of the woodlands." (152)

The theme of political movements sounding false alarms resurfaces in the USA, when this country was the oil king of the planet. As WWI concluded, the USA was the #1 supplier of oil in the world, with roughly 66% of global oil. As of 1929 the world supply of oil had increased approximately 225%, with the USA still supplying about two thirds. "Thus throughout the 1920's, but particularly after 1924, public officials, industry executives, and the man-on-the-street continued to speculate over whether or not the United States would soon run out of crude oil supplies, there was so much crude floating around in the States that such speculation seemed premature to say the least. Reserves kept pace with increased consumption. (153)

PART II

Chain the Beast, Unchain the Citizenry

"The central theme of this book is the conspicuous and disconcerting hiatus between accepted opinion and evident reality in major areas of academic and public economic discourse..." -Peter Bauer, referring to a work of his own (1)

The state or the government will be referred to, throughout this tome, as the Beast -the word will be capitalized throughout, to distinguish this use of the word from other uses. The state can be very powerful, indeed. A small, restricted, government which is kept in its proper place, can show tremendous strength once one of its shackles has been removed and it has been summoned into action. Such an exhibition can be tempting for the public and politicians alike. The temptation for politicians to become more powerful is self-explanatory, and will always be the case. *It is the public's clamor for further liberation of the Beast, that this book aims to quell*.

Imagine an 8,000 pound gorilla with 3 limbs chained to a wall inside of a building, its free arm turning a crank which generates and stores electricity -such as the stationary bike at the power reservoir which have been available to tourists at the hydroelectric plant near Niagara Falls, NY, for example. The beast, with a single arm, produces more electricity in 4 hours than 1,000 strong humans, laboring for 12 hours a piece, can produce in a month. To many come the thought that "if we can get *this* out of it with one arm, imagine how beneficial it would be to us to free *all* of its limbs!". That such a practice is a mistake becomes clear once the 8,000 pound gorilla is wholly unchained, as *the roles of master and servant are inverted. The Beast no longer serves the people, the people serve the Beast*; and re-shackling the Beast is quite a tall order once its gotten access to weapons and culled allies with empty promises of power for themselves, revenge upon their enemies, satiation of jealousies over those who have done more with their lives, material remuneration, and threats regarding their fate if they refuse alliance. This book shows *the importance of speaking the language of evidence* in the face of lavish promises, laced with ambiguities regarding the plan to fulfill those promises, while all known evidence shows the promised outcomes to be wholly unlikely, given the inputs. Take the shackles off of the citizens, and place them back on to the Beast.

"Equality", pursued as an end by central planners, *shackles the citizens*, in the name of shackling the Beast. Equality and redistribution lead to bureaucracies and *special privileges* -which are simultaneously *special oppressions*- doled out by those in government, which as illustrated throughout this volume do positive harm to the economy and citizenry as a whole -because they result in a detectable reduction of production, innovation, and choice for everyone- at the *behest* of the citizenry! The type of officials who a sensible populace should seek to systematically exclude -the shameless, power or office seeking, variety- are both encouraged and enabled by central planning schemes. The concentration of the power into the hands of the few by decree, which is the primary feature of all socialist governments -this being the key variable (see part VII, Key Variable), and the only factor to consider when voting, presuming that any candidate is championing such a scheme- allows and encourages government, particularly office seekers therein, to hamper the populace with additional restrictions in the name of their own liberation and empowerment. It is a bizarre and vexing mystery, the effectiveness of these political strategies. *Do you suppose*, as was posited by this author previously in another book, that *the mere envy of one's betters fuels the element of the populace who subscribe to this destructive religion?*

The best possible strategy -for one who is legitimately interested in harboring an environment in which the greatest liberty and prosperity for all can possibly be expected- is the precise inversion of the above model. Evil people will always exist, and shameless office seeking politicians will always be among their number, so the best strategy is to have a permanent model of government which is capable of doing the least harm while still carrying out its three legitimate functions, which are: to establish and defend/protect borders; to coin and regulate currency; and to provide a means for the mediation of disputes between private parties, which consists of the courts. Time and again, we see examples of the suffering, or at least the obvious hindrance, of the citizens once "equality" has been "redistributed".

"Equality" shackles the citizens, and we can observe this under conditions in which communal land use prevails. *Communal rights discourage people from putting in extra effort* -either physically in the cultivation of the land, or mentally in terms of innovation- *because they will not be rewarded*. The unproductive reap rewards equal to those of the productive, leading to *everybody having less; although their portions are equal*. Communal land edicts discourage proper conservation engagement, even among cost effective measures, because if everybody isn't going to participate, and the reward is equal irrespective of merit, then nobody bothers with it. (2) *The distinction between the equality of liberty, and the equality of material outcomes*, for "equality" movements, *is one of vital importance*. If one is pleased by the outcome yielding smaller portions for every plate at the dinner table, simply because nobody was able to enjoy a feast, then such a person has just confessed that their interest is not in the feeding of the poor, but rather their priority is the destruction of those whom they envy.

An observation of the Syrian village called mucha'a was completed in 1957. This communal village assigned each family its own particular plot which it may use as it pleased. Because the family plots were periodically re-allotted among the communal villagers, writers for the International Bank for Reconstruction and Development found this to provide "little or no incentive to permanent improvement of the land." (3)

"Equality" brought about less for everybody during the years 1645-1660 in Maryland. Maryland colony began this period with a small number of large investors who had correspondingly large holdings of land and laborers. By the end of said period, in an effort to attract and retain settlers by granting land to the servants, the colony was comprised of many small land holders, each with meager means to invest. Net production for the colony decreased as a result, for the reason that a grand scale of agricultural cultivation was demanded by both the crops grown, and by the soil; as was the case in Virginia. (4) "More" for everybody actually meant less for everybody -and all persons suffered due to the diminished pie remaining, along with its concomitant scarcity of money, food, and goods.

A chained Beast means better market efficiency, as we see in the textile industry of Germany from 1837-1850. In 1837, 3,345 separate spinneries housed the 345,894 spindles producing textiles, while just over a decade later 420,415 spindles spun in a mere 1,787 spinneries. The 100% increase in spindles per factory occurred as the less efficient or productive ventures were either bought out, or driven out, of competition by the better firms. *The market decided who would win or lose, who would bear the risks, and shoulder the burden of the losses*. Great gains were made by some. Many thousands were employed by all of these operations, with the winners often absorbing those formerly in the employ of the losers. In addition, the people throughout Germany -whether or not they had anything to do with the textile business- had access to more products; as did those in other parts of the world to which the goods produced were exported. The beneficiaries were many. (5) We also find a conspicuous example of a well-chained Beast producing rapid development of Hong Kong. This tremendous progress, and uplifting of the poor occurred in *absence of*: planning boards; planned economy; direction from abroad; the League of Nations or United Nations; substantial foreign aid; powerful bureaucrats; or rapacious taxation of high earners. (6)

It is a vexing situation that arises when great masses of supposedly intelligent people, who have their hands bound together by control over jobs and prices, their feet bound together by control over housing, medicine, and healthcare; their hands then bound to their feet by control over emigration and the press; are shocked that the shackled person's demands are not met by the party which has done the binding, this second party who themselves are left fully without restriction. Yet, we see this when the people demand policy which puts these and other vital measures into the hands of central planners, and out of their own, in the name of their own empowerment.

Please note that the following historical examples will, in the interest of preventing this volume from reaching the immense proportion numbering thousands of pages, be merely cursory, and will be absent many personal biographies of the individuals involved, and of certain other important and interesting details. Each of the following three episodes can be, and have been, the sole subject of books twice the length of this volume, while not being fully covered therein. The reader is encouraged to consult additional sources to learn more about these episodes, along with all of the others included in this book.

THE BEAST UNCHAINED:
FRANCE'S JACOBINS AND THE 1789 REVOLUTION

"Believe me, Sir, those who attempt to level, never equalize." - Edmund Burke, 1790
(7)

The episode known as the French Revolution of 1789 is one of the most clear examples of the dangers of leaving the Beast unchained; of the desire for a tyranny of the majority; and of permitting the least knowledgeable people, who have no financial stake in affairs, to make decisions for those who are knowledgeable and who have skin in the game. That this period is, as of this writing, frequently and successfully invoked as one in which the least-moneyed were uplifted, or were freed from tyranny, is both bewildering and troubling. Ignorance and arrogance are the only two explanations for touting such falsehoods; discounting, of course, dishonesty.

Some of the myths prevalent today regarding the episode which began 1789, were in existence as early as 1954. In a book published in that year, William W. Lockwood wrote: "The French Revolution, for example, despite its slogans, was hardly what we would today call a democratic revolution, in either its inception or its outcome. Its actual consequence was to complete the emancipation of feudal serfdom, to establish a unified nation-state, and to proclaim a new legal freedom and equality under the ascendant power of the middle class." (8)

In actuality, 10 years of horrific poverty and tyranny, leading to the dictatorship of Napoleon Bonaparte, are the actual outcomes of this 18th century French Revolution. Like bank robbers in a hostage situation, the pretenders of power and authority were mired in a predicament which they were ill-equipped to facilitate, and which continued growing further and further beyond their control, as desperation, betrayal, and despotism, filled the hours which delayed their inevitable demise. We now cure the ignorance of those in need, while refreshing the knowledge of those who are already familiar with this episode.

BACKGROUND AND INITIAL EPISODES

During the 1780s, the Catholic church, comprised of approximately 100,000 members, owned 5-10% of the land in France. (9) The job creating, and goods providing, merchants -bourgeoisie- were often resentful that their earned excellence was paralleled, or even surpassed, by the luck of the draw into which the nobility had been born. During the period 1713-1789 French foreign trade increased five-fold, thanks to the bourgeoisie. *Independent agrarian men, shop owners, as well as larger scale merchants, made up the majority of the so-called Third Estate*; however there were a contingent of wage-earners, who as a class had seen a pay increase of 22% by the 1780s, as compared to their wages during the 1730s, while prices obtained for consumer goods rose 65% during this period. (10)

During the 1780s, more than 80% of the French lived outside of the cities. The peasants were their own men, and certainly were not serfs enslaved to their lord on assigned lands; a contrast to the servitude that was the case in other lands practicing feudalism. The peasant either farmed his own land; farmed land which he rented, as a sharecropper; or farmed as a hired man for another. (11) Those who bought what were called "manors", which included peasants and merchants, served some functions which present day counties in the USA serve. Tracts of land within this manorial village could be bought or sold freely, but annual taxes, in addition to transfer fees when exchanged, were due to and collected by the owner of the manor. (12)

French Land Ownership 1780s:

Peasants   40%

Merchants   20%

Nobles   20%

Church   10%

Source for chart: R.R. Palmer and Joel Colton, A *History of the Modern World* (New York: Alfred A. Knopf, Inc., 1965), p. 336

The Estates-General was a quasi-parliamentary body in which the so-called three estates -the Church, the nobles, and the rest- each met in separate chambers, took separate votes, and which would be dominated by the nobles, as they occupied many high positions within the church, making them present in two of the three bodies. This body had been disbanded 150 years prior to 1788, and ideas were sought by king Louis XVI as to methods of re-constituting it during present day so that a re-organization of rights and taxation might take place. (13) As it turned out, this attempt at the leveling of lifelong, birth-determined privileges, would lead to the execution of the king at the behest of the very faction of people who would have no longer been excluded by such legal exemptions -the masses.

Winter of 1788-89 was a harsh one for France, with lows of -50 degrees fahrenheit. Work was suspended for a lengthy time; the paycheck to paycheck crowd couldn't buy any food or firewood because work was suspended. Bread was rationed, and trade heavily regulated, by government. Even those who paid were limited to small quantities from sellers. The bread shortage was not resolved until July of 1789. U.S. imports sold, at high prices, to the French, helped to weather the storm for

France. (14) By July of 1789, the price for bread in France was the highest seen since the death of Louis XIV in 1715. (15) *A lack of price controls outside of France facilitated access to the sustenance.*

Authors R.R. Palmer and Joel Colton list as characteristics of what might be termed a "classical liberal", as opposed to the "American Liberal" variety, liberal program: freedom from arbitrary arrest and confinement, constitutional government, and guarantees of personal liberty for all. (16) *This was not the outcome for the French revolution of 1789, though it is what was initially advertised.*

May 1789: the Estates-General was to meet in three distinct bodies at Versailles. The 3rd class had as many members as the 1st and 2nd classes put together, and wished to rig the game to their advantage by combining the three classes into a single body, and to take a simple majority of the vote as binding. Of course, this produced a standstill, and the 3rd estate sulked off to a nearby tennis court, there declaring themselves the National Assembly and arrogating to themselves the authority to draft a new constitution. (17)

May 1789: Advice from Thomas Jefferson, not taken: "I urged most strenuously an immediate compromise; to secure what the government was now ready to yield, and trust to future occasions what might still be wanting. It was well understood that the King would grant at this time 1. Freedom of the person by habeas corpus. 2. Freedom of conscience. 3. Freedom of the press. 4. Trial by jury. 5. A representative legislature. 6. Annual meetings. 7. The origination of laws. 8. The exclusive right of taxation and approbation. And 9. The responsibility of ministers; and with the exercise of these powers they would obtain in future whatever might be for them necessary to improve and preserve their constitution. They thought otherwise however, and events have proved their lamentable error." Jefferson notes that 30 years of war and suffering yielded less than was listed here. (18)

The great fear of 1789: peasants vandalized manor houses, destroying the papers within, or outright torching the homes. (19)

August 9th, 1789, the Jacobin wokers of the national assembly borrowed 30 million; on August 27th, another 80 million. September brought a 25% taxation of revenue, based upon the honor system, with each to pay immediately. (20) Ever desperate for funds, on December 2nd, 1789: "all the lands of the clergy belong to the State." *The desperate mob wanted money, so they stole it.* (21) This was done because the mob was broke. 400 million francs of credit -assignats- were issued using stolen land as collateral -the basis for issuance. On June 1st of 1790, these wokers were already broke, and issued another 400 million in notes on the land. (22) The church land was stolen, and sold off to the highest bidder in large blocks. *The least-moneyed peasants were excluded from such enormous sales due to inadequate funds.* (23)

August 26th, 1789, the Declaration of the Rights of Man and Citizen was unveiled. Though its promises were great, and undoubtedly strike the modern eye in a way which garners approval for the movement, *at every turn it was violated in practice*; an unmitigated defalcation of liberty which shall be detailed in the pages below. The hypocrisy is so flagrant as to be comical, so long as one can get over the revolting injustices, terror, penury, and murder, inflicted in its name. It declared that: "Men are born and remain free and equal in rights." Natural rights were "liberty, property, security, and resistance to oppression." *Among its promises*:

Freedom of religion to be guaranteed

Nobody to be arrested or punished except lawfully

No class barred from office by birth

"Liberty" meant the freedom to do anything not injurious to others

Laws to be made only by the people, or their representatives

Taxes raised by common consent

No amnesty for public servants

Powers of the government to be separated among various branches

Property only to be confiscated by the state with fair compensation (24)

October 6th, 1789: Edmund Burke:

"History will record that on the morning of the 6th of October, 1789, the king and queen of France, after a day of confusion, alarm, dismay, and slaughter, lay down, under the pledged security of public faith, to indulge nature in a few hours of respite and troubled, melancholy repose. From this sleep the queen was first startled by the sentinel at her door, who cried out to save herself by flight---that this was the last proof of fidelity he could give---that they were upon him, and he was dead. Instantly he was cut down. A band of cruel ruffians and assassins, reeking with his blood, rushed into the chamber of the queen and pierced with a hundred strokes of bayonets and poniards the bed, from whence this persecuted woman had but just time to fly almost naked, and, through ways unknown to the murderers, had escaped to seek refuge at the feet of a king and husband not secure of his own life for a moment.

This king, to say no more of him, and his queen, and their infant children (who once would have been the pride and hope of a great and generous people) were then forced to abandon the sanctuary of the most splendid palace in the world, which they left swimming in blood, polluted by massacre and strewed with scattered limbs and mutilated carcasses. Thence they were conducted into the capital of their kingdom." (25)

September 1789, the *National Assembly sought to violate its own declaration* by attempting to install a government consisting of a solitary chamber, providing an easily overridden veto to the king; these men being the so-called patriots. (305) Rioting during July, and again in October, led to the voluntary defection of many sensible members of the national assembly; some defecting from France altogether. (306)

Edmund Burke, then a member of the British Parliament, wrote a response to a Parisian's letter of 1789 soliciting Burke's opinion of the goings on in Paris. A response was begun in October of 1789, yet grew and grew so that it became book length -numbering 190 pages in your author's present copy- and was published in January of 1790. *Like a man before a crystal ball, Burke more or less predicted the future of France during the forthcoming decade.* Prior to detailing the cavalcade of horrid oppression, slaughter, privation, and horror, which accompanied this populist, redistributive, attack of their betters on the part of the envious masses, executed in the name of equality and of uplifting the poor, a few excerpts of Burke's sagacious observations, and prognostications which proved prophetic, will be provided for the reader, often accompanied by a label which relates *the accurate prediction* to a theme of this book:

Fallacy of the Lamp: "When I see the spirit of liberty in action, I see a strong principle at work; and this, for a while, is all I can possibly know if it. The wild gas, the fixed air, is plainly broke loose; but *we ought to suspend our judgment until the first effervescence is a little subsided, till the liquor is cleared*, and until we see something deeper than the agitation of a troubled and frothy surface. I must be tolerably sure, before I venture publicly to congratulate men on a blessing, that they have really received one. Flattery corrupts both the receiver and the giver, and adulation is not of more service to the people than to kings. I should, therefore, suspend my congratulations on the new liberty of France until I was informed how it had been combined with government, with public force, with the discipline and obedience of armies, with the collection of an effective and well-distributed revenue, with morality and religion, with the solidity of property, with peace and order, with civil and social manners. All these (in their way) are good things, too, and without them liberty is not a benefit whilst it lasts, and is not likely to continue long. *The effect of liberty to individuals is that they may do what they please; we ought to see what it will please them to do*, before we risk congratulations which may be soon turned into complaints. Prudence would dictate this in the case of separate, insulated, private men, but liberty, when men act in bodies, is power. Considerate people, before they declare themselves, will observe the use which is made of power and particularly of so trying a thing as new power in new persons of whose principles, tempers, and dispositions they have little or no experience, and in situations where those who appear the most stirring in the scene may possibly not be the real movers." (26)

Beast Unchained: "Compute your gains: see what is got by those extravagant and presumptuous speculations which have taught your leaders to despise all their predecessors, and all their contemporaries, and even to despise themselves until the moment in which they become truly despicable. By following those false lights; France has bought undisguised calamities at a higher price than any nation has purchased the most unequivocal blessings! France has bought poverty by crime! France has not sacrificed her virtue to her interest, but she has abandoned her interest, that she might prostitute her virtue." (27) Burke goes on to say "*They have found their punishment in their success*: laws overturned; tribunals subverted; industry without vigor; commerce expiring; the revenue unpaid, yet the people impoverished; a church pillaged, and a state not relieved; civil and military anarchy made the constitution of the kingdom; everything human and divine sacrificed to the idol of public credit, and national bankruptcy the consequence; and, to crown all, the paper securities of new, precarious, tottering power, the discredited paper securities of impoverished fraud and beggared rapine, held out as currency for the support of an empire in lieu of the two great recognized species that represent the lasting, conventional credit of mankind, which disappeared and hid themselves in the earth from whence they came, when the principle of property, whose creatures and representatives they are, was systematically subverted." (28) "The fresh ruins of France, which shock our feelings wherever we can turn our eye, are not the devastation of civil war; they the sad but instructive monuments of rash and ignorant counsel in time of profound peace." (29)

Burke observed that what was afoot was *a tyranny of the majority*; kings made of the populist politicians, in the name of eradicating privilege in government. The states-general of France was now composed of three bodies: 300 seats for the upper class, 300 seats for the middle class, and 600 seats for the lowest class. Because these three factions were to sit in the same body, and vote en masse, this effectively made "kings" of the representatives of the lowest class. (30) The placing of servile men into a position of supreme authority, rather predictably, yielded the immediate outcome of atrocious results caused by the commingling of a drunkenness with their newfound power, and their inexperience at applying said power. (31)

Contrasting the British House of Commons with the French National Assembly: "The power, however, of the House of Commons, when least diminished, is as a drop of water in the ocean, compared to that residing in a settled majority of the National Assembly. That assembly, since the destruction of the orders, has no fundamental law, no strict convention, no respected usage to restrain it. Instead of finding themselves obliged to conform to a fixed constitution, they have a power to make a constitution which shall conform to their designs. *Nothing in heaven or upon earth can serve as a control on them*." (32)

Describes the re-arrangement of the General Assembly, and the addition of the poorest clergymen, as having "completed that momentum of ignorance, rashness, presumption, and lust of plunder, which nothing has been able to resist." (33)

On the French wokers in the ILC (see part IV for more on the ILC): "*They despise experience* as the wisdom of unfettered men; and as for the rest, they have wrought underground a mine that will blow up, at one grand explosion, all examples of antiquity, all precedents, charters, and acts of parliament." (34)

On so-called equality: "For I am denying in theory, full as far is my heart from withholding in practice (if I were of power to give or withhold) the real rights of men. In denying their false claims of right, *I do not mean to injure those which are real, and are such as their pretended rights would totally destroy*. If civil society be made for the advantage of man, all the advantages for which it is made become his right. It is an institution of beneficence; the law itself is only beneficence acting by a rule. Men have a right to live by that rule; they have a right to do justice, as between their fellows, whether their fellows are in public function or in ordinary occupation. They have a right to the fruits of their industry and to the means of making their industry fruitful. They have a right to the acquisitions of their parents, to the nourishment and improvement of their offspring, to instruction in life, and to consolation in death. Whatever each man can separately do, without trespassing upon others, he has a right to do for himself; and he has a right to a fair portion of all which society, with all its combinations of skill and force, can do in his favor. *In this partnership all men have equal rights, but not equal things*. He that has but five shillings in the partnership has as good a right to it as he that has five hundred pounds has to his larger proportion. But he has not a right to an equal dividend in the product of the joint stock; and as to the share of power, authority, and direction which each individual ought to have in the management of the state, that I must deny to be amongst the direct original rights of man in civil society; for I have in my contemplation the civil social man, and no other. It is a thing to be settled by convention." (35)

Burke on the "rights of man" in France: "They have the 'rights of men'. Against these there can be no prescription, against these no agreement is binding; these admit no temperament and no compromise; anything withheld from their full demand is so much of fraud and injustice." (36) He goes on to say "In denying their false claims of right, I do not mean to ignore those which are real, and are such as their pretended rights would totally destroy." (37) Burke continues "Government is not made in virtue of natural rights, which may and do exist in total independence of it, and exist in much greater clearness and in a much greater degree of abstract perfection; but their abstract perfection is their practical defect. **By having a right to everything they want everything**." (38) He goes on to say "What is the use of discussing a man's abstract right to food or medicine? The question is upon the method of procuring and administering them." (39)

Burke on waiting for the cirrhosis of the liver, getting past the initial good feeling of taking the drink: "Nor is it a short experience that can instruct us in that practical science, because the real effects of moral causes are not always immediate; but that which in the first instance is prejudicial may be excellent in its remoter operation, and its excellence may arise even from the ill effects it produces in the beginning. The reverse also happens: and very plausible schemes, with very pleasing commencements, have often shameful and lamentable conclusions." (40)

Beast Unchained: Speaking of the National Assembly: "They sit in the heart, as it were, of a foreign republic: they have their residence in a city whose constitution has emanated neither from the charter of their king nor from their legislative power. They are surrounded by an army not raised either by the authority of their crown or by their command, and which, if they should order to dissolve itself, would instantly dissolve them. There they sit, after a gang of assassins had driven away some hundreds of the members, whilst those who held the same moderate principles, with more patience or better hope, continued every day exposed to outrageous insults and murderous threats. There a majority, sometimes real, sometimes pretended, captive itself, compels a captive king to issue as royal edicts, at third hand, the polluted nonsense of their most licentious and giddy coffeehouses. It is notorious that all their measures are decided before they are debated." (41)

Beast Unchained: "Already there appears a poverty of conception, a coarseness, and a vulgarity in all the proceedings of the Assembly and all of their instructors. Their liberty is not liberal. Their science is presumptuous ignorance." (42)

Private Property; particularly the theft of the Church's land to use as basis for their unstable currency: "This outrage on all the rights of property was first covered with what, on the system of their conduct, was the most astonishing of all pretexts---a regard to national faith. The enemies to property at first pretended a most tender, delicate, and scrupulous anxiety for keeping the king's engagements with the public creditor. These professors of the rights of men are so busy in teaching others that they have not leisure to learn anything themselves; otherwise they would have known that *it is to the property of the citizen*, and not to the demands of the creditor of the state, *that the first and original faith of civil society is pledged.* The claim of the citizen is prior in time, paramount in title, superior in equity. The fortunes of individuals, whether possessed by acquisition of descent or in virtue of a participation in the goods of some community, were no part of the creditor's security, expressed or implied." (43)

Magic Words: On the confiscation of land for the issuance of assignats: "Few barbarous conquerors have ever made so terrible a revolution in property. None of the heads of the Roman factions, when they established *crudelem illam hastam* in all their auctions of rapine, have ever set up to sale the goods of the conquered citizen to such an enormous amount. It must be allowed in favor of those tyrants of antiquity that what was done by them could hardly be said to be done in cold blood." The Romans "regarded them as persons who had forfeited their property by their crimes. With you, in your improved state of the human mind, there was no such formality. You seized upon five millions sterling of annual rent and turned forty or fifty thousand human creatures out of their houses, because "such was your pleasure". The tyrant Harry the Eighth of England, as he was not better enlightened than the Roman Mariuses and Sullas, and had not studied in your new schools, did not know what an effectual instrument of despotism was to be found in that grand magazine of offensive weapons, the rights of men. When he resolved to rob the abbeys, as the club of the Jacobins have robbed all the ecclesiastics, he began by setting on foot a commission to examine into the crimes and abuses which prevailed in those communities." (44) Burke went on: "All these operose proceedings were adopted by one of the most decided tyrants in the rolls of history as necessary preliminaries before he could venture, by bribing the members of his two servile houses with a share of the spoil and holding out to them eternal immunity from taxation, to demand a confirmation of his iniquitous proceedings by an act of Parliament. Had fate reserved him to our times, four technical terms would have done his business and saved him all this trouble; he needed nothing more than one short form of incantation---"Philosophy, Light, Liberality, the Rights of Men". (45)

It is recommended that the reader re-read these predictions and observations once they have completed the remainder of this section. Moving on from Burke, we resume illustration of the action in France, and the playing out of these negative consequences. There were a few splashes of encouraging signs during this decade of horror, and one occurred early on. During 1791, a prohibition was placed on all attempts at organized monopoly on the part of workers. Both *gilds* and *compagnonnages* -known today as labor unions- were outlawed, and this law enforced. All men had the right to work any job, in any trade, with any employer, provided that the employer came to amenable terms of productivity and remuneration, and that this mutual satisfaction persisted. ***Those seeking monopoly, and the exclusion of competitors from eligibility for employment, complained mightily.*** (46)

Suffrage: In order to prevent the ignorant unwashed from having too much sway, the assembly restricted the right to vote to those who paid above a denoted amount of taxes; this to be an indicator of having some "skin in the game", or having something to lose. While half of adult men met the initial criteria, electors made the only votes that counted in 1790, and 1791; these numbering 50,000. (47) These measures would prove ineffectual, in short order.

Summer 1791: Author F.A.M. Mignet, professor of history at the Athenee, in his work first published in 1824, tells us that the Jacobin club "could not want leaders; under Mirabeau, they had contended against Mounier; under the Lameths against Mirabeau; under Petion and Robespierre, they contended against the Lameths. The party which desired a second revolution had constantly supported the most extreme actors in the revolution already accomplished, because this was bringing within its reach the struggle and the victory. At this period, from subordinate it had become independent; it no longer fought for others and for opinions not its own, but for itself, under its own banner." (48)

July 1791: Assembly passes a resolution which more or less states that if King Louis XVI stays out of French affairs, and forgets about manning the throne, they will leave him be; but if he attempts to reclaim the throne, or make war upon the assembly's France, they they will prosecute him as a civilian. French republicans stirred up popular opposition, drawing a large crowd to sign the petition calling for a new king, this taking place at the Champs de Mars. The assembly sends men to disperse the crowd which had been agitated, against the wishes of the assembly, to rule without the monarch. Lafayette, *after sending the crowd away without the use of force, came back after a group decapitated a duo of suspected spies* -the severed heads adorning a pair of pikes. After a warning shot from the 1,200 man brigade at his command proved ineffective, Lafayette ordered a live round be fired into the unruly mob. The crowd fled -those who had not died in the shooting- and the assembly thwarted the will of the people in the name of delivering them from tyranny. (49)

The assembly's hodgepodge of decrees were made up into a constitution, upon which a three decade long amnesty from amendment was placed. King Louis XVI was returned to the throne, whereupon he accepted the constitution, while also renouncing any claim upon involvement in its composition. (50)

August-September 1791: The land of the nobility, having been previously stolen by the jealous mob who comprised the "Revolutionary government", was used as the basis of the issuance of *even more currency; further diluting the strength of the notes issued.* (51)

September 29th, 1791: The first national assembly concluded its session, and the king sent them off with the message that they should sell their neighbors on the constitution that they had enacted. (52) During its time from 1789-1791, the constituent assembly unilaterally decreed the abolition of the rights of Germans to collect manorial dues in Alsace; rights guaranteed by existing treaties. (53)

LEGISLATIVE ASSEMBLY DISPLACES
NATIONAL CONSTITUENT ASSEMBLY,
October, 1791

October 1st, 1791, the Legislative Assembly displaced the National Constituent Assembly. Writing in 1877, Stephen D. Dillage observed that "It fostered into power, by its subservience to demagogues, the influence of the clubs; so that the club of the Jacobins and that of the Cordiliers prescribed its laws, created its opinions and dictated its policy. It made hatreds immortal; legislative action, but ambitious revenges; and it laid down deep the foundations and the supports of the guillotine..." (54)

As the second assembly took their seats, the largely divided nation of France consisted of a variety of factions. Among them were:

1- Those who had fled, including those emigrating as their session was beginning, and who were plotting to return with foreign armies so that they might reclaim France.

2- Those fidelitous to the constitution crafted by the first assembly. These were called the Feuillant party, led by men such as Dumas and Vaublanc -referred to as "Right" by Mignet.

3- The Girondist party – the Jacobins, whom Mignet describes as being "Left"- who had a lust for anarchy, led still by Robespierre from outside of the assembly, as well as by others such as Chabot, Merlin, Danton, and Santerre. They aimed to create their own regime. (55)

Paranoid of conspirators abroad -group #1, above- thwarting the revolution; while also aware of the splintered factions within the French territory; the assembly, led by Jacobins under the title of Girondists, goaded the king to declare war against the King of Hungary and Bohemia on April 20th, 1792. (56) *Louis XVI was caught in an iron maiden*: to welcome the forces from abroad -who backed him and the strength of the monarchy- was to agitate his own, uproarious and violent people within France; to preserve his hide by cowering to the wishes of the national assembly, he eschewed those exterior forces who sought to rescue him from the blood-thirsty and violent mob. (57) The internecine squabbles within France from the outset of the second assembly led to this paranoid declaration of war. ***The hastily declared war by a paranoid assembly***, quickly spelled disaster for France's ill-trained forces. Consisting of three brigades or divisions, the first faction turned tail and ran at the first confrontation with enemy troops; the second group performed similarly; the third faction, with Lafayette at its helm, heard word that the other two brigades were not going to turn up, and headed back to headquarters. One of the two panicked groups killed their commander during their hysterical flight. (58)

During the ***summer of 1792*** a lack of confidence abroad in the provisional government of the French revolutionary assembly, commingled with the flight of gold from the country in the hands of those who had fled, caused a ***drastic reduction in trade and commerce domestically and a plummeting in the value of the assignats***. As the people shunned trading their food and other goods for the paper, its value eroded further. ***The least-moneyed were the most damaged by this consequence of redistribution***. (59)

The internecine squabbles intensified, following the military humiliation at the hands of Belgium. The Jacobin club accused their own people, the Girondists in the assembly, of sabotage. The assembly resolved that it would now sit permanently, and began to arm the masses with pikes, while also hoping to curry favor with the revolutionary sect of the assembly. An army of 20,000 men was recruited and situated just outside of Paris; the constitutionalist Feuillant party firmly opposed these measures of the Girondist and the Jacobin factions. The king was without any support at all in the assembly. (60)

The Girondists -who were a faction of ***the Jacobin club***, and consider by Mignet to be a "Left" party- in commemoration of the notorious tennis court oaths (see above, preceding section, page #96) taken June 20th, 1789, ***arranged for a mob*** to attempt to gain sanctions for the resolutions that the party had been denied through constitutional methods. 8,000 men crashed the assembly while in session. ***The Girondists among the assembly feigned ignorance of this mob***, for whom they had arranged, and a brief show was performed until this majority faction voted to permit the mob to make their statement threatening the king if he did not sanction the wants of the left. 30,000 people, including women and children, paraded through the National Assembly, en route to meet the king at the chateau. The mob gained entry to the king's residence, *Louis stood up to them* and persisted in his refusal to sanction their desires; though he did partake in ceremonial and superficial concessions to the mob by adorning their brand of cap, as well as by sharing a cup of wine with one of their number. The armed mob headed home without further incident. (61)

On the 28th of June, 1792, Lafayette made a surprise visit to the assembly demanding punishment of the rioters of eight days prior, the restoration of the legal authorities of the king, and the dismantling of the Jacobin club. Lafayette implored the national guard to join him in upholding the newly minted constitution of the revolution. The king sabotaged this effort however -playing the long game and betting everything upon rescue from foreign allies and ex-patriots, such a tactic leaving Louis XVI politically indebted to nobody within France in the event of a triumphant outcome- and 30 men turned up in his aid. Lafayette washed his hands of the situation, and returned to his troops. (62)

Continuing with their attempt at a coup, the Girondists dispelled their rival faction within the assembly, and had the Feuillant club shut down. Those factions of the national guard consisting of merchants -bourgeoisie- were sent home. The unwashed masses were all armed and ordered into service -either with firearms, or with pikes. The body of the serpent known as central planning choked off these obstructionist elements, placing in its clutches those who sought its unbridled state -*the illusion of safety concealed the reality of their imprisonment*. (63)

July 26th, 1792, the coalition of foreigners and French expats -upon whom the king had bet all of his marbles- begin their military invasion of France; on this same day, a writing was put out by these parties stating that French surrender would lead to moderate punishments, while armed resistance would bring the most brutal vengeance imaginable. The fully armed, largely ignorant, unwashed masses, erupted into an anarchic and riotous state. (64) These disorganized mobs made few successes. Beginning August 3rd, the members of the assembly *began to be swallowed whole by the monster* that they had let loose. The mob composed of those least thoughtful in the society were, unsurprisingly, thoughtless brutes. Homes of assemblymen were invaded by the louts, and angry mobs harassed legislators when they did not quench the thirst for blood possessed by the vapid majority. Disrespect for the rule of law accompanied the mob rule which had been cultivated by the Jacobins and Girondists -of the left- and the situation fomented on August 10th. (65)

August 10th, 1792, the Paris "commune" -a provisional government, outside of the assembly's provisional government- sought to usurp authority from the assembly, stealing the stolen authority; to overthrow the 1791 constitution; and through universal male suffrage, to *enact a tyranny of the majority.* (66) The commander of the national guard, Petion, was murdered by the power-drunk lower class on the steps of the Hotel de Ville. (67) Some foreign forces, which came to defend the king and the rule of law, were met at the hall of the national assembly after 6:00 a.m. by a riotous and unruly mob of greater than 20,000 armed savages. Some shots were exchanged, but resisting the mob proved futile, as the chateau proved to be the scene of a massacre after the *bloodthirsty rioters were ceaseless in their attacks, even after the opposing forces had surrendered.* The 60-80 members of the assembly who had honored their posts under these circumstances were unyielding in their fidelity to the rule of law. "Shots of victory were then heard without, and the fate of the monarchy was decided." (68)

"The assembly instantly made a proclamation to restore tranquility, and implore the people to respect justice, their magistrates, the rights of man, liberty, and equality. *But the multitude and their chiefs had all the power in their hands, and were determined to use it.* The new municipality came to exert its authority. It was preceded by three banners, inscribed with the words 'Patrie, liberte, egalite.'[translated into English 'homeland, liberty, equality'] Its address was imperious, and concluded by demanding the deposition of the king..." (69) King Louis XVI was taken prisoner and transferred to the Temple, there awaiting a September 23rd session of a new National Assembly, which was to decide his fate. (70)

"But royalty had already fallen on the 10th of August, that day marked by the *insurrection of the multitude* against the middle classes and the constitutional throne, as the 14th of July had seen the insurrection of the middle class against the privileged class and the absolute power of the crown. On the 10th of August *began the dictatorial and arbitrary* epoch of the revolution. Circumstances becoming more and more difficult to encounter, a vast warfare arose, requiring still greater energy than ever, and that energy irregular, because popular, rendered the domination of the lower class restless, cruel, and oppressive." (71)

Following August 10th, 1792, Lafayette "only saw the dearest hopes of the friends of liberty destroyed, the usurpation of the state by the multitude, and the anarchical reign of the Jacobins; he did not perceive the fatality of a situation which rendered the triumph of the latest comer in the revolution indispensable." (72)

In the wake of the events of August 10th, internecine squabbles again plagued the newly seated assemblymen, who each wished to have his own wishes granted, now that he was in possession of the lamp. Anarchy -masquerading as liberty for the masses- prevailed over France. All of the statues were taken down, along with the traditional emblems; *thus erasing any sense of history* which may have lingered since starting their own calendar. (73)

With all of the legislative power concentrated into the hands of the few by design, who in a state of paranoia and power-hunger had incited the general public into various riots -and had now lost control of them; like children playing with fire, the blaze had now gotten out of hand- their paranoia intensified enormously, as French cities began to fall to invading forces whose aim it was to put an end to the out of hand behavior of these misbehaving children. This is reminiscent of the scene in Disney's *Fantasia*, in which Mickey Mouse has gotten hold of the sorcerer's magical cap, thereafter misusing the power to his own detriment. The ruling group, known as the commune, received word of the enemy armies driving in on them on September first. The leader of the commune, Danton, possessed an unbound zeal when it came to his political cause; *like an outlaw bank robber* who has determined that to fall into the hands of the law means certain death, or a horrific life as a prisoner, *he would consider no means of perpetuating his life of crime as out of the realm of acceptability.* Said

Danton, "It is my opinion, that to disconcert their measures and stop the enemy, we must make the royalists fear." Mignet tells us:

"The committee, at once understanding the meaning of these words, were thrown into a state of consternation. 'Yes, I tell you,' resumed Danton, 'we must make them fear.' As the committee rejected this proposition by a silence full of alarm, Danton concerted with the commune. His aim was to put down its enemies by terror, *to involve the multitude more and more by making them accomplices*, and to leave the revolution no other refuge than victory.

Domiciliary visits were made with great and gloomy ceremony; a large number of the persons whose condition, opinions, or conduct rendered them objects of suspicion, were thrown into prison. These unfortunate persons were taken especially from the dissentient classes, the nobles and the clergy, who were charged with conspiracy under the legislative assembly." (74) On the night of September 1st, 1792, "The cannon were again fired, the tocsin sounded, the barriers were closed, and *the massacre began*. During three days, the prisoners confined in the Carmes, the Abbaye, the Concierge, the Force, etc., were slaughtered by a band of about three hundred assassins, directed and paid by the commune. This body, with a calm fanaticism, prostituting to murder the sacred forms of justice, now judges, now executioners, seemed rather to be practising a calling than to be exercising vengeance; they massacred without question, without remorse, with the conviction of fanatics and the obedience of executioners. If some peculiar circumstances seemed to move them, and to recall them to sentiments of humanity, to justice, and to mercy, they yielded to the impression for a moment, and then began anew. In this way a few persons were saved; but they were very few.

The assembly desired to prevent the massacres, but were unable to do so. The ministry were as incapable as the assembly; the terrible commune alone could order and do everything; Petion, the mayor, had been cashiered; the soldiers placed in charge of the prisoners feared to resist the murderers, and allowed them to take their own course; the crowd seemed indifferent, or accomplices; the rest of the citizens dared not betray their consternation. We might be astonished that so great a crime should, with such deliberation, have been conceived, executed, and endured, did we not know what fanaticism of party will do, and what fear will suffer. But the chastisement of this enormous crime fell at last upon the heads of its authors. *The majority of them perished in the storm they had themselves raised, and by the same violent means that they had themselves employed.*" (75)

NATIONAL CONVENTION
DISPLACES THE LEGISLATIVE ASSEMBLY
September, 1792

September 20th, 1792, the National Convention was put together, the following day *this body assumed total authority; as had the two preceding bodies.* The Jacobins again led this group, as they had the assembly, though they would change their veil from that of Girondists to that of the Mountain. (76) The power was all theirs, and they decreed the abolition of royalty, in addition to again altering the calendar in October of the following year, though it would retroactively date to the period beginning September 22, 1792: dating the year I of the French Republic, while refusing to label it year IV of liberty. Internal divisions were at an all-time high, as *more factions grasped for the complete authority* created by the [Left] Girondists -in the name of empowering the masses. (77) "The multitude had neither the intelligence nor the virtue proper for this kind of government. The revolution effected by the constituent assembly was legitimate, still more because it was possible than because it was just; it had its constitution and its citizens. But a new revolution, which should call the lower classes to the conduct of the state, could not be durable. It would injuriously affect too many interests, and have but momentary defenders, the lower class being capable of sound action and conduct in a crisis, but not for permanency. Yet, in consenting to this second revolution, it was this inferior class which must be looked to for support." (78) The Girondists eschewed the unwashed masses at this juncture, and their utility as a tool for the Jacobins was coming to an end, as they would be displaced by the Mountain. Historian F.A.M. Mignet:

"The Mountain, on the contrary, desired a republic of the people. The leaders of this party, annoyed at the credit of the Girondists, sought to overthrow and supercede them. They were less intelligent, less eloquent, but abler, more decided, and in no degree scrupulous as to means. *The extremest democracy seemed to them the best of governments*, and what they termed the people, that is, the lowest populace, was the object of their constant adulation, and most ardent solicitude. *No party was more dangerous*; most consistently it laboured for those who fought its battle." (79) Speaking about the Jacobins: "This club, the most influential as well as the most ancient and extensive, *changed its views at every crisis* without changing its name; it was a framework ready for every dominating power, excluding all dissentients. That at Paris was the metropolis of Jacobinism, and governed the others almost imperiously." (80)

The emphasis on perpetual "crisis", and their utter disregard for productivity in any areas other than tyranny, murder, and destruction, illustrate well the priorities of these people. Increasing commercial, or agricultural productivity, were nowhere to be found on the list of priorities of those who claimed to be fighting for the wellbeing of the least-moneyed, all while privation and hunger permeated the masses in an ever escalating degree of severity. *These were the priorities of criminals caught up in a bank robbery*, who know that the law and severe consequences await them as soon as the stand-off comes to an end, and so *they desire to prolong the situation by taking any lengths necessary to enable its perpetuation*; they see themselves as having nothing to gain by the completion of their botched caper, and therefore see themselves as having nothing to lose while taking measures intended to sustain the crisis. *Only the political class benefited*, and only so long as they remained in power within the realm of politics. *All others suffered the consequences.*

The Girondists, who had been complicit in the riots, now conveyed a comportment of rebuke regarding the terror of September, "and they beheld with horror on the benches of the convention the men who had advised or ordered them. Above all others, two inspired them with antipathy and disgust; Robespierre, whom they suspected of aspiring to tyranny; and Marat, who from the commencement of the revolution had in his writings constituted himself the apostle of murder." (81) Marat wrote and disseminated a pamphlet recommending dictatorship, and lauding the September massacres. (82) Robespierre, up to this epoch, had *consistently shifted his position* from the majority; contrarian, no matter where that course led him. His desire to be dictator was suspected by many, though little was done about it. (83) During September the animals looted 1,100 of their perceived enemies from the prisons, and executed them in the streets. (84)

Turning attention back to Louis XVI, Mignet: "Party motives and popular animosities combined against this unfortunate prince." (85) "For some time there had been a question in the assembly as to the trial of this prince, who, having been dethroned, could no longer be proceeded against. There was no tribunal empowered to pronounce his sentence, no punishment could be inflicted on him: accordingly, they plunged into false interpretations of the inviolability granted to Louis XVI., in order to condemn him legally." (86) The Mountain party, though a minority in the chamber, supported prosecution and conviction of Louis; wishing to plunge France further into chaos and tyranny. "This violent party, who wished to substitute a coup d'etat for a sentence, to follow no law, no form, but to strike Louis XVI. like a conquered prisoner, by making hostilities even survive victory, but had a feeble majority in the convention; but without, it was strongly supported by the Jacobins and the commune." This position was renounced as unlawful, the example of the Romans exiling the Tarquins, instead of executing them, was cited, attributing five centuries of Roman continuation to this decision. (87)

"The assembly," said Robespierre, "has involuntarily been led far away from the real question. Here we have nothing to do with trial: Louis is not an accused man; you are not judges, you are, and can only be, statesmen. You have no sentence to pronounce for or against a man, but you are called on to adopt a measure of public safety; to perform an act of national precaution. A dethroned king is only fit for two purposes, to disturb the tranquility of the state, and shake its freedom, or to strengthen one or the other of them.

"Louis was king; the republic is founded; the famous question you are discussing is decided in these few words. Louis cannot be tried; he is already tried, he is condemned, or the republic is not absolved." Mignet summarizes: "He required that the convention should declare Louis XVI. a traitor towards the French, criminal towards humanity, and sentence him at once to death, by virtue of the insurrection." (88)

The convention took it upon itself to make their own kangaroo court; *eschewing the supposedly precious constitution* created by the first revolutionary body -in the name of both securing liberty, and suppressing tyranny. (89) The Girondists "were about to determine, by an act of justice or by a coup d'etat, whether they should return to the legal regime, or prolong the revolutionary regime." The Mountain "pretended that, while following forms, men were forgetful of republican energy, and that the defence of Louis XVI. was a lecture on monarchy addressed to the nation. The Jacobins powerfully seconded them, and deputations came to the bar demanding the death of the king." (90)

Of the chamber comprised of 721 voters, a margin of 26 votes carried the death sentence of Louis XVI; an outcome which Louis had accepted as a foregone conclusion, irrespective of any evidence forthcoming, ever since the kangaroo court had been concocted. *The assembly voted against the rule of law, and therefore against individual liberty.* "Laws are made by a simple majority", a member of the Mountain was heard to have said at the time, in response to being alerted to the injustice being carried out. (91) January 21st, 1793, Louis Capet -King Louis XVI- was beheaded, after a trial before the Bar of the Convention. (92)

The Beast unchained gathered momentum following the killing of Louis Capet -Louis XVI. As Mignet tells us:

"But the Mountain, who then *directed the popular movement*, imagined that they *were too far involved not to push matters to extremity*. To terrify the enemies of the revolution, to excite the fanaticism of the people by harangues, by the presence of danger, and by insurrections; to refer everything to it, both the government and the safety of the republic; to infuse into it the most ardent enthusiasm, in the name of liberty, equality, and fraternity; *to keep it in this violent state of crisis for the purpose of making use of its passions and its power*; such was the plan of Danton and the Mountain, who had chosen him for their leader. It was he who augmented the popular effervescence by the growing dangers of the republic, and who, under the name of revolutionary government, *established the despotism of the multitude, instead of legal liberty*. Robespierre and Marat went even much further than he. They sought to erect into a permanent government what Danton considered as merely transitory. The latter was only a political chief, while the others were true sectarians; the first, more ambitious, the second, more fanatical." (93)

The Mountain snuffed out efforts to punish the criminal murderers within the ranks of the assembly; as they were themselves the most reprehensibly complicit. Like a group of misbehaving children, who slowed the pace of their misdeeds at the prospect of the lash, increased their pace and passion ten-fold once it had been ascertained that punishment was only a bluff; the masses and their leaders resumed their assault upon the quality of life of Frenchmen. Marat and the *Jacobins pronounced false accusations of monopoly* against the traders and merchants, duping the foolish rubes into *biting the hand that fed them; fanning the flames of chaos*. (94) Once the French army aided Belgium while thwarting the Austrian army, the Flemish felt just as oppressed by the *Jacobin demands of perpetual anarchy* in their own country, as Frenchmen were in France. (95)

February 1st, 1793, France declares war against Great Britain and Holland, making for a unanimous European coalition against France. (96) Perpetually panicky and paranoid, *the unchecked power of the assembly fostering ceaseless tyranny*, the Mountain party clutched at the formation of an even tighter authoritarian body within the assembly. This was to have the authority to trial and sentence, without a jury or an appeal. (97)

March 10th, 1793, the Jacobins hatched a plot to remove by murder the Girondists, who were not chaotic enough for the tastes of the despotic, destructive, and evil Jacobins. *Having served their usefulness to the Jacobins, the Beast now desired to swallow the Girondists up.* This plot was felled by the absence of their targets due to foreknowledge of the attack, as well as by the presence of fighting men to oppose those of the Jacobins. (98) President of the assembly, Vergniaud said:

"We go from crimes to amnesties, from amnesties to crimes. Numbers of citizens have begun to confound seditious insurrections with the great insurrection of liberty; to look on the excitement of robbers as the outburst of energetic minds, and robbery itself as a measure of general security. We have witnessed the development of that strange system of liberty, in which you are told: 'you are free; but think with us, or we will denounce you to the vengeance of the people.' Citizens, we have reason to fear that the revolution, like Saturn, will devour successively all its children, and only engender despotism and the calamities which accompany it." Mignet observes: "These prophetic words produced some effect in the assembly; but the measures proposed by Vergniaud led to nothing." (99)

Shortly thereafter, emigrants were forbidden from returning, their property stolen by the state, death to come to any who dared return. *Dumouriez, the military head, chose to stand up to the Jacobins* for the good of France and of the people. When the Jacobins sent messengers to communicate with Dumouriez, he was candid: "The convention is an assembly of seven hundred and thirty-five tyrants. While I have four inches of iron I will not suffer it to reign and shed blood with the revolutionary tribunal it has just created; as for the republic, it is an idle word. I had faith in it for three days. Since Jemappes, I have deplored all the successes I obtained in so bad a cause. There is only one way to save the country---that is, to re-establish the constitution of 1791, and a king." When a messenger rejoindered to the military leader the notion that Frenchmen would tolerate no royalty, Dumouriez proceeded undeterred: "My army---yes, my army will do it, and from my camp, or the stronghold of some fortress, it will express its desire for a king." He continued: "Should the last of the Bourbons be killed, even those of Coblentz, France shall have a king, and if Paris were to add this murder to those which have already dishonoured it, I would instantly march upon it." (100)

This defiance caused the convention to send four men to arrest Dumouriez, who had his troops assembled to receive the messages. Dumouriez quit his position within France, offering to return to Paris once the unchained Beast of tyranny had been subdued: "...we disfigure Roman history by taking as an excuse for our crimes the example of their virtues. The Romans did not kill Tarquin; the Romans had a well ordered republic and good laws; they had neither a Jacobin club nor a revolutionary tribunal. We live in a time of anarchy. Tigers wish for my head; I will not give it to them." Cadmus, one of the four dispatched to enact the arrest of Dumouriez: "Citizen general, will you obey the decree of the national convention, and repair to Paris?" After Dumouriez expressly refused, Cadmus replied: "Well, then, I declare that I suspend you; you are no longer a general; I order your arrest." *Dumouriez turned the tables on the henchmen of the assembly by arresting them instead*, as Germans transported the four men to Austria as hostages. The tyrannical convention responded by placing a price upon the head of Dumouriez, and encouraging the masses to assault him, if possible. (101)

In April of 1793, Palmer and Colton tell us that the unwashed in Paris "demanded price controls, currency controls, rationing, legislation against the hoarding of food, requisitioning to enforce the circulation of goods, in short a kind of regulated economy." This would involve the implementation of the "maximum", about which more will be said below (page# 124). The Mountain Jacobins betrayed the Girondist Jacobins -that is, *the new tyrants discarded their old implements, having served their master's purpose*- arresting them on May 31st, 1793. Men who today would be called community organizers -as former U.S. President Barack Obama was prior to his time in that office- were called *enrages*. Such people were domestic terrorist ringleaders, agitating unruly locals into a state of unrest. In France, they sent armed bands around to search the barns of peasants. (102)

Though some members of the assembly made an attempt to corral the Jacobins by bringing their leader, Marat, before them on charges, this only *emboldened the Jacobins*, who immediately began to fill the halls with their low class partisans, who not only brought the ever-present threat of mob rioting before the eyes of the assembly, but perpetually interrupted anyone who spoke against *their wishes for unbridled mob rule; a tyranny of the simple majority.* (103) A Commission of Twelve investigated the Paris commune, uncovering a conspiracy to be enacted on May 22nd of 1793, arresting several of the accomplices prior to the act taking place. On May 27th, a mob engulfed the assembly; at 12:30 am, the mob installed a new president, Herault de Sechelles, who declared "The power of reason and the power of the people are the same thing." The Committee of Twelve, which had broken up the Mountain/Jacobin mob's planned conspiracy earlier in the week, was disbanded. (104)

The following day, the mob actions were declared illegal, and the Committee of Twelve reinstated. Danton claimed a pretended victimhood for himself and his populist, redistributive cronies. Hebert, a jailed conspirator, was released. He was received as a hero by the commune and by the Jacobins. These louts, Robespierre amongst them, took up arms to again mob the convention in the wee hours of May 31st. (105) This mob received their demand that the Committee of Twelve again be disbanded. (106)

June 2nd, 1793, Marat, with the complicity of Henriot, who offered the armed forces to the use of the Jacobins -the Jacobins who on May 31st, stated "We have had but half the game yet; we must complete it, and not allow the people to cool- again mobbed the assembly, bringing a total force of 80,000 thugs. The half-filled body resisted the demands of the mob that a few might be spliced off as sacrifices to the blood-thirsty socialists, instead marching out in solidarity to meet Henriot and his ruffians. Again, the assembly refused to offer up to the mob their demanded two dozen members, daring the thugs to take them all. Henriot directed two cannon at the assembly members as they attempted to proceed from the area; this procession cut off at all points by insurrectionists further incited by Marat, the men returned to their chamber reconciled of the suicidal nature of resistance. The demanded men were offered to the masses, being placed under house arrest, and the crowd dispersed. Those demanded by the populist ruffians were Girondists, and members of the Council of Twelve. (107)

THE REIGN OF TERROR WITHIN THE DECADE
LONG DESPOTIC TERROR

"They [Lenin and Robespierre] expropriated the aristocracy and divided its possessions among the rural masses, bartering fields and flocks for votes and soldiers. Once the hungry farmer accepted their gift, he became their partner in crime. The French republic of virtue and the Russian soviet state were saved by peasants in uniform who valued a few acres of land more than the teachings of political theory." Theodore S. Hamerow (108)

During 1793-94, political leader Max Robespierre championed the Reign of Terror. The guillotine resembled a slaughterhouse with the government serving as the conveyor belt, feeding the blade a steady diet of its political enemies so that they would meet their bloody end. Robespierre himself was placed on this same conveyor belt, perishing July 26th, 1794. (109) This epoch began in the aftermath of the riot upon the assembly on June 2nd, 1793. Charlotte Corday attempted to quell the habitual and unrelenting unrest, by taking down Marat. When the tribunal asked of her, "You learned by papers that Marat was a friend of anarchy?", she replied, "Yes, I knew he was perverting France. I have killed a man to save a thousand; a villain, to save the innocent; a wild beast, to give tranquility to my country." Marat became a lionized hero to the riotous class, however. (110)

Others showed signs of resistance as well. The city of Lyons, against the revolution from the outset, executed the head of the local chapter of the Jacobins -Chalier-, fortified their town, raised a 20,000 man army, and acted as a safe haven for those fleeing the unchained Beast of communism. (111) Marseilles sent 10,000 men towards Paris to stand up to the convention, and the Jacobins who controlled it. (112) Forces came towards the convention from all sides, with England blockading all French ports, threatening confiscation of any neutral ships carrying provisions to the French. (113)

In Paris, *the Mountain party seized the moment following the violence* of June 2nd, feeding into the maelstrom of tyranny, by *implanting a constitution decreeing a tyranny of the simple majority of the ignorant masses*, unto the nation. Mignet: "The constitutional law of 1793 established the pure regime of the multitude: it not only recognised the people as the source of all power, but also delegated the exercise of it to the people; an unlimited sovereignty; extreme mobility in the magistracy; direct elections, in which every one could vote; primary assemblies, that could meet without convocation, at given times to elect representatives and control their acts; a national assembly, to be renewed annually, and which, properly speaking, was only a committee of the primary assemblies; such was this constitution. As it made the multitude govern, and as it entirely disorganized authority, it was impracticable at all times; but especially in a moment of general war." (114) *This constitution was suspended upon adoption*, a military state enacted in its place. Conscription of all men 18-25; all arms, munitions, and other combat items were requisitioned by the state. 1.2 million soldiers within France were gotten. All those who did not comply were imprisoned. All foreigners were arrested. (115)

These forces overcame those seeking to re-establish the crown. At Vendee, these victorious forces moved to fully exterminate the subjugated; terrorizing the assemblies, the town, and continued through the woods with continuous attack and arson bestowed upon those waving the white flag. (116) Once Lyons had been re-taken by the lawless, revolutionary assembly, the paranoia of the powerful and murderous body continued as it had before. The city was re-named, its buildings leveled, its people massacred with grape shot. Burrere, of the government, decreed that the history of Lyons was to be taught thusly: "Lyons warred against liberty; Lyons exists no more." Similar scenes occurred at other sites of resistance. (117) The laughable perversion of the word liberty, used in practice as a synonym of tyranny, is reminiscent of present day use of the word "liberal" in the USA, or of the phrase "free healthcare for all", or even of the brand name "woke"; as so-called liberal policies revoke individual liberties, monopolized medicine raises prices and increases scarcity, and there is nobody more asleep at the wheel than the so-called woke.

October 16th, 1793, Marie Antoinette was executed; October 31st, twenty-one Girondist deputies faced the same fate; 73 others who had spoken up when the 21 were arrested, were jailed. (118) A rash of suicides, and violent ends, ensued throughout France. On October 10th, the new revolutionary government had been announced by the convention. *It was an unabashed dictatorship. A 12 man committee of general safety was all-powerful.* Mignet:

"The committee did everything in the name of the convention, which it used as an instrument. It nominated and dismissed generals, ministers, representatives, commissioners, judges, and juries. It assailed factions; it took the initiative in all measures. Through its commissioners, armies and generals were dependent upon it, and it ruled the departments with sovereign sway. By means of the law touching suspected persons, *it disposed of men's liberties*; by the revolutionary tribunal, of men's lives; by levies and the maximum, of property; by decrees of accusation in the terrified convention, of its own members. Lastly, *its dictatorship was supported by the multitude*, who debated in the clubs, ruled in the revolutionary committees: whose services it paid by a daily stipend, and whom it fed with the maximum. The multitude adhered to a system which inflamed its passions, exaggerated its importance, assigned it the first place, and appeared to do everything for it." (119)

The Law of the "Maximum" came to be on September 29, 1793. This price-fixing scheme had four facets. The first, to pin prices of necessities at no more than one third above their 1790 price; the second, a fixed price for all transportation; the third, a fixed markup of 5% for wholesalers; and the fourth, a fixed markup of 10% for retailers. *As natural prices were already far above the prescribed levels, the rate of scarcity was propelled by the maximum.* Farmers abstained from purchasing any more than was barely necessary for their own sustenance; exacerbating the scarcity of food. Traders were ruined by this decree; exacerbating the scarcity of other goods. Black market trade was the only recourse, due to this law, and such tactics were met with execution if either party was found out; thereby skyrocketing prices, due to the risks involved. Anybody caught evading ensnarement in the play-money abyss of the wokers, trading in physical gold and silver as opposed to their assignats backed by stolen booty and the might of the state, were imprisoned in irons for 6 years; for twice refusing to accept the play-money in exchange for useful goods, 20 years imprisonment. (120)

The "populist" revolution infringed upon the rights of the masses, as Saint-Just, of the Mountain, made plain at this juncture: "You must no longer show any lenity to the enemies of the new order of things. Liberty must triumph at any cost. In the present circumstances of the republic, the constitution cannot be established; it would guarantee impunity to attacks on our liberty, because it would be deficient in the violence necessary to restrain them. The present government is not sufficiently free to act. You are not near enough to strike in every direction at the authors of these attacks; the sword of the law must extend everywhere; your arm must be felt everywhere." (121)

In October of 1793 a new calendar was introduced, supplanting the Christian calendar; this new calendar began with the 22nd of September, 1792. This calendar was made up of 12 months, each consisting of 30 days, with a 5 day period of festivals to round out the year. Each month consisted of three periods, each containing ten days, though there was still only one day of rest per ten day period; thereby cutting in to the leisure time of the masses, in the name of their liberation. Dates will be provided in accordance with the Christian calendar, in an effort to avoid cumbersome conversions of dates of an extinct, short-lived, time keeping system. Two new religions were proposed, one worshiping reason, the other the Supreme Being. (122)

On the 5th of December, 1793, Robespierre spoke in the assembly, successfully pursuing a decree against the constriction of liberty concerning religious choice; this, after just having forbade Catholicism in October! (123) **The Mountain, like the Girondists before them, now opposed the monster** that they had created and fostered, seeking law and order; and their leader, Danton, fled the scene to his home in Arcis-sur-Aube. (124) All the while the Jacobins continued to fan the flames of lawlessness, injustice, disorder, and terror. (125) Robespierre who, like Danton, would say anything to anyone at anytime, if he felt as though it would suit his present purposes, said "The government of the revolution is the despotism of liberty against tyranny." (126) In a private meeting with Danton, when confronted regarding the illegitimate murders in which the duo shared complicity, Robespierre denied that any innocent person had been put to death. (127)

In the assembly, Saint-Just: "Citizens, you wished for a republic; if you do not at the same time desire all that constitutes it, you will overwhelm the people in its ruins. What constitutes a republic is the destruction of all that is opposed to it. We are guilty towards the republic because we pity the prisoners; we are guilty towards the republic because we do not desire virtue; we are guilty to the republic because we do not desire *terror*." (128) The committee rounded up the anarchists of the commune, who cowered before the committee prior to their execution. After disbanding the army, the committee then summoned those remaining of the commune to give them thanks in exchange for killing their co-conspirators.

April 1st, 1794, Danton, along with several others, were arrested at the behest of the committee of public safety. The next day, after an inkling of courage displayed by assembly members was quashed, reversing their course back to cowardice following the exultations of Robespierre, the assembly unanimously voted to impeach Danton and company. Showing up the crooked tribunal of the revolution as they were paraded through en route to the guillotine, Danton predicted "but they will not long enjoy the fruit of their criminal victory. I draw Robespierre after me -- Robespierre will follow me." As Mignet put it regarding the assembly *"Every one sought to gain time with tyranny, and gave up others' heads to save his own."* (129)

The execution of Danton, concomitant with the cowardice of the assembly, *set forth a truly unrestrained and vigorous Beast throughout France.* Daily executions ensued as "The extermination en masse of the enemies of democratic dictatorship, which had already been effected at Lyons and Toulon by grape-shot, became still more horrible, by the noyades of Nantes, and scaffolds of Arras, Paris, and Orange." ..."*Inquire what became of the men of 1789 in 1794, and it will be found that they were all swept away on this vast shipwreck.*" Paranoia continued to permeate the ruling body, which was now the 12 man committee of public safety. They kept killing, *for fear that a cessation would turn the sword by which they lived into their own direction.* (130) On the 24th of May, 1794, (4th of Prairial) a woman turned up at Robespierre's home, planning to murder him. He wasn't in, but she was found out and executed. Her family was sought out, and executed as well. Robespierre was treated as a genius at the Jacobin club. (131)

June 10th, 1794, (Prairial 22nd), in events foreshadowing those of other central planners, such as Stalin, Hitler, and Mao, *the paranoid elimination of those deemed threatening to those running the crime syndicate of socialism* was amplified. Calling their tyranny "liberty", as had been the case throughout the episode -since 1789- the convention *passed a new law codifying the abolition of the rights of the accused*; no counsel, no individual trials, no amnesty for those of the convention. Couthon spoke in the assembly "All tardiness is a crime, all indulgent formality a public danger; there should be no longer delay in punishing the enemies of the state than suffices to recognize them." All were declared guilty who stood up to the so-called liberty of these central planners. (132) For two months executions took place en masse; 50 a day. (133)

The unwashed masses still enjoyed a lifestyle of perpetual destruction and pillaging; their hatred and envy of their betters taking precedence over any sensible measures regarding the enrichment of their nation, or of their class. Robespierre was their man, and he held all of the cards of power, lording over the Jacobins and all bodies: the

assembly, convention, commune, the committee of general safety, etc.. (134)
Estranged from the assembly, Robespierre colluded with a handful of political allies,
but mostly fanned the flames of the least sensible class, at the Jacobin club. (135) On
July 21st, 1794 (Thermidor 3rd), he spoke at the Jacobin club; on the 22nd, he wrote to
a messenger of the convention that both the convention, and the republic, must
perish. "As for me I have one foot in the tomb; in a few days the other will follow it."
(136) On the 26th of that same month, Robespierre enters the convention after a
prolonged absence, delivering a speech designed to lure the convention into his
control through demonization of the committees of safety; committees of which he
was in favor, and also a member. Nobody bought it. (137) Surprised by the resistance
of the convention, Robespierre sought comfort and refuge among the thugs of the
Jacobin club, inciting them with alarm, and instructing them to have men both at the
assembly and at the club the following day. (138)

July 26th, 1794, Robespierre and company were shouted down at the
convention, prior to their being arrested and sent to different jails. The Jacobins, and
Robespierre's accomplices outside of the convention, initiated tumult in the streets
and called to arms all those who loved the Reign of Terror and Robespierre. (139)
Jacobins amongst the commune arranged to have the various jailers disobey the
orders of the convention, and to release Robespierre and company upon their receipt.
Henriot was pried from the chamber of the committee of general safety by a force of
200 commoners, who then took aim at the convention. The commoners lacked the
conviction to obliterate the assembly. (140) Those of the assembly hastened to
summon armed men to their aid, and sent troops to avenge their near obliteration
"...we will march against the rebels; we will summon them in the name of the
convention to deliver up the traitors, and if they refuse, we will reduce the building in
which they are to ashes." Freron's statement was answered by Thuriot: "Go, and let
not day appear before the heads of the conspirators have fallen." (141)

Robespierre was at the Hotel de Ville, where he had been received with mighty
enthusiasm by the riotous masses, as they awaited the arrival of their conspirators so
that they might go forward with their plans of conquest of the republic. Plotting their

victory speeches, and their plans following what they perceived to be the mere formality of their victory, they grew alarmed at the lateness of the hour and the absence of the arrival of their chums. The thugs, armed with cannon, bayonets, and pikes, fled in a flash upon hearing the news that the convention lived, and at the sight of its troops. (142) Robespierre and 22 of his comrades were executed on the 26th of July, 1794 (9th of Thermidor). (143) Following the execution of Robespierre, the Jacobins incited another riot which descended upon the Assembly. The Jacobins were then displaced by Thermidorians, who continued the red wave of bloody terror. (144)

July 30th, 1794, in an effort to abate the conflagrated rage and provocation of the unwashed, sectional meetings were reduced in frequency from once per day, to once every tenth day; additionally, the paid to fail attempt at ingratiating the unwashed with their controllers -in the name of bestowing liberty upon them- of 40 sous daily, was discontinued. (145) We now find another clear instance of the supposedly populist movement suppressing populists. At this point the convention sought to obliterate the sway of the influential Jacobins via prohibition of all collective petitions, and of correspondence between Jacobin headquarters and all of its ancillary clubs. After some street violence with a rival gang, the Jacobin clubhouse was badly vandalized; appeal to the convention was met with stiff rebuke and hostility; another gang fight at the club, at which the Jacobins were bested, was followed by an official closing down of the clubhouse, accompanied by a revocation of its charter; the Jacobin club was no more. (146)

All told, the Terror, from the summer of 1793 through July of 1794, saw the execution of 40,000 people. Of that group: 70% were peasants/laborers, 8% were nobles, 14% were merchants, and 6% were members of the clergy; *harming most the very class that they pretended to be uplifting.* Several hundred thousand more were arrested and detained. (147) During this episode, assignats held their value steadily. The Jacobin government confiscated foreign currency, as well as physical gold and silver, from the people; forcing them to accept the assignats in exchange for the apprehended property. (148)

5 YEAR BENCHMARK:
LIFE AFTER THE REIGN OF TERROR; MORE TERRORISM

Writing in 1915 about the French Revolutionary episode which commenced 1789, L. Cecil Jane observed: "A movement ostensibly directed against despotism culminated in the establishment of a despotism far more complete than that which had been overthrown. The apostles of liberty proscribed whole classes of their fellow-citizens, drenching in innocent blood the land which they claimed to deliver from oppression. The apostles of equality established a tyranny of horror, labouring to extirpate all who had committed the sin of being fortunate. The apostles of fraternity carried fire and sword to the farthest confines of Europe, demanding that a continent should submit to the arbitrary dictation of a single people." (149)

Beginning with a proposal made on December 8th, 1794, legislative action was taken to return some of the land stolen by the French wokers to the clergy and nobility who had been victimized by the theft. Land which had already been sold, however, remained with the purchaser(s). (150) The "maximum" set maximum wages along with maximum prices for goods, though these prices were routinely disregarded. (151) This price control device, instituted in 1793 (see above, page# 124) by the populist redistributors at the helm, also mandated that goods and services be paid for in their new currency -which was created using land pilfered from their own countrymen as collateral- the assignat. This law was repealed in December of 1794, as the currency's value sunk like a stone. (152) *The inflation resumed at a pace far greater than the rate exhibited prior to the institution of these measures.* (153)

5 years into the revolution, in 1795: Mignet tells us "The general want was terrible. *Labour and its produce had been diminished ever since the revolutionary period, during which the rich had been imprisoned and the poor had governed.* ...To increase the difficulty, the assignats were falling into discredit, and their value diminished daily." The assignats traded at 1/15 their stated value, while physical gold and silver soared in value. The masses were perpetually starving, in severe penury, now that all of the

land had been stolen from the rich, and the poor had been directing affairs. Lengthy bread lines, and lousy quality bread, *were the realities of daily life* for the masses -whose displeasure was heard in loud complaints. (154)

Prices of Goods in France: Expressed in Concurrent U.S. Dollars

	1790	Mid-1795	End 1795
Bushel of Flour	.40	45	
Bushel of Oats	.18	10	
Cartload of Wood	4	500	250
Bushel of Coal	.07	2	
Pound of Sugar	.18	12.50	
Pound of Soap	.18	8	
Pound of Candles	.18	8	40
One Cabbage	.08	5.50	
Pair of Shoes	1	40	
25 Eggs	.24	5	
Pound of Bread			9
Bushel of Potatoes			40

Source for Chart: Andrew Dickson White, *Fiat Money Inflation in France: How it Came, What it Brought, and How it Ended* (USA: Jefferson Publication, 2015), p. 54

The trial of the ringleaders of the Reign of Terror was met with several riots among the unwashed: the first occurred on the 20th of March, 1795, two days prior to the scheduled beginning of the trial; their attempt at intimidation unsuccessful, they returned on the 31st with twice as many thugs, storming the convention hall with hatchets, shouting the slogans "bread", and "constitution of '93", but did not deter the assembly from sending the ringleaders on trial to be held at the castle of Ham. (155) The third riot took place on the 20th of May, 1795. This third riot was keen to enforce the constitution of 1793, ouster all of those presently in government, and to steal all property for themselves. (156) The Jacobin mob stormed the assembly, removed president Vernier by force, and beheaded Feraud in the lobby. They occupied the chamber and passed resolutions empowering the Jacobins, before their hour came at nightfall and they were expelled by La Jeunesse Doree, a rival gang. (157) The recent president, Boissy d'Anglas, stood up to the populist thugs even as they threatened him at pike-point, refusing to grant their requests. Although many assemblymen fled the hall, many remained, and a sect of those remaining usurped the presidency and awarded the armed men their desires; which included the re-establishment of the Jacobin club. This condition was short-lived, however, as friends of law and order soon arrived at the scene. The vandals fled. Their prizes, won under duress, were revoked; the conspiring assemblymen who granted the requests, along with several others, were arrested and sent far from Paris. (158)

The very next day, on the 21st of May, 1795, *the rioters were back*, and they brought their cannons. Negotiations prevailed which sent the insurgents packing, with nothing but promises that their demands would be kept in mind going forward. The convention loomed supreme in authority, and they executed 6 of the Mountain party involved with the riot on the preceding day. The presence of the unwashed was expunged from the area of the decision makers; this banishment would remain in effect thereafter. (159) Following the external Jacobin takeover of, and swift expulsion from, the Assembly, exiled church and nobles returned to France. The convention disarmed the populace. Revenge was taken on the political enemies of those returning; bloody revenge. (160)

August 22nd, 1795, a new constitution was decreed by the convention, independent of the 1793 constitution. The legislature was split into two bodies: the council of 500, for members 30 years of age or older, could propose or amend laws; and that of the Anciens, which contained 250 members, each being a minimum of 40 years of age, and was able to approve or reject the laws proposed by the council of 500 -though only once the law had been discussed in a minimum of 3 different sessions, each occurring a minimum of 5 days apart. There was also an executive directory composed of 5 members, appointed by the council of the Anciens, of which one member was to depart each year. The directory shifted the presidency amongst its members every three months, installed the military generals, and controlled government finances. Half of the council seats would come up for election every two years. Referring to the constitution of '95, Mignet: "It restored the two degrees of elections destined to retard the popular movement, and to lead to a more enlightened choice than immediate elections. The wise but moderate qualifications with respect to property, required in the members of the primary assemblies and the electoral assemblies, again conferred political importance on the middle class, to which it became imperatively necessary to recur after the dismissal of the multitude and the abandonment of the constitution of '93." (161)

The recurring theme, internecine quarrels, quashed this constitution, as it was more or less immediately disregarded by the rival factions, each continuing to seek supreme authority. The convention decreed that two thirds of its members must remain in their seats for the forthcoming session -without an election taking place- so that the current body could guarantee the votes necessary to perpetuate its rule. This was rejected by the council of the Anciens. Men took up arms, both in and out of the assembly, and Napoleon Bonaparte was called upon to take the second in command of the armed force, behind Barras. (162) September 23rd, 1795, the convention produced a constitution which was immediately unsatisfactory to both the returned nobility and clergy, as well as to the wokers. Arms were taken up at once, and Napoleon Bonaparte was summoned to the command. (163) Napoleon and company successfully fended off those attacking the assembly. Through these victories, and *a sense of exhaustion after years of perpetual conflict, terror, and executions*, some sense of lawfulness and or order had been restored. (164) The convention was closed after 3 years -9/21/1792 though 10/26/1795. The executive directory was installed the next day. (165)

Inflation: *As the executive directory began its duties, the assignats had lost all practical value.* People refused to trade goods and services in exchange for this paper, for the very same reasons that they would not accept toenail clippings; nobody would accept the mode of exchange further down the line, so that one would simply be left holding the paper. Commerce was impossible without a currency to enable the exchange, as specie in the hands of the masses had been forbidden. (166) 8 milliards of assignats had been issued by July 27th, 30 billion more since that date. (167) Mignet: "The directory then endeavoured to revive paper money; it proposed the issue of mandats territoriaux, which were to be substituted for the assignats then in circulation, at a rate of thirty for one, and to take the place of money. The councils decreed the issue of mandats territoriaux to the amount of two thousand four hundred millions [2.4 billion]. They had the advantage of being exchangeable at once and upon presentation, for the national domains which represented them. Their sale was very extensive, and in this way was completed the revolutionary mission of the assignats, of which they were the second period. They procured the directory a momentary resource; but they also lost their credit, and led insensibly to bankruptcy, which was the transition from paper to specie." (168)

The populists, unwavering in their desire for absolute equality of material condition, resumed their plotting. They brewed their conspiracy at the Pantheon, until the directory shut it down in February of 1796, without the consent of the legislative councils. The unwashed then recruited the police to do their bidding, so the directory disbanded the police. "Gracchus" Babeuf headed the Conspiracy of Equals, whose stated aim it was to abolish private property, declare universal equality, and thereby concentrate all power and property into his own hands. *As this dictatorship would interfere with the that of the directory, the latter beheaded Babeuf.* (169) Babeuf was the ringleader of the old Jacobins and their cause, aimed at stealing and redistributing all property -although half of France had already been appropriated by their efforts- and to establish pure democracy; a tyranny of the majority. (170) Fixated upon the constitution of 1793, they were betrayed by one of their own at the eleventh hour, this occurring during May 10th, 1795 (21st of Floreal), and the would-be rioters were arrested. From his shackles Babeuf affected a position of strength, but was mocked by his captors in the directorship prior to his execution. (171)

With factions plotting in both councils -the 500, and the Anciens- to overthrow the 1795 constitution, and to implement some other system and order, the directory of 5 took action with their own forces on the September 5th, 1797 (18th Fructidor year V), making arrests of council members, while also assigning each council a new meeting place. (172) This coup d'etat involved the establishment of a dictatorship of the directory, a mass deportation of council members, and of the press, and even of two members of the directory; *all perceived resistance to their grasp at power was expelled from the nation*. (173)

The September 1797 dictatorship, led by the directory, re-established the plebeian wants for satiating their envy of their betters: priests were exiled, all who dared speak out against the tyranny of the majority, and all who sought law and order, were exiled. The masses themselves were now abstaining from participation in the affairs of the country; the royalists and the middle-class traders had been quashed by the coup of the directory; the institution of new taxes, and the decision of the directory to pay off foreign debts in specie only, *coalesced to sink the French currency* -and therefore, those holding it; Napoleon's military conquests abroad, and their perpetuation, were deemed by the directory to be vital to the avoidance of retribution at the end of their dictatorship -hemmed in by their tyranny, and left without an exit strategy, *as had been the outcome for each preceding dictatorial, populist, regime since 1789*. (174)

NAPOLEON MAKES HIS MOVE

"Napoleon obviously owed his success to the nationalization and politicization of France in a revolution he had inherited and had not reversed. Even before Napoleon, the new French freedom and equality, its national democracy, had found admirers in Germany." -Sebastian Haffner on the influence of French episode which began 1789, on Germany (175)

In May of 1799 the directory was dismantled, and the resultant power vacuum attracted aspirants from all parties. (176) During this epoch, Napoleon made his move. Lurking in the weeds, biding his time for a year after first entertaining notions of ruling over an empire, on October 9th, 1799, he sailed to France and parleyed with Sieyes -now of the power-neutered directory. "Bonaparte was to gain the generals and the different corps of troops stationed in Paris, who displayed much enthusiasm for him and much attachment to his person. They agreed to convoke an extraordinary meeting of the moderate members of his councils, to describe the public danger of the Ancients, and by urging the ascendancy of Jacobinism to demand the removal of the legislative body of Saint-Cloud, and the appointment of general Bonaparte to the command of the armed force, as the only man able to save the country; and then, by means of the new military power, to obtain the dismissal of the directory, and the temporary dissolution of the legislative body. The enterprise was fixed for the morning of the 18th Brumaire (9th November)." (177)

The council of the anciens acceded to the wishes of the conspirators; the directory quit. (178) The council of 500 proved suspicious of Napoleon as a would-be dictator, with his brother Lucien as the council's president. This body rebuked Napoleon once while he was not present, and then once more to the man's face. During the intermittent period, occurring in between the two rejections, Napoleon returned to the council of the anciens, and made reference to the constitution of 1795 in his remarks to them: "The constitution of the year III has ceased to exist; you violated it on the 18th Fructitdor; you violated it on the 22nd Floreal; you violated it on the 30th Prairial. The constitution is invoked by all factions, and violated by all; it cannot be a means of safety for us, because it no longer obtains respect from anyone; the constitution being violated, we must have another compact, new guarantees." (179) The second, in person, rebuke of Napoleon Bonaparte by the council of 500, *was met with violent retaliation. Napoleon's men were outside of the hall*, and his brother Lucien incited them with the following line: "Citizen soldiers, the president of the council of five hundred declares to you that the large majority of that council is at this moment kept in fear by the daggers of a few representatives, who surround the tribune, threaten their colleagues with death, and occasion the most terrible deliberations. General, and you, soldiers and citizens, you will only recognise as legislators of France those who follow me. As for those who remain in the Orangery, let force expel them. Those brigands are no longer representatives of the people, but representatives of the poignard." *The hypocrisy of these men*, attempting to incite a violent riot so that they might overtake power, condemning men for utilizing violence to obtain power in government, *is blatant*. Napoleon proceeded to invoke the support of his men, to which they acceded enthusiastically, and ordered them to clear the hall of the five hundred. After recently claiming *in word* that the elimination of representative government would be sacrilegious, Napoleon Bonaparte *in deed* put an end to representative government in France on November 10th, 1799. (180)

December 24th, 1799, a new constitution was published. *The power, which since 1789 had in practice been concentrated into the hands of the few*, and subjected to the tyranny of the whims of the unwashed masses, *was now codified into the hands of the few*. The first consul could deliberate with his two deputies. These three consuls selected an 80 member senate, who selected impotent legislators and tribune members. As Mignet put it, there was "...an all-powerful consul, disposing of armies and of power, a general and a dictator...". (181)

FRENCH CONSTITUTION YEAR		POPULAR VOTES IN FAVOR
1791		No vote taken
1793	I	1,801,918
1795	III	1,057,390
1799	VIII	3,011,007

SOURCE FOR CHART: F.A.M. Mignet, *History of the French Revolution from 1789 to 1814* (North Haven, CT: ISBN: 9781507614303, 2022), p. 203

On May 6th, 1802, Napoleon was appointed first consul for another decade; on August 2nd, appointed to the position for life. (182) In between those two occurrences, on May 15th, 1802, Napoleon Bonaparte sought to restore the Ancien Regime with himself as the new monarch, his lineage to be the heirs to the throne; a restoration of the nobility; and to re-establish the legally preferential treatment of the clergy. (183) Bonaparte stated:

"I defy you to show me a republic, ancient or modern, in which distinctions did not exist; you call them toys; well, it is by toys that men are led. I would not say as much to a tribune; but in a council of wise men and statesmen we may speak plainly. I do not believe that the French love liberty and equality. The French have not been changed by ten years of revolution; they have but one sentiment---honour. That sentiment, then, must be nourished; they must have distinctions. See how the people prostrate themselves before the ribbons and stars of foreigners; they have been surprised by them; and they do not fail to wear them. All has been destroyed; the question is, how to restore it all. There is a government, there are authorities; but the rest of the nation, what is it? Grains of sand. Among us we have the old privileged classes, organized in principles and interests, knowing well what they want. I can count our enemies. But we, ourselves, are dispersed, without system, union, or contact. As long as I am here, I will answer for the republic; but we must provide for the future. Do you think the republic is definitively established? If so, you are greatly deceived. It is in our power to make it so; but we have not done it; and we shall not do it if we do not hurl some masses of granite on the soil of France." (184)

Another constitution was created on August 4th, 1802, which tilted the balance decidedly away from that of 1795. The 1795 document placed all power into the hands of the masses, subjecting the nation to the tyranny of the majority, while this newest document decreed the *exclusion of all classes* of the citizenry from decision making. Mignet tells us: "Towards the close of 1802, everything was in the hands of the consul for life, who had a class devoted to him in the clergy; a military order in the legion of honour; an administrative body in the council of state; a machinery for decrees in the legislative assembly; a machinery for the constitution in the senate." (185) On May 3rd, 1804, Napoleon was officially named the hereditary emperor, this decision confirmed on the 18th. The press, already heavily censored, was now nullified. Goings on of the government were not made public. (186) *On January 1st, 1806, the silly revolution was cast aside*. (187)

The series of dictatorships in this episode -the assembly, the commune, the committee of public safety, the directory, Napoleon, etc..- culminated in 1814, when Napoleon Bonaparte was deposed from the throne, and all of his hereditary rights to said throne were revoked. On April 11th, 1814, Napoleon was granted the isle of Elba for his exile, a far cry from the whole of continental Europe which he had ruled for years. (188)

1789, 40 years later, as told by Alexis de Tocqueville: "Democracy has thus abandoned to its primitive instincts; it has grown like those children who, deprived of a father's care, are left to fend for themselves in the streets of our towns and who come to learn only the vices and wretchedness of our society. We seem unaware of its arrival even when it has unexpectedly taken control of supreme power. Then each person has slavishly submitted to its slightest whim; it is worshipped as a symbol of force. When afterwards it was weakened by its own excesses, the legislators conceived the rash plan of destroying it instead of attempting to educate and amend it. ...Thus we have democracy minus anything to lessen its defects or to promote its natural advantages; already aware of the defects it entails we still remain ignorant of the benefits it can bring." (189)

"The renown of royal authority has vanished away without being replaced by the majesty of laws; nowadays the people despise authority while fearing it, and fear now extorts from them more than respect and love achieved formerly. "...I perceive that government has inherited by itself all those powers it has wrenched from families, corporate bodies, or individuals." (190)

*"The dividing up of fortunes has reduced the distance separating rich from poor...
[However,] each seeks to deprive the other of power; for both of them equally, the concept of
rights does not exist and power appears as the sole reason for action in the present and the
only guarantee for the future." (191) "Since democracy in France has been hampered in its
progress or abandoned, without support, to its lawless passions, it has overturned
everything that has crossed its path and has shaken everything it has not completely
destroyed. We have not seen it gradually taking over society in order to assert its power
peacefully; it has not ceased to march forward through the confusion and agitation of
conflict." (192)*

*"The central power created by the French Revolution has gone further than any
created by its forbears because it has been stronger and more knowledgeable than they:
Louis XIV committed the minutiae of community living to the whims of an intendant;
Napoleon left them to that of a minister. It is still the same principle but the effects were
more or less far-reaching." (193) The French during this period were simply destructive.
They did not take care to restrain the government, instead giving it total control over the
populace and then foolishly expecting the unchained Beast to obey the people;
"simultaneously republican and centralizing." While also both "populist and opposed to the
rights of the people, a closet servant of tyranny and an avowed lover of freedom." (194)
[Author's note: for more from Tocqueville on the aftermath of the debacle in France
beginning 1789, see his book, Le Ancien Regime.]*

THE BEAST UNCHAINED:
GERMANY'S 1930s-1940s NATIONAL SOCIALISTS

*"Their political bond, Liberal and Conservative alike, was opposition to the
destructive competition of untrammeled free enterprise and a belief that a moderately
authoritarian State could organize the nation's resources for the collective good." -Bentley
B. Gilbert on Germany during the 1900-1910 period. (195)*

A well-shackled populace, or an unshackled government, leaves the many dependent upon the whims or temperament of the few, as seen in Germany during 1870. About Bismarck, author Sebastian Haffner observes:

> "Now as before, he wanted to see Prussia as the dominant German power, but in the Reich this was not quite as self-evident as it had been in the earlier North German Confederation. On the contrary, once all the Lesser German hopes had been fulfilled, a Greater Germany was the next, so to speak natural, national goal.
>
> If one contemplates that the history of the German Reich led to a situation in which, in its last and most expansionist period, an Austrian became Germany's chancellor; that this last chancellor turned Bismarck's Lesser Germany into a Greater Germany; that this Greater Germany pursued an aggressive, expansionist policy diametrically opposed to Bismarck's; and that all this was greeted by an outpouring of enthusiasm unrivaled in Bismarck's Lesser Germany, even in 1870, one is tempted to say that Bismarck's greatest triumph, the founding of the German Reich, already contained the seeds of its collapse." (196)

A time-worn expression, "don't play with fire, because you just might get burned", warning of the dangers awaiting one if control over the blaze is lost, is apropos of the German National Socialist -NAZI- period, as a *domestically manufactured crisis* yielded an unexpected outcome. The drastic post WWI inflation of 1919-1923 was initially motivated by the desire of the German Foreign Office to evade the reparatory payments of the Versailles Treaty. (197) *It was the chaos caused by this strategy* from which Adolph Hitler and his socialists corralled power into their own hands, in the name of liberating the masses. Adolph Hitler fought for Germany, though Austrian by birth, during WWI. He launched the National Socialist party while the mark -Germany's currency- fell during 1922. His gang attempted to take over in 1923, an endeavor known to history as the Beer Hall Putsch. Hitler was imprisoned for a year. A British ambassador remarked to American newspaper man William Shirer in the late 1920s that: Hitler had "passed into oblivion." (198)

POST WWI GERMAN INFLATION
RATIO OF MARKS TO U.S. DOLLARS

YEAR	GERMAN MARKS	US DOLLARS
1919	10	1
1922	20,000	1
1923 (onset)	20,000	1
1923 (August)	1 million	1
1923 (November)	1 billion	1
1923 (December 31st)	4.2 trillion	1

Source for chart: Sebastian Haffner, *The Ailing Empire: Germany from Bismark to Hitler* (New York: Fromm International Publishing Corporation, 1989), p. 145-147

Haffner summarized this as a "sweeping redistribution of wealth from thrifty savers to property owners...". He continued, "At the expense of those who had been thrifty and saved their money, German industry was able to avoid the mass unemployment that other countries experienced after demobilization." (199) The French retaliated Germany's payment in worthless tokens by taking occupation of Germany's most vital industrial region. Germany responded by halting production in the commandeered area, thus necessitating that *more* currency be issued to replace the lost income from said region, further devaluing the German currency. Government had to appropriate -known alternatively as stealing- entire freight trains in order to meet the volume of paper currency being frantically printed and rushed off to disappointed hands. "Before 1923 the inflation had wiped out only monetary *wealth*, but now monetary *income* also lost its value. Workers and the thrifty middle class alike had become the victims of inflation. In effect, work was no longer compensated in money, or only in money that lost its value in one hour." (200)

Germany revalues its currency, then gets its payments lowered to 2 billion marks per year in a new treaty known as the London Agreement of 1924. (201)

The First World War had been financed by the USA. During the period 1924-1929 Germany paid out a cumulative 10 billion marks in war reparations, yet received 25 billion marks worth of new loans from the USA. Such a situation made for an ample supply of cash for Germany. The payment plan was arranged thusly:

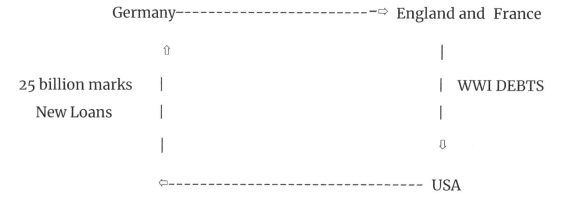

Source for chart: Sebastian Haffner, *The Ailing Empire: Germany from Bismark to Hitler* (New York: Fromm International Publishing Corporation, 1989), p. 150

October 1929: USA begins overreacting to Black Tuesday on the NYSE (202), veering from the relatively hands off approach, which had yielded so much plenty to the masses, concerning the federal government in regards to the economy. The USA ceased the issuance of new loans to Germany on such a grand scale, breaking the previous circle of payments (illustrated above). Germany's loan payments were suspended; bankruptcies spread over Germany like a rash; unemployment skyrocketed. Germany then ***intentionally engineered*** a deflation of its currency. Inflicting a crippling poverty unto its people -this deflation, and tanking of the economy, was done to evade the new reparations treaty. In 1932 a final settlement was reached on this score, calling for a final payment of 3 billion marks -though even this sum was not perceived as likely to be forthcoming. (203) Also in 1932, re-armament was sanctioned by the West. (204)

Behind the scenes political intrigue: General Kurt von Schleicher of the army, and Heinrich Bruning of the Center party; colluded to undermine the quasi-parliamentary republic and restore the monarchy. They planned to bleed the Reichstag dry of funds and energy through periodic dissolution of the body. They planned to make the Reichstag a bystander at best, and to make the president an emperor. In March of 1930, Bruning was named Chancellor. *The love of crises* on the part of oppressors was on display, as Bruning *utilized "emergency powers"* -as F. Roosevelt and the New Dealers would do shortly in the USA, as justification for their concentration of power and the ensuing saturnalia of tyranny known as the New Deal-, article 48 of the Constitution, to render the Reichstag impotent. The president could dissolve the Reichstag entirely if the latter's behavior displeased the president. (205)

Bruning goes rogue as he decides also to *engineer a severe economic crisis*, in an attempt to extract sympathy and payola from other countries. July of 1930 saw the dissolution of the Reichstag, and the September elections yielded a surprising outcome: Adolph Hitler and the National Socialists took 18% of the vote, and 107 seats. (206) This outcome was remarkable politically, as the proverbial David was becoming Goliath. In 1928 the National Socialists had taken 810,000 votes and 12 seats in the Reichstag; the 6.5 million votes in 1930 took the party from possessing the smallest representation, to the largest, in only two years. (207) Hitler's group progressed from 3% of the total vote in 1928, to 18% in 1930, over 30% in each of the 1932 elections, and finally to an astounding 92% of the ballots cast in the November 1933 vote. (208) The 44% of the vote captured during March of 1933 marked a 1,277% increase from their 1928 proportion of the tally. (209) During 1932, German unemployment was roughly 9.25% with 6 million out of work (210), and in July their remaining WWI reparations were written off. (211)

Spring of 1932 saw Hindenburg defeat Hitler in a tight contest, resulting in the former's re-election to the Presidency of the Reichstag. The incumbent took 19.3

million votes to Hitler's 13.5 million. (212) More political intrigue took place during June of 1932, as Bruning was ousted as chancellor by Hindenburg, at Schleicher's urging, and replaced by Franz von Papen. The July Reichstag elections yielded 37% of the vote for the National Socialists. (213) The 13,745,000 votes received yielded the NAZIS 230 out of the 608 seats in the chamber; the most heavily represented single party. (214) They, along with the communist party, joined to form a new majority in the body. This body proceeded to render a vote of no confidence in Papen -which, constitutionally, meant his ouster- to which Papen responded by dissolving the Reichstag. (215) Papen was left hanging by his co-conspirators, ruining him politically (216). November 1932 another Reichstag is elected, while Schleicher is appointed to succeed Papen as chancellor. (217) On December 2nd, 1932, General Kurt von Schleicher took the helm as the final chancellor of the Weimar Republic. (218) In January of 1933, Schleicher was denied the benediction of Hindenburg regarding the former's desire to again dissolve the Reichstag. (219) The conspirators now ditched their plan to restore monarchy in ram-rod fashion, instead opting to attempt to lure Hitler and the National Socialists into their circle of control: at first with a post in the Cabinet of Barons -rejected by Hitler- and then by meeting his demand of chancellorship with full presidential powers. (220) January 30, 1933, Adolph Hitler was installed as chancellor. (221)

The Beast unchained: 1933: January 30th, Hitler installed as chancellor; February 27th, Reichstag building torched; February 28th, Hitler given *full "emergency" powers of illimited scope*. Tyranny became the "new normal". The following week an election for the Reichstag was held, yielding a 42.9% share of the vote for the National Socialists; 81 communist were elected but none were able to serve, having been either hauled off to the camps or having chosen to flee the position -or even the nation. The National Socialists concocted a phony Reichstag via this maneuvering, and on March 23rd, the body granted a four year impotence of the Reichstag. June and July saw the banishment of two parties, these being the Social Democrats and also the Communists. (222)

Here, it seems useful to point out *the similarities of the NAZIS' time period contemporaries, the enthusiasts of central planning found in the USA, the New Dealers.* Frank Roosevelt's tyrannical, zealous, regime, featured such abhorrent acts as: Roosevelt setting the daily price of gold by his whims, even flipping a coin to decide its price; a record before the Supreme Court so poor that it was not approached again until the Obama administration, and in Roosevelt's second term he enacted the court packing scheme, which successfully removed a shackle from the government and placed it upon the people, infringing upon the liberties of individuals to privately contract thereafter; the establishment of monopolies and large holding companies in the areas of farming and of utilities, all-the-while claiming that demonic phantoms in the private sector were doing the same; the utilization of over 3,700 executive orders in just over 3 terms in office, or 307 per year, while no other president has exceeded 250 executive orders per year, and only 7 others have broken the 100 per year level (223); increasing by 50% the proportion of the people's income to be devoured by government. These outrages committed by the New Dealers were dwarfed by those of the National Socialists. (224)

The obstructionist nature of the USA's Constitution of 1789 –Supreme Court, Electoral College, Senate, etc..– *saved the USA from the same degree of tyranny at the hands of Roosevelt,* as was achieved by Hitler in Germany. Once the people have been shackled, and the Beast of government left wholly unfettered with its power, the people are at the mercy of the whims of whomever may happen to be in control of the reins. There is no guarantee that one person will behave precisely as another does, yet *a concentration of power into the hands of the few by decree makes for a mere waiting game, as the inevitability of an evil person manning the helm haunts such a nation until the inevitable conclusion comes to fruition.*

The Beast unchained; from servant to master: Three months after seizing the helm of government, with power now heavily concentrated into the hands of the few by decree, and with immense centralization of authority and planning, Adolph Hitler declared the standard Socialist European workers' holiday of May Day to be a national holiday, proclaiming May Day 1933 to be the "Day of National Labor". Prior to the festivities, Hitler spoke to a group of labor union delegates in the Chancellery in the Wilhelmstrasse, reassuring them of his commitment to the unions. In his speech to the six figure crowd at the gala in the airfield, Hitler stated: "Honor work and respect the worker". The following morning, May 2nd, 1933, S.S. and S.A. men occupied trade union offices nationwide, arrested the leaders so that they could be beaten and taken away to the camps. All workers, employees, management, employers, and the self employed, were now placed into a single, centrally planned and controlled, union called the Labor Front. State ownership of business means ownership of collective bargaining rights, along with private property rights. The People, through the mechanism of the State, owned -and controlled- everything; *which of course in practice meant that the handful of people in government positions at the time owned and controlled everything.*

Workers were chained to their assigned job at their assigned workplace; similar to Maoist China, and precisely what Frank Roosevelt had in mind with his NIRA and NRA in the USA. Workers were given papers without which they could never be hired by any employer -again like China would institute a few decades later. The finality of the job placement by the state was legislatively enshrined in 1938, though it had already been law in practice for some years prior. (225) Palmer and Colton tell us: "Strikes were forbidden. Under the 'leadership principle' employers were set up as small-scale Fuhrers in their factories and industries, and given extensive control *subject to the closest government supervision.* [New paragraph] The government assumed increasing controls over industry, while leaving ownership in private hands." (226) In other words: you pay for the car, I'll tell you when you may drive it, and how you may drive it when you do.

Although there were episodic exhibitions of arbitrary and homicidal use of government power, the full reign of terror did not commence until the 1938-45 period. August 2nd, 1934, Hitler succeeds Hindenburg as commander in chief on the day of the latter's death; this done in cahoots with, and with the benediction of, the Reichswehr -a body of military command which existed within, but independent of, the State. (227) From 1933 forward there was no Constitution, no Reichstag or

Parliament. A recipe for arbitrary rule -the Beast fully unchained- during which time the only certainty was uncertainty. (228) By August of 1934, whether you label them as S.A., or Sturmabteilung, "brown shirts", or street toughs, this faction numbered one million members. The S.S., or Schutzstaffel, black coats, or elite guard, numbered 100,000. The S.S. under Heinrich Himmler would increase its volume and "become the chief paramilitary arm of the party and dominate the police and the secret police." (229)

June 30, 1934, Hitler orders extermination of S.A. leaders, including his only personal friend and S.A. chief Ernst Röhm; also of various political enemies along with the previous chancellor General Kurt von Schleicher and the general's wife. On August 2nd of that year the president of the Republic, Field Marshal Paul von Hindenburg, died of natural causes at the age of 87. Chancellor Hitler assumed the presidency; doing so in violation of Hindenburg's will, which was a restoration of the Hohenzollern monarchy. The back-room politicking regarding the tanking of the economy, the destruction of the currency, was designed to terminate the Weimar Republic and to bring about a new rulership, they just didn't end up with the new regime that they had envisioned; *the fallacy of the lamp illustrated in practice*. Hitler promptly removed any semblance of checks and balances within the government in assuming this dual-role. Adolph Hitler was now dictator. (230)

During fall of 1934, Hitler imposed harsh censorship of the press, and also revoked recognition of labor unions in existence outside of the government's monopoly on control over jobs and employment. (231) On May first of the prior year, the German Day of National Labor, the National Socialist officials arrested the labor leaders. (232) *The role of slave-master and slave were inverted*, as the fantasy of individuals that the powerful central government will use all of its power to empower the individual, is shattered by the unsurprising and harsh reality of the powerful government retaining all of the power for itself. This abrogation of choice included all *employers as well as employees*. All freedom to choose had been revoked. (233) The monopoly in which its members accept the terms handed out uniformly from their union leader after negotiations, sometimes grumbling while so doing -imbued with the feeling of being protected from competition from others in the labor pool who are better candidates for the job, or perhaps protection from negotiating on their own, or of being responsible for their own employment and earning power through business ownership; while *always* free to choose to leave the perceived safety of the union nest in order to fly freely on their own– *was replaced by an all-encompassing monopoly.*

This second monopoly was controlled by politicians and bureaucrats; people controlling clothing shops who knew nothing of the business or of the job, people controlling mining or agriculture or anything else while possessing a tremendous wealth of ignorance on the subject. The Beast, with one or two of its four limbs unfettered, yielded a counterproductive interruption in the labor market which was perceived as acceptable to enough of the people. This was either because they enjoyed the special advantage of court protected exclusion of other members of the labor pool; or because although they were members of the overwhelming majority of the labor pool, and were therefore excluded from any possibility of employment in the jobs, yet they envied such an advantage and sought to one day gain it for themselves. *The temptation to unshackle more limbs overtakes those ignorant of the consequences, and before you know it the Beast becomes fully unchained, and the roles of master and servant are inverted.*

During 1934, Jewish owned shops were marked with yellow paint, designating them as "Not for Aryans". (234) That same year the National Socialists rolled out their version of what the New Dealers in the USA called the Civilian Conservation Corps (CCC), which the Germans called their Labor Service Corps (LSC) or *Arbeitsdienst*. While the New Dealers used the CCC to exacerbate the scarcity of cash in the USA, the Germans used their LSC to evade or to skirt the Versailles Treaty provision limiting the German army to 100,000 members. The Labor Corps imparted military training to its members. A chant heard during a parade of the LSC at Nuremberg in 1934: "We want one Leader! Nothing for us! Everything for Germany! Heil Hitler!" (235)

An eyewitness among the Germans, American newspaperman Bill Shirer, said of the natives in 1934: "I heard no mention at Nuremberg of the loss of personal freedom and of other democratic rights. Apparently this was not much of a sacrifice.

They couldn't have cared less. They had committed themselves to Adolph Hitler and his barbarian dictatorship." (236) Shirer went on to state that "What surprised me at first was that most Germans, so far as I could see, did not seem to mind that their personal freedom had been taken away,...or that their life and work were becoming regimented to a degree never before experienced even by a people accustomed for generations to a great deal of regimentation." (237) *As the unleashed Beast progressed in its subjugation of the very people who had freed it* by giving the government too much authority and centralization, women were barred from holding public office, from workplaces, as well as from all positions of authority. The National Socialist *Frauenschaft*, or N.S. League of Women, was headed by a man. (238)

Spring 1935: Inflation was *voluntarily and willfully imposed* upon the masses, to serve the ends of those into whose hands power had been concentrated by socialism. Dr. Schacht, minister of economics, informed Hitler that the buildup of the military, for the sole purpose of conquest, would require "use of the printing press". Having stolen funds from Jews and foreigners who had German accents, Schacht boasted: "Thus, our armaments are partially financed with the credits of our political enemies". (239) That is, those who were not socialists or who stood in the way of "the Beast unchained".

The National Socialists made their own foray into the territory of selling off the property of their hated minority group; just as the Jacobins in France took from the clergy, the merchants, and the nobility; the Maoists in China took land and agricultural necessities from the so-called landlords, and capitalist roaders; and the communists in Russia took from the so-called rich peasants; the German NAZIS "aryanized" the property of the Jews, forcing its sale to non-Jews. (240)

1935, Beast Unchained: Central planner Goebbels had the final word on all paintings and sculpture exhibited, all books published, which movies were produced, which music played and who played it, and which plays could be brought to the stage. All this, in addition to control of state radio and newspapers. The name of the bureau he headed was called the Chamber of Culture. (241) As is customarily the case, private property and individual enrichment, which are forbidden to the masses, are a mundane matter of daily occurrence for those into whose hands the power has been concentrated in the name of uplifting the masses. *The unchained Beast robs the securely bound populace blind.* During a time of professed distrust for those all outside Germany, Goring sold articles to the press -the foreign press at that!- at high prices. After demanding a high price initially, he would constantly up the fee on subsequent submissions. Citing well known publishing giant William Randolph Hearst's wealth, Goring stated "what's a thousand or 2 more dollars per article to him?" The per capita income in the USA during 1935 was $583 (242). Goring offered to sell, in the spring of 1936, some of the stolen -or confiscated, if you prefer- paintings that the National Socialists had taxed away from the museums and the Jews, to an American journalist at very low prices in US dollars. After all, they hadn't cost Goring a cent! (243)

Hitler's Germany was highly compartmentalized, with department heads acting freely -within the boundaries set by Hitler. Speaking of Hjalmar Schacht, head of the State Bank, going on to head Hitler's Economic Ministry, Sebastian Haffner tells us: "Schacht stimulated the economy through rigidly compartmentalized domestic economic measures -through credits without immediately felt inflationary consequences." The 1936-39 period was highly prosperous for Germany. (244)

During 1937 some sham trials were witnessed in the "dictatorship of the proletariat" by newspaperman Bill Shirer. Shirer reports witnessing the People's Court in session multiple times. He described them as "a travesty of justice". 4 of the 5 judges overseeing the affair were party members, hurling accusations from the bench while the appointed defense attorney stood idly by. The verdict was always guilty, the sentence almost always execution. (245)

The Labor Front was a "labor union" with inverse proportions when compared with the traditional type. Ordinarily, a labor union or guild, consists of a minority of the labor pool excluding the majority, nearly always with the sanction and enforcement of the state; in the name of benefiting the laborers as a class. In this case, we find the majority of the pool excluding a small minority -the Jews. 1935 Nuremberg laws "deprived Jews of all civil rights". This, after excluding Jews from many professions. (246)

A state orchestrated attack upon the Jews -or pogrom- occurred in the 1938 *Kristallnacht*. Synagogues were set ablaze, homes of Jews leveled, and Jews were carted off by the thousands to death camps. Sebastian Haffner records that the German masses held their noses regarding the Jewish preoccupation of the government, since other phases -jobs, material quality of life- were going so well. (247) Hitler responded by putting the camps in Poland, in an effort to keep the death camps quiet within the German press. (248) The Final Solution, initiated 1941 on occupied land in the Soviet Union, seeping into the whole of the German occupied territory during 1942. (249) ***The love of a "crisis" for those interested in shackling the citizens***, while simultaneously unshackling the government, was evident within the National Socialists as revealed in the diary of Joseph Goebbels, who noted that wartime afforded options to those in government which were not available during peacetime. One could cover their tyranny by invoking claims of national security, or accusations of espionage. (250)

The death camps, and the horrors of the war years within Germany, are well chronicled elsewhere. The route to the tyranny and despotism are pertinent to the scope of this volume. Let no election go by without a crisis (see intro page# 12), as we saw in the USA during the 1930s, led to let no day go by without a crisis in Germany during this period, as it had in France in the 18th century, and as would occur in China a couple of decades later. The true crisis is the invocation of the word "crisis" on the part of those in government, and this leading to a parting of the legislative Red Sea protecting the people from tyranny. To put a stop to such cause and effect is to truly solve the problem.

THE BEAST UNCHAINED:
CHINA'S MID-20th CENTURY "LIBERATION"

"The rule of law, real judicial institutions, banks and businesses independent of political pressure, and respect for promises and contracts. It is now thought that the existence of such institutions, in varied forms adapted to local cultures, is the foundation of all development." Guy Sorman, 2009 (251)

A few tales of woe will be repeated here to illustrate the horrors of the so-called dictatorship of the proletariat which concentrated power into the hands of Mao Zedong -in the name of liberating the masses- along with some horrid statistical performance. Individual liberty, along with material well-being, were sacrificed upon the altar of so-called social justice.

The "equality of poverty" delivered by supposed equality schemes, along with the reality that the power has been concentrated into the hands of the few by decree in central planning, were apparent to the legions who trekked across China in 1942. That year, a five-figure amount of volunteers traveled on foot to join the communist party, expecting the fulfillment of promises of liberty, equality, and democracy. Historian Frank Dikotter relays that:

"They were quickly disillusioned. ***Instead of equality, they found rigid hierarchy***. Every organisation had three different kitchens, the best food being reserved for the senior leaders. From the amount of grain, sugar, cooking oil, meat and fruit to the quality of healthcare and access to information, one's position in the party hierarchy determined everything. Even the quality of tobacco and writing paper varied according to rank. Medicine was scarce for those on the lower rungs of the ladder, although leading cadres had personal doctors and sent their children to Moscow. At the apex of the party stood Mao, who was driven around in the only car in Yan'an and lived in a large mansion with heating especially installed for his comfort." (252)

Dr. Bill Gao, a man born in the United States to Chinese parents while his father was studying engineering at the University of Michigan during 1923, preferred his Americanized first name although he had been raised in China. At the age of 21 Bill studied at Harvard medical school, and during the 1949 Communist takeover of his homeland he voluntarily chose to return to China so that he may use his aptitude as a surgeon to help his country. The onset of China's Cultural Revolution in 1966 brought false accusations of espionage from empty-headed thugs in the Party. Gao's challenge to *bring forward any proof, or reason* for legitimate suspicion, was met with nothing of substance. Bill was arrested and confined to a room in the hospital, where he was only permitted to leave on work detail assigned by the Communists, which often meant sweeping floors or scrubbing toilets but never meant performing surgery.

Meanwhile, elsewhere in the country, his parents were also accused of espionage due to their having studied in the USA decades ago. Bill's 70 year old father was locked in a basement and forced to endure the struggle sessions -beatings as a result of failing to comply with obvious fabrications put forth by Party men after their heated beratement. The elder Gao's character and integrity were too strong to be taken from him by the advocates of central planning, as he was beaten to death after 5 months of this routine. When we in present day West realize that the ILC (see chapter IV) may require such treatment in order to *give up* their fidelity to fiction, and to *comply with the plain reality* dictated by the weight of the evidence in regards to central planning and the forced pooling of resources, it becomes clear that such people are truly overcome by evil; or that the level of education, and of character, in the present-day industrialized West, are markedly inferior to the levels found in those residing in the boonies of mid-20th century China.

The younger Gao was released from his wrongful imprisonment in the hospital room after enduring it for two years, at which time he was exiled to the desolate wasteland known as Xinjiang province, where this immensely competent surgeon was assigned to spend his days teaching the people how to brush their teeth, and not to share handkerchiefs.

One day he and his wife and all the people in the village, a ramshackle collection of mud-walled buildings, were called out to attend a mass trial. Several policemen, marched out an *ah-hong*, a Moslem holy man, into the main square in front of the crowd, consisting of perhaps 1,000 people. "One policeman read out a document that accused the *ah-hong* of leading a rebellion against the government," Bill said. "But it was not really a trial. They just read out the charges, then the verdict, then shot him in front of us. It was all over in a few minutes."

Having concluded three years of being wasted teaching rudimentary hygiene to desert dwellers, Bill Gao was sent to work in a hospital located in an industrial town founded by Chinese immigrants in Xinjiang province. This hospital had a ratio of 80 beds to 60 doctors. This embarrassment of riches led to more waste, as the doctors spent the overwhelming majority of their time twiddling their thumbs. *The supposed genius and superiority of a planned market, over the free market, strikes again!* In 1976, Gao heard word that he was wanted back in Shanghai, where he could practice surgery on a regular basis again. Butterfield's *China, Alive in the Bitter Sea* relays a passage regarding Gao's trip to Shanghai:

" 'It was like a bucket of ice water poured on my head,' Bill said. He could see that his own personal friends in the hospital, the older men, wanted him back, but many of the young leftist doctors and cadres promoted during the Cultural Revolution were still in key posts and they didn't want him. They were afraid he would try to "settle accounts" with them; they also knew he was a better surgeon and they might lose their jobs. Some of them had gone through medical school in the Cultural Revolution *when classes were devoted to politics* and were hardly qualified for the title of doctor. 'They were good at shouting slogans but not much else', Bill asserted. The Cultural Revolution was not really over — it never would be. The internecine wrangles would go on. And China had missed a generation of doctors, a serious blow to the Communists' plan to expand the availability of medical care." (253)

Any illusions of "gentle"communists, merely concerned with the aiding of the most vulnerable and least-moneyed, will quickly evaporate when perusing the results delivered in practice. One such instance occurred during the civil war battle of Changchun, when 160,000 *civilians were starved to death*; communists refused to permit fleeing civilians -known alternatively as refugees- through their barricades, which surrounded the city. Communist soldiers watched civilians hang themselves after having been refused passage -many pleading on bent knee. Military honcho Lin Biao discovered a few soldiers mercifully permitting the innocents passage through communist barricades, and in his own words "corrected" this behavior through reprimand. (254)

The civil war between the nationalists and the communists began 1927. 1934. Mao and his forces flee to Yan'an. Mao builds a regiment of 900,000, over the ensuing decade. At the conclusion of the Chinese war against Japan during WWII, Mao took on the reigning nationalists. (255) October 1, 1949, in Beijing, Mao Zedong ceremonially announced the formation of the Central People's Government. (256) Days after victory in the civil war against the Nationalists, the Communists sent party workers to permanently patrol areas, and to routinely grant themselves unannounced entry into residences, strictly to harass people and to rummage through their property in search of items that they wished to steal -such as weapons and radios. These agents were called police. (257) *When property is "everybody's", it's also "nobody's".*

In 1946, we saw an episode depicting so-called equality in practice. Mao calls for an all out class struggle, to unleash the revolutionary potential of the countryside. He also called for confiscation of land by the peasants, through the use of force against the landowner. In the town of Yuanbao, nobody gave a damn about the communists, or about communism. "They had no idea", recalled Han Hai, a then twenty-two year old cadre. The first thing that the communists did was to impose themselves upon the villagers, and divvying them up into the 5 classes that had been derived from the Soviet model: Landlords, rich peasants, middle peasants, poor peasants, and laborers. This task proved arduous, as the villagers were all more or less financial equals; equals who had all been minding their business beforehand, and who never once requested that anybody intervene on their behalf. Han Laoliu was collected as a landowner, though he owned no land himself -just the same as all of the others in the town. Weeks of intense brainwashing sessions were necessary prior to *any* of the townspeople expressing a sinew of a desire to hate their neighbor out of envy or jealousy, or to show an iota of interest in utilizing theft and violence as a means towards vengeance.

Each of the five classes were assigned an identifying stripe to wear in perpetuity. Those who were ginned up to be "rich", or "landlords", from the town of peacefully living financial peers, were publicly mocked during the fabricated hate fests which were orchestrated by the communists. Afterwards, all of the food, and goods, in the town were rounded up for the purpose of redistribution; *the communists took all of the booty and left town*, while the villagers received a few small items from what, mere days prior, had been their own property. (258) The Yuanbao system of arbitrarily assigning classes, while knowingly designating innocent people as scapegoats, was repeated en masse. Kang Sheng, who in 1934 had worked for Stalin in Moscow, liquidating the Chinese, was sent to Yan'an in 1936 and promptly pledged allegiance to Mao as chief terrorist via security and intelligence, remaining there until 1945. In 1947, Kang Sheng was sent to Shanxi province to head *the domestic terrorist operation known as land reform*. Sheng instituted methods of torture and execution whose intensity was greater than the methods preceding, which promptly swept the nation. These new methods included burning the victim to death by pouring hot oil over their head, along with drowning in salt water. Fighters for the Mao cause were betrayed: Sixty-one year old Nin Yonlan was tortured on stage, then led by his son to a cave where he was abandoned for eight days until his death. In Xing county 25 children were murdered during a class envy demonstration, as they were branded "little landlords". (259) In 1950, Pingyi county, Shandong province, a mere 25% of arrested "landlords" actually owned any land. (260)

1949-50: Mao's men take over the pre-existing system of mandatory personal identification cards, along with information on file with the police regarding the residents of various homes in their district; to which they added food rationing of households based upon the number of people listed as residing therein. People were also given one of 60 officially prescribed class designations. Specifics are as follows:

Good Class	Middle Class	Bad Class
Industrial workers	Petty Bourgeoisie	Landlords
Revolutionary cadres	Professionals	Capitalists
Revolutionary soldiers	Intellectuals	Rich peasants
Fallen Revolutionary fighters	Middle peasants	
Poor peasants		
Lower-middle peasants		

Source for chart: Frank Dikotter, *The Tragedy of Liberation: A History of the Chinese Revolution 1945-1957* (London: Bloomsbury, 2017), p. 47

During this period police routinely raided houses of the so-called "bad classes", without provocation or reasonable suspicion of wrongdoing. The communists would help themselves to the property of the "bad class"; radios, guns, and ammunition, were popular targets for theft. Approximately 20,000 citizens were sent to Hebei for execution. The entire population was sent to brainwashing sessions -mindlessly regurgitating slogans. Those deemed "bad classes" were forced to submit a written confession of their so-called sins. Some of these were published in the newspaper, while a few "confessors" were made to hold court before a large audience for hours. Each person's permanent record then reflected their "confessions" of guilt. (261) These brainwashing -sometimes called re-education-centers in 1949 usually featured the "friendly liberators" bringing "equality" to the masses by beating their captive "students" and stealing from their already meager provisions. These facilities were staffed with negligent and irresponsible nurses and physicians. Sodomisation of children was also known to go on. (262)

The Marxist or socialist promises of love for the poorest, and of delivering a dictatorship of the proletariat, or a worker's paradise, once they have concentrated the power into their own hands, are often met with outcomes precisely anterior to those promises. The central planners during the 1949-50 period made sure to segregate the poorest, along with the most derelict of the poorest -thieves, beggars on the street, whores, paupers- rounding them up and sending them to work camps in an area well partitioned from the slave laborers deemed to be of different classes; fearing loss of order with any dispersement of the lumpenproletariat into the remainder of the camp. This, after just having emptied the prisons for the purpose of saving the cost of heating the building. It is likely that many of these people were simply transferred from one internment to another, in the course of no greater than a few months. (263)

Mao's regime promptly issued a paper currency, and in short order ruled that it is the only currency -including gold and silver- to be accepted. It was called the People's Dollars, or renminbi. (264) Now that everybody was in one, enormous, "labor union" -as we would call it today-, instead of a handful of workers being dictated to by the union leaders, while they presume that it is worth the advantage of monopolizing the labor pool of their customer, knowing that if the worker really wanted to he could leave for another source of income; everybody was now simply dictated to, and had forgone their freedom to choose to leave. Shortly after the "Liberation", the workers revolted when the empty promises of communism -a position as a leader, better compensation, better material quality of life- were replaced by demands for greater output in order to offset the shortages occurring due to the tightened hand of central planning's strangling of the economy; and this output demanded at the same, or *even lower,* rate of compensation as they were receiving before. (265)

Heavy taxation and arbitrary justice were major problems in China. Citizens, and cities, could be taxed more than they brought in -a fledgling attempt by government to ameliorate their perpetual shortage of funds, *exacerbated by their hatred of productivity and of personal gain.* Some were taxed so heavily they could not eat, themselves. Businesses were attacked the hardest, leading to many closed doors and their corresponding additions to the ranks of the unemployed. (266) China would later go to a 100% income tax for grain farmers. *It seems counterintuitive that very much force would be required to enforce a dictatorship of the proletariat*, particularly when the worker comprises the overwhelming majority of a country's population, *because the people should be willing to comply with their own edicts*; if in fact the source of the dictatorship were their own, monolithic, uniform, edicts. But since in practice the power is concentrated into the hands of the few by decree, the masses do what they're told by people who know no competency other than politicking and ruling. Total governmental authority, and control of all property -by its "ownership" of that property which is "the People's"; and since it's "everybody's" money, it is "nobody's" money- *means concentration of that property into the hands of those few who occupy seats in government.*

Because the bizarre religion of Marxism asserts that success in business and finance requires no more than access to capital, and that managing the money to create and perpetuate jobs is not real work or not valuable work, the communist government placed inexperienced and unlearned proletarian soldiers at the heads of existing companies, as well as at the heads of banks in important places. These -what would today be called "token hires", or "diversity hires"- decisions had adverse consequences, as one ought to expect. The destruction of the once mighty trading hub of Shanghai was facilitated by fidelity to superstition, *as socialist promises were substituted for the evidence of their practices.* Prior to 1949, Shanghai was perhaps the pre-eminent commercial hub in Asia; had more foreign investment than London or Paris; second only to New York City in foreign residents. The jewelry shops on Nanking Road soon saw the fine jewels and extravagant accessories they customarily featured replaced with ordinary soaps, underwear, and medicines. All over the nation, factories shut down due to want of business, and Shanghai was no exception. One estimate out of Hong Kong at the time placed the amount of bankruptcies in firms in the area of 4,000 in Shanghai alone, 25% of which were factories. (267)

During their institution of so-called "land reform", the communists used what I call the "hate system", of arbitrarily assigning class distinctions, thus concocting a minority to use as their scapegoat -sometimes literally sacrificing their lives during beatings, or performing outright executions- having the rest voluntarily give up their own rights -albeit unwittingly- as they informed on their neighbor in an effort to revoke their neighbor's rights. All food was looted by the party cadres and sent to Beijing for the government officials' purposes; much was sent to the USSR in exchange for industrial equipment. The land was "redistributed" to the masses, each portion assigned a production quota, and taxed heavily. Hundreds of thousands starved to death in Manchuria, alone. (268)

It is worthwhile to *note the absence of feudalism, or of a landlord class,* immediately preceding the mid-century takeover by Mao. No derogatory term for a rapacious landlord existed in China. During the period 1929-1933 a study was performed by a team from the University of Nanking, which surveyed over 16,000 farms spread out over 168 villages across 22 provinces. *Land Utilization in China* found that fewer than 6% of farmers were tenants, more than half owned their farm outright, while many farmers had partners. No farmer surveyed noted exorbitant interest rates, or land tenure, as being in existence. (269) Outside of the scope of that study, we note that all land arrangements of the period were handled by contracts, which were honored in the courts. Farmers who owned their land were abundant in supply. (270)

October 1950, "Paranoia was intrinsic to the regime, which lived in fear of its own shadow. The party had long developed the habit of blaming every setback on *real or imagined enemies.* Behind every poisoned well or granary that went up in flames lurked a spy or landlord. Every act of resistance by ordinary farmers –and there were many– was seen as proof of a counter-revolution. Tension was also deliberately cultivated to keep people on edge and justify ever more intrusive forms of policy." (271) *Such a statement could easily be made about the Jacobins in France.* Also like their predecessors in tyranny and oppression, the Chinese order of terror throughout the land was issued on the 10th of October. The promised "dictatorship of the proletariat" had no allies, and the party cadres ruled the proletariat by coercion. By April of 1951, 60% of provinces had murdered, minimally, 0.1% of their population. (272) Lest this amount be dismissed by present-day socialists as paltry, this amount, extrapolated at the same rate over 12 months, makes for double the proportion of population officially killed by the Covid Monster in the USA during the year 2020, which many socialists lamented with horror as they *utilized this "crisis" as a pretense for deliberately sabotaging the economy, and for eliminating civil liberties of the masses*.

Internal records of this period in China, which may very well have contained accounting which was suppressing the actual damage inflicted, show that baseless arrests and executions of the innocent were rampant during this period. In Guangdong 33% were wrongly accused; 50% in segments of Guizhou; 66% in Congjiang county. One man born in 1928 was accused of having murdered eight people during 1929. In Sichuan province 4,000 government workers were jailed for having brushed elbows with nationalists, no matter how benign or distant that contact may have been. One party man stated "You must hate even if you feel no hatred, you must kill even if you do not wish to kill." Mao's stated guideline quota of 0.01% to be murdered in each province -so that a message would be received by the others, without robbing the nation of necessary manpower- was pursued in earnest, while some go-getters sought to curry favor with the helmsman by surpassing this mark. (273) And many succeeded in obliterating this benchmark.

Motivation for suppressing the totals in the official reports may be found in the secret killings by party cadres, conducted to settle personal scores, and so going untabulated. The widespread application of the murder spree ordered by government, on the part of the unruly gangsters of the proletariat who were now in power, led to many unaccounted murders. Death totals for the period are skewed somewhat by the civil war, occurring prior to October of 1950, as the deaths are not neatly segregated into separate periods. In late 1952, Bo Yibo estimated 2 million were killed. Out of a population of 550 million, that makes for a 0.36% voluntary slaughter of the nation's people, merely to establish authority *so that the fictions of socialism might not face resistance from the able-minded and empowered masses*. The official report of Luo Ruiqing, made August 23, 1952, estimated the total murdered to be 301,800. (274)

Mao's Communist Terror of Oct 1950 – November 1951
Official Report:

PROVINCE	DEATHS	IMPRISONMENTS
Guanxi	46,200, 0.256%	Minimally, 5%
Hubei	45,500, 0.175%	
Henan	56,700, 0.167%	
Guizhou	0.3%	
Hunan	61,400, 0.192%	
Jiangxi	24,500, 0.135%	
Guangdong	39,900, 0.124%	

Source for chart: Frank Dikotter, *The Tragedy of Liberation: A History of the Chinese Revolution 1945-1957* (London: Bloomsbury, 2017), p. 86-88 + p. 99-100

The danger of substituting pretension for factual evaluation, of superstition for conclusions founded on evidence, was exemplified during this episode of orchestrated terror. What contemporary readers will recognize in the "I identify as" crowd, who arrogantly demand that the use of this deflector shield phrase be able to transform fiction into fact, and vice versa, was clearly present in the wokers of China during the period 1950-51. Frank Dikotter tells us: "As the politics of hatred tore apart the social fabric of community life, tens of millions of people were permanently branded as "landlords", "rich farmers", "counter-revolutionaries" and "criminals". These were the black classes, who stood in opposition to the vanguard of the revolution, called the red classes. But the label was inherited, meaning that the offspring of outcasts were also subjected to constant persecution and discrimination, all sanctioned by the party." (275) *Those to whom such labels were affixed were rarely wearing accurate monikers.* The magic words were spoken, the party leaders "identified as" knowing such things about individuals, and *all interjections of facts and reality were met with swift rebuke.*

Parallels to the present day situation in the USA, which one can only hope seems a bizarre footnote of history to future readers, pertaining to the legal codification of the reality altering phrase "I identify as" -giving the words magical powers in the eyes of the law- are inescapable. In the age of the electron microscope, outer space exploration, and other scientific and technological advances which remove much of the mystery from life that supplied past generations of people with comparative license to bend to superstition and make-believe, this phrase must be accepted by citizens of this country as accurate, even when it is clearly and irrefutably -irrefutable when one is speaking the language of evidence, that is- false. *Speaking the plain truth when confronted by such fraud and duplicity results in the legal rebuke of those obeying the evidence.*

Sadly, the Supreme Court has failed to protect the people from such tyranny on the part of sleazy politicians, and the lowest proportion of the population for whom they fetch. As of this writing, in *a clear case of the special interest taking precedence over the general interest*, the phrase only pertains to gender fraud, and mostly attacks the minority group who are business owners. However, unless it is snuffed out in short order, it is not difficult to foresee the expansion of disrespect and disregard of the law on the part of competently minded adults, concomitantly with the expansion of disrespect for the rights of the citizens on the part of legislators. The horrid New Deal legislation metastasized into the Great Society and War on Poverty monstrosities; the Interstate Commerce Commission, initially for codifying monopoly of railroad transportation, expanded to include automobiles once they came into competition and provided consumers with an alternative; it should surprise absolutely nobody to witness such expansion of this perverse law. If the phrase truly does transform water into wine, according to the lawmakers and judges, then each party in a court of law will rise, and in unison proclaim "I am the winner of this case". How will such a case be decided? By whomever spoke first? Or spoke the loudest? Perhaps they'll just draw straws; but then, wouldn't each party simply "identify as" having pulled the winning straw? Every employer tells their employee on pay day "I identify as having already paid you", every person walks into a bank and states "I identify as having $30 billion on deposit at this bank". The unacceptability and impracticability of such a practice is glaringly obvious to all adults with competent minds. The shunning of such a class, those who are adults with competent minds, by people in government, is an alarming development in the USA.

An obvious strategy for either forcing the legislation to be outlawed, or rubbing the noses of those perpetrating this crime against justice into the illegitimacy of their behavior and thereby making their departure from legitimacy as flagrant as possible, involves bringing the law back before the Supreme Court. Once there, the party representing the grown-ups opens by stating : "I shall utilize this supposedly magical phrase, 'I identify as', in order to usurp the seat of each justice on this court. As I proceed to each justice, individually, they will have but two choices: the first, to comply with this fiction and to move aside, at which time I will render an opinion in my favor which must be honored by the existing law; the second, to refuse to comply with this fiction, thereby voting through their behavior that the phrase does not transform fiction into fact, thus leaving the justice with no legitimate alternative but to render an opinion in my favor. A unanimous outcome in my favor is the only legitimate outcome possible."

In China, the promised "dictatorship of the proletariat" delivered a situation in which the proletariat were dictated to, as they were beaten and berated into complying with fiction. After months of enclosed and monitored behavior, forcing false confessions; false reports on friends, family, and neighbors; starving people as a consequence for refusing compliance with the government's falsehoods -similar to the so-called "social credit system" proposed by some people today- Dikotter tells us that:

"By the end of 1952 virtually every student or teacher was a loyal servant of the state. The food they received depended on their performance. And like all other government employees, they were required to accept any form of employment to which the party directed them. The state needed millions of young people to help build up the border areas such as Inner Mongolia, Xinjiang and Manchuria. It also wanted experts to provide technological advice in the countryside. Thought reform thoroughly crushed any resistance to assignment to a job in a distant and often unappealing place. Socialism lauded the collective, *meaning that the government's needs now took precedence over individual preference*. On the other hand, young assistants with more reliable political qualifications replaced foreign-trained professors in the cities. Others with degrees from some of the world's best universities were sent to such posts as assistant clerk in a village library or cashier in a distant bank. 'None of them received assignments of any real dignity or service,' to quote Robert Loh." (276)

During 1951, the "I'd rather burn it than have you steal it" phenomenon, witnessed so frequently throughout this volume, was again on display. Word of the confiscation and redistribution of socialism moved more rapidly than the cadres doing the plundering, and many citizens destroyed their property rather than permit the government cadres to take it for themselves; in-so-doing reducing the supply of said property. In droves, people burned their own homes in Sichuan. Elsewhere, party officials recorded 27,000 fir trees chopped down by their owners, prior to the arrival of the cadres. (277) In 1952, as cadres carried out "land reform", distributing murder, torture, and poverty, rather than equality, government agents pilfered the homes and food storage reserves in each town and city -the party slogan was "To be Poor is Glorious". Agricultural output declined by one third in North China. Being productive, and working the fields, which is done for personal material gain of food and/or currency, was behavior that was acutely contrary to the Party slogan "To be Poor is glorious." (278) After the torture, murder, and theft, at the hands of the socialists during "land reform", the survivors would understandably wish to comply with party slogans in the immediate aftermath, for the purpose of self-preservation. Historian Frank Dikotter estimates that a minimum of 1.5 million were murdered during the years 1947-52, as a result of the domestic terrorism operation called "land reform". (279)

Also during 1952, the communists put all of the physicians in the hospital in which Dr. Bill Gao was assigned to work, into thought reform class. Gao described the thought reform classes later as "what you Americans call brainwashing." The Communist Party conversion -via coercion- was to be executed, one by one, until every citizen of China was in lock step conformity with the Party's dictates of "equality". (280)

These brainwashing sessions went on for six months. The "liberated" Chinese were required to discredit and berate their elders -an enormous contradiction with their wishes, as honoring one's elders was of gargantuan import within the Confucian Chinese culture at the present time- with Dr. Gao forced to disparage his own father, in writing. *It was all a lie.* Dr. Gao: "Thought reform was a fraud, it didn't work." "You always ended up pretending, not really telling what you thought." For the ensuing three decades, the cavalcade of political campaigns in China had unintended consequences that included a pervasive state of psychological repression among the masses, as well as a widespread cynicism and distrust of government. Bill Gao: "Because of all the thought reform meetings, you could never even tell your wife what was on your mind. For the next time a campaign came along, the first thing the cadres would do was turn to her and ask her to help you confess. So we hid our true feelings." (281)

In 1955, Mao stated that "Socialism must have a dictatorship, it will not work without it...This is a war: we are opening fire on peasants with private property." (282) From summer of 1955 to July 1956, the farmers, enticed with promises of land ownership -land appropriated from other Chinese in the name of the condemnation and *punishment* of those who owned land while others did not, was now being offered as a *reward* so that these recipients might own land while others did not- so that they would accede to participating in the theft of property from the targeted minority group, were betrayed by the socialists who had blandished them. Upon completion of the task of these servants for their evil master, *the master perverted their reward*; the land was now to be taxed at a rate of 100% by the state, converting the promised co-op into a collective farm, so that none of them owned anything and all were slave laborers at the hands of the state. (283) By December of 1956, 89% of all peasants households in Kwangtung province were engulfed by collectivism in farming. (284)

The outcome was, unsurprisingly, negative. The amount of land sown with crops for food was reduced by an amount ranging between 3 and 4 million hectares. The voluntary slaughter of farm animals, unceasing since the onset of "Liberation", was amplified in its occurrences. Population expanded more rapidly than the grains produced to feed them, and Mao's war on peasants with private property was accompanied by another wave of terror, this consisting of mass arrests. High officials were routinely sacrificed, as Mao's perpetual paranoia resulted in frequent purges from within his circle. (285)

October 1955, the current terror, commingled with the nonstop thought reform, theft, and arbitrary arrests and executions, proved sufficient to intimidate the heads of businesses into "requesting" that their businesses be taken from them by the few in power -under the guise of turning them over to the masses. (286) Dikotter:

"Mao left, promising to give serious thought to their opinions. But he warned them that he would have to consider carefully their best interests before deciding to accelerate the pace of nationalisation. A few weeks after the meeting, the authorities announced that the transformation to socialism was to be accomplished not in six years, as most had anticipated, but in a mere six days. Shock teams were sent around the city to nationalise all industry, forcing businessmen to give up their enterprises and become members of the Federation of Industry and Commerce. Most did so out of fear, but they had to demonstrate wild enthusiasm in public. The reason for this was simple. Every entrepreneur knew that, *once his property had been handed over to the state, his only means of livelihood would depend on the whim of the party*. And many remembered the brutality of the campaign against them in 1952." (287)

In 1957 psychology was abolished. The Communist Party asserted that studying Mao's works would cure any and all mental ailments. Because the existence of any studies during this period are lacking, as a direct consequence of this "canceling" of psychology, observations are all that we have to examine the psychological consequences of these "woke" Communists. Dr. Bill Gao: "Contrary to what you might expect, there was no rise in mental illness during the Cultural Revolution." "People either snapped all the way and committed suicide or they survived. It was something like what I've heard about the Jews in the concentration camps. There was very little you could do about it when they started attacking you - it was all arranged. So the main thing was to try and stay alive." In one hospital with a staff of 300 people, 20 doctors committed suicide during the Cultural Revolution. Dr. Gao: "But if a person committed suicide, it was worse for his family. Then the Communists automatically considered you guilty. It was terrible. They would hold a ceremony, not to mourn the person but to formally condemn them." (288)

In 1958, an emboldened plot to collectivize China, in all facets including agriculture, was enacted. The collective farms of 1955-56 were now transformed into massive communes, as all private property and free markets were eliminated. The authors of the 1978 book, *Village and Family in Contemporary China* tell us that although they glued a bird's wings onto their pig, no matter how many "magic words" they might have chanted, they couldn't make it fly:

> "Everything went wrong. The commune leaders were not equipped to manage the activities of such a huge and complex organization, and in the enthusiasm of the moment they diverted too much labor from farming to a variety of untested schemes: backyard steel furnaces, roadbuilding, and large construction projects. Peasants had to work together with people from other villages with whom they had no history of cooperation, and the former poor-peasant allies of the government *realized that those who did not work as hard as they or who lived in poorer villages were reaping undue benefits from the new system*." (289)

The collectivization of farms came with more promises, and delivered more disappointments. To palliate those who might have inner objections to the forfeiture of their rights to provide for themselves, those in government promised the "five guarantees", which were food, housing, clothing, funerals, and medical care. *The failure to deliver on these promises was immediate.* These so-called guarantees were promptly limited to the aged, and the overtly indigent, though efforts were made to throttle the supply of even this class of applicants who expected the socialists to deliver on their empty promises.

The propaganda instrument of the wokernist government, the *People's Daily*, ran material designed to shame the people for expecting to receive the payola assured to them, all while displaying an absolute absence of shame on the part of those in government for failing to hold up their end of the so-called bargain: "...some collective members use the 'five guarantees' system to divide their parents off as they please. They push the responsibility for the livelihood of the old completely off on the agricultural collective..." This condemnation of people for utilizing, while inferring abuse of, the fruits of the stolen property and labor, which they had been assured would be their own to utilize as they needed when it was taken from them, is appalling. *Is it guaranteed, or is it an abuse to expect what was promised?* You may have one, or you may have the other, but you may not have both while remaining credible. Imagine confiscating a person's entire earnings each month, and then condemning that person for their inability to financially support their family; or stealing a person's car, assuring that person use of the car whenever they like, and then shaming them for their desire to use what is now "our" car. Such was the case with the socialists in China. (290)

Certain families, if the administrators in their local unit deemed, were permitted to take small loans at 4% interest. (291) Using money to make money was not permissible to the masses, yet was perfectly acceptable for those who condemned the behavior, and stole everybody's property in order to prevent such so-called abuses. *Capitalism -in the sense of utilizing capital to replace muscle and to free up time- would enable those who are aged to earn money while sparing their bodies from the expenditure of physical exertion, and therefore remove them from dependency upon anyone else; yet this is anathema to wokers.*

The 1958 tightening of the grip of the Beast upon the windpipe of the nation included their efforts pertaining to the control of housing. The dictatorship *over* the proletariat forbade the movement of workers from country to city, even though the jobs in the city were often much more coveted than those performing work in the fields. One regulation regarding this matter read:

"A citizen who wants to move from the countryside to a city must possess an employment certificate issued by the labor bureau of the city, a certificate of admission issued by a school, or a moving certificate issued by the household registration office of the city of destination, and must apply to the household registration office in his or her permanent place of residence for permission to move out and fulfill the moving procedure." (292)

One had to gain permission from the place in which they presently lived in order to depart, along with gaining the benediction of the place in which they wished to move in order to enter. *As opposed to living the lives of free adults*, able to do as they pleased, *the Chinese masses found themselves living the lives of beggars*; bumming from one couch to another, dependent upon the permission of the responsible parties in order to make any changes.

The 1958-59 attempt to provide "free" medical care for all was met with the delivery of prolonged waiting times, and financial insolvency; with the rural outfits, upon which approximately 80% of the Chinese population were dependent, performing far worse than those in the cities. (293)

Many other political campaigns -known alternatively as episodes of domestic terror- and their details exist, perhaps most notoriously the Cultural Revolution of the late 1960s. Much has been written of these episodes, and the reader is encouraged to seek out these texts, if they are not already familiarized with these goings-on. In the interest of space, we now skip ahead to the period in which the Beast remained unchained, continuing to act as master over the forced servitude of the masses, even after the death of Mao Zedong.

The post-Mao loosening of the grip remained fairly tight, and although the relaxation of the grip around the windpipe permitted much alleviation from poverty, the roles of master and servant remain unaltered as of this writing. In 1978 Mao dies, Deng Xiaopeng soon takes over as leader, the grip loosens as an amount of private property rights are re-introduced. The authors of *The Bamboo Network* tell us that, as of 1996:

> "Although China's Communist Party continues to monopolize political power and suppress any opposition, it has loosened its grip on the society. Individuals are allowed, to a degree unheard of during the Maoist era, to make career, travel, and lifestyle choices. Living standards for the average Chinese are much higher than they were in 1978. Millions are escaping from poverty and filling the ranks of a new middle class." (294) "The problems encountered by U.S. businesses in China seem endless. Rules and regulations are often not publicized by Beijing, and those that are may be changed without notification. Currency is not freely convertible, so many firms have difficulty bringing their money home. Signed contracts are not legally binding, and judicial recourse is very limited. Copyright infringement and other forms of intellectual piracy are widespread. With a few sporadic and well-publicized exceptions, this form of economic theft is rarely punished by government officials who look the other way—and on occasion profit from the piracy." (295)

As has been illustrated up to this point, and will continue to be shown throughout the remainder of this book, ***an environment prioritizing collective rights over individual rights makes for no human rights***. A party cadre and his wife lived in Peking, but were required to move to Tibet. The failure of Communism made for immense scarcity of food all over -especially in Tibet. Their children remained in Peking for access to slightly better rations from the central planners. The parents were permitted to see their children once every two years. The Chinese government forcibly suppressed the amount of cattle available to the citizens of Tibet -and elsewhere. Although the masses were tremendously malnourished, socialism is based on preying upon the class envy of the most base citizens, combining this envy with an ignorance of the fact that central planning routinely delivers the opposite of its promises, or an arrogance which expects impossible outcomes to occur via magic, and therefore farmers with more cows than others created envy due to this inequality.

Instead of teaching the envious child that there is somebody out there with only one arm, and is therefore jealous of the child's two arms, so that they might realize that envy is not a justification for theft; or that private property rights and the inequality in terms of both remuneration, and of wealth and property accumulation, are the keys to leaving the most for everybody; or that the artificial depletion caused by the indulgence of their desire to steal harms the least-moneyed most of all, and that **the natural plenty caused by the absence of laws and bureaus which exist ostensibly to satiate their petty envy benefits those presently least-moneyed better than any other remedy ever has**; instead Mao and his cohorts confiscated from everyone in the name of redistribution, and so everybody got to be poor and hungry so that none of them would *have* anything of which anybody else could be jealous. (296)

Voluntary defections were common in the horrid reality of this promised "worker's paradise". In China, during the period 1975-1980, 460,000 Chinese escaped to Hong Kong. This figure accounted for nearly 10% of Hong Kong's 1980 population of 5.08 million people. Most of the defectors did so illegally. The escapees had to walk -sometimes for days- to the heavily guarded -by Chinese- special border zone, then choose between traversing shark infested waters for hours worth of swimming, or scaling the double walls of barbed wire on the 25 mile, hilly, land border. The final hurdles were the British and Gurkha mercenary soldiers on patrol in Hong Kong.

During 1979, three hundred and twenty bodies of fleeing Chinese were reportedly found in the ocean or on Hong Kong's beaches. When questioned by Fox Butterfield, their stated motivations for defection were: *escaping the hopeless poverty assigned to them by socialism*; lack of choice in jobs, housing, and schooling; all cited the immensely higher standard of living in the free-trade dominated city of Hong Kong. (297) By November 1980, Hong Kong had to shut their door much more tightly as they simply could not accommodate the massive inflow -as high as 500 per night- to their small territory. (298)

The aftermath of Mao's death, 1975-1980, left a power vacuum in the all-powerful central government of wokernism. Eyewitness Bill Gao relays that following the death of Mao, and the arrest of the Gang of Four, the reaction was jubilant but cautious due to the decades of false alarms, indicating calm and safety just prior to a new political campaign's commencement. Several of Bill's friends drank so heavily that they gave themselves brain hemorrhages; one laughed hysterically for weeks. Bill's wife's disbelief in the displacement of the radicals left her silent for one month. All of the Gao family heirlooms -letters, photos, yearbooks- were burned by the wokers, then called Red Guards. The family did manage to salvage and smuggle a handful of old photos, including one of Bill's father when Bill was a baby. (299)

Collective rights, over individual rights, means no human rights. Under Deng Xiaopeng, in approximately 1980, Henan province was said to have a "surplus" of pregnancies, exceeding their quota of 3,000 set by the central planners. An order was given to initiate a "clean out the stomachs" movement. All of the women were ordered to have abortions at once, without regard to their stage of pregnancy. At a minimum, one of the women in this province were nine months along. While many women fled in terror, to evade the Party officials' groping their village in search of pregnant women upon whom they might perform forced abortions, some children formed a group and went around warning any pregnant women to flee, so that they might have a headstart on the communist cadres who would inevitably come for them. "It was a shocking story, just like during our war against the Nationalists and the Japanese, only now the Communists were the enemy," remarked a reporter for the *People's Daily* (300)

Zheng Peide -who had previously served very hard prison time during the Cultural Revolution because one of her relatives had a romantic escapade with Mao's then-current squeeze, Jiang Qing, during the 1930s- hosted the most popular television show in China in 1981. TV was new for most Chinese, as sets were limited to

5 million in quantity until 1979. At that point, they began adding a few million sets per year. *Peide's show was popular because she taught English, which was key to a successful life after exiting China for good.* For the first time in three decades, Chinese were being exposed to the West through their televisions, and this underscored mightily the inferiority of the tight regulatory grip of central planning, and socialism, to the comparatively loosened grip of the capitalist and free market dominated West. (301) Punishment for a crime or action taken in which the convicted, it is acknowledged, had absolutely no involvement whatever, but rather was committed by a relative or ancestor, is akin to ancient Jim Crow law code in the United States, along with the present demand for so-called slave reparations in the United States.

The Press: Following the death of chairman Mao, and the rise to power of Deng Xiaopeng, the loosening of the grip of the communist central planners around the windpipe of the nation included not only an introduction of individual incentive for personal gain financially, but also extended to the press. The *People's Daily* began to attempt the establishment of an iota of credibility -a tall order based on their paltry prior performance, combined with three decades of the enslavement and impoverishment under the tyranny of the so-called dictatorship of the proletariat- by admitting the paper's complicity in the deaths of millions, along with the suffering of hundreds of millions more, which resulted from the socialist scheme known as the Great Leap Forward when, in 1958, the paper admitted that they spread what they could now describe as a "premature Communist wind" designed to advance *public acceptance of their servitude, masquerading as equality*. The paper also admitted their complicity in the horrors and oppressions of the Cultural Revolution of the 1960s by making a substantial amount of what they described as "false accusations" against good officials. (302)

In the 1970s, China arranged the press into four levels of availability to the masses and of accuracy; the more widely available the periodical, the less forthright it was.

Level 1: Being the most widely available, the *Reference News* was a four page paper which contained the **only** foreign news permissible for ingestion by the masses. The only people in China who were forbidden to consume it were foreigners, as they could readily dispel the inaccuracies contained therein. China did not pay Western, or Japanese, wire services for re-publishing their work, thereby violating international copyright laws. This paper's circulation of ten million in 1980 was roughly double that of the official Party paper, the *People's Daily*.

Level 2: More scarce than the aforementioned *Reference News* was a publication called *Reference Material*. Printed in two editions each day, the volumes providing a cumulative 150 pages between them. Party members and cadres could access them through their *danwei*, known alternatively as their official office, but could not personally subscribe.

Level 3: The next step up the chain of secrecy was the *Internal Reference* paper. Only those above the 12th step on the 24 tier communist ladder -it is fascinating that those claiming to deliver "equality" in fact deliver rigidly imposed, intricately designed, inequality of liberty, over and over again, isn't it?- could access this publication. The *Reference* contained government reports from the various sectors -agricultural, industrial, railways, crime, etc.

Level 4: The newspaper most strictly forbidden from consumption by the rank-and-file slaves -or citizens, if you prefer- of China was the *Cable News*. This paper was available to the Central Committee members, and those in charge of large military regions, only. This was akin to the information contained in the daily meeting that the president of the United States has with his top advisors. (303)

The grip of the Beast loosened a little more, as during the middle and late 1990s, China instituted even more de-regulation of commerce and of life than they had in the late 1970s -loosening the grip of the Beast upon this once proud nation's windpipe- and even in the remaining oppressive tyranny of the flexibility of private property rights, which were subject to unannounced confiscation at any time, this permission to have property rights and the opportunity for personal gain or loss -even though gains may be short lived prior to being taxed away, although gains could potentially extend for decades- the great mass of people experienced gains which by that epoch were extremely easily predictable. In what ought to rattle the cages of many present day Westerners with degrees in race studies, or diversity, occupying positions concocted for them by government either within its own bureaus, or in the very universities in which these people were awarded their certificate in the first place, regarding what happens when counterproductive bureaucracy is dismantled.

Readers should bear in mind that when such people appear in the media, these people have nothing but their own interests at heart when advocating the perpetuation of these same bureaucracies, and their tax and spend schemes, as the speaker would have to go out into the world and do something productive; a task for which that person is wholly unprepared and untrained. Murray Weidenbaum and Samuel Hughes observed that:

"Never before in recorded history have so many—literally hundreds of millions of people—risen from poverty so quickly. At the same time, however, *large numbers of uneducated, unskilled workers currently employed in the unproductive state sector face a threatening future in the form of large-scale unemployment.* Change is often painful, and the rapidity of change in mainland China has placed great strain on that country's social and cultural foundations." (304)

The people of China, as of this writing, are bristling for evasion of the grip of the Beast. *Each relaxation of controls by government has resulted in the alleviation of hunger and privation in China, as they have throughout the rest of the world and throughout the rest of human history*, yet the masses are still unable to be their own masters. Chaining the Beast remains elusive.

PART III

The Fallacy of the Lamp

"The successful pursuit of the unholy grail of economic equality would exchange the promised reduction or removal of differences in income and wealth for much greater actual inequality of power between rulers and subjects. This is an underlying contradiction in egalitarianism in open societies." Peter Bauer (1)

One of the incredibly successful prevailing popular fictions apropos of socialism, though insultingly false, is what can be described as the fallacy of the lamp. This moniker draws from fables which tell of a person rubbing a magic lamp and having their wishes granted. ***Many are suffering under the delusion*** that all of the power will be concentrated into the hands of the few by decree, and ***that all of this concentrated power will serve themselves, personally.*** Their own myopia masquerading as charitability. The United States is a nation which in 2020 had a population of 330 million people, and the world in that same year had an estimated population of approximately 7 billion. ***When hundreds of millions, or billions, of people each make their own individual, self-serving, wishes, they are bound to conflict with and to contradict each other ceaselessly.*** The farmers wish for sun and rain, while petty burglars wish for darkness and dry conditions in order to provide cover for their movements. In the end, the concentration of power into the hands of the few by decree, a necessity of wokernism, only grants the wishes of those holding power in the government. All others have no rights other than to obey the whims and dictates of the bureaucrats, their wish for socialism having been granted, and now results in eternal privation of future wish granting; a classic example of another old fable, involving "a pact with the devil".

As central planning takes a more prominent role in a country, the strings attached to the handouts inevitably infringe upon the human rights of the citizenry; the citizens become property of the government, which in practice of course makes them property of whatever small group happens to occupy seats in the government at the present moment. Promises of "free healthcare for all" inevitably lead to both rationing and slavery; since the planners never do a better job than those who function in a diverse assortment of much smaller groups, each planning for its own benefit, are able to do. The evidence dictates this conclusion, and no other. The prevalence of death panels, in which the rationing of the state-seized healthcare goes to the length of having meetings in which bureaucrats look over the patient folders of those who have been diagnosed as near terminal, and who are in need of life saving care, then decide which are going to be denied; irrespective of means to pay, or the willingness of a physician to accept said payment for the job.

The limitation on child births, including executions of infants -known as infanticide- and forced abortions, are well known under such conditions. People are still denied care in centrally planned healthcare schemes; this is not a problem that is solved by implementing monopolized medicine. Freedom of choice is certainly not present, in any aspect of healthcare, under such a scheme. One is always perpetually limited to the menu provided by the state, and on whatever terms are dictated by the state. One cannot simply work harder, or use their ingenuity to create something useful to people, so that the inventory of said products could raise money to buy what one wants. If it's not your money, it's not your choice. For more on this, see note (108)

An interesting example of a populist movement delivering negative outcomes to its followers took place during the 1970s in the USA. The populist trend known as "Women's Lib" drove down female wages in the immediate term. In a book first published in 1975, Bradley Schiller notes that the media campaign called "Women's Lib" increased female demand for jobs, in response to their being prompted to do so by a massive advertising campaign, simply for the sake of having a job and thus participating in the trend. With an abundance of supply, combined with their eagerness to be a part of the fad, coalescing to make for a buyer's market, in which a reduction of the dollar value of the wage rates necessary to satisfy the applicants was resultant. (2) The already eager sellers, when coupled with a glut in supply, drove down prices for those doing the buying; delivering a negative outcome to those who rubbed the lamp and wished for high paying jobs. Some will merely show an average wage for women, contrasted with an average wage for men, to conclude that gender discrimination, or that the phantom monster called "The Patriarchy", must be the reason for any differences. In fact, market forces are the most reasonable explanation for such inequalities.

LABOR MONOPOLIES, CASTES, WAGE CONTROLS
(See also: Part I, Government Makes
Monopoly in Jobs, page# 72)

The labor market is just another market, and when central planners get their hands on it, negative outcomes ensue for the very class of people that they claim to be assisting. *Attempts at micromanaging outcomes for others*, and particularly for large segments of people, *by egomaniacal individuals who are arrogant in their ignorance* of the mountains of evidence regarding the documented outcomes resulting from the inputs that they are threatening to install, yield nefarious outcomes. Number of jobs: reduced. Mobility between trades or industries: reduced. Ability to put one's self "on sale" in an attempt to win new customers -labeled as "employers" in the case of the labor market, but in its practical function, the terms employer and customer are interchangeable- the way that a dress merchant, restaurant, or any other variety of business or corporation opening in a new location might do: forbidden. We all know of the success of such tactics which are enjoyed by those with corporations, yet those affecting an interest in the upliftment of workers as a class, deny their flock access to this instrument of trade.

This known and proven tactic, discounting the price per sale in the hopes of increasing the volume of sales, which has delivered the breath of life and vitality into so many enterprises, while also delivering and perpetuating so many jobs, goods, and services, is removed from the arsenal of a person who simply has their "worker" card. The individual, presently a worker in the employ of another, is free to choose to go into business for themselves, to risk some or all of the fruits of their labor, in an attempt to increase overall productivity by having some mechanism to produce better than the person can in absence of said mechanism. Those who such people envy and want to steal from utilize price-cutting as a tactic for increasing profits, yet the envious forbid themselves and their members from taking the very steps which elevated the current "bosses" from their former status as "workers". This elevation occurs in a free economic setup, but *the chains of servitude and exclusion are all which are delivered by central planning*. The man who wishes to enter the job field is rendered, by minimum wage laws and by artificial restrictions on the creation of jobs, to a *maximum wage of zero*, as the number of positions are strictly forbidden from being expanded, and thus a man without employment who wishes to gain some at a price which is presently desirable to him, is permanently denied. All this in the name of strengthening the "worker" as a class!

As illustrated (in part I, Government Makes Monopoly in Business page# 66, Government Makes Monopoly in Jobs page# 72; part VI, Grip tightens, Masses Suffer Monopoly page# 350), *lasting monopolies*, whether among producers and sellers of goods, or whether among those employed by the prior faction, *exist only when government makes them so*; and this always done under the auspice of benefiting the class as a whole. The fastening of the shackles made of regulation and of the erosion of private property rights for others, delivers adverse consequences to the class upon which they have been fastened; while their removal delivers positive outcomes to the class formerly restrained.

In their writing published 1957, Peter T. Bauer and Basil S. Yamey observe:

"But *economic progress* cannot be accelerated simply simply by imposing restraints either on employers or employees to force them to specialise. Enforced specialisation may in fact be a serious obstacle to economic development. In parts of India a person's economic activities are often defined and limited by his membership in a particular caste. Even if the market or demand for his services may not be adequate to occupy his time fully, he never the less cannot take part in other activities because of restrictions of caste. Such restrictions conduce to a less efficient deployment of available labour resources; they also prevent the most economic use of capital accumulated by members of a particular caste. Again, the enforced division of work between the members of different trade unions or categories of labour, whether in the United Kingdom or in Southern Africa, increases occupational specialisation but *reduces productivity*." (3)

The imposition of so-called strong worker's rights, resulting in a lack of work, was also evident during the 18th century in England, when we saw migration of businesses -and even entire industries- from one area of the country to another, often motivated by a desire to be rid of "irritating restrictions imposed by the craft traditions of the older towns". These traditions are known alternatively as tax, regulation, and difficulty with obtaining liberty in regards to the labor he is purchasing. (4)

The necessity of teaching the fallacy of the lamp to the general public is evidenced by the undeniable populist trend, from the 19th century onwards, *clamoring for regulation and oversight as a means of warding off monopoly, when in reality such arrangements are the only ones under which monopoly exists or perpetuates*. During Medieval times, trade monopolies permeated the nations of Europe. Whether called *arte* in Italian, *zunft* in German, *metier* in French, *ministerium* in Latin, craft-gild in English, or a host of other names, they all performed their similar function: subjecting the masses to monopoly, and giving said monopoly legal protection, under the guise of protecting the masses from monopoly. Historian Henri Pirenne notes: "The pressing necessity to stand by one another, *so as to resist the competition of new-comers*, must have made itself felt from the very beginning of industrial life." (5)

Evidence is known of mayors of towns exercising control over which products may be sold, as well as over who may enter into various professions, beginning during the early 11th century. By the 12th century these horrors were well ingrained all over Europe. Pirenne: "They were thus essentially privileged bodies, as far removed as possible from industrial liberty. They were founded on exclusivism and protection. Their monopoly was known in England by the name of *gild*, in Germany by those of *Zunftzwang* or *Innung*." (6) Governments were eager to grant the evil-doers monopolies because prior to that, this element rained violence upon those who dared to offer consumers an alternative competitor, and to attempt to elevate the new hires above the very bottom of the career ladder, in absence of government doing the job on their behalf. (7) One of many *clear instances of the minority group in power trading the rights of one class of the population, to satiate a second faction of the citizenry*; which gives credence to the plan to eliminate institution of a ruling class, and to have all involved view themselves as private sector people permanently, while being public sector people sparingly if at all, discussed in part VII of this book.

Gild monopolies eventually ruined their own members, as the bill came due for the Faustian pact made in allegiance with the state. As each town -founded in the first place by the merchants (see part VI, social mobility page# 393), who themselves rose from the status of outcasts or of runaway serfs, and which provided a safe haven for peasants/serfs who sought escape from the feudalism of the manor so that they may pursue a better life- became more prosperous, it attracted those who sought to enact control through administrative techniques, and *that administrative bureaucracy* -populated and heavily influenced by *gild* members- gripped ever tighter as it *squoze the life out of their businesses and jobs*. These sources of goods were crippled by regulations and jealousy. A prevailing notion that no member should have a more profitable operation than another - "Income Equality" for their class; and *a state enabled and perpetuated price fixing monopoly in practice*- saw to it that harsh rebuke awaited any who were found to have deviated from centrally dictated policy regarding: hours of operation, prices and wages, that each operation be subject to frequent random and thorough inspections, the forbiddance of advertisement, and a strict cap upon the amount of both workers and industrial tools. Pirenne:

> "The counterpart of the privilege and monopoly enjoyed by the *gild* was **the destruction of all initiative**. No one was permitted to harm others by methods which enabled him to produce more quickly and more cheaply than they. Technical progress took on the appearance of disloyalty. The ideal was stable conditions in a stable industry." (8) "For almost all of them, the economic organisation meant the same kind of existence and the same moderate resources. It gave them a secure position and *prevented them from rising above it*. It may, in fact, be described as a "non-capitalistic" system." (9)

Outside the clutches of the administrative zeal which impacted the trade within the town, were the large operations which sold to the wholesalers engaged in trade abroad. Such outfits are analogous to "steel towns" of the late 19th and early 20th centuries in the USA, with cloth manufacture taking the place of steel. In the mid-14th century, at least 10% of the total population of Ghent was engaged in the production of cloth. In Ypres 1431, 51.6% of all engaged in trade were in the cloth business; 16% of workers at Frankfurt-on-the-Main. Layoffs accompanied slow periods. In such cities the administrators were international merchants of the *haute bourgeoisie*, who utilized the administration ruthlessly and harshly as the rough treatment fell down each rung of the bureaucratically erected classes: from the customer/foreign trader, to trade master, to journeyman and apprentices; gaining momentum as it descended the proverbial hill. (10) (11)

If such monopolistic arrangements are so beneficial, then why do people shun them? In the early 1950s, 35% of US jobs were controlled by union monopolists; by 2020, only 6% of US jobs existed under such conditions. (12) Stated alternatively: in the early 1950s a mere 65% of US jobs were open to all applicants legally eligible for employment in their area, in which a business owner was free to choose whose services they may or may not purchase; while in 2020 the number of jobs absent the barrier to entry imposed by union monopolists, who claim to exist to benefit workers as a class, had swelled to a comparatively robust 94%. When a mountebank attempts to swindle you with the pathetic ruse that "trade unions exist to benefit the worker", ask them "which worker?". As with all government imposed cartels, this monopoly exists only to benefit its members to the detriment and exclusion of **all others**. 100% of jobs ought to be free from such artificial walls, which arbitrarily bar citizens from entry. This does not prevent a group of people from voluntarily acting in concert with one another, in an attempt to bargain collectively. It merely removes the strong-arming of government from becoming involved. Such attempts at the monopolization of jobs and industries are routinely broken up by the beauty of free competition, as is illustrated in several places throughout this volume.

Another method of implementing a systematic barrier to entry into the workforce, or into certain industries, that happens to have been progressing in a negative direction, is called occupational licensing. During the 1950s, only 5% of workers were required by the state to show their papers if they wished to retain the employment that their customer -employer- was happy to extend in absence of government interference, while the proportion swelled to 18% by 2000, and then to 29% by 2020. Morris M. Kleiner, in his article published the year 2000, "Occupational Licensing" in the *Journal of Economic Perspectives*, found a wage premia as high as 30% in licensed vs unlicensed work. This means, of course, artificially higher costs for all consumers, in the name of their benefit. (13)

Africa mid-20th century: As noted elsewhere (page# 378) the only certain negative impact of European colonialism in Africa was the transportation and implantation of the political strategy which teaches one seeking power *to take the rights of the many in the name of liberating the few*, and so cultivating a willful concentration of power into the aspirant's own hands, on the part of the very people over whom this person seeks rulership. The Victim Politics Industry opened several branch offices throughout Africa, concurrent with the departure of the Europeans.

Tyranny and monopoly ensued. *The promises of a worker's paradise were promptly revealed to be empty.* A smattering of examples of obstruction to commerce follow.

Ghana 1959: unionists from multiple African nations convened at Accra to formulate the All-African Trade Union Federation. This was intended by Nkrumah to be an instrument for control of, and indoctrination of, the masses. Strikes were forbidden. (14)

Liberia 1966: A four year plan for development was forced to traverse strikes by those who were employed by Lamco iron ores, and by Firestone rubber company. Striking was declared illegal. Force was used to quell the disobedient workers, and their ringleader was jailed. (15)

Guinea 1950s: Sekon Toure had been in politics since the mid-1940s. In 1952 he became secretary general of the PDG, and by 1958 was prime minister of Guinea. *Toure used communism as a veneer to gain control and popular support, then pushed it aside when it was no longer politically advantageous.* Each town and village had strong, autocratic, governing bodies. Toure on individual liberty: "Liberty is only a tool, a tool for organising and orienting our activities to conform with the popular will." The prime minister also said:

> "We have used certain parts of the Marxist doctrine to organise rational foundations for African trade unionism. We have adopted from Marxism everything that is true for Africa...We formally reject the principle of class struggle...In fact the new African society cannot depend on European-inspired doctrines if it is to succeed. If we prove that without the class struggle a profound transformation of our country is possible, we will have made our contribution to political science...Communism is not the way for Africa. The class struggle here is impossible because there are no classes."

This statement was made while the speaker, himself, was of a separate class! A class which was strengthened in power under the guise of empowering the masses, as the scriptures of the Marxist religion yielded the only outcome that they ever have, or ever will. In Guinea, all deviation from the party doctrines were to meet stiff rebuke from those around the offenders, as was the wish of Toure, who *upon taking the helm abolished all obstacles in between party headquarters and the towns*. All those who worked for wages were lumped into a single, massive, labor union, in order to ensure ease in controlling not only their options for employment, but also of controlling their minds for use politically. (16)

Labor strike: An example of the entitlement culture, in which a would-be worker refuses to work a job, while simultaneously refusing to part with said job, and also forbidding any competitor within the labor pool a chance to work the very job which the striker refuses. Historically, such people have often resorted to physical violence and acts of terrorism. *The arrogance required to sincerely exude an entitlement to dictate policy regarding property owned by another, is gargantuan.* The selfish disregard, on the part of such a striker, for the well-being of other members of "the worker" class, is undeniable.

Some regard the legal interference with, and obstruction of, a property owner's replacement of employees who do not want the jobs offered, with employees who are clamoring for these very same jobs, as being of benefit to workers as a faction. In actuality, notes Lee Ohanian, "...A strike is a tax on investment. By idling a firm's capital stock, a strike, or even the threat of a strike, lowers the expected return to investment, which in turn lowers investment, innovation, and productivity growth." (17) This tax upon the property owners, *in fact represents a tax upon those who are refusing to work the jobs*, while also refusing to part with the jobs -which is what a labor strike consists of. There are fewer jobs to go around, as the return on investment is being artificially compacted via such legislation. In addition, there are fewer products, and those remaining products at higher prices, which of course negatively impacts all members of the labor pool, who after all are in fact among the potential consumer pool for all products.

Prussia was decimated by the terms of the Treaty of Tilsit. After they were reached in 1807, Prussia lost approximately 50% of its population and territory, the nation was broke, and occupied by France. From this trough, the hierarchy of Prussia *set about a course of de-regulation*. Guilds -unions- were targeted specifically. Legislation of November 2, 1810, did impose a new tax upon those partaking in trade and manufacture -this enacted as an attempt to pay the French as they extorted the Prussians- but also *revoked the ability of guilds to stand between the buyer -employer- and the seller -job applicant-*, as well as rendering impotent the previous ability of the labor monopolies to control production and prices for the populace at home and abroad. Payment of a nominal fee, along with an employer's consent to hire, were all that stood between a man and a job. *Workers were now free* to pursue work in any area of employment they desired; and to engage in multiple types at once, if desired -both of which were impossible beforehand.

September 7th, 1811, new legislation forbade the police from having any regulatory hand in commerce. Guilds became purely social clubs. Government included a clause giving it authority to order any guild to disband at once if they behaved contrary to the general welfare, as the organizations colluded with one another. Individuals were left much more free to pursue their objectives, change course more expediently if desired, to suffer failures in competition, and also to reap its rewards based on a good job done -as opposed to through government enabled extortion, known as union strikes.

During 1813, the previously demoralized nation ousted the French. Post victory, some municipalities within Germany briefly reinstated guild power, particularly in rural areas where industrialism was absent. Legislation reinstating freedom to choose returned as soon as May of 1819 in Nassau, 1825 in Bavaria and Wurttemberg, while being delayed until 1848 in Hanover. *The condition of the worker was one of steady employment and high wages*. Those still hanging on to their old craft, unresponsive to the market in many cases as they obdurately plodded on, were *out-earned by the factory worker at a rate of 5:1*. Some artisans may have continued living well, though unemployment among their class was high, and many were now low earners. About half of all shoemakers in Berlin earned enough to pay income tax on their trade, while only 32 of 1,100 shoemakers paid in Elberfeld-Barmen (1840s). Old tradesmen outnumbered industrial workers within a range of 2:1 and 3:2 in the cities, while the former dwarfed the latter in the countryside; the oversupply of those selling obsolete products and services further depressed their prices. By mid-century, there was great political unrest agitated largely by non-industrial citizens, the former monopolists turned paupers, whose sect committed many acts of terrorism through violence. (18) Read on to learn more about this episode.

19th Century Germany

During the middle of the 19th century, Germany experienced an episode of drastic internal strife, which evoked, on a reduced scale, memories of the tyranny and adolescent misadventures with adult implements, of the French experience during the final decade of the 18th century (see part II, page# 93). A featured theme of this period in German history is the so-called liberation of the worker, *which in fact involved little more than the centralization of authority, the implementation of monopolies, and violent rioting.*

During the first half of the nineteenth century, Germans saw several regimes commence and dissolve. The Germanic Holy Roman Empire dissolved in 1806. In 1815 the Congress of Vienna yielded the German Confederation, consisting of 38 distinct states and city-states, headed by both Austria and Prussia. In 1848 the Greater German Reich set out to overthrow the German Confederation, in an attempt at greater centralized control of the more or less independent entities. (19) In 1849 Prussia formed the new German Confederation, consisting initially of 28 German states. (20) We will examine more closely the details of the mid-century activity in Germany.

During the first half of the 19th century, we find another example of private infrastructure; once again affirming that in cases of free trade, oftentimes "greed is good", as *the desire for personal gain builds infrastructure through private investment*. From a starting place of a mere 5 joint-stock companies in 1800, the Germans embraced industry, and with tremendous exhilaration. The industries felt that railway transportation would improve their operations, and so between the years 1834-1848, Prussians invested nearly 60 million marks in shares of stock in heavy industry. During the first half of the 19th century, private investment in rails topped a cumulative 450 million marks. (21)

In 1835, the first German rail completed ran 7 kilometers. By 1850, Germany's railroads -the most vast network in Europe- brought goods to people in areas with regularity, who had only been afforded scarce opportunity to encounter the products prior. The rail was also a less costly mode than horseback over the distance transported. This system of goods not only afforded greater opportunity to consumers, but *enabled many of the same to become producers as well*. New firms were established due to the increase in the availability of goods, as well as the ability to ship their own goods produced, and these firms employed many. The cost of shipping coal was reduced from 40 to 13 pfennigs, or by 67.5%. (22)

The 1835-1850 period saw the German rail system progress from its germination, to the largest in Europe. This period began with private investment building the rails, and then government slowly slithered its tentacles around the lines, as their success and popularity became undeniable. Some German nations were better than others in this aspect. Wurttemburg and Oldenburg were among the worst offenders, as they intruded upon the railroad industry most egregiously; Saxony and Bavaria played it halfway; while private ownership prevailed until 1848 in places such as Prussia and Mecklenburg-Schwerin. An attempt at monopolizing the German rails and imposing uniform rates -or regulation known in today's terms as nationalizing- was proposed in 1847, but was thwarted by the legislative body known as the Diet of the Confederation. (23)

Concurrent with the German rail expansion and increase of its transport of goods and passengers, the Rhine saw a doubling of the amount of goods shipped through its waters between 1836-46. (24) Commerce and transportation were booming in Germany during this period.

Some more information may be useful to the reader, introducing them briefly with the financial state of affairs for the Germans. 1825-1850 pig iron output increased five fold, while coal production tripled. 1840-1850 the amount of horsepower that industry found at its disposal grew nearly 500%. (25) 1846-50: pay for miners increased 4%, printers 9%, construction laborers 10%. A mill hand in an Augsburg textile factory was paid 278 marks in 1845, but 372 in 1850. In 1850, as measured by inflation adjusted dollars, industrial, agricultural, and transportation, workers were receiving their highest income in two decades. (26) Nonetheless, riots broke out just prior to mid-century.

Trade unions are for the enrichment of their members, to the detriment of all others, including the "worker" as a group. While a new government was being established, a Constitution was being drafted granting citizens new found freedom from the controlling regulation of arrogant and selfish central planners, a committee prepared a document which acted as a list of demands for the Frankfurt Parliament. Enumerated #1: "We declare ourselves most *firmly opposed to industrial freedom*, and we *demand that it be abolished* insofar as it exists in Germany by a special paragraph of the fundamental law of the nation." (27)

The benefits of industrialism to the lowest members of society were manifested in jobs, wages, goods, and improved convenience. By the mid-1840s, the skilled weaver of linen in Westphalia commanded one mark per week, while the unskilled help in the mill producing textiles commanded double that, or better. (28) Theodore S. Hamerow concludes that during the tumult of 1848-49: "The truth was that the industrial worker refused to play the role of downtrodden plebeian which socialist theory had chosen for him." "...he resented the insistence of the left that he was a proletarian." (29) *The envious and obsolete crafters aimed to destroy the precious instruments which uplift the masses*, known as industrial factories. Terrorism and violence were among their preferred methods.

In March of 1848, a Schmalkalden nail factory was decimated by forces of Thuringian handicrafters. The vandals sought to cease the progress brought on by mechanization -mechanization which would provide greater amounts of goods at lower prices for all people of the earth; including themselves. The jobs provided by the nail factory were also threatened by the attacks. Similar terrorism and destruction were delivered to mills in Mittweida and Elterlein. In Berlin the police stood guard of the job providing, and goods creating, factories, to save them from the ungrateful union monopolists (30); *seeking to destroy jobs* under the guise of "helping the worker" as a class. That this is routinely present in so-called union behavior gives a clear indication that *the motivation of these monopolists was to protect their own monopoly*; that is, to protect the members of their select few at the expense of *all* others, including all of the others in the classification of workers. These behaviors are precisely the same as we observe in government enabled and perpetuated monopolies consisting of business owners. *Monopolies only exist when government codifies them into law*, and when they are in existence they serve their own members alone, to the direct detriment and expense of all others. This also makes such a person perpetually at the mercy of bureaucrats and politicians, who at any time can revoke entirely their membership in the club, and cast them down into the pit with the rest; wholly incapable of climbing any way other than by begging to curry favor with a person who often hasn't any competence or aptitude for the job at hand -farming, mining ore, making garments, etc.

An episode involving riotous behavior when monopoly "rights" are revoked occurred 15 years prior in Germany. January of 1832, in Hanau, rioters were upset about others having the opportunity to compete freely with them, requiring the use of military force to quash their efforts. (31) 1832-33 rioters in Bavaria terrorized the populace for nearly one full year in protest of the freedom afforded their competitors and the increased selection for consumers. (32) And returning to our present episode, during March, 1848, the animals -still upset that their government enforced monopoly, once the government's mandate had been removed, crumbled because customers chose others over them, and former members of the group chose to pursue other ventures instead of sticking to the old shops- simply burnt, looted, and vandalized the area. Westphalia, along with the Rhineland, saw *self-absorbed citizens set fire to the productive mills that provided jobs and goods to the people,* in addition to witnessing this egomaniacal bunch throwing debris such as rocks at the private residences of those whom they envied. Dusseldorf, Krefeld, Bonn, Cologne, the highland of Berg, and Coblenz, were all scenes of reported malfeasance. (33)

Historians R.R. Palmer and Joel Colton opine that the hatred of and attacks upon the merchants as a class, by the wage-earning class, pre-dating 1848, created and perpetuated a schism between the two groups which would render any mass insurrection impotent: "...social revolutionaries had already declared war on the bourgeoisie, and the bourgeoisie was already afraid of the common man. It is the common man, not the professor or respectable merchant, who in unsettled times actually seizes firearms and rushes to shout revolutionary utterances in the streets." (34)

The violent gang activities in the Germanic lands continued. In April 1848, after the animals had rioted in the streets for weeks undeterred by the state, and *private property rights had been disregarded via the refusal to prosecute those guilty of destroying property* during their rioting, this unruly behavior was rewarded through the granting of monopoly "rights" to the rioters. Order was then restored through the use of the armed forces of the state. Moreover, the *private charity* of German citizens -themselves having just been thoroughly violated- nevertheless founded employment bureaus and charitable fund centers to disburse cash to the destitute.

A newly minted ministry of commerce, industry, and public works -independently operating within the German government- made loans to the banks, mill-owners, and other citizens who owned businesses. Economic recovery was swift, as the job creating class of the citizenry returned to industriousness now that private property rights were once again held in some esteem by the government. Within weeks, bonds rallied from a price of 61 marks to 80, a 30% gain. (35) Now that they could expect personal gain from investment and exertion, the entrepreneurial element once again saw reason to risk capital and exert effort so that the workers might be afforded the opportunity to advance themselves, *on the backs of the businessmen*.

During the July-August period of 1848, a group of artisans seeking to obtain monopoly (unions) for themselves, codified into law by the new Confederation's

Constitution, prefaced their proposal thusly: "Can anyone blame...the German hand-craftsman...if he fathers his last reserves of strength and pronounces before Germany and before his representatives in the German parliament *a solemn protest against economic freedom*." The so-called Artisan Congress went on to put forth the well established falsehood that absent strong dictatorial oversight by central planners, power would be concentrated into the hands of the few, while in the same document demanding: codified restriction to entry into the business -regulated by the businessmen (workers) themselves; high taxes for their domestic competitors (factories); a codified limit to factory production; and that the petitioners were to advise the Parliament of any changes in policy. (36)

This group also, laughably, referred to the 18th century French Revolution as an example of *insufficient centralized authority,* which then permitted the unrestrained merchants and manufacturers to oppress the proletariat through the former's resultant unfair accumulation of wealth and property; and that this was what kept the unwashed perpetually agitated and rioting, which would be the fate of Germany at this epoch without the granting of legalized cartels for these petitioners! The tyranny and terrorism perpetrated by the paranoid and criminal usurpation of power by the Jacobins -comprised of merchants, in concert with the unwashed masses- the theft of property from those in the Church, the squandering of this ill-gotten booty through the issuance of bad currency, and the perpetual terrorism and oppression generated from within those occupying the government, are the story of the French Revolution of the 18th century. (see part II, page# 93 for more)

Among the outcomes of the summer 1848 constitutional convention, were that the newly minted federal government was authorized to:

Supervise all venues of trade, industry, and transportation

To have judicial power over roads, rivers, rails, and telegraphs

To establish uniformity for the nation in respect to weights and

measures, along with currency, and tariffs; though those adjacent to the

Hanseatic sea were given liberty to go their own way on this matter; these lands having a predilection for free trade.

Also removed the state taxes upon domestic freight within the borders of the German confederacy. (37)

An absence of uniformity of outcome desired, on the part of those within the realm that was attempting to be unified by the German National Assembly, has been deemed by authors R.R. Palmer and Joel Colton to be vital to its failure to achieve this unity. (38) This may be a fortunate outcome for everyone involved, as the trading of one class's rights for the supposed benefit of another, and the doling out of monopolies, were consistently present in the proposals of various groups. In January of 1849, the parliamentary constitution, having been overturned, was now *replaced with legislation severely restricting, if not entirely eradicating, the freedom of the workers* who were not self employed. In no fewer than 70 crafts, employment was contingent upon approval from monopolists -*gild*/union- who did not own the enterprise doing the hiring, and who had made no investment of stake in the company whatever. For a worker to engage himself in multiple lines of work -broadening their skills, increasing their earning power going forward, enabling themselves to have legitimate options while negotiating with customers (employers)- was forbidden. (39) March 28, 1849, the Frankfurt Parliament officially recognizes Frederick William IV as king, including recognition of his authority as such. (40) August 23, 1851, the revived German Confederation, having displaced the ousted Frankfurt Parliament, passed a resolution which nullified the Fundamental Rights of the German People document. (41)

In the 1850s, post defeat of the insurrectionary Frankfurt Parliament, life went on. Despite welfare legislation enacted by the state as a measure to quell the riotous under-class -including job holder's monopolies (*gilds*)- private investment and entrepreneurialism were ample, and explosive economic growth resulted. As measured in German marks, pig iron output, by 1857 was 2.5 times as great as that of 1848. More than three times as much coal was sold, while coal mines tripled in estimated value. Overall capital and commercial production doubled. Foreign trade was up 150%. An important factor, the discovery of gold in California brought many speculators, and those with new found capital served to artificially inflate German conditions somewhat. (42)

During the 1850s, we see an example of the common lesson taught to children and adolescents, filled with complaints of a lack of autonomy, yet too immature to handle the tasks which are best left to competent adults: "It's easy to complain about the boss, or to demand the "right" to steal his property; it's not so easy to *be* the boss". As droves of former serfs, tilling soil under feudal manorial taxes, were liberated and afforded the opportunity to purchase the land from their former master, they found that *being a successful businessman was not as easy as simply having access to capital* -contrary to the sermons of Karl Marx. Extended mortgage loans by creditors, the overwhelming majority of this class failed as entrepreneurs, and either sold or abandoned their land in search of the safety of the womb employed as dependent wage slaves, known alternatively as being of the proletariat. Contrary to the fabrication asserting oppression of the worker by industrialization, brutally squashing this class beneath their evil overlord employers, *these people flocked to factories, eager for entry level employment*. Factory cities swelled in population by two, three, and even four times in some cases. (43) (see also: page# 408)

This pattern of flocking to the cities and factories is far from unique to Germany, or to this particular regime. The time of Bismarckian oversight, culminating 1895, saw more of the same. "Bismarck's era was still a time of westward migration, of a steady flow from the Prussian agrarian areas to the western industrial regions." (44) We also saw this pattern of migration into the towns, with a desire to work in the shops, in Medieval Europe. (109) If things were so bad for the workers in the cities, then why did they remain there? Do you suppose that it had anything to do with the significantly higher incomes, and the ease of accessibility to goods, to be had in the city?

During the decade of the 1860s, thirty German nations removed restrictions on trade, production, and investment; while the *gilds* were kicking and screaming against it. (45) On July 8, 1868, a decree permitted the freedom to choose for consumers of any legal goods, from any market, and from any seller they wished. Also removed hiring restrictions from employers, which had left able and willing workers jobless. All this was done in defiance of union/guild demands. In 1870, joint-stock companies were liberated from their prior restrictions concerning their formation. (46)

WAGE CONTROLS

The dictation of prices from on high results in shortages, in absence of disregard for such edicts. When minimum prices for hourly labor are dictated by members of government, in the name of enriching "the worker" as a class: a diminution in the rate of the growth of jobs at which one may work is triggered, as $1,000 to spend on payroll must necessarily be split up amongst fewer payees when prices are artificially increased, reducing the overall volume of workers employed; *an exclusion altogether of the workers* attempting to enter the workforce, or who had been members of the workforce, but who are *not presently worth the price mandated by their supposed benefactors*, occurs with the imposition of prices above their present value. If the minimum wage was set to $500 per hour, then hardly anybody would work; unless the edict was disregarded en masse, or unless the value of dollars were watered-down to the degree that all prices would rise in concert, so that, in terms of spending power, $500 would be equivalent to the present minimum wage; making the recipient no better off.

"The minimum wage relative to average worker productivity gauges how many workers may be negatively affected by the minimum wage because their employment cost exceeds the value of their production. Specifically, if the minimum wage is higher than a worker's productivity, then the worker will not be hired because the hiring organization will take a loss on that worker. Instead, it will focus hiring efforts on workers whose productivity exceeds the minimum wage." -Lee Ohanian, of the Hoover Institute (47)

"The preponderance of evidence indicates that minimum wages reduce employment of the least-skilled workers….More definitively, though, it is indisputable that there is a body of evidence pointing to job losses from higher minimum wages. Characterizations of the literature as providing no evidence of jobs loss are simply inaccurate." -Researcher David Neumark in 2019 (48)

A 2015 study conducted by Isaac Sorkin, "Are There Long-run Effects of the Minimum Wage?", found that a 10% increase in the minimum wage yields an *immediate* 0.02% reduction of employment in such jobs, while yielding a 2.5% reduction in the existence of such jobs *in 6 years*. This inequality of outcomes, based upon the length of time after the implementation of the market interference by central planners that the damage is measured, in this case being multiplied 100 times, seems evidentiary of the delay in industry's ability to mechanize and streamline their operations, thereby reducing their employment cost and substituting equipment instead. (49) *Notice that this delayed effect occurs long enough afterwards* so that it does not impinge upon any positive press coverage the central planners may have received when the harmful measure was passed, while also offering an opportunity to blame some other scapegoat for the outcomes yielded by the measures of the politician or bureaucrat, and so affording the ne'er-do-wells to offer a socialist "solution" to the *problem created by* the prior socialist "solution". The larger check in the mail received by the wage earner today trumps the unemployment to come in a few years, while those unemployed today due to such measures being implemented in the past, have no idea that politicians caused their joblessness several election cycles ago.

All throughout history, an attempt to rig a market in a way which provides an enduring benefit to all, through the tight regulation and micromanagement of prices and procedures by those who are outside of the two parties directly involved in given transactions, always misfires and usually harms the very people who are supposed to be aided by such behavior. *The fallacy of the lamp is evident in all cases*. Minimum price laws are no exception to this universal truth. Yet, in 1994, two men -one of whom would go on to be an Obama era economic official- claimed to have found the elusive proof showing that simply mandating higher prices could bring prosperity. It was later revealed that they "cheated on their homework', as it were, yet the positive headlines enabled many office seeking politicians to profit off of their deprivation of the masses. The 1994, USA, study "Minimum Wages and Employment: A Case Study of the Fast-food Industry in New Jersey and Pennsylvania" by David Card and Alan Krueger, published in *American Economic Review*, stated that in 1992 New Jersey increased their mandated minimum wage from the former price of $4.25/hr to the new price of $5.05/hr, this while neighboring Pennsylvania remained steady at $4.25/hr. The study *shocked the world* as it reported that NJ restaurants added 3 full time equivalent workers, while PA showed no change. Card and Krueger obtained their "results" by calling the businesses in the area via telephone, and asking for their results; simply taking their word for it *without an iota of substantiation*. If the results reported were in line with the entirety of the existing body of evidence on the subject, perhaps their laxness or laziness might be excused by some, but since the reported results were precisely *contrary* to the entirety of the body of evidence in existence, these results should have set off alarm bells for an honest person and induced said person to seek legitimate substantiation of the results. Card and Krueger did nothing of the kind.

David Neumark and William L. Washer, 2000, "Minimum Wages and Employment: A Case Study of the Fast-food Industry in New Jersey and Pennsylvania: Comment", also appeared in *American Economic Review*. Neumark and Wascher used *actual payroll data* from the restaurants, and found that the NJ restaurants in fact showed a 4% *reduction* in employment as compared to those in PA. (50) These results, of course, are par for the course and surprising to absolutely nobody other than those possessing a tremendous wealth of ignorance on the subject. Attempts at the micromanagement of outcomes by central planners yielding precisely inverse results to those claimed at the outset, and harming the very group or individuals that the planners claim to be helping, is the norm.

Another example of price fixing occurred in 18th century England, as officials set out to uplift the masses through the imposition of maximum prices, and of outputs, on the part of food suppliers, yielding an outcome which did nothing but harm the masses. Prior to 1710, the price of bread -per loaf- was set according to the price of wheat. Beginning 1710, magistrates dictated that bread prices be based upon the price of flour, as well as the price of wheat. In 1758, central planners dictated the number of loaves to be produced per sack of flour. Beginning 1797 bakers were prescribed a set price received per sack of flour, designated as being used to produce bread, irrespective of each baker's other costs. (51) The fixed prices tempted -if not outright forced- bakers to reduce quality by mixing in filler, consisting of less than desirable ingredients, in order to get ahead. After all, if it's illegal to earn more money by doing a better job -selling a better product- then the laws of central planners dictate that the only way to earn more money under a system of fixed prices is to do a worse job -selling an inferior product. Lower quality food was the only result that one could reasonably expect -in lieu of perpetual scarcity- under a fixed price scheme; said scheme in place ostensibly to "empower the masses" with "consumer protection".

All of this despite the study of the prices of wheat, flour, and bread, during the period indicating that there was, as T.S. Ashton tells us "no ground for believing that there was widespread exploitation of the public." (52) That is, the central planners went about *solving a problem that did not in fact exist*, but created a problem as a result of their interference; harming the very people that the power mad zealots affected to be aiding.

Price controls pertaining to the rate of interest charged by lenders, particularly edicts requiring lending at rates which are deemed to likely be unprofitable, and therefore unsustainable in the long run, harm the least-moneyed most of all; as they are the ones who are dependent upon the ability to rent the money of others. Due to their presently penurious position, they are of course unable to utilize their own funds for use in their proposed ventures. Moreover, those who are without funds at that juncture are dependent upon those with money to find profitable uses for it, so that jobs may be created and sustained which can supply the destitute with an opportunity to earn funds. In England, *during the early 17th century, the prohibition of the lending of money at interest was lifted*. From this nexus, legislators would still centrally plan rates of interest -or at least the boundaries within which rates were permitted to range- but would not outlaw the practice entirely. ***The stimulating impact was felt and displayed by industry immediately***. Overseas exploration and trade were among the varieties of industry demonstrating beneficial impact, due to the lending of money at interest. In 1613 £400,000 -$8,000,000 1908 value; $274,000,000 2024 value- was raised in two weeks to finance a journey seeking profit in the Far East, while a mere £30,000 had been mustered in 1599 to finance such a venture. (53)

Centrally planned interest rates are noted again in England during the 18th century. Interest charged for lent capital was fixed by government at a maximum of 6%, prior to 1714, and at 5% thereafter. Government itself was able to offer any price it wished for capital, leaving the private businessmen -their superiors- to cope with a scarcity of obtainable funds as national market conditions drove rates to, or near, the legal limit prescribed by government. War and peace were powerful forces, including speculation thereupon, governing business decisions. (54) This undoubtedly stifled commerce, suppressed the amount of jobs and goods in existence, stifled the supply of food, and resulted in an overall reduction in the quality of life, all to some degree greater than zero, as is evidenced throughout this text.

Mortgages were not issued with a defined length or interest rate. Either party might, at any time during the life of the loan, insist on a change in interest as a condition of continuance of the loan. Rates throughout England were impacted by the government's offered yields for the funds it borrowed to finance its wars. This would most immediately impact London, and permeate entirely to the outskirts of the nation within approximately six months. (55) Interest rates, fixed at a maximum by government, did very obvious harm. "The violence of the fluctuations by which the century was marked is to be attributed less to the speculative tendencies of producers and traders than to the operation of the laws against usury." (56)

In addition to food and nutrition, housing is another area often intruded upon by government, placing its members in between the parties pertinent to the transactions, ***and doing more harm than if they had abstained entirely from involvement***. So-called ***"tenants' rights"***, which trample upon the property rights of the minority group called landlords -in the modern use of the word; *rentiers* during the feudal period- who actually own the dwellings, **lead to the "right" to lower quality housing, in lesser supply, and at higher prices.** Eviction difficulty, including so-called squatter's rights: in which a person can simply enter a presently unoccupied dwelling without the consent of the dwelling's owner; in-so-doing preventing a person from entering who has the benediction of, and who will pay, the landlord; in addition to keeping the actual property owner from utilizing his own property; and also imposing legal fees unto the landlord in order to lawfully remove the thief.

Imagine that your automobile was without any person inside of it, and a person simply entered it without your consent, whereupon you were **legally forbidden** from utilizing the vehicle for your own purposes, and had to seek the permission of the court in order to remove the thief from your stolen automobile! Other common actions taken for the ostensible benefit to renters as a class are to impose lengthy delays between the filing of papers by the property owner and the actual eviction date, a lack of accountability in practice on the part of the court when it comes to property damages caused by renters, and so forth, of course have a detrimental impact upon the rental housing market.

Such laws and practices, which may provide the renter with a feeling of possessing a license to steal, or cause them to feel as though the renters as a class are "getting one over" on the landlord class -and thus benefiting politicians- *in fact diminish the return on invested dollars for the property owner.* This can cause the property owner to make up for it in other ways, *such as reduction in the quality of the housing* in terms of updates and repairs, *such as an increase in the monthly price tags of the apartments* across town -making up for the loss of money imposed by the courts when booting out those who are stealing housing- and eventually in *an increase of abandoned buildings* that nobody wants to invest in because the "tenants' rights" laws cause the investment to be unappealing. Additional harm is done to the tenants as a class, in the name of their empowerment, when it is declared illegal for the property owners to ask certain questions of applicants; questions which will enable the owner to steer clear of those unlikely to be good customers, such as their method of payment, whether or not they have animals, these in addition to being forbidden by law to run a credit check which will enable the owner *to prevent known thieves from forcing losses which must be passed along to the good customers.*

During 1960, Egypt implemented rent controls. Investment was curtailed, leading to a decline in the supply of housing. Some renters who otherwise would have paid for their own, individual, housing, were forced by this law to bunk up with other parties because the supply of housing was artificially suppressed -under the guise of helping the renters as a class! Half of a century later, the impact remained evident. (57)

Milton Friedman points out to us, in his fine book *Free to Choose,* the negative impact which government involvement had in the USA during the 50 year period from the 1930s to the early 1980s. Citing the initial government housing programs during the horrid and tyrannical New Deal period, the addition in 1965 of the Cabinet department HUD, which by 1980 employed 20,000 people so that they could be certain not to devote their energies towards anything productive, who were supplemented in their endeavor by some city and state interference as well. The politicians were first using Treasury funds as payola to buy the votes of low-income people, then moving on to bribing middle-income families. "In terms of the initial objective, these programs have been a conspicuous failure. More dwelling units were destroyed than were built." The Pruitt-Igoe public housing project, covering 53 acres in St. Louis, began with a nice ribbon-cutting ceremony and an award for architectural design. After a few decades, 1,400 of the 2,000 housing units were vacant, violent crime was rampant, and a portion of the project was detonated. (58)

During October of 1883, a thin pamphlet was produced in an effort to further the cause of socialism, which just so happened to detail the failures of central planning. The writing was called *The Bitter Cry of Outcast London: An Inquiry Into the Condition of the Abject Poor.* The findings were summarized by its authors thusly: "The effect of municipal housing and sanitary regulation appeared to have been only to raise rents." There was the curious reporting of a single street on which 32 of 35 domiciles were cathouses, along with the expected reports of unsanitary conditions and of neglect. (59)

PAID TO FAIL SOCIALISM:
THERE'S NO SUCH THING AS A FREE LUNCH

(see also: part VI, Paid to Fail, page# 402)

"The dangerous spirit of the lower classes is nourished by an application of philanthropy to statecraft which does honor to humanity, but which in its consequences is most pernicious. We insist that no one suffer distress, and so one institution after another is founded to feed and clothe the poor, to educate their children, to care for the old, to help poor mothers, etc. And almost all the poor to whom aid has been given in this fashion achieve for a shorter or longer period of time or even for their lifetime a much better position than those needy persons who struggle against unfortunate living conditions with their own earnings or those of their families. Here lies the most direct, the most open invitation to wastefulness and laziness, the two vices which will most effectively nourish among the lower classes good-for-nothings dangerous to the public safety. And that nothing may be lacking to arouse in these classes the belief that as a matter of duty they must be taken care of very nicely as soon as they find themselves in some measure destitute, the alms of Christian charity are in many places transformed into annually increasing poor rates." -David Hansemann, 1830 Germany (60)

Duplicitous preachers of political sermons often convey the message that, through their facilitation only, their flock of sheep can wholly evade the opportunity to engage in productive behavior as they pursue their own survival, by reaching their hands into the pockets of those whom they envy; and that through this magical arrangement, civilization may survive, while the cache of supplies remains ample. As the old saying goes "there's no such thing as a free lunch", and such handouts for the healthy always carry a price far greater than the nominal value of the loot obtained via this pilfering. Only the most sadistic and cruel people on earth could fail to be made unhappy by **the plain fact that health and prosperity cannot be decreed by simply writing upon a piece of legislative paper** that it must be so. The fact that we do not like this reality does not make it any less factual. A responsible and caring person, sincerely prioritizing the well-being of not only themselves, but also of all the others in the world, *must obey the evidence and follow its lead* when it contradicts their favorite incantations and tee-shirt slogans. During the 21st century, in what has been dubbed the "information age" since the explosion of the popularity of the internet occurred around the turn of the century, *scientific explanations must prevail over superstitious conclusions*.

The entirety of this book (see France page# 93, China page# 152, American Indians self-destruct page# 337) confirms the lesson that paid to fail socialism brings scarcity rather than plenty, while failing to deliver conditions which yield the greatest bounty or the greatest uplifting of those who begin without much treasure, and here follow a handful of explicit examples, which have been isolated for the reader.

The fallacy of the lamp is evidenced by the juxtaposition of the Americans, and of the French, beginning with the late 18th century and following each for 100 years. France attempted to solve the tyranny of the state -in the hands of a monarch, and a small cadre of his chosen stooges- by ousting the monarch from its all-powerful position, and replacing it with an assembly; an assembly who had all of the power. The French falsely supposed that concentrating power or authority into the hands of the few by decree, would result in "angels" using this power to grant all of the wishes of the masses. Precisely the opposite occurred. (for more see part II, page# 93) Conversely, the United States of America at this epoch placed little power into the hands of the federal government, ensuring greater liberty for citizens by leaving the power in their own hands; independent of the mechanism of the state.

In ancient Athens, Demosthenes in *On Organization* "...while the sum of money that we are talking about may be slight, *the habit of mind which it creates is a serious matter*. Now if you lay it down that the right to receive distributions should be related to the performance of duty, not only will you not harm, but you will even do a great deal of good to the city and to yourselves. But if every festival and every pretext becomes an opportunity for getting a distribution, *while you refuse to hear a word about what ought to follow after*, then beware lest what seems to you right now will appear to you later to have been a serious mistake." (61) An accurate prophecy which did not carry the day, unfortunately. It is worth noting that festivals were put on by the municipality, and attendance was considered a reward or privilege.

This paid to fail counterproductivity is evidenced by recent data pertaining to European unemployment. Ljungqvist and Sargent (1998) find that unemployment checks with high values, combined with a lengthy period of availability, coalesce to yield a higher rate of the instances of long term unemployment in Europe. A long duration on the dole *led to a deterioration of training and ability for the individual*, which consequently led to a diminution of the individual's value, to the level of, and eventually beneath, the monetary value of the handouts received from the paid to fail, socialist unemployment bureau. That is, *the person becomes unable to earn more than welfare pays because the welfare program paid them to become that way*, in this case it is the unemployment welfare bureau that is the culprit. Your author will interject that it is worth noting that *the individual was not this way before the welfare bureau got their hands on the citizen*. The findings of Ljunqvist and Sargent were confirmed by Bernal-Verdugo, Furceri, and Guillaume (2012) who studied 85 countries; also confirmed with similar results by Botero, et al. (2004). (62)

European unemployment during the years spanning 1985-2020, in France was 9% per year on average, while in Germany this figure averaged 8% per year. (63) Blanchard and Wolfers (2000) found European unemployment to be artificially increased by 1.3% because the average unemployment check was such a high percentage of the average wage check; long duration of access to these checks increased unemployment another 0.75%; so-called worker protection laws, laws making the dismissal of redundant or inadequate workers more cumbersome and expensive increased instances of joblessness by 1%; unionization worsened the problem by another 0.6%. This cumulative 4.6% per year is "The difference between a very healthy labor market and one that is perpetually in a severe recession." (64) While affecting to benefit those who are being paid to fail to engage in productive activity, they are instead paying such people to abstain from productivity, and so *the process in fact retards and even regresses the individual's value as a worker*.

"Why a man who first neglects his duty as a father and then defrauds the State should retain his full political rights is a question easier to ask than to answer." -A.V. Dicey, in reference to parents of children, who said parents have failed to provide adequate nourishment, who were made able -by a Bill made Law in December 1906 by the British government- to reach into the pockets of their neighbors without their neighbors' consent -even despite their protestations- to pay for their child's needs. (65)

The fallacy of the lamp is again evident in governmental actions which purport to take from one party who has, and deliver this booty to those who have not, in the name of benefiting the poor as a class. In England during the 17th century, a redistributive action required the more wealthy residents to incur the welfare costs of the poor, if any, within their own parish of residence. ***Ostensibly***, such an edict was to force the wealthy and productive people house, feed, employ, and clothe, the poor and unproductive people. ***In reality***, the edicts yielded the pulling down of cottages in which the economic underclass might live, or live in the future; and the exporting of the children of the poor, sent off to apprentice in other parishes so that they would be removed from the bill due to be paid by the first parish. Another outcome was the hiring of workers from outside of their parish so that, if work became scarce, the worker would not become eligible for welfare in the employer's zone of burden. 11.5 month contracts became standard, as 12 months were required to establish residence -and welfare eligibility- in the parish. The Act of Settlement of 1662 was designed specifically to keep paupers away from the productive people and in the areas in which there were, among other things, "the most woods for them to burn and destroy." Local authorities could remove from the parish any newcomer who seemed likely to become eligible for welfare, within 40 days of their arrival. This practice served as a deterrent for the economic underclass to seek handouts through parasitic migration. (66)

Prior to this epoch, unemployed persons in England, without skills deemed acceptable to the government, were sentenced to one year husbandry after which time they must obtain a certificate to leave their parish -which was, in practice, also acting as a modern-day municipality or township. After years of these statutes, the rulers increased the disincentives of the unproductive by whipping them and burning their ear with a one-inch-wide hot iron. An idler found with such an ear burn was executed. This occurred 1572-1598. Thereafter, vagabonds found outside of their last town of employment were whipped until their upper torso bled, prior to being sent back to their last place of employment. *This town that last employed them was to be responsible for providing for the vagrant*, and for tolerating their presence. (67) This initiative was put in place during the year 1598, only to be emboldened in 1601. Not surprisingly, *this "assistance" in fact discouraged the hiring of those who were presently the lowest people* in the society, as it imposed this additional cost for so doing, and thusly *ensured* that the vagrants would be less likely to move up the social ladder to a better lot in life. (68)

A codified defense against the uplifting of the masses, masquerading as a measure to ensure their welfare. An insulting falsehood, to be sure. The fact that such a pathetic charade is still just as effective at this writing -in terms of its effectiveness in convincing the citizenry to accept their shackles, purporting to be the key to their liberation- is a distressing reality. Whether it is by creating barriers to employment through this voucher scheme, by the institution of a minimum price law which is above the value of what the presently lowest are attempting to sell, via the governmental creation of monopolies which act to ensure that those presently on the outside remain on the outside, or by any of the various other methods cited in this book, *the shackles are always shackles. Magic words, wishing hard, and chanting, have never converted them into anything else.*

At the end of the 17th century, the Act of 1697 was passed in England. This Act was similar to the legislation referred to in the preceding paragraphs. The 1697 edict was less harmful to the presently-lowest in the country, because it was discretionary as opposed to mandatory. In some cases churchwardens and overseers would issue a certificate to an aspiring emigrant, indicating the church's responsibility for the certificate bearer in the event that said bearer may become eligible for handouts for the healthy, while also stating that the responsible church would remove the failed migrant from the new parish and return said migrant to the responsible church. *This absolved the new parish of any potential obligation* in that area so that the traveler represented more clearly an opportunity for providing a net gain, as opposed to presenting an incredibly obvious opportunity to provide an impact which resulted in a net loss through poor behavior and leeching from the Exchequer. (69)

Until 1795 the cost of removing a pauper fell on the pauper's parish of settlement -that from which they came- as opposed to the parish demanding his ouster. Certificates of responsibility were rarely issued for a distance greater than 15 miles. (70) This last fact obviously limited immensely the potential opportunities for those presently in a penurious condition. Although traveling 15 miles in short order may have been unlikely for a person in such a state, one could travel 15 miles and find nothing to improve his condition, and then desire to continue further in search of a trade or shop at which to work. Imagine if today, Mexico guaranteed that any of the people who pass through the southern U.S. border who ended up eligible for handouts, would be returned to Mexico at the expense of Mexico. The apprehension to the permitting of border crossings would be largely alleviated, though the incentive of Mexico to permit such emigrations would be reduced by this potential new cost.

As often occurs in cases of paid to fail redistributionism, whether pertaining to politicians and bureaucrats, or to those on the dole: if you give them an inch, they take a mile. Sir Henry Peck, in Rousdon in Devonshire, beginning 1876, provided five hot meals per week to school children, at a nominal cost of one penny per meal. The program was successfully self-sustaining under these parameters. Then there came an instance in which a child was permitted to pay with a story, instead of paying with a penny. The child merely gave an excuse such as "I spent it elsewhere", "I lost it", or some such tale. The first time that this was permitted proved to be the single loose thread which unraveled what had been a fine garment. Before long the proportion who paid with pennies dwindled, as the proportion who paid with stories swelled. The charitable operation ceased to be self-supporting as a result. (71)

"WORKER'S PARADISE"
"DICTATORSHIP OF THE PROLETARIAT"
(see also part VI, Karl Marx Stuff, page# 405)

China late 1970s: "Nothing still holds true now, not a single element of Marxist theory." – Li Shenzhi, one of Deng's brain trust, director of the freshly minted Institute of the United States. (72)

Nearly always promising the upliftment of those presently lowest on the ladder of success, power, and notoriety, when one rubs that lamp and wishes for such outcomes, the results delivered are Faustian, indeed. What is advertised, prior to the enshackling of the populace and the unshackling of the Beast, as a worker's paradise or a dictatorship of the wagearners, *most often delivers tremendous oppression of this very class.*

The performance of the USSR is among the glaring examples of Karl Marx's predictions going unfulfilled. Although the incongruities between his predictions and the actual outcomes certainly are not limited to the USSR, as several instances from elsewhere will be listed here, as well as in a later section (see part VI, Marx Stuff), and can be found throughout most of this book. Writing of Marx during 1944, Carl L. Becker, Professor Emeritus of History at Cornell University: "His philosophy aimed to prove that the forces of history would bring about a social revolution which would establish a democratic government and social equality. But the course of events has been very different from what Marx predicted. Only in Russia has there been a "proletarian" revolution; and the Russian revolution has failed to establish either a democratic government or equality among the workers." (73) Soon to come would be similar outcomes in China (see part II, page# 152), Cuba, and in the 21st century, Venezuela, to cite a few "name-brand" examples. Some say that the French experience of the late 18th century was one propelled by the middle class, yet the proletarians carried much of the weight of that proverbial log, as detailed above (part II, page# 93).

In Bolshevik Russia, after having made promises to deliver a dictatorship of the proletariat, the behavior of those into whose hands the power had been concentrated -in the name of empowering the masses- *was decidedly anterior to this promise*. Stalin bemoaned some articles printed in the already tightly controlled press during 1929, because the articles seemed "a call for a review of the general line of the party, for the undermining of the iron discipline of the party, for the turning of the party into a discussion club." (74) *Shouldn't the people be free to dictate* the general line of the party, as opposed to being condemned for even considering questioning or improving that party line, *if they are in fact masters of their dictatorship?*

1929 USSR: A major theft of land (peasant revolution) had occurred 12 years prior to the Bolshevik pilfering, the first making land "owners" -or possessors- of 25 million peasant households. (75) A mere 1% of arable landowners voluntarily submitted to the state confiscation of their property. (76) Bukharin (a high official) complained during a closed door party meeting that although 12 years into the so-called revolution, no province had been permitted to elect a local representative -all party policy came from mission HQ/central command. (77) Steve Kotkin tells us that "Stalin cited Lenin to the Manichean effect that everything came down to 'who defeats whom', us or the capitalists....Every advance of capitalist elements is a loss for us," and that these planners considered the peasantry to be "the last capitalist class." (78) In response to the suggestion that grain be imported, Stalin: "It is better to squeeze the kulak and extract from him surplus grain, which he has in no small quantity." The 1928-29 harvest yields 20% less grain than had the prior year -10 million compared to 8 million- in the state collection. Food rationing kicked off as early as November 1928 in Leningrad, spreading speedily to Moscow, and throughout the cities. Potatoes, meat, bread, and tea were among the restricted foods. (79)

If it's a dictatorship of the proletariat, or worker's paradise, or liberation of the masses, *then why are they being dictated to?* And in every avenue of life, not merely the workplace? Also, is this "right" or "left"? No private property (traditionally, left), hating your betters (traditionally, left), use of coercion (both). (for more, see page# 427) Kotkin says of Stalin, which could just as easily be said of Stalin's contemporary

Frank Roosevelt in the USA "...he had created his own moment, taking advantage of a crisis that his emergency measures had helped create to force through permanent emergency-ism."(80) *This illustrates one of the central themes of this book, the love of crises by those wishing to expand government and to corral the people.*

Exemplifying the absence of liberty in 20th century "liberalism", during the fall of 1929, amid suspicion that the state would steal the livestock of the peasants, the latter naturally attempted to sell off the animals. As the resulting boon in supply crippled the prices, peasants slaughtered the animals, *preferring their property be destroyed, rather than enjoyed by thieves*; denying the latter the satisfaction or reward for maltreatment. This exacerbated the already precarious food supply problem. (81) 1,300 uncoordinated peasant riots were recorded by the secret police during 1929. (82) Confessing the impossibility of central planning well, in 1929, Stalin derides a critic of the lack of thought afforded to the actual implementation, or practicability, of party edicts, chiding "You think everything can be 'prepared beforehand'?" (83) Illustrating the fallacy of the lamp, we find the so-called dictatorship of the proletariat being dictated to during March of 1930. 6,500 instances of group resistance to the confiscation of their property, while collectivization of agriculture was being imposed, were recorded. 2.5 million peasants were reported by the secret police -OGPU- during 1930 as having partaken in anti-Soviet activities, resulting in a mere 1,100 deaths of the oppressive officials sent in by the central planners. Stalin published in the *Pravda* of March 2nd, 1930, an article condemning the theft of the farms by force; although he had, of course, ordered that very theft. The voluntary and intentional, wasteful, *killing of their own livestock by the peasants* -seen as preferable to permitting the thieves to prosper from their being taxed away- *was rampant.* (84) Of course, centrally planned material "equality" yielded its customary outcome, as in July of 1930, *while the masses were suffering under forced privation, Stalin had a Rolls Royce.* (85)

Very quickly, socialism yielded results similar to an animal being fed its own leg; unsustainability. During 1930, Ukrainians were not being paid in food by the central planners, and refused to work the farms in absence of their remuneration in kind. This, of course, would exacerbate the food shortage. (86) From January 1, 1930, through the end of September of that same year, there were over 250,000 arrests by OGPU -the secret police. The official record showed a decline in the proportion of households that were collectivized by half, between the beginning of March, and the summer; from a level of 56% to a mere 24% of households. *Desperate, Stalin and company grudgingly acquiesce to the will of the people, and their desire to remain unenslaved.* Some private ownership was permitted among those who stayed on at the government farms. 3.5 million tons of grain were permitted to be retained by each household, along with plots set aside for household production. Some estimate that one third of all fruits and vegetables grown during 1930 were raised on these household plots. These farmers were even permitted to *sell* some of their crops if they wished -my, what a worker's paradise! This, along with improbably conducive weather, saved the Soviets' bacon during the fall 1930 harvest. (87) Just as we saw in the New England region of the New World during the first thanksgiving (page# 219-220), *a reduction of so-called equality*, and the accompanying repeal of the forbiddance of personal gain, *caused land to be tilled and seeds to be planted* which would not have occurred otherwise; fortuitous rains also occurred in both cases, which would not have yielded as ample of a bounty had not the people sought to plant seeds for their own gain prior to the arrival of the downpours.

During the famine of 1932-33, 6 million died of starvation in the communist territory. Russia was a net exporter of grain during this episode, while its own people starved to death. (88) *Stalin admitted that individual gain feeds the masses; while redistribution* from those who are productive, to those who are not, *starves the masses.* In February of 1950, Stalin warned Mao in China not to eliminate all of the rich farmers, as Stalin had 20 years prior, so that scarcity of food would not be so widespread. (89)

"Class" struggle persisted among the workers, despite the assertion that they were a monolithic body. During 1932-33, the Dniester River served as a divider of Soviet Ukraine from Romanian Bessarabia and Moldavia. Workers *fleeing* the "dictatorship

of the proletariat" crossed the iced-over river during the winter, and traversed the running waters thereafter. From the town of Tighina, red guards patrolled the Soviet border *-to prevent escapes, from the so-called paradise-* as peasants plowed the fields behind a team of horses. Though sometimes "their tales of woe seemed almost incredulous", Bill Shirer continues, "I quickly perceived that there was no love lost between the richer kulaks and the poorer serednjaks and bednicks - a distinction they themselves had pointed out to me - their accounts of hunger and persecution on their side of the frontier held together." (90)

Soviet Ukraine escapees in Romania, despite Ukraine being the breadbasket of Russia, complained vehemently of a lack of feed. Their grain, livestock, and farm tools were all confiscated by government officials and redistributed. *This use of the state as an instrument of theft* from the workers, in the name of their own benefit, was repeated by Mao and Deng in China. Approximately half of the 2,000 who attempted to flee the "worker's paradise" were cut down by Soviet machine guns. "Used to misery and hardship though they were, in Soviet Russia that year they had found the limits of their endurance." (91)

The old phrase "actions speak louder than words" is illustrated as people vote with their feet, and run from the nominal paradise of socialism. The necessity of preventing flight from the theft ring perpetuated by collectivism, illustrated above, persisted after the Second World War. In 1949, East and West German entities were put into place. (92) West Germans predicted that the inferiority of the much tightened grip of the Beast's hand upon East Germany's wind pipe would lead many eyes to gaze lustingly at the much more free West Germany, and voluntarily defect; the same phenomenon observed in the American Indians centuries prior, as well as in other now extinct cultures. During the 1949-1961 period, millions made the trek from East to West. (93) The Berlin Wall was erected in 1961; acting as the wall of the socialist prison of 20th century "liberalism", manned with armed guards. (94) Such flights from socialism were also evident during the late 1980s in the USSR: "from the Baltic Sea to the Caucasus Mountains political movements aimed at dismantling the Soviet system rode the powerful wave of nationalism, fusing the goal of an exit from the union with that of an exit from communism." (95)

The fallacy of the lamp is evidenced by the rank incompetence resultant when people are forced into places into which they have no qualification other than a contrived "class" qualification, and who are not buttressed by competent people surrounding them; as all others in their environment were misplaced via the identical process. Bureaucrats, often plucked from "the masses" to occupy positions controlling industry and commerce in which they do not belong, in addition to being rampant in Russia during the Soviet period, in China beginning 1949, was also pervasive in Germany during the 1930s. Socialism forced the masses to suffer under the reign of incompetents who have been permanently placed in positions of great import. During the 1930s, the German National Socialists had Hitler appointing braindead thugs from "the masses", many of whom had been with him since the early days, to important posts for which they haven't any experience and are inept. This is similar to the behavior of Mao Zedong in China, and of Stalin in the USSR. Examples in Germany include: Ribbentrop, Hess, Ley, Himmler, Goebbels. (96)

In Russia, Joe Stalin himself was improperly positioned as the head of all industry, all agriculture, and all other affairs. ***He was fit to advise only in the areas of ineptitude and of enduring imprisonment.*** Stalin's preoccupation with manufacturing, and his desire to attain goals plucked from the air, were among his numerous deleterious impacts upon the USSR. In 1957 it was noted that the USA had 25% of employed people working in the manufacturing industry, which was much less than the United Kingdom, yet the USA had a much higher per capita income than the UK. USA, Canada, New Zealand, and Sweden, had a higher percentage of those employed working in agriculture than the UK, and all four had higher per capita incomes than did the UK.

Not until the later stages of the 19th century did manufacturing comprise a prominent proportion of the US economy, with the proportionate size of the US agricultural labor force increasing until 1910. In the year 1941, the manufacturing workforce exceeded the agricultural workforce in the USA for the first time. This, after several decades among the planet's most wealthy nations. (97)

In China, near the year 1980, *the dictatorship of the proletariat was notably absent* when it came to the realms of occupation and of residency. As all jobs and living quarters were assigned by the state, no individual had any choice regarding either. Husbands and wives were routinely assigned to work in locales distant from each other, and in separate domiciles. Although there is a joke which might be made by television characters Ralph Kramden, Al Bundy, or Ricky Ricardo, regarding the desirability of such an arrangement, the Chinese example was *decidedly counter to the desires of the people*. The persistent housing shortage was no doubt exacerbated by this practice, conducted by a system of governance which is advertised as being the most efficient. *The roles of master and servant are made clear* in Fox Butterfield's statement: "There is no official rationale for it, except that it is the way the labor offices have decided to assign people, for the convenience of the state." (98)

"Equality" produces massive inequality for the masses, as is evident in the USSR during the late 1980s. Sergei Chudinov, deputy secretary for ideology of the factory's party committee, "Pay at the plant averages 310 to 330 rubles a month [about 50 percent, or 100 rubles, above the average for the city]. Blast furnace operators and steel smelters earn up to 650. Some engineers make even more. The director probably makes about 2,000." The suppression of information available to their own people was of primary import to the wokers, as ignorance of the superior outcomes yielded by competition, and the possibility of gain and of loss, was crucial to preventing rebellion. Chudinov, the party official at Magnitogorsk Works, told Steve Kotkin that permission for trips out of the country "has been declining." Less than 250 per year to non-capitalist countries. "The number of trips to capitalist countries is too small to mention." (99) During this period, at Magnitogorsk, ration coupons regulating the disbursement and acquisition of goods were needed, in addition to sufficient currency,

in order to procure new items. (100) The same practice was used in China during Deng's reign.

In the USSR during the late 1980s, in the cities of Rybnitsa, Moldavia; and Komsomolsk-na-Amure; Soviets copied the blueprints used concurrently by Austrians in Zhlobin, Belorussia, to construct a "miniplant" to fill small orders of specialized steel. The Soviets used twice as much land in Rybnitsa, and built a structure three times as large in Komsomolsk, than the Austrians had in Zhlobin. Soviets chose land with exquisite topsoil -ruining the soil in doing so- while the Austrians set aside their topsoil for agricultural use, prior to beginning construction. The Austrians utilized fewer than 2,000 workers while building their structure, while both Soviet sites used greater than 6,000 workers and finished over one year tardy of their scheduled date of completion. The Austrians slowly tested machines for optimum efficiency, while the Soviets tried to beat the prescribed maximums -thereby breaking the machines. (101)

A RESPONSE TO MARXISM

"Assume a Mr. X in the context of a deserted wilderness. X is unquestionably faced with...the fact that life sustaining commodities are not "free"; he must somehow transform the land and its natural resources into consumable goods." –B.T. Armentano (110)

Your author will now briefly respond directly to Marxism; another section (part VI, Marx stuff) will also provide elaboration. The claim that all material capital is the result of labor -termed "stored up labor"- and therefore belongs to all who labor, is among the unsubstantiated claims of Karl Marx and his followers.

1- Under what conditions was the labor of the now-complaining laborers performed? If this was involuntary, forced by threat of direct violence against the laborer on the part of the party for whom they labor [such as occurs once Marxism, or socialism, has been implemented], then and and only then, might such a claim be worth taking seriously. If labor was performed after mutually agreed upon terms had been known and agreed to by both parties in absence of coercion, then a fair bargain had been struck; the laborer has received his "fair share". Please note that the potential duress awaiting either party in the bargain due to risks present in nature, such as: starvation; illness or death as a result of unsheltered exposure to nature, including hypothermia or sunstroke; potential harm or death as a result of unsheltered exposure to the other living beings, such as bears or snakes; or other naturally occurring dangers; are not relevant because *neither party is the reason that such dangers exist*. "Work for food and shelter, or starve to death" was man's reality long before the advent of employers or of industrial machinery, and was indubitably not an invention of man or of "capitalism".

2- How was currency converted into material capital? One party sacrificed luxury today -food, housing, nights out- to accumulate greater sums, preparing for a better tomorrow; while the other party lived "better" in the moment, but sacrificed the quality of their tomorrows -*creating a perverse cycle* in which the individual bets that they will not live to see tomorrow, and so exhausts their resources today, thereby creating a situation in which waking up to another day of precious life is *bad news; the person has lost their bet*- sentencing themselves to a lifetime of low funds as a result, and so held themselves back from being in a position to invest in machinery or inventory in the event that they lived to see another day, another month, or another decade. *As we can plainly see, there is nothing unfair or ill-gotten* contained in this illustration of the time prior to measuring their "wealth inequality", as the first party is now living a life in which their capital has replaced the labor of their body, as a business owner offering jobs and manufacturing products; while the second party is now their job seeker or dependent employee. Both people got what they deserved.

3- Even if we permitted the employees to violate the private property rights of the people that they envy -in this case their employer(s)- taking care of machines/buildings impacts their lifespan and effectiveness. These presently un-moneyed people -who may also be unwilling to start pooling their limited funds for use in the operation of the business, particularly when they are forced to receive the same remuneration as those who contributed less, or even nothing, from their own pocket; in the name of "equality"- would seem ill prepared to maintain the buildings and machines once it became their responsibility. Material capital *not* in existence today might be so because it had been neglected or misused. Are the thieves going to have the money to keep up the machines? Or to keep paying everybody during sales downturns? Will they make the appropriate layoffs to keep the ship afloat? These very laborers affecting to own property which they clearly do not own, simply because they were hired to work on said property, would be likely to take the previously good operation and convert it into an awful one. We have seen, in the USSR during this section and elsewhere, China (part II, page# 152), 19th century Germany (part III, page# 188), as well as in Panama (part VI, Marx, page# 408), famous instances of this very outcome; the New Dealers in the USA did as much through indirect interference such as the undistributed profits tax, NIRA, NRA, TVA, and others. (102)

I wonder if we asked a person of such a mind today whether or not the auto mechanic owns their car as a result of being hired to change the tires on it, what their answer might be? The mechanic would be responsible for absolutely none of the costs put into the car, but is entitled to a percentage of the proceeds from its sale, as is the case with labor unions in the USA. Or whether, under the same conditions of remuneration, the person the laborer hired to mow their lawn now owns their house? Either the person must admit legal ownership of said property has been transferred to the other party, or they must admit that *the entire premise for their theft is nothing but a venal, pathetic, concoction*. To adhere to the fiction that one may steal and the other may not after such a confrontation with reality, *is to confess that equality of liberty is their nemesis*.

Marxism's demonization of the merchant (bourgeoisie) class, and capitalist bankers, who uplift those who are presently the least-moneyed, is astounding. The expansion of credit and loans for the lender's profit have been shown to uplift commerce and the masses, one such instance of which occurred in 12-13th century Europe. Merchants acted as lenders, not only amongst themselves -sell a load of wool at a bazaar, on credit, collect with interest one year later at the same fair. Interest rates ranged from 5%-24%, though generally hovered in the range of 10%-16%. (103) (For more, see part VI, Social Mobility, page# 393)

The conversion from Marxism to markets saves the Pilgrims: USA 1621-23: The Pilgrims in the New World were founded by private enterprise; made possible by capitalists paying for the journey of refugees of religious persecution who had fled England and Holland prior, in the hopes that the investors might profit financially. However, *the system of remuneration in place for the people in the colony, was quite evocative of Marxism, or socialism*. While those who were solely capital investors remained overseas, the colonists -who each owned, at a minimum, the one share of stock in the company each was awarded by the investors as incentive for making the trip and performing the labor; while they were as free as anybody else to purchase additional shares out of their own pockets if they so desired- in effect governed themselves and served as the de facto "state".

The agreement struck prior to setting sail for the New World provided that for the first seven years all gains were simply added to the common stock of the venture -the disbursement of which, in correspondence to the amount of shares owned at that time, was not to occur until the 7th year had culminated. *During the meantime, each was clothed and fed equally from the kitty; irrespective of their productivity or effort.* In such a situation, seeing your neighbor, who does not employ you, eat as well as you even though you produced most of the food, perturbed many. Some reached the conclusion that being productive was for suckers because it wouldn't make you any better off. It wasn't as though the laboring party was in the employ of the slothlike, so that the slow mover's capital was doing the work for him; under these latter conditions, complaints about a dearth of fairness due to this lack of physical movement would be unfounded.

Facing imminent starvation, a tweak in the system of immediate remuneration during 1623 rescued the Pilgrims, and the company, from death. After *the abolition of* what would today be known as *the Marxist, collectivist, arrangement* of immediate pay, each family got their own parcel from which their fate would be determined by their own success or failure at cultivating that land. *Productivity and responsibility flourished.* The very same people, in the very same territory, suddenly and markedly improved the planting effort. These religious refugees prayed and prayed for rain, and for God to save them. Substantial rains did in fact come, and the now well planted fields produced a bounty of crops. The colonists survived, and all in the company made money. (104) Although the weather would have been the same with or without the work in the fields, the additional work, done in the pursuit of individual gain, yielded a far greater harvest from the rains than would have occurred otherwise. *"Equality" nearly killed them, but they were rescued by the desideratum, the incredible power, of private property and of the incentive for personal gain.*

China ca. 1980: 24 year old Lu Lin: "Before, I used to believe in Marxism, but that was forced on me and I was blind. I didn't understand what it meant. Now I can see Marxism has not brought China any benefits." "The people are not masters of their own country, there is no democracy." (105)

The myth of a dictatorship of the proletariat following rioting was plain to see in Germany during March of 1848. *After the animals had burnt and looted with impunity* throughout the states of Germany, because the statesmen had neither stood up to them, nor stood up for private property rights, which resulted in a devastation of the economy and the exacerbation of the plight of the masses, the new statesmen in power had no further use for these miscreants. *The useful idiots ceased to be useful to those seeking power*, and the senseless, destructive, proletarians, eager to steal in the name of redistribution, now proved a liability. As historian Theofore S. Hamerow observes: "In their eyes plebeian violence had done its work...and now its persistence would only undermine the new order as it had destroyed the old." The task of those freshly minted in power was, according to Hamerow: "to effect the transition from proletarian lawlessness to constitutional stability with dispatch". (106)

The absence of a dictatorship of the proletariat was abundantly evident in China circa 1980. A Jilin province coal mine was 100,000 tons short of the centrally planned target. *Workers* -who were supposedly in a dictatorship of the proletariat- though they may have been dismayed or displeased with their job assignment or compensation, *were left without competitors from which to choose*, as their work was rigidly assigned by the central planners; *they were all in one, massive, labor union* controlled by the state. So too was their housing, food, and everything else, assigned to them by the socialist overlords. Workers were forced -actually forced, not to be confused with those in other areas, and at other times, who have the freedom to choose otherwise, but nonetheless choose a dirty or dangerous job in pursuit of the better compensation possible, who are then falsely portrayed as having been "forced"- into the dangerous mine as protests from the gas inspector, as well as of the deputy chief engineer of the mine, who both cited an excessive concentration of gas present, were cast aside. In a matter of days an explosion killed 52 miners and seriously wounded 6 more. The engineer, who protested the entry of the miners into the gas pit, was *reprimanded* and criticized for "shirking his duty" by warning the miners and thereby jeopardizing the central planners' quota. (107)

PART IV

The Intellectual Lower Class:
a Matter of Attitude,
as Opposed to Aptitude

*"He **must** come out victorious in any argument, regardless of where the truth lies. His thoughts in this matter are the exact opposite of Socrates: '...for surely we are not now simply contending in order that my view or that yours may prevail, but I presume that we ought both of us to be fighting for the truth.' The compulsiveness of the neurotic person's need for indiscriminate supremacy makes him indifferent to truth, whether concerning himself, others, or facts."* (1)

Obstinate: 1 stubborn, intractable. 2 firmly adhering to one's chosen course of action or opinion despite dissuasion. 3 inflexible, self-willed. 4 unyielding; not readily responding to treatment, etc. (23)

Sophistry: a sophism, or evasion.

Sophism: a false argument, especially one intended to deceive.

Sophist: one who reasons with clever but fallacious arguments

(24)

The obstinate sophistry industry, which consists of most of today's prominent politicians as well as the mainstream media's coverage thereof, can be observed to be mimicked by a large portion of the general public in the USA today. Whether the chicken or the egg came first -that is, whether it's simply a case of "monkey see, monkey do", as the media campaigns mold the masses; or whether the general public are sincerely inferior to the intellectual standards to which we hold our single digit aged children in our much maligned government school system, and so such tactics are reflecting their natural level- is a question which will go unanswered by this chapter. One hopes that the people are capable of asking for, and examining honestly, the breadth of evidence relating to public affairs. If not, the solution is obviously to restrict immensely the opportunity to participate directly in the deciding of such matters.

Workers -this word is the presently fashionable new shade of lipstick on the same old pig, which may age as rapidly as the word "hippie" when referring to this very class, or the word "tomato" when referring to an attractive woman, or which may endure for some time; whatever word is presently in fashion during your reading, feel free to substitute it, as it is synonymous- or American liberals, display the effrontery of preying upon, and financially exploiting, the ignorance of their audience; or of exploiting the deficiency of character possessed by their audience, as they refuse to behave like educated adults, and to speak the language of evidence. Using words such as "view", "ideology", and "belief", as deflector shields which they cower behind, *seeking a cocoon into which reality cannot pierce* through and interrupt their obstinate sophistry, the Intellectual Lower Class (ILC) behave as though they were mentally ill or mentally handicapped, while in fact comprehending precisely that they are purveyors of falsehoods who *knowingly peddle poison as though it were health tonic*.

One is reminded of a joke in the observational style made popular by the comedian Jerry Seinfeld: "Who are these people who go around chanting these slogans without any proof? Wheeeeere is the secret proof? Whyyyyyy are they hiding it? And where is it being hidden? I mean: hey, if you want to go around making demands and blocking traffic with your demonstrations, then you ought to have *some* proof! It seems to me that if a person was actually serious about solving any of these problems -healthcare, hunger, poverty- that they would be waving the proof right in everybody's face. I see these other people who don't chant the slogans, all they ever do is show you their proof. It's everywhere! Who aaaarrrre these people!?!"

An, often intentional, drastic shortening of historical perspective is directly attributable to the preponderance of the prevalence of ignorance -masquerading as knowledge, altruism, or concern- over education amongst the ILC. The obstinate clinging to, and repetition of, tee shirt slogans, in the face of evidence, *as though a superstitious faith in the power of "magic words" could overturn scientific results*, is certainly not a trait foreign among those holding college certificates as of this writing. Karen Horney, M.D., in her book *Neurosis and Human Growth*, place the distinction between a healthy person exhibiting an isolated neurotic characteristic or a solitary thought, and a *problem neurotic who is unwell and in need of reform*, describing a problem neurotic as "a person in whom neurotic drives prevail over healthy strivings." (2) When it comes to obstinate sophistry, they describe in the problem neurotic:

> "He *must* come out victorious in any argument, regardless of where the truth lies. His thoughts in this matter are the exact opposite of Socrates: "...for surely we are not now simply contending in order that my view or that yours may prevail, but I presume that we ought both of us to be fighting for the truth." The compulsiveness of the neurotic person's need for indiscriminate supremacy makes him *indifferent to truth*, whether concerning himself, others, or facts." (3)

The solution, of course, is to make clear that "victory" in the argument is impossible when utilizing such tactics, as *disqualification* of tee shirt slogans, once the language of evidence is introduced, renders their plans impotent towards the end of attaining victory. The *arrogant disregard for the evidence* -illustrating an intellectual inferiority to the standard which we hold single digit aged people in our much maligned government school system; that is, if there are four wooden blocks before you, no matter how many ways you arrange those blocks, you must admit that *the evidence dictates the conclusion* that 2+2=4, otherwise you don't pass through elementary school- while also wearing as a badge of pride what is in fact shameful evidence of their embarrassing ineptitude; specifically that they are willfully clinging to what they know for certain is a falsehood, while affecting to be superior in their knowledge, honor, character, intellect, and good intentions.

One example of such irresponsible obstinate sophistry as described by the doctors, and its consequences, can be observed in China during the later 1970s. There, we witness political motives and a closing of ears to reality, taking precedence over facts, evidence, and proof. Dr. Niu Man-chang persuaded Chinese officials that he could bioengineer and alter human characteristics by making use of ribonucleic acid (RNA). Niu's work at Temple University in Philadelphia, experimenting with goldfish, was a failure, and an honest assessment based on the evidence left him slotted into his rightful position as that of a quack; except in China.

China's isolation of its scientists from the outside world during the 1960s and 1970s, coupled with the Communist government's perpetual heavy handed, torturous and murderous, behavior, with an ever-wandering shifting criteria when it came to actions of which it might approve or disapprove, made their scientists easy prey for the "pretension over evidence" approach of the proponents of slavery -POS- (see part VII) style of governance known as central planning. The Chinese scientists put out fraudulent reports of their achievements in this area. Legitimate assessment spotted the nonsense with stupendous ease. As nobel prize winner Walter Gilbert stated simply, "What we found when we looked at their papers was that their experiments were entirely uncontrolled and were not doing what the people claimed they were doing." (4) Perhaps they just hadn't discovered the magic words necessary to allegedly bring fiction to life: "'I identify as' the person who achieved this unachievable nonsense."

Karen Horney, M.D., continues:

"The more his irrational imagination has taken over, the more likely he is to be *positively horrified at anything that is real, definite, concrete, or final.*" (5) "There are endless ways in which he *disregards evidence* which he does not choose to see. He forgets; it does not count; it was accidental... Like a fraudulent bookkeeper, he goes to any length to maintain the double account..." (6) "For these reasons it seems advisable to speak simply of irrational or neurotic claims. They are neurotic needs which individuals have unwittingly turned into claims. And *they are irrational because they assume a right, a title, which in reality does not exist.*" (7)

By "claims", these authors mean claims upon, such as land claims; a rightful ownership of, and entitlement to, whatever it is that they seek to "claim" -such as housing, moral superiority, historical knowledge, food, steel, etc..

Workers are to "America" or "whites (inferred to be white supremacists)", as Nazis are to "Jews", and as Maoists are to "capitalists" or "capitalist roaders". Their targets are nothing more than scapegoats -which in reality do no harm, and even benefit the complainers and their prey- *used as a license to disqualify anything factual which disproves the sacred chants, claims, and traditions* of the religion of socialism/communism/wokernism; particularly those at the head of the religion -Mao, Stalin, Hitler, F. Roosevelt, Danton.

We see Jew scapegoats utilized in Germany during the National Socialist era, as a basis to justify the neurotic claims of the preachers of socialism. A class known as "science and race" was a course in every German high school during the tyranny of the National Socialists. A distinction was made between "German" and "Jewish" science in the schools. The University of Berlin added 25 courses in racial science *Rassenkunde.* On Einstein's Theory of Relativity being published: "The Jew conspicuously lacks understanding for the truth...being in this respect a contrast to the Aryan research scientist with his careful and serious will to the truth...Jewish physics is thus a phantom and a phenomenon of degeneration of fundamental German Physics.", asserted Professor Phillip Lenard. Professor Wilhelm Müller of the Technical College of Anchen characterized the Theory as an attempt at "Jewish world rule". Professor Lenard, of Heidelberg University: "Science, like every other human product, is racial and conditioned by blood." (8) This sounds just like the prejudice displayed by people in America today who make statements such as "blacks are genetically unable to achieve coherent thoughts", or that "men can't make laws about women", or even that "whites cannot relate to possessing a familial history of enslavement" (see part V, Slavery Around the World, page# 258). *Such people will do anything to disqualify reality, and to reinforce their false claims to entitlements.*

Horney continues:

"The person establishes a title which exists in his mind only, and he has little, if any, consideration for the *possibility of the fulfillment* of his claims. (9)

The communists like to start with the universities, and in so doing hamstring the efficacy of such as the instruments of the instillation of productive competency into their students, and thereby making highly improbable the outcome of a strengthened school system. After all, if facts and evidence are removed from the educational process, how could anything other than ignorant diploma bearers result? And if such are told that bearing the diploma certifies the graduate as superior in that field, or as being of superior intellect, how can one expect other than a tremendous arrogance in their ignorance, coupled with an incompetency regarding anything other than repeating the slogan ingrained while at the university? During 1934 in Germany, Dr. Bernard Rust, minister of education, spoke openly of "liquidating the school as an institution of intellectual acrobatics." Rust was molding the curriculum so that it then became "according to the great ideas and ideals of the Fuhrer." Quality suffered and declined mightily from their previously lofty place. Enrollment fell from 127,920 down to 58,325, after 6 years; institutes of technology in particular declined by half -from 20,474 to 9,554. Trade publications, in a variety of businesses, openly decried the new generation of graduates as being of poor quality, and of possessing substandard performance capabilities in their jobs. (10) This is similar to the experience of the USA in the 21st century, the USSR, and of Maoist China.

After citing several examples of unrealistic expectations -perpetually irresponsible people expecting others to drop what they are doing in order to bail out the claimant, among the examples. The authors continue:

> "These illustrations point implicitly to a second characteristic of neurotic claims: their *egocentricity*. It is often so blatant that it strikes the observer as "naive", and reminds him of similar attitudes in spoiled children. These impressions lend weight to theoretical conclusions that all these claims are just "infantile" character traits in people who (at least, on this score) have failed to grow up." (11)

After pointing out that such behavior in *a child is justifiably excused, as it is age appropriate behavior* at that stage of development, they remark of the egocentric adult that:

> "He is consumed with himself because he is driven with his psychic needs, torn by his conflicts, and compelled to adhere to his peculiar solutions." (12)

Ph.D. Ruby K. Payne observed in those who exemplify a pattern of behavior which emphasizes so-called pride in the short term -obdurately refusing to accept the ineptitude of their initial efforts- among those who voluntarily keep themselves financially destitute, via their chosen cycle of making an attempt, this attempt meeting with an unsuccessful end, refusing to collect evidence regarding this failure, engaging in some attempt at "face-saving" via joking or otherwise evading productive and healthy behavioral patterns, refusing to apply said evidence towards future behavior, and so repeating the same inadequate method while expecting a different outcome– among people who are voluntarily penurious as a result of this behavior, as *they perceive the embarrassment of admitting fault in the present as being too great an indignity to bear, and so engage in sophistry so as to evade admission of fault*, and who then proceed to carry the much more damning badge of knowingly repeating the same mistake for the rest of their lives: "Reality is the present - what can be persuaded and convinced in the present. Future ramifications are not considered by anyone." (13)

It is so that nearly every human being engages in two, wholly divergent, activities. The first, involves the experience of coherent and productive thoughts; attempts at problem solving, at learning, of growth. The second, involves defecation; the necessary elimination of human waste from the body. Many people seek to reduce the second of these activities to a bare minimum in their daily experience; they wash themselves clean of the experience as soon as it occurs, and seek to remain free of it for the duration of their day, as they bask unfettered in productive and useful thought, and desire to go to bed that night an improvement upon the person that they were when they awoke that morning. *There exists an alarmingly large proportion of the population who invert this prioritization.* Such people wipe their minds clean of coherent thought as soon as it becomes evident, and wallow in the lowest and least desirable portions of human life. Such people usually seek to lower others to this plane of existence as well; always looking to bring someone "down a notch", or to remind them that "we all put our pants on one leg at a time" when they notice a person excelling beyond their own level, as *these people seek to deter the advancement of all people*, making their friendship and allegiance conditional upon participation in *a culture which ensures that when the person goes to bed that night they are no better off than they were when they woke up that morning.* A confederacy of the voluntarily inferior.

The Intellectual Lower Class routinely cloak themselves in the banner of selflessness, altruism, or concern for the weak (see part I), while exemplifying a self-absorbed myopia which is all consuming. We have all spoken to people who embrace the fallacy of the lamp, expecting that a heavy taxation and redistribution scheme will act as their own perpetual piggy-bank, enabling them to reach their hands unabated into the pockets of their countrymen, say things such as "but I've paid taxes all my life, and so I should be able to...", and then insert whatever desire that they may have into the remainder of that sentence. The psychologists remark about this aspect, as well as strategies for curing these sick people:

> "Both acceding and refusing can make the condition worse—that is, in both cases the claims may become more emphatic. Refusing usually helps only if the neurotic has begun or is beginning to *assume responsibility for himself*.
>
> Perhaps the most interesting basis for claims is that of "justice". Because I believe in God, or because I have always worked, or because I have always been a good citizen—it is but a matter of justice that nothing adverse should happen to me and that things should go my way. Earthly benefit should follow from being good and pious. Evidence to the contrary (evidence that rewards do not *necessarily* follow virtue) is discarded. If this tendency is presented to a patient, he will usually point out that his feeling of justice also extends to others, that he is just as indignant if injustice is done to others. To some extent this is true, but *it merely means that his own need to put claims on the basis of justice is generalized into a "philosophy"*." (14)
>
> "The overemphasis on justice may be, but is not necessarily, *a camouflage for vindictiveness*. When claims are raised primarily on the grounds of a "deal" with life, usually one's own merits are stressed. The more vindictive claims are, the more the injury done is stressed. Here, too, the injury done must be exaggerated, the feeling for it cultivated, until it looms so large that *the "victim" feels entitled to exact any sacrifice or to inflict any punishment*." (15)

Author Joseph Schumpeter is guilty of this behavior, as he states in one of his books: "I beg leave to repeat that the moral aspect is in this case, as it must be in every case, entirely unaffected by an economic argument." (16) In this case "economic argument", of course, is merely code for "evidence" or for "reality".

The matter of the importance of record keeping has been mentioned at the outset of this book, along with the dramatic increase of it during the 3 most recent centuries, in addition to the tremendous increase in the accessibility of this evidence during the most recent century -first with the spread of mechanized aircraft to transport books in the early 20th century, then with the explosion of electronic accessibility provided by the spread of the information superhighway occurring at the turn of the 21st century. For a supposedly educated and enlightened race to resort to superstition in the face of tangible proof, and *to act as if mankind were perpetually doomed to grope blindly in the darkness seeking the results yielded by hypotheses which have been carried out dozens of times, is unacceptable*. Evidence based conclusions, and predictions based thereupon, are incontestable in the face of sacred chants; or so concludes *a truly educated and enlightened race*.

Why ignore reality as though no evidence exists, when failing to keep track of outcomes has proven so harmful? Peter Bauer and Basil Yamey, in a book first published in 1957, inform us that: "The term "under-developed countries" usually refers loosely to countries or regions with levels of real income and capital per head of population which are low by standards of North America, Western Europe and Australasia. In under-developed countries there is no large-scale application of the fruits of scientific and technological advance to agriculture and industry..." (17) To disregard and ignore the fruits of scientific and technological advance regarding finance, governmental structure, agriculture, and industry is criminal; to adorn such behavior as a veneer of concern for the best of the masses, insults all who are encountered by such behavior.

As late as 1970, zero West African countries kept records of births or deaths. The region was largely illiterate, and sparsely populated with vast tracts of undeveloped land separating the population clusters. Reliable counts of population were impossible. Record keeping in other important areas -agriculture, industry, income, spending- were also absent. Nonetheless, population was estimated to have increased 150% during the period 1940-1970 in the region. (18) *This was a region whose only technological and agricultural advances had been implanted by colonists*, mostly from Europe. Did wallowing in ignorance benefit the Africans?

The importance of bookkeeping is evidenced during the mid-9th century AD, when the chief magistrates in Genoa and in Venice kept accounts. Sailors likely adopted the practice at a roughly concurrent date (19), though surviving records date 1110 AD. (20) Written contracts accompanied the practice of record keeping in Europe, as Pirenne relays: "From very early times, commercial profits had created a class of rich traders, whose operations already present an incontestably capitalistic character." Noting the origin of the *commenda* during the 10th century, this written contract between investors and workers on ventures had roots in Byzantine customary law. (21) Record keeping aided these people in creating and sustaining prosperity, alleviating the would-be hunger and privation of hordes of individuals.

"Wholly unacquainted with the world in which they are so fond of meddling, and inexperienced in all its affairs on which they pronounce with so much confidence, they have nothing of politics but the passions they excite." -Edmund Burke (22)

Membership in the Intellectual Lower Class, I suspect, is a matter of attitude as opposed to aptitude. When a person brakes at a stoplight, and does so prior to striking any other cars on the road, such a person exemplifies the competency of their mind when confronted with information which they might disdain. Such a person would likely prefer to proceed unimpeded to their destination, and if they must stop at the traffic signal, would likely prefer to be the first in line to resume forward progress. When such people, on the same day, pretend to be unable to process the information dictating the conclusion that redistributive schemes labeled as "free healthcare for all" deliver outcomes in which healthcare is significantly more costly, and is available to fewer people; or that handouts for the healthy do nothing but suppress social mobility, and hinder overall productivity of goods and services, thereby leading to increased privation, as opposed to the upliftment promised by slogans; *it is clear that the individual in question is deliberately arriving at what they know for certain to be incorrect answers.*

This author hypothesizes that the costs in the example of the automobile are more obvious, immediate, and directly traceable to the individual, and it is the coalescence of these factors which motivate the individual to accept the conclusions dictated by the weight of the evidence; yet in the case of public affairs, the costs are more subtle and less obvious, are delayed in their negative impact, and are not directly traceable to the offending party, and the coalescence of these factors enable the person to do what they know for certain to be the most harmful to themselves and to others, yet perceive themselves as evading direct punishment. This is a matter of character, as opposed to I.Q. We can presume that this individual, while cloaking themselves in a banner claiming themselves to be in favor of the safety of the average road traveler, would undoubtedly crash into the other cars on the road, if they felt that they could evade accountability for so doing.

Such people are not good people, and do not have the best interests of their fellow humans at heart when they feign ignorance of the consequences of their behavior. The eradication of the ILC seems best accomplished via discrediting and shunning this faction until they reform their behavior. *In the event that their bizarre religion and fidelity to superstition in the face of evidence persists*, then the failure of non-violent solutions will have to be admitted, and resorting to organized violence -warfare- will be the only route available. For the adults to surrender to the children, for the learned and informed to lay down before the ignorant and the superstitious, is an outcome which can never be deemed acceptable by an enlightened and educated culture, one which desires the best possible conditions for the people of this earth.

Your author hypothesizes, through mere observation, that there are two large factions of people in the USA today, each enriching and perpetuating their separate cultures which are anterior and contradictory:

The first, consists of *people who cling to fiction* and to a self-defeating disregard of facts; arrogantly *eschewing those who* confront their pretension, with evidence, and who *would elevate their development* in pursuit of fulfilling their potential as individuals; and thus leaving only a self-perpetuating cycle of inferiority, ineptitude, and counterproductivity, conducted under the guise of excellence, progress, and care for others.

The second, consists of people who are fidelitous to the *speaking of the language of evidence*, and who are *humble before the weight of said evidence*; *eschewing those who* cling to fiction, and who *would retard their development* in pursuit of fulfilling their potential as individuals, and of best serving their fellow man.

The first group are the ILC, and the second are the adults whose place it is to make the decisions for the whole. Because *membership in each group is voluntary and therefore can be transient*, as honesty and integrity are traits which people either utilize or disregard as a matter of choice, it is my most ardent desire that the second group vastly outnumbers the ILC, so as to render this cancerous element, this societal plague, impotently gasping for existence on the very fringes of society, if not wholly foregone by the people. *Non-violent solutions, brought about via the expostulation of works such as this book, which make these matters a mere question of a sober and judicious appraisal of the thousands of years worth of trials and experiments which have been undertaken by humans in the past, are this citizen's preferred tonic for the remediation of this sickness.* Only their recalcitrant refusal to behave like adults, obstinately engaging in their sophistry and prevarications, participating in violent outbursts in the streets, as such people have been well-chronicled to do, will render unavoidable the odious necessity of organized violence undertaken to remove this cancerous tumor from society, *and to replace it with nothing* (see page# 454) other than a life free of the cancerous tumor.

PART V

Victim Politics and the Race Industry

"We are here dealing only with civic equality, not that crude, materialistic, communistic equality which seeks to do away with all natural differences in intellectual and physical endowment and to neutralize their consequences in employment and in the acquisition of wealth." -Heinrich Ahrens, Frankfurt parliamentarian in Germany 1848-49 (1)

As opposed to focusing on achievement, making the best of one's self, and admiring the success of others, societal elements such as the Victim Politics Industry, and the Race Industry, *demonize success and the successful*, thereby encouraging their prey to voluntarily become and remain losers themselves, lest they become one of the vilified achievers, which would result in the forfeiture of their "victim" status. By maintaining and encouraging *a culture of historical ignorance*, as well as of ignorance of even contemporary evidence, the leaders of such factions are able to extract lucrative outcomes for *themselves*, despite their insistence that the prosperous have somehow wronged their followers; in fact, *the only party guilty of wronging these "victims"* on their way to riches, *are the very leaders of the Victim Politics Industry themselves*. Unsubstantiated claims abound which assert that: state ownership of businesses; centrally planned economic activity, including artificially set prices for goods, services, and wages; rapacious taxation of the minorities who have sacrificed and worked so that they have presently achieved financial success, which will then be handed out to those who have not made the sacrifices or achieved the same success;

and other similar measures, are the keys to making winners out of the voluntary losers.

Of course, the willfully downtrodden have themselves to blame ultimately for their own choice in accepting whatever bizarre temporary comfort they find in the acceptance of a mountain of insultingly fictitious claims which they swallow whole –even a cursory examination of evidence *at the very least raises questions about the assertions* of the shysters swindling them, and it doesn't take long to *disprove the insulting falsehoods entirely.* Contemporary readers will likely bring first to mind the *bizarre claims that*: not only has Africa been the only continent whose people have ever endured slavery; that the U.S. is unique in its, very limited, participation in slavery; that African slaves who ended up in what became the United States were captured by white men; that people who are alive in the 21st century are guilty of, and ought to be punished for, actions which occurred in the 17th, 18th, and 19th centuries; and that people alive during the 21st century were personally wronged and are due compensation for actions which occurred centuries ago. Such claims should be embarrassing for any adult to make, as the overwhelming reaction ought to be that they are laughed out of the room and shamed, yet the Intellectual Lower Class or ILC (see part IV) –*many of whom have at least one college certificate*– are convinced of its accuracy in distressingly large proportions. This chapter will chronicle in detail, and with statistical evidence, the actual outcomes of the loosening and the tightening of the Beast's hand upon the windpipe of a people. That is, the liberty providing deregulation or the subjugation of tight regulation, and their impacts upon quality of life and financial progress of a populace. Also illustrated will be the pervasiveness of slavery around the world, and the exposure of many fallacies purported to be facts by preachers of the religion of socialism.

The ignorance, and/or amnesia, of the masses is a prerequisite for the success of the tactics utilized with an aim to purvey fiction which is wholly refuted by any semblance of the weight of the evidence regarding a particular matter. Contemporary readers will recall that in the USA during the presidential election of 2020, during which an intentional shutting down of the economy occurred, with an accompanying surge of handouts for the healthy as they were paid to fail to be productive, in the name of saving the people from the Covid Monster -a virus called COVID-19- which took a mere 0.1% of the US population according to the official statistics [330,000,000 Americans at the beginning of year according to census bureau, 360,000 deaths per the Centers for Disease Control (CDC)], *the shutdowns themselves* -as Scott Atlas, M.D., reported in his article published midway through that year- according to data obtained from the actuarial tables used by life insurance companies, *caused the loss of far more life years than the Covid Monster ever did.* This virus is derisively termed the Covid Monster within this volume because it was portrayed as a living villain, which complied with curfews municipalities requested and with which people complied; steered clear of the socialist and race riots which took place throughout the summer; agreed to stay 6 feet away in countries in which that was the prescribed distance between people, 2 feet away in those countries which requested this distance, and so forth. All one had to do was to examine the substance beyond the claims of the evil doers in the USA alone, many of whom were running for president at one point or another during the summer, to notice that at a minimum these claims warranted further scrutiny. As we learned during the hysteria of the shutdowns *"compliance with nonsense is the virus, stop the spread".*

Dependency upon ignorance or amnesia was again in the air regarding the outcome of the presidential contest. A close contest during which the democrat party strongly advocated staying away from the polls -which was consistent with their message promoting the fear of fresh air, as well as their customary message demanding and promising handouts as a reward for the concentration of power into the hands of the few by decree, in the name of empowering the masses- made for much speculation regarding the legitimacy of the vote tally, with allegations of van loads of phony ballots arriving at vote counting centers in the dark of night. *Many behaved as though no such thing could have ever happened before*, that nobody had ever flagrantly attempted to tamper with an elective contest for the presidency, and that such behavior was unthinkable. In fact, such had occurred during the contests of the years:

2000, with the so called "hanging chads" controversy involving the accuracy of the tabulations made by voting machines in the state of Florida, wresting the contest from Al Gore, delivering it into the camp of George W. Bush.

1960, with a close contest in which it has been alleged many times that, much like the contest of 2020, van loads of illegitimate ballots arrived through the back doors of polling places, delivering the presidency to John F. Kennedy instead of Richard M. Nixon.

1824, with the controversy known as "the Compromise" in regards to the alleged backroom deal involving representative Henry Clay of Kentucky, who is said to have sold his vote in exchange for some considerations, which stole the close contest that had been sent to the House of Representatives to be decided, from Andrew Jackson while delivering it to John Quincy Adams.

1800, with the controversy caused by Aaron Burr as he attempted to usurp Thomas Jefferson as the president rather than to accept the vice presidency. Burr would of course go on to commit treason in an effort to overthrow the Jefferson government and to establish his own empire; a treason which was begun while still in the office of the vice president, and which would very controversially result in the judiciary not only sparing Burr the gallows, but also sparing him any conviction of guilt in the plot.

During the Democratic National Convention of 1844, the rules of the contest via which their presidential nominee was chosen were changed in an effort to discriminate against a candidate. Martin Van Buren, with a well deserved reputation for skullduggery and sleazy behavior, had a majority of the votes prior to the convention, and so the standard was elevated to a two thirds vote from the simple majority that had been the benchmark previously. It was Van Buren's resistance to the annexation of Texas which was said to have cast him out of favor with those at the DNC. (2) James K. Polk would emerge with the nomination.

BEHAVIOR DETERMINES OUTCOMES

One common falsehood purported to be fact by those in the business of Victim Politics, is that behavior does not determine outcomes. Instead, the priests of this backwards religion assert that arbitrary factors such as: one's variety of skin tone, the amount of "natural resources" in the land upon which one stands, one worker's wage on a given day, the price tag on certain goods on a given day; determine one's outcomes. Reality dictates the conclusion that focusing one's energies upon productive habits and enriching behaviors, or deciding to waste one's time focusing on the search for scapegoats as is encouraged by Victim Politics ringleaders, play the most decisive role in determining one's outcomes.

If lucking into being the people or country who happen to occupy the space with the great natural resources is the key to national wealth, and its concomitant impoverishment of the nations outside of such regions, then why didn't any of the American Indian nations rule the world and possess immense riches? Why was Europe conquered by Muslims for three centuries, beginning in the 8th century AD? The European land also changed hands several times besides this; there wasn't any lucking into possession, so isn't success or failure predicated upon its utilization once possessed? How does this system of superstitions account for the recurring rising and falling of China throughout the centuries, if natural resources are the key variable determining prosperity or penury?

Q: How much oil did the USA have in 1858?

A: None. Oil wasn't first discovered until 1859

How does one reconcile the Chinese experience with Hong Kong, with that of the British, if possession of the "lucky" land is all that it takes to attain prosperity? The island is not what one would ordinarily call plentiful in the realm of natural resources.

Peter Bauer and Basil Yamey tell us that: "It is easy enough to list the personal qualities which help in the process of economic change and development; such a list would include an interest in material things, responsiveness to new ideas, willingness to learn, perception of economic opportunity, mobility and general ability to adapt to change, ability and willingness to take a long view, resourcefulness, industry and thrift." (3) Pertaining to India during the mid-20th century: Profesor Tax reports that boys 8-20 years old are in business, independently of their parents. 12-14 year old boys are often experienced and cunning in their trading. "I doubt that I know even one man in the region who is not interested in new ways of making money, who does not have, typically, an iron or two in the fire, and who does not make his living partly as a business enterpriser." They continue: "..the Indian is perhaps above all else a businessman, always looking for new means of turning a penny." Conversely, in a South African nature reserve, two economists concluded that "It is, however, in the matter of entrepreneurial ability that the Bantu peasant shows the greatest deficiency; economic enterprise and initiative are most noticeably lacking. This fact presents the greatest obstacle to any improvement in the situation." (4)

Another illuminating example occurred during the 9th century in Europe and Italy. After the *loss of access to the Mediterranean Sea*, and of the nordic ports in the Baltic Sea, the Western Europeans were largely secluded in terms of international trade. The Carolingians, *segregated from trade with the Orient*, regressed to a purely agrarian subsistence economy. Conversely their neighbors, the Byzantines, *continued on with oriental trade without interruption* -and without such an economic regression. Historian Henri Pirenne: "To pass from the latter [Carolingians] to the former [Byzantine], was to pass into another world." "No more striking contrast could be imagined than that between Western Europe, where *land was everything and commerce nothing*, and Venice, a landless city, living only by trade." Byzantine towns in Venice and Italy traded heavily with the East. Constantinople (approximate population 1 million people), Africa, and Syria, were among their trading partners. Venetians would capture or purchase slavs on the Dalmatian coast, selling there to Egypt and Syria. This slave trade with arabs, in addition to selling them timber and iron, comprised some of the commerce between the Christians and Arabs. (5)

Another example of behavior determining outcomes is found in 12-13th century Europe. Even under the remainder of the intense controls of feudalism, those who began with money ended in penurious condition. As the new class of vagrants-now-merchants (see part VI, social mobility) brought about a new wealth of goodies to the locale, *many in the nobility consumer spent themselves into poverty*. (6)

BLACK "VICTIMS" AND THE 1619 PROJECT, USA

"Underprivileged is a nonsense expression akin to under - or overfed. Privilege connotes special advantages conferred on some people and denied to others." -Peter Bauer (7)

There is a bizarre fabrication, commonly mistaken for fact, which states that blacks in the United States of America were enslaved due to their variety of skin tone; that the country was built upon the fruits of the labor of blacks obtained, free of cost, by white slave owners; that many or all whites were slave owners on profitable agricultural plantations; that all white people in the USA have many generations of familial wealth upon which to draw and to gain supremacy, while blacks in the USA are forced to begin each generation penniless because two centuries ago some of them had ancestors who were enslaved in the USA; that in 1619 the white man imported blacks who they had themselves enslaved, and that from that moment whites have lived the lives of kings while blacks have been kept in chains.

Of course, the plain truth is that many people who are not black -including white people- have come to the USA penniless, famously so during many epochs, and continue to do so to this date. Many families who are not black -including some who are white- have children while possessing hardly any wealth, and this has been the case for centuries. Many families who are black have children while in possession of some wealth, sometimes immense wealth, and of them an amount have wealth which has passed on from one or more preceding generations. Following are many examples which sort the truth from the fallacies.

Non-African labor pre-dates the recently publicized 1619 shipment of 20 black slaves -captured by Africans prior to being sold to Europeans. In addition, outright enslavement in the New World pre-dates the 1619 date, as the Spanish had previously enslaved the Indians of the West Indies; and cases of Indians enslaving other Indians are common, though the recording of such is spotty, several instances are relayed during the forthcoming pages. It is noteworthy that the Northern Indians, and the Europeans whom they encountered, were initially even matches for each other, and that is why neither party enslaved the other. (8) The eventual subjugation by the sword was skill predicated, as opposed to racially so. This mirrors the history of Eurasia for thousands of years preceding.

Non-negro labor was brought in to work the fields of Virginia during the first quarter of the 17th century. Tobacco was the lifeblood of those European invaders, or immigrants, to the New World that were able to survive. Tobacco planting required new soil frequently, so that the hard labor of clearing trees on new farm land was added to the hard labor of planting and tending the tobacco crops. Prior to 1616, the entrepreneurs with money invested paid the way for the un-moneyed and unskilled British to come over, and to perform this hard labor in their employ. After 1616 indentured servitude became a common arrangement by which people without money, skills, training, or good standing in society -such as ex-cons- could afford themselves an opportunity to make something of their lives and to pay the expensive cost of transport overseas to the New World. It also afforded investors with an opportunity to be potentially repaid, and perhaps handsomely, for their investment. Thus providing actual opportunity for advancement to a better life to the lowest of British society, without coercion.

Contracts of service were not uniform. With exceptions, generally of 5 years for those 19 and older, while those under 19 would typically be under contract for service until the age of 24. Criminals served longer. Although the work was often very hard, and the lifestyle unappealing to most contemporary readers, they were better off in Virginia than they had been in England. They ate better, lodged better, and were eventually free to make their own lot in life; perhaps even, to own land. This was an all-but-certain impossibility for them in Britain. (9)

In 1708, a man by the name of Doyle reports: "In Virginia and Maryland there are but few traces of any attempt to enslave the Indians." Commenting on the state of affairs in South Carolina *"As late as 1708 the native population furnished a quarter of the whole body of slaves."* (10)

"RACISM"

In the hands of the Race Industry in the United States of America, "racism" has come to be a term which in practice denotes *a blanket legitimization of any grievance brought forth by anybody who is not white*, and which refers only to one's variety of skin tone. For decades prior to the present day, "racism" was code for anti-black, prior to its current expansion of definition. Skin color being the method of determining one's caste in the world, according to the scriptures of these preachers, and *any examination of evidence regarding the accuracy of such claims is considered to be blasphemous* by its most zealous devotees.

In reality, "race", much like "liberal", has been perverted and re-defined by shysters in the West. Just as liberal has traditionally been an indication of being in favor of individual liberty, but beginning the late 19th and early 20th centuries has come to denote a condemnation of individual liberty, instead condoning tight regulation and micromanagement; race has traditionally been utilized to denote *behaviors* or cultures, with skin color being an ancillary consideration, if considered at all. We see this evidenced by Edward Channing when, writing in 1908, he refers to the English, Swedish, and Dutch, as being of different races. Citing the New York and New Jersey territory as multi-racial, due to the presence of these three groups: "...the diversity of race which prevailed therein..." (11) and referring to areas of both Dutch and English settlement as possessing "both races". (12) In today's USA, they're just "white". Contrary to fictitious claims that the USA is the most racist and oppressive nation which ever existed, and is worse today than it has ever been, there exists much less racism in the USA at present.

Channing also referred to the English and French as being of different races: "In the epoch under consideration began that contest between two races in America which was to continue for nearly one hundred years until it ended disastrously for France on the Plains of Abraham." (13) Edmund Burke in *Reflections on the Revolution in France*, states that the French deemed the English to be a "...dull, sluggish, race...". (14) A race of people, when the term is usefully utilized, *denotes culture, habits, and behaviors, irrespective of one's physical features*. The Race Industry, which has existed prominently in the USA from, minimally, the mid-20th century until this writing, focuses solely on each person's variety of skin tone, and defines them by this aspect of their appearance -which they cannot control- *thus ascribing invariable castes and character traits to individuals*; be they victims, oppressors, or anything else.

Racism is not unique to the West. In fact, it is incredibly common throughout the world, and *is least prevalent in the West*. In 1635, the Western Mongolian peoples murdered Khara Khula for being appointed Khan -their leader- in 1634, as they did not approve of his ancestry/bloodlines. (15) In 1957 several East African countries -most notably Kenya- forbid non-Africans from helping their economy and keeping their supply chain moving, as well as from lowering the prices for consumers, by establishing trading posts. The *East African racial discrimination* also hindered the development of farmland, reduced sales for existing African farmers, and served to "prevent new combinations of land, capital, labour and skills which are essential if the economy as a whole and opportunities for all its inhabitants are to expand." (16)

On a smaller scale, we can find evidence of racism in the USA which is quite similar to the racism in Western Mongolia during the preceding paragraph. American blacks are absolutely capable of discriminating against others based upon their variety of skin tone, just as all other people are. An incident in Georgia during 1865 involved freedmen -blacks who had formerly been enslaved, but had now been alleviated of this status- laboring voluntarily as wage earners, walking off of the job -and out of town- because the supervisor was a white man. (17) Can you imagine if a group of workers today uniformly quit because an Asian, or black, or homosexual, or any other presently accredited "victim" group member, was hired as their supervisor? *Let's call the behavior what it is: bigotry and racism*.

The fallacy put forth by the Race Industry, and the president elected on that ticket, Barack Obama, that the USA "oppresses" blacks is disproven by the following data -in addition to a heap of other evidence- which is collected from the very year that Obama was first elected to the office of president of the United States. In 2008 the cumulative income of American blacks -as measured by taking the per capita black income, and multiplying by the number of black Americans- was $726 billion. When one peruses the the reported GDP of all of the countries in 2008, one notices that the figure $726 billion would place #16. That is, this small faction of the United States population had a gross income that was approximately 50% greater than the entire countries of Switzerland ($491 billion) and Sweden ($478 billion); approximately 50% as much as Russia ($1.6 trillion) and Canada ($1.5 trillion); while bringing in approximately 75% as much as India ($1.1 trillion), Australia ($1 trillion), and Mexico ($1 trillion). (18) That is some mighty, if I can borrow a term from the Race Industry, *"privileged" oppression*, is it not?

ACCUSATIONS OF PRIMACY IN OPPRESSION: FALSEHOODS FUEL UNFOUNDED HATRED OF THE USA

*"If I wanted America -or any nation- to fail, I would **never** teach children that the free market is the only force in human history to uplift the poor, establish the middle class, and create lasting prosperity for all classes. Instead, I would just demonize prosperity itself, so that they will not miss what they do not have." -Paul Dayton*

The United States of America has long been a place where people could come, often penniless or at least without much treasure, to *escape the oppression and restrictions of the highly taxed and regulated nations* elsewhere around the globe. Ignorance of history, as well as of current events, are vital prerequisites to the success of any campaign aimed at convincing a person that the United States is particularly oppressive, compared to the actual conditions prevailing in the other nations of the world at any given time. Only in comparison to an imaginary and unrealistic standard can the USA, particularly prior to the 20th century, be deemed appropriate for condemnation as an elite oppressor of its people.

I hope that readers of the future, even the very near future, haven't any familiarity with the 1619 project. This so-called project is a publicity stunt on the part of both the Victim Politics and the Race Industries, which is only a couple of paragraphs long. It states that in 1619 a boat arrived to the New World carrying black slaves. It doesn't say much else. The reader is left to infer that blacks are especially oppressed, and that the USA is inherently evil; but more than anything, the reader of this brief statement is left needing to buy other items sold by the preachers of this religion. *"Accessories sold separately", as advertisers of other consumer products have traditionally put it.* Only a person who steers clear of even the most simple and banal records of history, while consuming only the unsubstantiated claims of the Race Industry, could be duped by the sermons of their preachers. The universality of slavery throughout history will be illustrated below (page# 258). For the moment a few surveys of the population in the colonial germs of the USA, illustrating both the diversity of the population, and the decidedly absent wave of black slave laborers making everyone else rich, will be provided.

The cases of Bosnians and the Serbs during the 1990s, and of the Palestinians and the Israelites of present day, are but two of a myriad of glaring, name brand examples, of hatred and oppression due to ethnic differences in other parts of the world. The case of the 1930s and 1940s National Socialist government in Germany (page# 139) is referred to in this text, along with several other instances. Nonetheless, *the wokers in the USA, arrogant in their ignorance of evidence*, engage in the opprobrium of asserting that their own nation has been an exemplary oppressor, as opposed to an example of tremendous commingling of diverse peoples, and the undeniable triumphs of those with meager beginnings attaining tremendous ascensions; in absence of populist, redistributive, schemes. These imbeciles demand an increase in counterproductive handouts for the healthy, government creation of monopolies through regulation, and the shackling of the people via taxation and regulation, as a means of uplifting the masses.

Diversity of the population was evidenced on the island of Manhattan in 1643, when Father Jogues, a Frenchman and a missionary, tells us that he encountered 400 men on the island, who spoke no fewer than 18 languages. (19)

Population of New World English colonies in 1660:
75,000-80,000 Englishmen, 6,000-7,000 Netherlanders. New England had a small faction of huguenots and Scots. Maryland had some Irishmen to labor. New Netherland was split amongst Swedes, English, and Dutch, with a potpourri of minute factions besides. *A minute quantity of black slaves were also present, in scattered locations*, with a concentration in the Chesapeake region. (20)

Population of Virginia in 1670:
Total population of "settled Virginia" 40,000. *6,000 white indentured servants, 2,000 black slaves*. Periods of indenture varied, some 3, 5, 7, 14, and 21 years. Indentured servants received small land plots as a condition of their service. Many worked their land, while others promptly employed others to toil; *an upward transition likely impossible in England, or elsewhere*. During the seven year period culminating in 1670, three slave ships came to Virginia, while 1,500 indentured servants were imported per year. (21)

Population of the Carolinas 1700: Total population 8,000. Hardly any black slaves in Southern Carolina, even fewer in Northern Carolina. (22)

Population of the Carolinas:

	South Carolina			North Carolina	
	Whites	Blacks		Whites	Blacks
1719	9,000	12,000	1717	9,000 combined	
1734	15,000	22,000	1732	30,000	6,000
1749	25,000	39,000	1754	62,000	15,000
1763	30,000	70,000	1760	77,000	16,000

Source for chart: Edward Channing, *A History of the United States, Volume II, A Century of Colonial History 1660-1760* (New York: The Macmillan Company, 1908), p. 366

Free blacks were quite common prior to the 1860s, and we will see more examples of this in the forthcoming section on slavery (page# 266). During 1807 in Richmond, Virginia, using approximate figures, 33% of the city's population consisted of purchased and cultivated slaves, while 10% of the population consisted of free blacks who commingled with the whites regularly. (23) While the false claim that blacks in the USA today are uniquely handicapped because their ancestors 100 or more years ago began life in this country while penniless and illiterate, as though the same could not be said of ample people of other varieties of skin tone, author David O. Stewart tell us that:

"Daily life in the West involved hardship and risk, and the people who lived there posed some of the risks. Though European arms and diseases had greatly reduced the native population, the remaining Indians could be hostile. The whites were just as scary. Cutthroats lurked on trails and in settlements, ready to separate the weak and careless from their valuables, or their lives.

A traveler in 1804 found the residents of Mississippi Territory "illiterate, wild and savage, of depraved morals." Recent arrivals, he continued, "are almost universally fugitives from justice, and many of them felons of the first order" or bankrupts hiding from their creditors. A Virginia politician referred to Kentucky as "Virginia's Botany bay." (Botany Bay in Australia was settled by British convicts.) A visitor to Kentucky found that wealthier citizens were "immersed in infidelity and dissipation" gathering in crowds for horse races. The lower classes, he reported, "were downright fanatics and zealots in religion." Kentucky's settlers, according to one of them, "were illiterate... and all were poor or in moderate circumstances."

English visitors of the American West -at that time, "West" meant west of the Appalachian Mountains- went on to relate tales of savagery in fights, without any respect whatever for each other's chances of going on to live another day after the sparring. Eye-gouging, and the ripping out of testicles, were among the common tactics utilized by these roughneck white men from Europe. (24)

One of the phantoms concocted by the Victim Politics Industry, they have named "The Patriarchy". This is the title given to a supposed club which has throughout the ages, and up to present day, been comprised of all men, these men covertly acting in concert to suppress women and to keep them down within society. Most of the preachers of this dogma can be exposed as frauds by simply pointing out that prior to medical advances occurring during the 20th century, pregnancy and childbirth were extremely dicey propositions -with many complications during pregnancies, a much greater chance of perishing as a result of giving birth, along with a higher infant mortality rate which necessitated an increase in the number of pregnancies necessary to yield a given amount of adults, coalescing to keep most women occupied with these matters much of the time, and thereby making it unlikely that they could be expected to work jobs or to gain enough familiarity with the political scene to be entrusted to vote responsibly. *Nature made this so, not any secret club*. Only those with historical amnesia -an aversion to anything that happened beyond their lifetime; and sometimes averse to anything that happened more than 10 minutes ago- would expect the incredible medical standards of the most recent century to be applicable to all of the centuries prior, in which women did not work paying jobs and were not permitted to vote in elections.

Even those who are acquainted with statistics in the United States during the most recent half century certainly are aware of the large thefts women have been extracting from men via divorce courts, while also being enabled to keep a man's children from him. During certain years of that period, women have also been reported to have years in which they earned more on average, as a class, than men. Going beyond that, to one of the landmarks in the legal sovereignty of individuals, the Magna Carta in 1215, provision #7 guarantees women can receive inheritance upon their husband's death within 40 days, and without subjecting that inheritance to taxation. (25)

Four centuries later in England, during the years 1603-1625, there were 92 women in Middlesex sentenced to be hanged. In the country, theft of goods valued at 12 pence was punishable by death. There were a slew of women found "guilty of stealing eleven pence half penny", and thus dismissed with a fine; illustrating preferential treatment for women. Towards the end of Elizabeth's reign -ruled 1558-1603- a woman charged with stealing 6 shillings worth of property received a reduced sentence of a mere fine upon conviction of eleven pence one half penny's worth of goods. Concurrently, two men charged with theft of a tablecloth and a napkin -whose cumulative value was deemed 6 shillings- received death sentences. One of these men was pressed, while the other was hanged. In England 1611-1616 the minimum amount stolen, making one eligible for punishment by death: for men 1 shilling; for women 10 shillings. (26)

To counter the assertion that the USA is paramount in oppression of the people within it, a few of the contemporary norms of decorum in England circa 1619 will follow here. Three men were convicted of stealing goods whose value was deemed just beneath the level set for punishment via execution. Their sentence required them to be whipped from Newgate to Bridewell, after having spent three days in the stocks, themselves adorned with signs denoting their offense. This trek was merely the initiation to their lifetime sentence of hard labor at Bridewell. Ear cutting, public whippings, and the pillory, were all common in England during this era. Vagrancy was punished by public whipping at the post. (27)

English laws for the *privately funded Virginia colony* included punishment by death in response to speaking against the holy trinity; new arrivals received daily floggings until they had satisfied the minister of their adherence to the state religion; profanity was punished with a whipping after the first offense, a second instance resulted in a bodkin through the offender's tongue, while a third instance brought an execution. The gallows, the lash, and other similar methods of negative reinforcement, awaited those who were deemed to have engaged in idleness, theft of tools or of food, or to have slaughtered any of the company animals. (28) In England during the first quarter of the 17th century, in the House of Commons, Sir Edwin Sandys proposed the allowance of providing all accused of crimes with the option of choosing to *employ* counsel in their legal defense. This was swiftly disposed of by that body, because it was asserted that such a provision would "shake the cornerstone of the law." (29) At the time, feudal tenures and wardships were common in England, though scarce in the colonies of the New World. (30)

Religious freedom, or lack thereof, outside of the USA is evidenced by goings on during the 16th century in England. The year 1559 in England brought the Acts of Supremacy and Uniformity, which provided that the Roman Catholic Church was distinctly separate from the Church of England. In 1563 Roman Catholics were barred from: universities, legal work, and teaching. By 1593 any Roman Catholic found within the kingdom was to be executed; this after having been expelled from the territory once prior. Exceptions were made for Roman Catholics who were landed, with wealth of some substance. These people were fined £20 per month, and were constricted to an area 5 miles surrounding their land in any direction. An oath was required to ensure submission to the religious requirement. In 1610, women who refused this oath were jailed in absence of a payment of £10 monthly. (31)

Additionally, *the supposedly oppressive USA boasted, in 1798, a whopping 49% of adult males who owned land*. For centuries, land ownership had been coveted by many throughout Eurasia, and this has been cited as the motivations for many violent outbursts in the countries contained therein. During that same year, Scotland, Denmark, Sweden, and Finland, each showed percentages in the 20s. (32)

"It is only in this way that justice can be done to the memories of those who have gone before and have left for us a splendid heritage. They treated the problems which arose in their time by the light of the age in which they lived. To estimate them by the conditions and ideas of the present day is to give a false picture to the reader and the student."
-Edward Channing, 1905 (33)

A common falsehood put forth by the frontmen of the Race Industry -who only make money when people identify themselves, and others, primarily or solely by their variety of skin tone; preferring that people hate each other due to these differences- *is that the American Civil War was fought over slavery*. A conversation with one of their converts usually has the slave to superstition telling you that there was a situation in which the Southerners, each with their plantation full of ill-treated slaves, lash in hand as he is rolling in opulence while starving the dozens of black slaves, stating earnestly "Free the black man? The hell you say? We've got to keep those niggers in chains!". Meanwhile, the Northerners dropped everything that they were doing, picked up their muskets, abandoned their enterprises and families, all because of their inner-feelings that blacks should go free. Nothing could be further from the truth, as the issue of slavery was one of many, and not even the primary, reason that secession occurred and a war was fought. *Since the colonial days, the issue of alliance has always been a sticky one.* During the Constitutional Convention, the evidence of the differences in priorities and of ambitions of each state were glaring; the famous ⅗ compromise being perhaps the most conspicuous example thereof. Ever since the founding of the nation, secession plots and ambitions were rampant right through 1860.

As the USA was first organizing, Creek Indians, in league with and under the direction of the Spanish in Louisiana, routinely terrorized residents and travelers alike. Attacks began in January and continued throughout the year -women and children were not spared. *During 1789*, the Creeks averaged 1 murder per 10 days in Nashville. During September of 1789, the Spanish offered "protection" from the very

Indian attacks that they had been ordering, along with plots of land, to the Cumberland Mountain inhabitants. *This was all arranged in an attempt to curry favor with, and draw them in from, the prostrated Atlantic Confederacy.* (34)

Some mention has already been made of *the secession plot of 1804.* Federalist party members of the New England states, eager for separation from the perceived monopoly of the Republicans of Virginia in national politics, approached sitting vice president Aaron Burr with a proposal to secede, along with New York and New Jersey, to form an independent nation. Months later, in August, Burr -now a "man without a country": out of favor with the Jefferson administration in Washington, governor Clinton in New York, wanted for trial on the charge of the murder of Alexander Hamilton in a duel, was also dealing with the British minister to the USA regarding a proposal to overtake the land west of the Rockies. (35) *Burr engaged in a plot* over the course of years *which fell just short of a war*, and only so because he couldn't get the forces together which could fulfill his ambition. The 1805 New Orleans fiasco, during the Louisiana Purchase episode, is mentioned below (Free Blacks USA, pre-1860, page# 266; also part VI, Myth of Pillaging for Living, page# 383)

During the year 1810 Tecumseh visits Red Eagle -born Alexander McGillivray- a 7/8 white man, selling his dream of a confederacy spanning all the territory from the Gulf of Mexico to the Great Lakes. This confederation's ambition would be to unite against the invaders who were defeating them. Having not forgotten the war two decades prior, Americans were furious that the British continually interfered with their foreign commerce, which spawned a battle for control of land and of the waterways during the years-long conflict known as the War of 1812. (see Indian Claim #2, Mixed Racial Alliances, page# 308)

During the 1820s-30s, Northern, industrial, states favored tariffs; while Southern, agricultural, states favored free trade. (36) Another instance of a sitting vice president of the United States of America prominently featured in a plot to break apart the unity of the USA (Victim Politics Introduction, page# 238; also above) was begun via the tactic of politicians, involving the proposal of extreme legislation which they expect will never be passed into law, but which will garner the politicians headlines and support therefrom. In this case, the unexpected occurred, and the tariff

Act of 1828 became law. Vice President John C. Calhoun, of South Carolina, sought to nullify the law in his home state, and threatened to secede from the union over the matter, raising an important question regarding the power of the central government over the local -or of states' rights. (37) President Andrew Jackson refused to stand by and permit the states to pick and choose which federal statutes they would obey. Vice president Calhoun, who was leading the secessionists of South Carolina, was a political rival for the presidency, not only in the completed 1828 contest -which had gone to Jackson- but also looking ahead to the 1832 race. (38)

This matter became commingled with the Indian removal matter in the southeast, as Georgia, Mississippi, and Alabama acted in licentious disregard for federal statutes in their grasps at the land previously assured to the various Indian nations of the region (see page# 332). The key matter at hand was the power of central authority, and whether or not a state possessed the latitude to disregard federal edicts which it deemed unsuitable to its peculiar circumstances, while remaining in the union.

Due to the violation of federal treaties by Georgia, Mississippi, and Alabama, the Indian removal issue became entangled with the tariff issue, in terms of states' rights and political parties. In 1831 the Choctaws went back on their agreement to vacate their land. The Cherokees and the Creeks were unwavering in their refusal to leave. The Supreme Court was roped into the matter of Removal during 1831 when one Indian killed another on the Cherokee land which had been "annexed" by Georgia. Georgia sentenced the killer to be hanged, and an appeal was made to the Court due to Georgia acting outside of its federally prescribed jurisdiction. The state of Georgia thumbed their nose at Washington, refusing to respond to their inquiries into the matter. The matter was "settled out of court", so to speak, with the use of a strong rope and firm tree limb, as Corn Tassel, the condemned Indian, was found dead.

This disrespect of federal authority called into question the strength of the union of states. *Vice President Calhoun embraced secession*, and championed the right of the states to nullify federal laws. Georgia would not join South Carolina in their threats to secede, as the former wished to steer clear of a civil war. Calhoun, and the

S.C. legislature, declared Jackson a tyrant, and asserted secession to be neither treason nor insurrection. (39)

Whites within the Cherokee territory were required to take an oath of allegiance to the USA. Two missionaries from New England refused, and were imprisoned by the State of Georgia. The Supreme Court issued a writ of error to Georgia, with which the state blew its figurative nose. In February of 1832, the case of the imprisoned missionaries was brought before the Supreme Court, at which proceedings Georgia was conspicuously absent. The Supreme Court ordered the release of the captives, and the State of Georgia once again blew its nose with the judgment. When confronted with this disobedience, president Jackson remarked that if Chief Justice John Marshall wants the prisoners released, he ought to go down there and enforce his mandate himself. Nullifiers in S.C. were bolstered by this sequence of events. (40)

September of 1832, the Nullifiers swept the state elections in S.C. *Troops at Charleston were ready to accede to the takeover by the secessionists*; Jackson ordered their replacement with men in whom he had confidence. Historian Marquis James: "Ominous tidings awaited the President at the capital: South Carolina hopelessly in the hands of extremists; the staffs of the customs houses corrupted; a call out for a convention to proclaim nullification of the revenue laws; demands for troops to "defend" the State against Federal "aggression". " (41) November 24, 1832, South Carolina declared that beginning February 1st of 1833, the tariff acts would not apply to them. (42) *Both Jackson and the secessionists in S.C. made plans for battle, and arranged for forces.* Days prior to the first of February, South Carolina blinked, and thus ended the episode. (43)

"Minorities" has come to serve as a synonym in practice for the word "victims", among those claiming to champion the upliftment of their audience. China, 1980: Fox Butterfield himself gives some irreconcilable information about the ethnic composition of Xinjiang Autonomous Region, first stating that 66% of its 12 million inhabitants were "Turkish-speaking Moslem peoples including Uighurs, Kazakhs, Kirgiz, closely related to the natives of the Soviet Central Asian republics across the border" (44), and later that the Chinese proportion of Xinjiang was 42% (348), nonetheless this would put the so-called intruding -or so it is clearly inferred and presupposed when Butterfield describes "This ready assumption of cultural superiority, not unlike Americans' treatment of the Indians" (45)- people clearly in the minority amongst the subjugated. Yet he complains, with a presupposed expectation of outcome based not upon ability, interest, or aptitude, but rather on a dispensation strictly adherent and proportionate to the ethnic or racial population composition, that "Despite Mao's successors' proclaimed policy of being more respectful to the minorities' rights and giving them greater political power, the Party boss of Xinjiang is a Chinese. So is the army commander and six of the right provincial Party secretaries. Only 40 percent of the 400,000 Party members in Xinjiang are minorities, most of them working at the lowest village level." (46) Minority had already become a code word for victim in the U.S. Race Industry at the time of Butterfield's writing. The Chinese were, by his own account, the minorities in the province, yet because they were not victimized, they were not labeled as "minorities" by the author. Preconceived notions, and their accompanying labels, trumped the reality staring him right in the face.

Another group of accredited "victims" have been those who have borrowed money in order to purchase college certificates, thinking these certificates to be their golden ticket to a life of ease and opulence. When 5% of American adults had certificates in the middle of the 20th century, *they clearly advanced their bearers to the front of the line during job openings*. When by the turn of the century 25% had one, and by 2019 33% of adult Americans had at least one certificate, these no longer became the VIP pass enabling their bearer to "skip the line" and get to the front. (47) People continue purchasing the certificates anyway, even as the news broadcasts dissatisfied customers who shout loudly that the certificates are worthless, and who wish to evade their payment obligations to their lenders. Many point to interest rates on these loans; often stunningly asserting that companies such as ExxonMobile, who are well established, have enormous assets, and a proven track record of profitability, should not be able to borrow money more cheaply than college students. Most applicants for student loans are teenagers or those in their early twenties, whose assets, at best, consist of a car on its last legs with half of a tank of gas, a bank account with fewer than $500, and no other tangible assets aside from half of a pack of cigarettes. *That such a person can obtain a loan at all is a miracle, for which they should be immensely grateful.* Moreover, that such an undesirable applicant for a loan should be *charged a higher rate of interest due to the higher risk* that a prompt repayment will not ensue, and that a total loss may be realized on the loan, is the best way to assure that such loans *will continue to be worth making for lenders.* Complaints to the contrary are unfounded in the practical experience of all businesses, in all countries, and during all of recorded human history. Only fidelity to the fictitious sermons of the preachers of the religion of Victim Politics, on the part of the ILC, could render such complaints remotely plausible, let alone to seem valid.

Charging high interest rates reflecting the high risk of the loans, or unworthiness of the borrowers, was evident in Africa during the 1930s. Before getting to that, we see an example in which the market dictated higher rates of interest due to the scarcity of funds in Africa, and particularly in Lagos and the Western Provinces of Nigeria during the 1950s. The sparse availability of capital caused high rates of interest which reflected this scarcity. An established customer with an importer -who may obtain 30 days credit with them- receives a shipment of goods, and immediately resells the goods for currency; even at a loss. The middleman uses the currency to engage in money lending or other trading. Similar practices were utilized by Italian wool buyers in medieval England. (48) Another obvious reason for high rates of interest charged to borrowers is their unlikelihood of repayment due to experience or track record. H.S. Booker studied a cocoa village in the Gold Coast during the 1930s. He found the bulk of debts to be increasing in size, while *no interest* was collected, all due to non-payment. (49)

Slavery:
A Pervasive Global Phenomenon

The asinine and insulting popular myth regarding Africans being unique as peoples enslaved, will be dispensed with first. Throughout the world, for at least 4 millenia of recorded human history, slavery and subjugation have been the norm; and so has the norm been that the slaver and enslaved were of the *same* variety of skin tone. As has been illustrated elsewhere in this text, prosperity is neither the natural state of affairs nor does it come automatically to those who happen to be in possession of land with natural resources. Mechanized human transport only came to be during the 19th century AD, and then only in certain parts of the world, and in the hands of certain peoples [does everyone in the U.S.A. today own a motor vehicle? Of course not.]. Throughout the world, *geographical convenience has been the predominant factor* in choosing who one might attempt to conquer, ally with, subjugate, or otherwise commingle.

It is true that Africans have been no exception to this plain reality. That is, *Africans have been capturing and enslaving Africans* for as long as anyone has been keeping track. To think of these diverse peoples monolithically as Africans, is incorrect and misleading. The many African tribes or nations have been far from a unified group acting in concert. Quite the opposite has been the case historically, and the northern Africans have always been closest to Europe and Western Asia (Middle East) and have absorbed the superior technology and culture to some degree, which of course advanced these Africans; while the *southern Africans were insulated from nearly all contact with the outside* world by the geography of the land -smooth coasts and rough waters surrounding made docking boats hazardous- *and therefore were less advanced* and made for easier prey at the hands of their continental neighbors to the north. The Africans who were sold, winding up in North America, were southern Africans that were captured and enslaved by the northern Africans.

Interracial relations have been unfathomable to all cultures; *the USA*, from its outset, even during the colonial period, *has been the most well integrated multi-racial society in world history*. Occurring during 1539 in Mexico or "New Spain", on the West coast of the north region, a small search party comprised of a French friar Marcos de Niza, several Indians, a black named Estevan, and others, set out to explore in search of wealthy cities. Estevan went ahead of the others, and was murdered by local Indians in short order. These *Indians could not believe that interracial comity could be legitimate*, as they met the negro man's story about his traveling companions with disbelief. These Indians also found Estevan to be cowardly, deceptive, greedy, and without morals. (50)

The origin of the term describing an enslaved person is described by Pirenne: "The word *slave* is, of course, simply the word *slav*." (51) The Slavs have always been getting subjugated and traded by one culture or another, so much so that even as the ordinary enslavement of locals permeated every land, *merchants and traders traveling far and wide noted the ubiquity of Slavs among the subjugated*, so that the term for the condition was derived from the name of their race. If Africans were in fact the pre-eminent candidates for slavery around the world, and for all times, wouldn't we expect those in the condition to be termed "afros", or something else derivative of their particular characteristics?

Brazil imported far more slaves than the U.S. (52) *One million Europeans*, at the very least, *were enslaved by Northern African pirates during the timespan 1500-1800.* (53) In ancient Eurasia, from minimally the 8th century BC, the Royal Scythians divided their society into 4 layers -as was customary in Central Eurasian societies until the Mongol Empire's rule- plus one ruler. The dominant class viewed all others as their slaves, as would become customary in Central Eurasia by succeeding cultures. (54) During the 19th century in North America, Indians were enslaved by Mexicans. In January of 1846, Jim Clyman wrote of Californians being more or less aimless drifters, with minimal skill for hunting. They enslaved Indians to perform the hard labor. (55) The California territory was owned by Mexico at the time

Were the Egyptian pyramids built by slaves? Author Kevin Shillington asserts that evidence has been unearthed which shows that 1,500 skilled stone masons shaped the stones used, while the men of each village rotated onto duty as those tasked with moving the massive blocks. He states that this description of events refutes the commonly held notion that the pyramids were built by slaves. (56) While it is so, according to Shillington's own accounting of events, that purchased, chattel slaves, were not utilized, the utilization of force -through conscription- on the part of the state amounts to slavery or enslavement. That is, the people did not receive any compensation for their efforts, and had no choice but severe physical punishment, or execution, if they refused to perform the work assigned to them by their master. From the standpoint of individual right to contract and to negotiate his own terms to buy or sell his property and services, access to remuneration for his sale, or freedom to turn down an offer to sell, were these men any less enslaved than the Africans in the USA? Or the Chinese after 1949? Or the Russians after the Marxist movements began in the early 20th century? Does this revelation -in the event that it is one- to the reader alter their verdict regarding whether or not slavery was utilized to build these temples, or regarding the odium of utilizing slave labor? *Socialism is slavery*, and one cannot be outraged at the thought of past African slaves in the USA, while desiring mass slavery of all people today, and continue to be worth taking seriously.

In ancient Greece, *Ecclesiazousai* by Aristophanes tells of a communist regime implemented by the women -who have seized the reigns of power. That nobody would bother to work once they knew that they could not profit, was obvious. The need for slave labor under such a system was acknowledged explicitly by the women themselves. Aristophanes, in *Women of the Assembly*, points out the same trouble in Athens. His analysis further pointed out that nobody would take on the task of purchasing and/or subjugating slaves for sale -engaging in the enterprise of slave trading- since the conditional absence of possibility of reward would preclude him from taking on the risks involved with attempting to capture, transport, and sell off, humans. He acknowledges that the slaves would have to be purchased and imported from elsewhere in such a system, yet there would be an absence of sellers, and so *the person wishing for the communism will find themselves doing more backbreaking work than they were before they had wished for the system*; as it will be impossible to buy anything from anybody, because they themselves will not be interested in working when they expect to live just as well by sitting idly all day and night. (57) Of course this tale is also evidentiary of the existence of slavery in Greece during this time, as it was supposed a prerequisite of life, and that no society would exist without it.

What if the entire known world had employed a uniform system forbidding gain from one's labor? The human race would have likely ceased its existence at that very point, unless this scheme was cast aside in favor of one which encourages productivity by offering potentially limitless material gain, along with the risk of loss and potentially of destitution, to any free -that is, not presently incarcerated as punishment for a crime- person among the nation's citizens. It is the coalition of liberties present in the latter system which have been shown repeatedly to yield greater bounty in material wealth and food, while it is the forced servitude of the masses under the monopoly of the small coterie of central planners holding office in such a government, which has been shown to yield destitution and hunger to the masses. As this book has shown, and will continue to show, these outcomes have been occurring for at least 4,000 years. In all geographical conditions, encompassing the most extreme varieties of climate and of so-called "natural resources", during an incredible array of states of technological development, along with a slew of other variables often clung to by those in the business of selling the people their shackles under the guise that the shackles are key to their liberation, and nonetheless the outcomes promised by central planners are sparsely evident at best.

For thousands of years, nearly everybody has had paid servants in less wealthy countries due to their affordability, but less so in more wealthy countries in which opportunity is more plentiful and the overall level of wealth is greater. In 969 AD, Liuprand, Bishop of Cremona, visited Byzantium. Being from a poorer land, he disdained that the Greeks were "...Rich in Gold, but poor in servants." (58) An example of Europeans enslaving Europeans can be found during the Carolingian era -the time of Charlemagne. So-called adventurers would purchase Carolingian prisoners of war, thereafter selling these men as slaves to the pagan Slavs on the Elbe and the Saale. (59) In Europe, back in the year 376 AD, one nation was so destitute that they *volunteered* to be enslaved. The Visigoths fled their former land after defeat at the hands of the Huns, where the Romans agreed to permit them to enter the Eastern Roman Empire as refugees. The Romans promptly robbed them blind, and broke up Visigoth families, eventually leading to Goths consenting to self-enslavement in Rome. (60)

During the 8th-6th centuries BC, historians M.M. Austin and P. Vidal-Naquet tell us that it seems likely that "the subjection of native peoples was more or less the rule in all the Greek colonies around the Black Sea." (61) The Arab slave trade of the 18th-19th centuries AD is evidenced by the existence of Mombasa as a key Arab slave port while in the realm of the Sultan of Oman, which began in the middle 18th century. (62) Evidence of slaves outside of the USA, and not involving Africans, can be found in the 9th-10th centuries AD: "The country conquered by them [the Scandanavians, having won land in Southern Russia] put at their disposal products particularly suited for trade with rich empires leading a life of refinement: honey, furs, and above all slaves, the demand for whom Moslem harems, as well as from the great estates, promised the same high profits which tempted the Venetians [who were a trading partner of the Arabs]." (63)

Beginning, at the latest, during the early Medieval period in Europe, Jews traded Christians. Speaking of the Jews, Pirenne remarks: "They even seem to have engaged in a clandestine traffic in Christian slaves up to about the end of the tenth century." (64) During the 12th century Barcelona, Spain, began to engage in trading of the Moors as slaves, captured in Spain, returning the favor to the Moslems of generations prior. (65)

COLOSSALLY EXPENSIVE, "FREE" LABOR

Returning to the United States of America, we note that In October of 1562, Englishman John Hawkins purchased African slaves from Africans. (66) And also that the Atlantic slave trade was organized by Africans and Arabs. The Arabs castrated the males, killing, by Karl Barth's estimate, 90% of them in the process. (67) We know of an Indian ordered to be sold into slavery in the west indies by authorities on Manhattan Island. (68) Another instance of non-black slavery in the USA took place during 1669 in Carolina. Private funds in the neighborhood of £6,000 were spent on 3 vessels, and so 100 colonists departed from England on an arduous journey. A stop was made in Ireland, at Kinsale, to pick up 70 Irish servants -though only 10 were acquired. The convoy then landed near today's Port Royal, though Indians there shooed them to Charleston Harbor -enticing the immigrants, or invaders, with tales of better land. Indians were again a factor as the English chose their first settlement at Albemarle Point, with an eye to defense against Indian attacks. (69)

It is necessary to reiterate that *there were many free blacks in the country prior to the American Civil War in 1860*. Blacks have not been selected due to their skin color to be kept down at all times by the phantom known as the "White Supremacist" club, or as the "Negro Suppressionist" group. *These silly titles are as foolish as the tales of fiction which are attributed to these apparitions*. At the founding of the country, and throughout its development leading up to 1860, around half of all states outlawed slavery altogether, and in the states which permitted this incredibly expensive practice of acquiring labor, there certainly wasn't any requirement to own slaves. Most people did not own any slaves because slaves were so expensive to purchase and to maintain, and also because very few people owned enough farmland to justify the purchase of a fleet of fieldhands. *An incredibly small minority of Americans owned slaves to work the fields*. In 1774, splitting the 13 colonies into three geographic regions from, north to south, the southernmost colonies owned 94.8% of all slaves and servants within the colonies, these valued in concurrent money at £20.3 million. (70) While the bureau of the census does show that in 1790 17.2% of white American families owned at least one slave, a mere 3.9% owned the 10 or more slaves that would be necessary to run a large-scale and potentially lucrative plantation. (71)

Many American Indian nations -the Iroquois and others- *were perpetual slavers for centuries* (see part V, page# 300, and page# 345). During the last quarter of the 18th century, the USA was formed and slavery was forbidden in these lands. In 1774, Thomas Jefferson complained to the king of England about the crown's refusal to permit the colonists to abolish African slavery -and also their attempts to ban the importation of new slaves, and to tax the slave trade so heavily as to create a virtual embargo. Jefferson lists these specifically in his "A Summary View of the Rights of British America." (72) In 1778, Thomas Jefferson proposed successful legislation to ban importation to Virginia of *new* negroe slaves; passing without opposition. (73) Roughly 20% of those toiling in the colonies in 1774 were slaves, while 2-3% were indentured servants. During the years 1763-1775, of all *Europeans* immigrating into the colonies, 56% were unfree laborers -either convicts working as a condition of their sentences, redemptioners, or indentured servants. The *average price of male indentured servants* sold in a Philadelphia auction house during June through September of 1774 was £18 for males, and £15 for women. More than half of male convicts sold in Maryland during the years 1767-1775 fetched between £10-14. (74)

As you can plainly see, slave labor was not "free (of cost) labor", simply because the labor was not paid for with wages. Buying the "unfree labor" was certainly not free of charge. At Nashville in 1790, an advertisement read: 28 year old sawyer, man, 250; 32 year old woman, 150; 3 underage bring the total for the family as a package to £710. (75) *To provide the reader with a sense of proportion*, during the years 1797-1801, theft of anything over $12.50 was considered grand larceny in New York. (76) U.S. dollars of that time were less valuable than English pounds, and so *the cost of one adult slave* advertised in Nashville *would exceed the threshold for grand larceny by between 10-20 times* its value! During the latter quarter of the 17th century in Pennsylvania, William Penn was practically giving away the privately owned land, in an effort to entice men to purchase more and to develop it. 5,000 acre lots in the wilderness of PA were £100 down, with annual quit rent of 1 schilling per 100 acres. (77) In 1805 one riverboat, sixty feet by 14 feet, cost $133, or $5,000 in 2011 value. This amount was not quite enough to purchase the adult woman slave offered for sale in Nashville, but could buy 5-10 male indentured servants of much shorter duration. The handsome boat had two bedrooms, a dining room, and a kitchen with a fireplace. (78) The cost of Henry Thoreau's house on Walden Pond in Concord, Massachusetts, in the 1840s was $28 and 1 shilling. (79) You could buy more than ten such houses, or you could buy a solitary adult male slave advertised above, for the same price.

One assertion that the slave labor in the USA was "free" of cost, or "stolen", came from Willis Hodges, black minister in the 19th century: "If they were to pay us but twenty-five cents on the dollar, they would all be very poor." (80) Slaves were tremendously expensive to purchase, requiring additional expense to maintain. As opposed to paying a massive initial outlay of cash in order to purchase the labor, paying wages to employees would instead only involve a *comparatively minute outlay of cash*, thus leaving the remaining large chunk of money in the pockets of the plantation owners. The net impact of the money exchange would be far different than the minister was intimating. Also, the change in likely productivity, as wage-earners have been shown to be more productive than slave laborers (see China, USSR, English colonies in the New World, and others; particularly parts III and VI), would positively impact the return for the plantation owner; thus fattening his pockets in comparison to the profit realized as a result of the productivity yielded by the same laborer as a slave. *Nothing about the minister's statement rings true*.

Another quote: "We have been working all of our lives, not only supporting ourselves, but we have supported our masters, many of them in idleness." An unnamed ex-slave dimly states that "We used to support our-selves and our masters too when we were slaves and I reckon we can take care of ourselves now." (81) Slaves in that era were to farms what modern farm equipment is today, from an investor's standpoint. The purpose of making the investment is to increase output in production, while decreasing input in terms of exertion on the part of the investor; the money supplies the muscle. The farm owners will simply hire workers or machines to perform the work, and will be spared the enormous out of pocket costs involved with purchasing and caring for slaves; instead able to make comparatively much smaller weekly payments to wage earners. The owners were supporting themselves, and had been throughout the duration of their slave ownership, just the same as if they had paid for the powerful mechanized farm equipment used today. *The assignment of undue burden which is affixed to such people is an insult to the actual oppression that they endured* while living as a piece of someone else's property, instead of as their own property as a free person lives. For the congregation of the Victim Politics Industry to advocate socialism, which revokes one's status as a free person, and which renders that person's life as no longer being their own property, is vexing.

FREE BLACKS USA, PRE-1860

In 1805, immediately following the Louisiana Purchase, the U.S.A. initially imposed a ban on all importation of foreign slaves into the Orleans Territory; the portion containing the port of New Orleans. This measure was met with considerable discontent on the part of the French locals, who knew that manpower was the key to the success of their agricultural operations, and in absence of modern machinery, incredibly expensive slaves were utilized. As the devil that you know is most often considered preferable to the devil that you don't know, the French resisted creating a new wage and hours system, instead sending representatives to Washington pleading their case. The other territories were not banned from such imports until 1807. (82)

During January of the year 1806, in Orleans Territory after the Louisiana Purchase added the region to the possession of the United States, a free black man reported overhearing rumblings of a conspiracy to overthrow the USA, and to establish a new kingdom headed by Aaron Burr. The report consisted of information that the plotting included many others amongst *the free blacks of the region*. The man reporting the rumor was far from an isolated example of a rarity in the USA. (83) *Black slaves greatly outnumbered free blacks because*: blacks were only native to the islands of the southeast, not the mainland; black slaves had been imported -after being purchased from their African captors- by an extreme minority of moneyed people to work their farmland, which required great numbers; Africans did not choose to emigrate to North America during this period due to their own lack of wealth, ignorance of the land, and a general lack of interest in migrating across the ocean towards anyplace; thus doing nothing to elevate the number of free blacks in North America during this epoch. It is sadly necessary to point out to many people that in the USA blacks were not enslaved merely for being black; skin tone was not the reason for the enslavement of those who were enslaved.

In 1774 it was reported that 17,761 *legally free black people* were within the 13 colonies. (84) The census of 1790 partitioned people into the following classes: free white males 16 years and upwards, free white males under 16 years, free white females, all other free persons except Indians not taxed, and slaves. Presumably, the

4th of these classes would be comprised of free blacks, who in that year were numbered at 59,481. (85) Of the 20 states, as well as the District of Columbia, in 1800 the census recorded 110,072 in this same category. (86) In the New England colonies of 1774, nearly one in ten blacks were legally free, numbering 1,350. (87) Of the 50,000 slaves imported to the 13 colonies during the period 1763-1775, one in every five were from the West Indies. (88)

By the arrival of the years 1860-62, nearly half -44%- of blacks in New Orleans were free, and many were prosperous. (89) New Orleans blacks of this time owned property estimated at a value of $2 million. (In 1875, Standard Oil bought out two major competitors, at generous prices, each of which cost approximately half of this $2 million figure; see part I, Combination and Terms of Takeover, page# 42) *Negro Antoine Dubuclet owned 100 slaves on his sugar plantation.* Others excelled at shoe making and bricklaying. (90) The free blacks in New Orleans considered slaves to be less advanced than themselves; as an entirely separate unit of humanity. (91) At the outbreak of the American Civil War, the Maryland population consisted of a roughly 1:1 ratio of free blacks to enslaved blacks. (92) The preceding section (Accusations of Primacy in Oppression, page# 245) gives more information about this matter.

UNPOPULARITY IN THE USA:
A FRAGILE UNITY PRESERVED

Practical experience has proven that it is, regrettably, necessary to prevent the possibility of sincerely accepting the false overstatement of the proportion and pervasiveness of slavery, and/or mandated segregation by pointing out the following to readers. When the term "The South" is utilized: 1) the phrase does not denote 50% of the present day USA; 2) the phrase does not denote a developed and populated USA, as existed during the second half of the 20th century. In 1846, "California" was Mexican territory. Largely undeveloped, sparsely populated, California consisted of more or less the territory west of the Rockies, excluding the Northwest Territories, then known simply as "Oregon". No known detailed map upon which one might rely for veracity with his life was known of, as there was an element of the risk one undertook if they ventured too deep into harm's way, prior to 1846. Coastal towns, which drew frequent trade, were a distinct exception from this cloud of mystery. (93)

Many in the Race Industry assert that the United States has been nothing more than an instrument of so-called white supremacy throughout its history, and that those who were prominent in the founding of the nation prioritized suppressing blacks above little else. Of course both charges are absurd. Most people know that George Washington freed all of his plantation and domestic slaves in his will. Aaron Burr, while serving as vice president in 1804, prior to dueling with pistols against Alexander Hamilton, placed his affairs in order in case he were to perish as a result of the contest. Burr left one of his slaves, Peggy, $50 and a city lot. Burr saddled his own daughter with a balance sheet which yielded a negative balance.

Coming back to Thomas Jefferson, writing about a Bill concerning slavery, Jefferson describes the reasoning for his having submitted the Bill "without any intimation of a plan for a future & general emancipation. It was thought better that this should be kept back, and attempted only by way of amendment whenever the bill should be brought on. The principles of the amendment were agreed on, that is to say, the freedom of all born after a certain day, and deportation at a proper age. But it was found that the public mind would not yet bear the proposition, nor will it bear it even at this day." He added, "Nothing is more certainly written in the book of fate than that these people are to be free. Nor is it less certain that the two races, equally free, cannot live in the same government." (94) Jefferson knew well the world's history, which contained no examples of successful or prolific multi-racial societies. In 1784, the Committee appointed to lay out a temporary plan of government for the Western territory, included in their plan provision #5 which states "...there shall be neither slavery nor involuntary servitude in any of said states..." except for as punishment for a crime which the person had been convicted of after due process and a trial. (95)

In 1769 Jefferson, as a member of the county legislature, pre-revolution, obviously: "...I made one effort in that body for the permission of the emancipation of slaves...". (96) Why would the matter be considered at all if there were not an interest among the legislators, or at least an interest perceived as existing in the minds of great enough of a proportion of the general public, so that its suggestion might curry favor with voters? During July of 1776, there was a committee of five men -John Adams, Ben Franklin, Roger Sherman, Robert R. Livingston, and Thomas Jefferson- which was tasked with drawing up the Declaration of Independence. Jefferson, as a member of this committee, authored a document that he describes as "reprobating the enslaving the inhabitants of Africa." This first draft was altered in many ways by the Congress, and this section's removal was one of many omissions and additions made prior to the final draft. The amputated quote? "...violating [human nature's] most sacred rights of life and liberty" by "currying them into slavery in another hemisphere, or to incur miserable death in their transportation thither." (97) They knew that the heavy investment in the slaves necessary to work the plantations of several southern colonies was too great, and that without any method of substituting machinery for muscle, while also lacking any method for reimbursing these farmers in the event that slavery was declared punishable by law, rendered such measures -the removal of the quoted material- precautions against violating the property rights of the citizens, and also precautions against famine ensuing from the ruination of those who were responsible for growing the food necessary for sustenance and for cash to obtain necessities and luxuries, all coalesced into a situation in which the committee knew that it could never strike a pact between the food growers with immense capital investment involved, and those food consumers without a single penny of capital investment involved, in order to form a nation which might be able to survive its birthing and reach maturity.

This state of fragile unity persisted consistently up to 1860, with several incidents of near-disunion already noted on (page# 253-255). The USA was too fragile to have any effective, heavy, federal power for many decades. The country, as opposed to being bonded together by sturdy rivets and the most durable adhesives, was instead one held together by band aids and dental floss. On November 4th, of 1783, Jefferson took his seat in the Congress. He noted the body to be small, with sparse attendance. A majority of states were not even represented -due to absenteeism- until December 13th. (98)

It may seem easy to sit in one's 21st century chair, in a world full of mechanization and automation, of ample luxury and of relative plenty, while condemning those who owned slaves in any of the nations covered in this volume, and in particular the USA, or disapproving of the aforementioned changes made by those drafting the Declaration. *Without paying any cost* for making the immense financial sacrifice that the individual plantation farmers would be forced to make, while *also paying no cost* for the mass food shortage that would result from committing agricultural suicide as a nation by *intentionally bankrupting those who own the means of growing the food supply*, and who are competent in their operation. The colonies couldn't afford a war amongst themselves, as well as with England. The course of history, featuring the plenty and prosperity as a result of the successful germination of the Virginia company in the early 17th century, to the 13 colonies, and then the first 13 states, prior to *blossoming into the greatest machine for the upliftment* of those least statused at birth, of feeding the hungry, of technological innovations and advancements, that the world had ever known, this course of events may have been altered entirely for the worse in absence of this compromise. Sitting in a 21st century chair, even one mildly acquainted with any banalities of the most prominent and easily researchable figures and events in the history of the United States, ought to render any judgment upon this matter a *positive* judgment.

PROPOSED SLAVE REPARATIONS "TURN BACK THE CLOCK" ON CIVIL LIBERTIES

"We might ask the high cadres who have come out of Qin Cheng, when you suppressed the rights of others to express freely their political views, did you secure your own? When you persecuted others using political pretexts, did you foresee yourselves being subjected to the same kind of persecution?" -Wei Jingsheng. Note that Qin Cheng was a notoriously rough prison in China during this epoch. (99)

Some preachers of the religion known as Victim Politics advocate for a populist, redistributive, scheme known as slave reparations, often referred to simply by the title "reparations". Reparations violate basic civil rights, in the name of so-called social justice. One of the most celebrated documents in history when it comes to elevating the legal position, and protection from tyranny, of the least-moneyed in a society, is the Magna Carta of 1215. This code, in provision #20, provides that *any punishment must fit the crime.* (100) Since nobody is alive today who participated in the slave trade, either in Africa or in the New World/United States of America, hundreds of years ago, then *to punish the descendants of the Africans who captured and sold* the slaves, or *to punish the descendants of those who purchased and utilized* these same slaves in the USA, would be to punish a person who is, without any shadow of legitimate and factual doubt, not guilty of having anything to do with the act in question. Additionally, with reference to this provision, neither the capture, the sale, the purchase, nor the utilization of, these slaves was forbidden by any law in either land. Furthermore, provision #38 of Magna Carta provides that credible *witnesses* to the commission of any crime must be produced. (101) *Nobody can witness a crime that never occurred*; and even if a crime had occurred, nobody alive today would have been able to bear witness to acts having taken place, minimally, 150 years ago.

Another landmark for the rights of the rank-and-file citizens occurred 1679 in England, as the Habeas Corpus Act guaranteed a *fair trial* by jury prior to being sentenced or punished. (102) *A fair trial could obviously never convict a person of an action committed prior to that person's birth*; nor of an action which was not a crime at the time of its commission. The trial is also to be a *speedy trial* before a proper court. (103) *Centuries after an act was committed hardly seems a speedy trial.* This prodding to violate the civil rights of others -whether it be in the case of reparations, satiating envy of those who resent people who are more wealthy, incentivising poor behavior such as laziness and irresponsible spending, incentivising single parent homes in which the father is absent, or any other- via Reparations, imbues the "victims" with a blanket permission to steal, *while the grievance is never settled as no definition is declared of the amount of debt owed*, so that there is always another tax and spend campaign which can be justified by the claims of the sermons. There can always be another cry of the failure to "pay their fair share". (see the ILC, page# 222)

Absurd pleas for sympathy from the audience have been made by many people. In reaction to a remark made by an abolitionist entrepreneur that "no man... appreciates property who does not work for it", in response to a proposal to give low prices to people solely based upon their skin color, Eric Foner speciously states that they "had worked for the land during their 250 years of bondage." (104) Who was 250 years old at the time? Does working at a building for a certain amount of time make that worker the owner of said building? Does belonging to the third generation of a family who have been employed scrubbing toilets at Standard Oil, or at Microsoft, make the third generation worker the majority shareholder, or the sole shareholder, of the company? *Even the most minute subjection to critical thinking or analysis reveal such tactics to be an effrontery to the dignity of their audience*.

A black owned newspaper, the New Orleans *Tribune*, denounced former slaves being afforded their opportunity to enter the workforce, and to labor for wages which may perhaps be supplemented by non-monetary compensation such as housing or groceries, stating that "Every man should own the land he tills", in 1864. (105) Of course, this is preposterous. The oodles of citizens who have labored on land, in factories or shops, or elsewhere, *often go their entire lives without working for themselves*. Some may be poor savers, eschewing extra work today in favor of leisure, or opting to enjoy additional consumption of goods today, as opposed to delaying gratification; they may not be interested in the element of risk, or in the additional responsibility, that come with owning one's job; they may prefer the steady income which comes with being in the employ of somebody else. The motivations are many, and are familiar to nearly every member of the rank-and-file in the USA, so that the rate of success when employing such tactics ought to be minimal, if any.

Reparation demands reveal the economic ignorance of those advocating such a scheme. During 1865 in Alabama, a convention of blacks asserted of the landowners -as this convention campaigned for federal land theft, known alternatively as appropriation or redistribution, as a reparation- that "The property which they hold was nearly all earned by the sweat of *our* brows." (106) Of course, hardly any

Americans owned slaves, as they were incredibly expensive. The few who did only had any interest in purchasing slaves because they owned arable land in the first place. Why would one purchase laborers to work land that one does not possess? What's more, what if the efforts of the laborers had been insufficient to make ownership of the land -the cost of purchasing and maintaining slaves, animals, fencing or irrigation, property tax- worthwhile for the investor? Who is then responsible for paying the cost? *Like children, members of the ILC disregard evidence, state anything that they think will garner them sympathy, and envision terms in which they can reap endless rewards but can never suffer losses.* Such preposterous claims are both familiar and insulting; so long as people stand up to them, such claims will dissipate. The land, in fact, had already been earned, or achieved, by the owner prior to the purchase of a single slave laborer; just as it has been rightly earned upon the purchase of mechanized equipment, or upon the hiring of people to work the land who are paid by wages.

The so-called White Supremacists Club, invented by the purveyors of Victim Politics, must have disguised itself awfully well in the USA, as the systematic oppression of non-blacks took place during the decade following the American Civil War. Sympathizers to the Confederacy, and also those who had been part of the Confederacy, were systematically kept from government positions, as well as from voting, upon returning to their home states; the newly freed former slaves were treated similarly. In Tennessee, a man was arrested for having been simultaneously elected judge of a Circuit Court, and also of being sympathetic to the Confederacy. (107) Can you name an important difference between this, and a man being elected by the people, and then removed from office because it was found out that the man was black? Or that he was a member of a vanquished political movement or group?

Another feather in the cap of this systematic oppression, abrogating the right to representative self government from such states, was the 10% rule of the post-war Confederate states. This was designed to give politically opportunist outsiders rule of the roost by requiring the recital of an unpopular oath, the recital of which a mere 10% of the voters in 1860 partook. One does not doubt that many oath takers traded dignity and honesty in return for power, just as they do today; yet 90% of voters in

1860 retained their integrity by abstaining from making statements contrary to their character, while under political duress. It is vital to express to modern audiences that **Abolition was almost never motivated by noble concerns** pertaining to the injustice of humans being owned as the property of another, **but rather by jealousy** of the wealthy, extreme minority class, who **could** own slaves; this, in addition to their obvious desire for power. (108) The injustice of a human being owned as the property of other humans never seems to bother the advocates of socialism, does it? American liberals frequently advocate that the fruits of the labor and investments of others be appropriated through the mechanism of the state -thereby making slaves of those from whom the fruits have been extracted- to be redistributed, so that what began as rightfully gotten gains may be transformed into ill-gotten gains for both the recipients of the handouts, as well as the middle men doing the stealing and taking their healthy cut of the booty.

The child's version of history which states that America existed for the purpose of keeping the black man in chains, until the wonderful people of the North during the Civil War freed the blacks so that they could be free, is a fairy tale. After all, if the USA hated blacks, why would half of its states take up arms to liberate the blacks, as the fairy tale claims? And if the USA's hatred of black people was cured by the American Civil War, then how would one reconcile that with the alternative sermon claiming that the USA hates colored people during the present day, and that the country has never ceased to function as a mechanism for negro suppression? As has been briefly illustrated, the USA had been at the forefront of multicultural nations in the world, a far cry from the wokernist assertions that the USA is the most hateful and oppressive nation in the world; this supremacy is perhaps most clear when compared to nations who actually pursue the religion's vaunted measures of "equality". During the mid-20th century, China fully enslaved the entirety of their people, implementing a 100% income tax, dictating where one may reside, controlling all luxury goods through requirement of special permissions, implementing strict travel restrictions, forbidding emigration, forcing people into locked rooms to endure beatings until they complied with known falsehoods, and so much more. The USSR was stealing farms, assigning via dictation laborers to jobs and remuneration, confiscating all goods at the pleasure of those in government, and more. But in the USA, in a small pocket of the southeastern portion of the country, there were separate water fountains for white people and for colored people. The Victim Politics Industry, and the wokers, assert that the USA is the apex of oppressors, while socialist centrally planned nations -such as those in China and Russia- are the champions of freedom. My, what little respect they have for their audience.

American Indians:
Just Another Group of Failed Nations;
Slavers, Warmongers, Land Conquerors, Treaty Cheats, and More...

A "crisis" of so-called injustice is attempting to be manufactured, so that populist redistributive politicians can get their hands on power and treasure. The American Indians have been swept into the "innocent victims" basket by the ILC (see part IV), the Race Industry, and the wokers. This unsubstantiated claim is decorated by a few key assertions which prey upon the ignorance of their intended victims:

- that the land in North America *belongs* to the Indians perpetually, simply because they happened to inhabit the land at one time

- that the land therefore could only change hands through a means of wrongdoing or theft; and also that the Indians could never themselves be guilty of attaining these very lands, lost next to the Europeans, through such nefarious means

- that the American Indians were a monolithic, united, people; a great nation who were somehow cheated, and uniquely so, of their greatness simply by crossing paths with Europeans. That the Indians were somehow free of all sins, and even that they were the only successful communist society in history who have ever experienced a half century or greater period of growth and prosperity; summarized as: *the peacefully living, while sustainably living off of the land, in harmony with nature, fallacy.*

Each preposterous assertion will be taken in turn, and disproven through mere banality. The evidence is not always neatly segregated according to the specifics of each claim cited, due to the fact that much of the body of evidence is applicable to each of the three claims. The American Indians warred with each other almost constantly -just as every other group of nations has in every other part of the world- and shifted territorial rights amongst the winners and losers frequently. As they encountered other nations, of different varieties of skin tone, the behavior amongst the humans was no different in these aspects -which is surprising *only* to a mind which is itself prejudiced and racist in its assumption that people of one skin color will inherently behave in a better or worse way than another, *due to no variable other than that of their variety of skin tone.* Of course, the history of the American Indians is no different from the history of all of the other peoples.

Unsubstantiated Claim #1: that the land in North America *belongs* to the Indians perpetually, simply because they happened to inhabit the land at one time.

FACT CHECK: Land changes hands almost constantly throughout history, and peoples or nations disappear due to their own misdeeds and/or being overtaken by a superior people or nation on a routine basis. Where are the Alans, Sarmatians, Scythians, or the Roman Empire? *For the nearly 4,000 years of recorded human history* that are chronicled throughout this text, *one of the glaringly obvious patterns is the changing of hands of lands; another is the emergence and disappearance of cultures and nations.* In fact, the recorded history of the American Indians is itself punctuated quite generously with instances of the distinctly separate and individual -this will be expanded upon in the following section- Indian nations taking land from one another. Dishonest treaties entered into by Iroquois Indians during the French and Indian Wars, in which the Iroquois knowingly and purposefully sold land to the English that belonged to other Indian nations -without the knowledge or consent of the second Indians, and in absence of official authority which would grant the Iroquois the right to such territory- *in order to secure land concessions for themselves* are many, and will be encountered specifically in response to claim #2, below.

Land and Power Succession Around the Globe:
The Mundane Reality of this Common Occurrence

Let's take the geographic area near the Elburz Mountains, and to the east, northwestern Iran. Beginning in the late 8th century BC, the people or nation known as the Medes were defeated by a coalition of the Cimmerians and the Scythians. The Cimmerians took down Urartu in 714 BC, and then the Phrygians in 696; prior to being defeated at the hands of the Assyrians a few decades hence. The Cimmerians defeated the Lydians in 652 BC, prior to being extinguished by the Scythians in the 630s. A few decades afterwards, the Assyrian Empire fell to an alliance of the Medes and the Babylonians. In 585 the Medes took down the remnants of the Urartians, massively expanding their possessions of land simultaneously. The Medes fell to the Persians in 550 BC, as the Persian Empire established itself. By 539 the Persians acquired Iran and Anatolia, thus establishing Persian rule over all territory in the Near East with the exceptions of Arabia and Egypt, defeating the Babylonians in 539. (109)

Can you imagine if someone presented the position of various nations and their possessions in terms of land at any given point during this two century period, asserted that the land had always belonged to these peoples simply because they *happened to be holding the land at the time of the presenter's assessment*, and claimed that it was a unique historical crime that these people should not hold said lands perpetually? It would be insultingly false, and the presenter would be entirely dependent upon the complete and total ignorance of their audience, in order to evade exposure as a shyster. What's more, such a person would require an audience which was so incredibly intellectually inept, that they themselves would strongly parrot such a fiction which they did not know was true or false, *and* they would need to be too lazy to ever look into the evidence regarding such a claim at all. The reader is asked whether they can ever recall someone asserting, particularly violently or militantly so, that the American Indians have been "victims" of a similar "crime"? And that the land should be forfeited by posterity of the involved winning parties, into the hands of the descendants of the involved defeated parties? Such behavior is exposed as embarrassingly inappropriate, even flagrantly so, by the above snippet of a particular area possessing a radius of a few hundred miles, covering a duration of a mere 2 or 3 centuries.

During the mid-first millennium BC control of the territory called the Pontic Steppe, which is in the area of present day Ukraine, changed hands from the Cimmerians, to the Scythians, and then to the Medes. After having been ejected from power by the Medes, the Scythians were able to conquer a stretch of territory above the Black Sea, from the Caucasus Mountains between the Black and Caspian Seas, to the Danube River to the west of the Black Sea. During this time, *the Scythians unearthed a trade network* already in existence. The Scythians were able to *improve upon the quality of this network in the interest of enriching themselves* through the improvement of commerce, due to their own talents and influence which made them great and powerful for many years, and so the creation of a gold and grain route stretching from Greece to the Altai Mountains in present day Eastern Kazakhstan and Western Mongolia was the result.

This route, without any doubt, improved, enriched, extended, and sustained many lives as a result of the commerce which exploded as a result of each separate party and group *wanting to enrich themselves materially.* Greed, as they say in the movies, is indeed good in many cases. Production of all demanded goods of course increased; the variety of goods available to the populaces of areas spanning across Eurasia was vastly increased, making available products which originated hundreds and even thousands of miles away; hunger was obviously greatly alleviated by the existence of this network of merchants and producers seeking riches, as food itself was transported great distances, while the monetary gains one might accumulate as a result of participation in the sale or production of goods enabled more people to obtain food from abroad during shortages at home because others knew that money could be got for supplying the food. (110)

The trade route substantially improved the quality of life for the Scythians. All parties involved benefited to some degree. The Royal Scythians always kept up the cultivation of grain for export -known today as cash crops- as part of their economic structure. *Plundering was not at all their primary, or even secondary, source of income.* (111) The Silk Road, as this network would come to be known (learn more page #370-372), brought salt to Greece from the Sea of Azov, directly north of the Black Sea. The sale of grain to the Greeks, which was farmed largely by Thracians in the Pontic Steppe -known also as the Western Steppe- in vast quantities during the great famine -circa 360 BC- was vital, as Greeks in the homeland and living abroad paid gold for grain. (112)

LAND/POWER SUCCESSION: B.C.

One example of vanquished nations, and the succession of territory, took place near the Ch'i-lien Mountains, in west-central China, around 2,000 BC. The Tokharians settled into Kansu and *remained there for 1,800 years* until they were felled and displaced by the Hsiung-nu during the 2nd century BC. The Tokharians were split into two bodies as they fled, with the great bulk heading westward to Jungharia. These Tokharians defeated the people who were presently inhabiting Jungharia -the Sakas- before being turned away in defeat themselves at the hands of Asvin. The Tokhars fled further to the west and occupied Sogdiana, defeating the adjacent Bactria in the late 2nd century BC. They established a government or society in Bactria known as Tokharistan. *Midway through the first century BC the Kushun defeated the Tokharians* and established a Kushan empire that would stretch well into India, establishing rule over the valuable trade of the Indus river, which connected the region with Roman territory in Egypt. *The Kushuns would reign until the early portion of the 3rd century AD.*

(113) The flight of the Tokharians from Kansu to Bactria was approximately 1,000 miles by way of the crow. (114)

In Egypt during the Middle Kingdom (2040-1670 BC) period, after more than a century of an absence of centralized authority, unification of Egypt was re-established around 2040 BC. Trade with outsiders -previously the sole territory of the state- was now handled by private merchants. This trade was taxed by the state. (115) *After 1.5 millenia of unmolested possession* of the Valley of the Nile, the region was invaded in 1670 BC by western Asians known as the Hyksos, with their chariots and bronze weapons to overtake the Nile Valley. *Having been caught without a standing army, upper Egypt was severed from access to lower Egypt.* After approximately one century, the northern faction of Egypt rounded up an army and drove the Hyksos from the region, thus reunifying Egypt. Beginning 1570 BC Egypt became an international power-house, overtaking Palestine and Syria while also venturing deep into Nubia. This went on for approximately 500 years. *Beginning around 1,100 BC the tables began to turn.* Centuries of foreign invasion, vacillations between rule of regions by foreign conquerors, along with their ouster by the Egyptians, coalesced to weaken Egypt and led to its defeat at the hands of the Grecian Alexander of Macedonia in 332 BC. Three centuries later, the Romans came to town. (116)

Losing does not have to spell tragedy for the defeated. One case of a loser moving on and prospering occurred in Asia, during the period 127-119 BC. The Hsiung-nu are repeatedly defeated by the Chinese, and are displaced from China to Sogdonia. They remained strong, and subjugated lands too far westward to be within China's ability to control, still trading with China, and thriving as nomad warriors; just as the Scythians had before them. (117)

It is not always so that conquerors destroy all in their path, or that the conquered always either perish or flee. Christopher I. Beckwith: "But most of the ordinary people, the rank-and-file survivors of the defeated group, who were largely pastoralists (animal farmers) and agriculturalists, would normally merge with the members of the new nation." Beckwith adds: "This pattern occurred over and over in Central Eurasia from the beginning of the historical record down to modern times; it is exactly the same process... that characterize the history of the peripheral agricultural-urban cultures of Europe and China." (118)

LAND/POWER SUCCESSION: 0-500

Around 100 BC, Romans ruled Greece, Anatolia, Southern Gaul, Italy, and territory in North Africa. By later in the century, the Romans were in Spain, raided Britain, and assaulted the Germans in Germania. (119) Then, in approximately 200 AD, Germanic peoples overtook much of the former Western Roman Empire -present day Europe- while Mongolic speakers became dominant in eastern Eurasia. (120) *In just a few hundred years, the same lands changed hands multiple times.* The continued Germanic migration from the *4th-6th centuries AD reveals many changes in the habitation of lands*, as the Western Roman Empire became populated by Germanic orders of people. 410 AD, Rome abdicated its former colony in Britain. The Irish settled on the west coast of Britain, particularly in Scotland. The Angles, Jutes, and Saxons -all Germanic- settled in Britain after passing the English Channel, soon becoming the dominant power in Britain. Elsewhere in modern Europe, the Vandals -Germanic- devastated their way through Gaul and Spain on their way to Carthage in North Africa, where they ruled until the middle of the 7th century; at which time they were overthrown by Arab peoples. (121) Are the Arabs guilty of "wrongfully" taking this land from the Vandals? *Did the Arabs "steal" the land, simply because an audience might be presented with a historical timeline in which the world begins when the Arabs entered upon land which was presently inhabited by the Vandals?*

Another Germanic nation, the Visigoths, took over the Iberian Peninsula, based in Gaul, until they were ousted by the Franks, and so migrated southwest in defeat. Nonetheless, the Visigoths presided over a strong rulership of Spain for some time, until they were defeated by Arabs at the onset of the 8th century. Back in Gaul, where the Franks had conquered the land formerly held by the Visigoths, the Franks built the first agrarian-urban empire in Europe north of the Mediterranean, during the Early Middle Ages. The various Germanic rulers, and their Romanized subjects, coalesced to begin what would become a "distinctive new European civilization". (122) *Over the course of 3 centuries these lands all changed hands, some more than once.* New civilizations sprung up where the old ones had perished. The strong, who became so due to their methods of cultivation, and of incentivisation, which made them more wealthy and therefore stronger -they could always have weapons, feed people, feed an army traveling great distance, motivate soldiers to fight- displaced the weak, who were so because they had inferior methods and were therefore less wealthy and unable to sustain themselves. *Conditions were improved for the humans who populated the new civilization because the superior methods displaced the inferior methods.*

One example of what had been a great nation being wiped out, is the example of the Huns. The Huns first appeared around the year 200 AD. From 370 to 455 the Huns expanded their land and power immensely from their first known home northeast of the Sea of Azov, eventually heading west and south, overtaking the territories between their starting point and the Roman Empire. Giving the Romans plenty of trouble, the Huns weakened the fading empire by putting a dent in the Roman forces during the Battle of the Catalaunian Fields in 451. The Huns took cities in northern Italy, including those in the Po Valley during 452, causing Roman Emperor Valentinian III to flee the then-capital of Ravenna. By around 500 AD, *just half of a century after this achievement, the Huns disappeared as a people altogether.* (123)

The Victim Politics Industry will often denigrate interculture rulership. There are some people who claim that it is not right for a person who is an ethnic or racial minority to preside over the majority in a given land; some refer to the Europeans in Africa during the 19th and 20th, and of the Europeans over the American Indians in the New World from the 17th century through present day, as horrifically unjust and even "racist". Christopher I. Beckwith in his wonderful volume *Empires of the Silk Road*, describes China during the mid-first millennium AD: "For two centuries the Chinese cultural area of East Asia remained divided into a number of Kingdoms, with dynasties largely of foreign origin ruling over mostly ethnic Chinese in the north and ethnically Chinese dynasties ruling over Chinese and non-Chinese in the south". (124) We might ask those members of the ILC whether or not it is "racist" when the yellow man engages in this activity, or is this reserved exclusively for when the white man does so?

LAND/POWER SUCCESSION: 501-1500

During the Roman-Persian wars of the 7th century AD, at which time the prophet Mohammed died, and Islam was founded, *the same land changed hands multiple times within a single century*. (125) The Arabs, who were then the masters of Africa, took Sicily in 878 with their conquest of Syracuse. Arabs ventured no further into Italy. (126) Sicily again changed hands four centuries later, as from 1029-1091 the Normans had their time in Sicily and in Italy. (127)

In Europe during the 8th century, Charlemagne conquered most of continental Western Europe as leader of the Franks (Germanic), as well as Pannonia and Savony, and Avar Kingdoms. (128)

An historically accurate account of *the toleration of immigration, outside of the present day USA*, can be found in China during the 9th century AD. Infighting amongst the ruling elite of the Uighurs resulted in one of said group turning coat, and leading their sworn nemesis, the Kirghiz, in a surprise attack upon the Uighur capital; obliterating the attacked in 840. The portion who survived the invasion fled in all directions, the majority of whom fled to territory slightly north of the Yellow River at the Ordos. China wanted the uninvited intruders to vacate. *When the Uighurs refused, while also refusing outright submission to the Chinese, the latter attacked and slaughtered the majority of those Uighurs in 843*. (129)

The Iroquois Indians of the 17th century onward are suspected, due to archaeological evidence, of having begun as the Owaslo; who were known to occupy the same territory below Lake Ontario 900 AD - 1,350 AD. (130) These people, evidently, were displaced from this territory and then recaptured it at a later date, only to be displaced once again by the Europeans.

Many locales changed hands in the battles between the Arabs and the Christians during the 11th and 12th centuries AD. At the onset of this sequence of events, the Tyrrhenian Sea was under the control of the Saracens (Arabs). Arabs pillage Pisa in 935 and again in 1004, thwarting a potential uprising of the locale into a competitor. 1005 the Pisans launch a victorious attack upon their foe in the Straits of Messina. Pisa joins with Genoa and attacks Sardinia victoriously in 1015. 1034 Pisans overtake Bona (African). In 1052, having engaged for some time in trade with Sicily, the Pisans infiltrated the nautical port of Palermo and destroyed its ships. 1087 Christians attack Mehdia; pillage the mosque, impose trade terms between the two parties which favored the Pisans, and wipe out the "priests of Mohammed". By 1096 the Tyrrhenian had been pried from the clutches of the Arabs. 1097 Genoa obtains the first of many commercial agreements with towns along the coast of the Holy Land; following the capture of Jerusalem, rapid expansion of such relations with Eastern Mediterranean peoples ensued. 1104 Genoese make colony of St. John of Acre. Venetian counting-houses -customs depots- sprout up at Tyre, Kaffa, Sidon, and St. John of Acre. 1136 Marseilles -French port- found settlement at St. John of Acre. Barcelona, Spain, begins to engage in slave trade of the Moors, captured in Spain, returning the favor of the Moslems generations prior. (131) Key islands conquered: Sardinia 1022, Corsica 1091, Sicily 1058-90 (132)

During the forthcoming century, Western European control of the Mediterranean Sea was maintained, as *Arabs recaptured much of the land* and with it many of the cities. The towns established by the Crusaders went to the Arabs: the country of Edessa in 1144, Damascus 1154; Saladin took Aleppo in 1183, then during 1187 Acre, Sidon, Ascalon, Caesarea, Jerusalem, Beyrout, and Nazareth. The Silk Road trade between the Mongols and the Turks, by way of India and China, supplied ample goods and funds with which to trade with Europe -all taken via the Italian fleets. This trade with Europe, made possible due to possession of their key Mediterranean islands, funded the hapless Crusades through their futile conclusion in 1270. (133)

The French used their clout as a trading partner to set up shop at various points on coastal Asia Minor, Palestine, as well as on some Aegean islands -using them militarily before long. (134) The expansion of stock of vessels by the Europeans due to the increase in commerce -via trading, as well as via military contracts to transport crusaders- along with the expansion of important Mediterranean possessions, combined nicely with a lack of Turkish competition in this phase of commerce, to fortify European hegemony of control over trade in the Mediterranean Sea. (135) This reversed the negative pattern caused by the stifling of commerce due to prior isolation from Mediterranean trade, as the commercial and profiteering spirit of enterprise permeated inland from the trading towns at sea. (136)

1017-1035: Canute the Great united England, Denmark, and Norway, in an ephemeral empire. (137)

In Russia, following Tokhtamish's attacks on Tamerlane, the latter's devastating retaliation demolished the Jochi -Golden Horde- successors of the dukes of Muscovy, splitting those of the Golden Horde into a variety of smaller governments/civilizations by the mid-15th century. The locales of those various khanates -governments- ranged from the Astrakhans near the Volga Rivers's divergence from the Caspian Sea, the Volga-Kama confluence locale of the Kazans, and Central Steppe nomads south of the Urals -known as the Blue Horde- ranging from the Volga to the Irtysh in Siberia. In 1547 Ivan IV -Ivan the Terrible- crowned himself the first czar -caesar- in Russian history; claiming Russians to be rightful heirs to the Byzantines (Eastern Roman Empire). The Russian Empire then took down the dispersed and separate khanates of the former Golden Horde peoples; taking the territory of the Kazans in 1552, and the Astrakhans in 1556. (138)

A name-brand example of territory changing hands, of people rising or falling, is known as the Fall of Rome. May 29th, 1453, the Turks take Constantinople -then a much humbled city of approximately 20,000 inhabitants- declaring it to be their new capital and thereby officially bring an end to the Byzantine (East Roman) Empire. Over the course of the subsequent century -culminating 1571 when they lose to Christian Europeans at the Battle of Lepanto- the Turks (Ottomans) *re-took for themselves* old territories of the Eastern Roman Empire under Heraclius, *prior to the Arabs' taking* of the territories -Greece, Anatolia, northwest Persia, Syria, Kurdistan, North Mesopotamia, Egypt, Hungary, and according to Beckwith "most of North Africa and into the Red Sea". (139)

The Seas are no exception to the winds of change shifting the power about, passing along supremacy and destitution amongst various parties just as occurs on dry land. During the Middle Ages, as certain Christian Europeans developed improved seafaring technology and skills, the balance of power shifts from the Arabs to the Christians. In 1492 the Spanish *reconquista* capture the Arab capital of Granada, and boot the Muslim Arabs from the country for good. The Christian nations of Portugal, Spain, Holland, England, and France, *each take their turn at the forefront due to their dominance of the seas.* (140)

In the New World, the re-discovery of the Americas was motivated not by "imperialism for the purpose of exploitation and subjugation of non-whites; nor by racism or so-called 'white supremacy'", as practitioners within the Race Industry of the 20th and 21st centuries might assert; but rather by factors noted by Edward Channing such as: "Religious enthusiasm, human affection, the pursuit of gain". (141) The Americas were first known to be discovered, containing non-white inhabitants, in 999-1,000 AD by Leif Ericsson in a misadventure which occurred during an attempt to sail from Norway to Greenland. The sailor made a wrong turn someplace -perhaps the sailor should have made that left at Albuquerque!- and landed in the present day New England/Nova Scotia region. Ericsson donned the land with the name of Vinland and set back to find his way to his destination. Foreign voyages to the Americas seem to have ceased for half a millennium or so thereafter. (142)

During the late 15th century Kristopher Columbus, quite famously, made an inadvertent voyage to the New World. The *promised remuneration* from the Spanish rulers for his voyage to the Far East included: Columbus and his heirs declared Admirals in all lands and islands discovered or procured for Spain; one tenth of all gold and silver found; in return for putting up one eight of the cost of the expedition, he could receive an eighth of the profits. (143) *He didn't get paid.* Historian Edward Channing summarizes the experience: "For years all things were evil with him; his colonists rebelled; gold was only won in small quantities and with great difficulty; and island after island, peopled with naked savages, appeared where Cipango [Japan] with its silken-clad princes should have been." (144)

LAND/POWER SUCCESSION 1501-PRESENT

An example of a region being labeled as rightfully belonging to a nation, who occupied it only briefly, but happened to be located there at the isolated moment presented by a shyster, leading to the spurious assertion that it was "always their land", occurred in the pre-revolutionary USA. An Indian nation, the Susquehannocks, said that their tribe had been members of the Iroquois Confederation in the New York and Pennsylvania regions, but in the late 16th century a faction out-migrated to new territory -the Susquehanna Valley- and started their own tribe. Subsequently, they warred with the Iroquois and eventually the English as well. By 1680, the Susquehannocks had been reduced to nothing; their number having been dispersed and disbanded, each going their own way. *The river and valley which bear the namesake of the Susquehanna today, was named for a people who occupied the territory for a mere century.* The land was then occupied by a coalescence of Indian immigrants/refugees: a ragtag bunch of misfit cast-offs from other failed nations/tribes, who by 1710 had created a trading hub -present day Lancaster, PA- named Conestoga, after its inhabitants. (145)

In Mexico during the early 16th century, Hernan Cortez -a defector from a search party dispatched to explore the northern and western shores of the Gulf of Mexico- conquers Mexico for himself. The search party that Cortez abandoned had been sent by the Governors of Jamaica and Cuba. (349)

China 1616: Jurchen leader Nurhachi forms a Chinese-style dynasty, to become known as the Later Chin Dynasty. The moniker changed to Ch'ing Dynasty in 1636; though Hung Taiji -then ruler- decreed in 1635 that their ethnic group be labeled Manchu. This group presided over Southern Manchuria, moving their capital southward to Shenyang in 1625 after taking Liaotung from the Ming. With the Ming unable to abate a rebellion which cost them possession of Peking, they sought military aid from the Manchu -Ch'ing. Dorgon headed the Manchu force that won Peking from the rebels in 1644. Aptly discerning the weakness of the Ming, the Manchus went on northward and took the remainder of China as their own by 1662. The conquering Manchu assured their victory by seeing to it that *ethnic Chinese were forbidden in practice from holding the highest offices* in the administration, though they were permitted to advance to the height of provincial governor in some cases. Manchus adopted Chinese culture. The Ch'ing would go on to annex East Turkistan (Xinjiang), grow China in population, exert influence over some Central Eurasian lands, and make a kingdom which impressed European visitors as being superior to themselves both culturally and materially. (146)

Elsewhere during the 17th Century in Eurasia, Western Mongolians, known as Oirats, conquer territory and exert power over much of Eurasia, establishing the Junghar Empire. In 1641 they use their strength to exact a duty-free trade arrangement from the Russians -who had been their nominal subjugator twice within the past 50 years- setting off a boon in transcontinental commerce benefiting all peoples involved -of course- and especially the Russian trade cities of Tobolsk, Tara, and Tomsk. In a land in which a leader had been *executed in 1635 for being of unlike ethnicity*, merchants came in from Islamic Central Asia to prosper as intermediaries; or middleman minorities.

Drawing peasants from Central Asia to cultivate fields adjacent to monasteries constructed in various towns for the purpose of agricultural production, the Junghar capital became a trading hub of international exchange. More food, goods, and coin, existed which fed and clothed people due to this free trade. (147)

Of course, the land throughout Europe has undergone many changes in rulership during the 19th and 20th centuries. The Napoleonic Wars, the territory in Alsace has changed hands several times during that span, the First World War, the Second World War, the expansion of the USSR; all of these are well documented elsewhere, and the reader is encouraged to pursue this information if they wish to learn more about *the gargantuanly pedestrian occurrence of land and power changing hands*.

INDIAN NATION LOCATIONS BY DATE

The following will list some Indian tribes, and their known region of residence at given dates. This is primarily a codicil to satisfy those who may be curious about Indian tribes, and who may decide to take up further reading on a particular nation or region. If the reader is a consumer of the material disseminated by the purveyors of Victim Politics, do you find that any of the tribes or lands mentioned here specifically, or anyplace else throughout this book, differ from the material that you possess or have consumed previously? *Let such conflicts be further evidence that no land is always anybody's land*; one must perpetually and vigilantly maintain their culture and habits so as not to lose what is at present their own. The following list is anything but complete, and is not purported as such.

1607-1669: Virginia: Thomas Jefferson gives an account of Indian nations or tribes within Virginia during this epoch:

WEST	EAST
Mannahoac Confederacy	Powhatan Confederation

WEST	EAST
Whonkenties	Tauxenents
Tegninaties	Patowomekes
Ontponies	Cuttawomans
Tauxitanians	Pissasecs
Hassinungaes	Onaumanients
Stegarakies	Rappahanocs
Shackakonies	Moraughtacunds
Mannahoacs	Secaconies
	Wighcocomicoes
Monacan Confederacy	Nantaughtacunds
	Mattapoments
Monacans	Pamunkies
Monasiccapanoes	Werowocomicos
Monahassanoes	Payankatanks
Massinacacs	Youghtanunds
Mohemenchoes	Chickahominies
	Powhattans
	Arrowhatocs
	Weanocs
	Paspaheghes
	Chiskiacs
	Kecoughtans
	Appamattocs
	Quiocohanocs
	Warrasqeaks

Nansamonds

Chesapeaks

Accphanocs

Accomacks

Outside of These Alliances

Nottoways

Meherrics

Tuteloes

SOURCE FOR TABLE: Thomas Jefferson, *Writings* (New York: Literary Classics of the United States, Inc., 1984), p.218-219

1666: habitating the recesses of Lake Michigan, were the Potawatomies, Sacs, foxes, Illinois. Sioux, west of Illinois, Iroquois to the east. Sioux west of Lake Superior. (148)

1671: The "remains of one branch of the Huron nation" were at Point St. Ignacious, Michigan; 1672 the Mascoutins and the Kickapoos in Milwaukee, Wisconsin; Miamis at the "head of Lake Michigan" (149); Foxes on the Fox River (150). 1673, Marquette finds red men in Des Moines who identified themselves as Illinois, though the word has a literal translation to mean "men". (151) At the intersection of the Mississippi, Missouri and Ohio Rivers were the Shawnee Indians –who, incidentally, mentioned fearing the Iroquois due to prior experience. (152) Further downriver the Chickasas (153). 1675 approximately 2,000 members of the Illinois tribe were on the Illinois River. (154)

Cenis nation in Texas/northeastern Mexico 1686 (155)

1690 the Abenaki Indians inhabit Piscataqua (156); 1691 Micmac Indians near Penobscot (157) in Canada.

1768, East of the Mississippi:

Nation	Region
Abnaki	Maine, VT, NH
Catawba	SC
Cherokee	Carolinas, GA
Chickasaw	Miss, TN
Choctaw	Miss, Ala
Creek	GA, Ala, FL
Dakota	MN
Delaware-Munsee	PA–OH
Illinois	ILL
Iroquois	NY, PA
Kickapoo-Mascouten	ILL
Mahican	OH
Menominee	Wis
Mesquakie (Fox)	Wis
Miami, Wea, Piankeshaw	Ind–OH
Mingo	OH
Missisaga (Chippewa)	Mich–OH
Ojibwa	Minn, Mich, Wis
Ottawa	Mich–OH
Potawatomi	Wis, Ill, Ind
Sauk	Ill, Wis
Shawnee	OH, PA
Winnebago	Wis
Wyandot	OH

SOURCE FOR TABLE: Thomas L. Purvis, *Revolutionary America, 1763 to 1800* (New York: Facts on File, Inc., 1995), p. 24

1806: Chickasaw Indians inhabit present day Memphis, TN. (158)

Mid-19th century: Fort Snelling, erected 1820 under the moniker Fort Saint Anthony, at the intersection of the Minnesota and Missouri Rivers, housed many Europeans who were combating Indian nations; the Pawnees, Flatheads, Sioux, and Mandans, among their number. (159)

1882: Apache Indian tribe in the Arizona Territory. (160)

See also: the subject index of this book, for more about Indian nations and their locales at various periods, as many are not listed in this section.

Unsubstantiated Claim #2: that the land therefore could only change hands via wrongdoing or theft; and also that the Indians could never themselves be guilty of attaining these very lands, lost next to the Europeans, through such nefarious means.

FACT CHECK: throughout nearly 4 millenia of recorded human history, land has most frequently changed hands in a transaction that involves a nation who undertook a more self defeating way of doing things, losing out to a nation who used their resources in a manner which was more effective in yielding improved economic production; which could afford them the money necessary for a well fed, and equipped, national defense.

Strictly "pillaging for a living" has not been common for nations historically; not for extended periods, anyway. (see part VI, pillaging for a living, page# 383) Superior methods in agriculture were the key to national superiority for thousands of years. From the Egyptians in the 16th century BC, the Greeks in the 13th century, the Scythians of Eurasia in the 9th century BC, to the American Indians of the 16th century AD, a well fed people were key to prosperity. The best societies eventually traded in large quantities for other goods from abroad, to multiply their prosperity through the addition of luxuries transported from great distances, and through forms of readily exchangeable wealth such as gold. This was so, just as widespread and pervasive dearths of food, seemingly constantly accompanied by other general penury and misery over periods of two decades or longer, were certainly a sign of an unprosperous people.

Often, physical combat and warfare are involved in deciding who will rule over and inhabit tracts of land which can be both large and small in scale. The surviving historical record shows that the American Indians were not exempt from this pervasive trait of humanity. We also see that the motive was almost always an interest in participating in the existing, or in attempting to generate new, commerce in a given region. Commerce which, as we see expressly detailed in the aptly named section (part VI, commerce uplifts the masses, page# 370) as well as throughout the entirety of this volume, uplifts the masses. Additionally, it is also plainly true that the arrival of the Europeans, and/or their attempts to overtake any Indian territory or trade, *did not arouse a new behavior of warfare in what had been previously tranquil North American Indians*. These Indians were just people, and they had combative nations along with docile nations, the same as have existed in the other regions of the globe.

The Massachusetts Bay Company, for example, was formed in England as a commercial venture -as opposed to one designed to steal territory, and to murder Indians for no reason other than because they weren't white- which would provide investors with a return on their money invested; these profits derived from trading furs with the Indians, fishing off the coast of the Atlantic, and in agricultural development and use of the land. Land for the privately funded company was granted by the king via the Council for New England, during the spring of 1627 or 1628. (161) Although this "grant" was supercilious; as the English hadn't any possession of the land, the king was arrogant in presuming that he had any place in the matter; this arrogance compounded by the fact that the crown hadn't put up any of the money -not even money from the exchequer, which in truth belongs to the citizens.

The supposedly "peaceful Indians", claimed by iniquitous purveyors of fiction to be in perpetual harmony with nature and with each other, *have an awfully high amount of* both instances of violence at first brush with newcomers, as well as of *combat history with other nations which pre-dates regular contact with the white man*; this exemplified by the pre-existing military rivalries of the various Indians, which have been recorded in this volume. There were many warlike Indians, exhibiting a strong national defense, as has been evidenced to be vital to the success of any nation. The importance of a strong national defense had been previously illustrated in 1526 when the Indians fought off a 600 person caravan, arriving by sea, headed by Lucas Vasquez de Ayllon. In so doing, these Indians were turning away the would be invaders -or immigrants (162), if one were to utilize the terminology presently being pushed forth by wokernist politicians regarding those who are currently illegally invading the USA, mostly through its border with Mexico. There was an instance recorded during 1549 in Florida, south of Tampa Bay in which missionaries there were murdered by Indians upon arrival ashore. (163)

An example of the existence of conflict between nations in the New World, prior to the permanent arrival of Europeans, occurred during 1540 in the general vicinity of what were then the northwest New Mexico and Arizona territories. Vasquez de Coronado, governor of the northwest province of New Spain, led an expedition composed of anywhere from 300-1,000 Indians who themselves, without any coercion, were heading out seeking treasure and conquest; in addition to 300 Spanish on horseback; 70 on foot; 1,000 horses; along with vast herds of sheep, cattle, and mules. This combined force reached the plains of Southern Arizona, and they were spotted by four Zuni Indian scouts. Having some advance warning of the oncoming invasion, the Zuni fought well prior to giving way to their attackers. The Zuni village was no longer their own. (164) That the Zuni would be in the practice of having advance scouts is, in and of itself, evidentiary of a pre-existing condition in which danger of invasion by attackers was ordinary. *Why would perpetually peaceful Indians know anything at all about strategizing for counter-attack, if tranquility was the only state of affairs that they had ever known?* Another episode occurred during the 1540s wherein an Indian force of "thousands of men" beset the crusading Spanish brigade, which began its journey with about 600 men. The battle was fought, and the Spanish were hurt mightily -losing all of their clothing and military equipment in the exchange. (165)

Evidence of commerce, and the desire for individual profit, serving the masses, can be found in the fact that on January 1, 1562, there was not a single white man of record on the mainland of what would later be the U.S.A. (166) A desire for trade, and for tremendous profits as middlemen merchants, brought men to the wilderness of North and Central America during the 15th and 16th centuries. As they sought passage to or from the Orient, the discovery of fishing in the later New England and Western Canada regions kept them coming back, as did rumors of treasure inland from the Gulf Coast/Florida. The French had been in and out of Newfoundland for fish and furs during the early 16th century, but none remained who could be counted by 1562. (167) Of course, the bounty of plenty which was gradually cultivated, *though hampered by redistributionism*, persists through present day, having *done more good for those who began life as the lowest members of society than any of the Indian nations ever did.*

INDIANS VS INDIANS

A smattering of instances exemplifying the various Indian nations fighting against other Indian nations will follow. All those who are of the faith that the Indians were always peace-loving, and only fought the white man upon provocation, ought to take heed as a cure for their ignorance is outlaid, so that they will be able to combat the torrent of lies which have been utilized to make fools of themselves. Others may take an interest in perusing these instances as a refresher, or may elect to skip ahead to the next section.

Historian Timothy J. Shannon relays to us that remains of the bodies from the 15th century AD: "show evidence of ritual torture, execution, and cannibalism, supporting the conclusion that the fifteenth century was a time of endemic warfare between neighboring peoples in Iroquoia." (168) "Before the arrival of the Europeans, the Iroquois traded and warred with other peoples in eastern North America.", says Shannon. (169) In 1735, a person speaking on behalf of the Iroquois at the Albany treaty council made it plain that this nation saw rival factions as either trading partners, or war nemeses: "Trade and Peace we take to be one thing." (170) During 1564, at the St. Johns River, Rene de Laudonniere docks with men. An amicable existence occurred at first blush between the newcomers and the local Indians. However, *the pre-existing condition of the separate Indian nations being engaged in a hostile diplomacy towards one another* drew the French into the fray, as they too began to take sides in the Indians' skirmish. (171)

1613: An Indian war party from Canada, with Champlain and a few other white men tagging along, made an attack upon the Iroquois fort near Lake Oneida. Having arrived at the base following a route that began with the Ottawa River and made its way through Lake Ontario, it's fair to say that the northern Indian brigade was looking for trouble with the redoubtable Iroquois. (172) In present day Ontario, French Jesuits allied with the Huron Indians during the 1630s, engaging in the fur trade. The Iroquois warred with the Huron during the 1640s. In the 1650s, the Iroquois warred against the: Petuns, Eries, and Wenros. The Mohawk Indians -of the Iroquois Confederation- instigated wars with some Indians of the St. Lawrence valley, such as the Montaignais and Algonquins, over control of the trade routes connecting Montreal to Lake Ontario. To their eastern side, the Mohawks warred with the Mahicans over primacy in trade with the Dutch at Fort Orange.

The Iroquois enslavement of their vanquished foes, after having transported said slaves from their native land to the Iroquois base, *has been said to account for as much as two thirds of their population in some villages*; and has also been estimated at 6,000 over the course of the 17th century. (173) Based upon the proportion to the population of the area at the time, that is a substantial number of kidnapping victims turned slaves. New York in 1678 was reported, by its then Governor Andros to the Lords of Trade, to have 24 settlements, a militia of 2,000 men, value of province of £150,000.

(174) In 1701 the population at Albany was estimated to be 1,000; at Montreal also 1,000. (175) The entire Iroquois population in 1700 was 5,000. (176)

Of 17th century Virginia, Thomas Jefferson gives an account of Indian tribes (see above, Indian Locations, page# 289-291) at this time -passed forward to him, obviously- being named specifically at a number of 43, individually named and cited; and those *split into three confederations*, each bearing the namesake of its most dominant tribe: The allied duo comprising the Mannahocs and the Monaccans, along with *their mutual foe* the Powhatans. Jefferson writes that the duo "...waged joint and perpetual war against the Powhatans." Jefferson mentions a "most powerful confederacy" of tribes under the leadership of the Massamowecs. This nation was said to have territory west of the mountains, ranging to the Great Lakes. Massawomecs "harassed unremittingly the Powhatan and Manahoacs." (177)

During the 1670s, the *Iroquois invaded and attempted to capture and enslave* the Susquehannocks, Foxes, and the Ottawas, among other nations of the upper Mississippi Valley and western Great Lakes. They drew the ire of the French Jesuits, who had allied with the Hurons, the former attacking the Mohawk territory of the Iroquois confederation in 1666; causing much damage and provoking an offer of peace from the Iroquois, which resulted in more commingling with the French. The French won many Indians over with their ways, and during the late 1670s a large voluntary out-migration occurred; numbering 1,000 by 1700. *Constant warfare disrupted the Iroquois economy, causing their own fragility.* The habitual warmongers now needed peace in order to have any prayer of survival. (178)

An instance illustrating that Indians had fear of other Indians occurred during January of 1680. LaSalle and his men encountered Illinois Indians at Lake Peoria, who eagerly sought protection from the ever-looming Iroquois confederation. The red men sought this protection in the form of both the acquisition of arms, along with the formation of alliance, and *were pleased to hear of LaSalle's desire to establish a permanent French presence in their area through the establishment of colonies.* The Illinois Indians also offered to express kinship by acting as tour guides on the rivers. (179)

EUROS ATTACK/TERRORIZE

To portray the immigrating, or invading, Europeans as peace-loving and meek, would of course be just as dishonest and absurd as it would be to portray the various Indian nations as such. Instances of 19th century treaty breaking in the American West seem to permeate the sermons of the priests of Victim Politics, seemingly rendering a recitation of such as unnecessary if the reader is of that cult. In the interest of fetching for all audiences, and of refraining from the vitiation of this work in the eyes of the most captious of elements via omission of the European wrongdoings, a handful of examples in which various groups of Europeans engage in terrorism, or at least in seemingly unprovoked attacks, follow.

In 1535 Jacques Cartier, having kidnapped a pair of Indians at Gaspe the preceding year, camped for the winter with his men in Quebec. 25 Frenchmen succumbed to scurvy. The Indians aided the remaining French by sharing knowledge of a medicine, perhaps saving them. Cartier kidnapped the amiable chief of the Indians, carting him to France. The chief's demise occurred shortly thereafter. (180) July 17, 1609, in Maine, Henry Hudson dropped anchor near Penobscot Bay. On July 25th, Hudson's men stole one of the two boats they had spotted in the possession of some local Indians. Hudson's men came later with a dozen armed men to go ashore and *drive the Indians from their dwellings, so that the English could ransack their goods unperturbed.* (181) During the first quarter of 17th century, Dr. John Pott killed Indians by means of deliberate poisoning. (182)

1676, Maryland: During the course of battle, the Susquehanna Indians were cornered in an abandoned fort by the colonists. 5 chiefs descended upon the fort, seeking negotiation on behalf of the troubled Indians. These 5 were executed by the colonists. The colonists impeached the responsible officer. The act set off an intense Indian war. Indians murdered an overseer at Nathaniel Bacon's plantation. Tepid response from the Virginia Governor led to *Bacon's rebellion.* (183)

In Virginia a series of poor harvests, beginning 1670, combined with shortages experienced in the New England colonies due to King Philip's War, resulted in a drastic increase in the scarcity of food, and by extension, other material goods and cash. This exacerbated the comparatively penurious material condition of the newcomers to the backwards country. An Indian attack upon the plantation of Nathaniel Bacon, Jr., occurring during 1676, in which an overseer was killed, sparked this powder keg of niggardly people living under arbitrary rulers; revolution and independence were in the air. Bacon led a mob of like-minded Virginians, who torched Jamestown. Bacon died of natural causes, and the rebellion was quashed shortly thereafter; Bacon's government was removed and his conspirators were captured, killed, and relieved of their property. (184)

INDIANS ATTACK/TERRORIZE/ENSLAVE

"The standards of those days were not the standards of our day, and the standards of three hundred years hence will doubtless be unlike those of our time." -Edward Channing, 1907, *speaking of religion, and Christianity specifically. (185)*

The supposedly "peaceful Indians" were purported to have a rather ornery and violent temperament in the 1540s by Luis de Moscoso. Having assumed leadership of the remaining forces originally headed by De Soto, he expressed his desire to see himself in a place where he might sleep his full sleep rather than govern a country like Florida; the warlike Indians driving these Spaniards westward. (186)

Some examples of *attitudes towards uninvited immigrants -or invaders- exhibited by those other than the citizens of the United States of America* can be found in the behavior of some American Indians during the early 17th century. In 1603 the English sea voyager, Bartholemew Gilbert, was murdered by Indians at an unknown point located between Chesapeake and Sandy Hook. (187) During May of 1607 the

Englishmen of the first Virginia Company arrived at Chesapeake Bay, having first departed England in December 1606. *On the first day of their arrival, local Indians assaulted the English* immigrants/invaders. The Indians were said to be "creeping on all fours from the hills, like bears, with their bows in their mouths." The attack wounded two English, while the aggressors escaped unscathed. (188) *Such realities conflict directly with* both the assertions that American Indians were peaceful and welcoming to outsiders, and **the claims that the 21st century USA is uniquely opposed to unwanted intruders**.

Edward Channing on the state of affairs in Virginia during 1607: "Indians, intent on killing, behind every convenient bush and tree." (189) The situation wasn't much different up north during 1610, as the French Canadians and the Huron Indians, took up combat against the *perpetually ornery Iroquois*. Hurons tortured Iroquois prisoners, and cannibalized one of those slain during battle. On the way back to Huron headquarters they selected one of the captives being transported, rebuked him for the poor treatment of Huron captives in Iroquois hands, and tortured the prisoner -ignoring the protests of the French. The Huron warriors made efforts to emphasize their trophies by attaching scalps from the heads of their enemies to the ends of long wooden sticks. *The Huron ladies went wild, adorning themselves with the scalps around their own necks.* It is also worth noting that Champlain lived in an area surrounded by these same Indians without incident. (190)

One *Indian massacre of the English* took place during a 12 month period 1622-23 during which 347 English were killed by Indian attackers. This amounted to approximately *40% of the Virginia immigrants at the time.* (191) A man named Bartram, who was a colonist from Virginia, visiting Onondaga in 1743 described the Iroquois as existing in an "uninterrupted state of war" with Indians and Europeans alike; said them to be "the most warlike people in N. America"; purported that they inspired fear and posed a formidable deterrent to people "1000 miles distant." (192) This, in a time before radio and photographs.

The warmongering culture of some Indian nations, the voluntary defections which would ultimately end the existence of many nations, as well as their customary place as slavers, are all evidenced during the 17th century "Beaver Wars" involving the nations of the Iroquois Confederation in New York. Warfare was a part of their community vibe, or culture. Much like the Eurasian "Nomad Rulers", the Royal Scythians', warriors had been in their day, Iroquois warriors were respected in the community and held in higher esteem than others -even during peaceful times. The families *encouraged their sons to go to war*, seeing it as a rite of passage, *expressly for the intended goal of returning with P.O.W.s to enslave* and use to replace those of their number "ravaged by disease, internal strife, and out-migration." After being sent by family matrons, mourning the loss of a loved one, in order to replenish their numbers, the manhunters were brutal to their prey -scalping those P.O.W.s who had been too badly wounded to keep pace during the trek from the battlefield to the Iroquois home base. Other captives were frequently tormented en route; the removal of a thumb, or burning off of fingertips, were among the routine methods employed by the Iroquois.

Upon arrival at their new "home", the entire village stripped them naked, then forced them to take a blow from each of the Iroquois -the latter having formed two parallel columns. The freshly captured slaves were divvied out to the respective families while being forced to hold hot coals and be poked with firebrands. Women and children were integrated into the community, but men were tied to a stake and tortured to death for hours -amputation of limbs, burning of the feet, and the like. Then, the man's corpse was cooked and eaten by his tormentors. (193)

Another massacre at the hands of Indians occurred during the Mid-17th century. French Jesuits, intent on spreading the word of Christ to all of the North American Indians, were stoutly resisted by the mighty Iroquois. Owing to a distaste of the "softening" effects of the teachings, the Indians brought forth a persistent affront as they made war upon the French Jesuits, their converted Indians, and the missionaries. The Iroquois drove the Huron from their home near the Great Lakes, chasing and continuing to slaughter their prey all the way to the Island of Orleans, near Quebec.

The Huron were killed by the Iroquois wherever they were captured -including the streets adjacent to the seat of the government of New France. The blood thirsty Iroquois took to torturing and killing, including burning alive, all of the white men they could get their hands on once the supply of Huron Indians grew slight. By 1660 there were less than 3,000 whites altogether, between Acadia and New France. (194)

Within the regions inhabited by the nations of the Iroquois Confederation, interwoven into the multitude of testimony on the part of missionaries and colonial officials alike, were **complaints of Indians making war for sport**. The Europeans derided what this author might describe as a "war for war's sake" culture of the Indians, as they felt that it inhibited the Indians and prevented them from pursuing more useful things -such as planning for self sufficient survival and growth; growth which would aid in their future prosperity and weal. This may likely account for a large segment of the credit -or blame- for the extinction/demise of these Indians. (195) Jefferson thought so (see page# 338). (see page# 337 for more on Indian self-destruction)

The Indians as slavers are evidenced again during the 1680s, when Frenchman Louis-Thomas Chubert de Joncaire was captured by Seneca Indians. The prisoner was sentenced to torture and death, for committing no offense other than having been taken captive by the Senecas. Prior to their carrying out his sentence, the French captive attacked his oppressors -breaking one of their noses, and gaining their respect, in so doing. They enslaved him among their number and forced him to assimilate. Joncaire later became a diplomat between various nations. (196) In a separate incident during the year 1680 a group of Frenchmen, associated with LaSalle's travels on the Mississippi River, were briefly held captive by Sioux Indians. (197)

One example of the results of Indian terrorism can be found during the late 1780s. 10 miles outside of Nashville, TN, the widow of John Donelson -whose husband had been driven from at least two areas by Indian attackers, and may have been killed by Indians- would take on boarders even though she was not in need of the income, or the assistance from their labor in farming. She was selective in her choices, with an eye on good defenders against Indian attacks. One such boarder was future president Andrew Jackson. (198)

Aggressive Indians were out West, too, during the 1820s. June 1824, Near Devil's Gate, Jim Clyman was captured by Indians after leaving his impromptu camp that he'd lived in for eleven days; having been surrounded by the Indians. Having captured Clyman during his attempted escape, they brought their prisoner to their home camp, intending to extinguish his existence, but a chief intervened -choosing to turn Clyman loose on the restoration of his firearm. (199)

INDIANS EXTORT EUROS

The apparition constructed by those unscrupulous beings selling fiction cloaked in the label of non-fiction, portraying a peace-loving and righteous people who were cheated and murdered out of existence by the white man, is dispelled quite readily by the mass of evidence depicting their time as extortionists; *some nations eventually became professional extortionists, leaving themselves without any other means of support.* A listing of a few examples follows.

Indian terrorism was utilized as a mechanism for extracting loot from those nearby during the first quarter of the 17th century. In order to give the English any prayer of cultivating their crops -in particular, tobacco- it was necessary to procure assurance of safety from vandalism at the hands of the nearby Indians; who relentlessly attacked those nearby no matter their appearance, in their fight against nature for survival. The English were able to use their superiority in battles with the Indians as deterrence. A price of 2.5 bushels of corn per Indian was negotiated, and an 8 year period of peace was inaugurated. (200) In the 2nd quarter of the 17th century, we see a Mohawk chief demand bribes from outsiders in exchange for civility. 1634-35 the Dutchman Harmen Meyndertsz van den Bogaert was cursed out by the

Indian chief for arriving without any gifts, while the same chief lauded the French for their "generous gifts". (201)

1738: William Johnson, of Anglo-Irish descent, settles in the Mohawk Valley. Thereafter, Johnson had thriving real estate and merchandising interests. Johnson became the benefactor of the Mohawk Indians, and they his loyal followers -this is reminiscent of the comitatus of Ancient Eurasia, a fighting force flocking to a provider. By 1746, Johnson is leader of the Canajoharie Mohawks, heading their representatives at an Albany treaty conference; even donning the garb of an Indian war chief. Albany Governor Clinton enlists Johnson's services as colonel and commissary for all Iroquois warriors who sided with the British. Johnson lavished the Iroquois to the tune of £3,500 per year during King George's War. To provide a sense of proportion, typical treaty conference pay from New York was £400; a year's worth of routine bribe money from the Albany commissioners amounted to £170. While other Iroquois nations observed neutrality, *war hungry Mohawks mounted an attack* on the French; expecting allied forces to bolster their efforts, it soon became clear that the promised *New York troops were not forthcoming, as was their habit*. As a result, the Mohawks tell the English goodbye forever: "You are not to expect to hear from me any more, and Brother we desire to hear no more from you." (202) *The Mohawks had sold their loyalty to a higher bidder, anyhow.* William Johnson, their benefactor, made gifts valued in the thousands of pounds. (203)

During the 1740s, the Mohawks, of the Iroquois Confederation, use King George's War as a *chance to increase their take from the English*, by exploiting the latter's vulnerability. Trade with the French from Montreal to Albany, as well as vice versa, was quite lucrative for the English, and the Iroquois occupied much territory in between. The English at Albany needed the Mohawks big time, and the Indians knew it. *These Indians openly shopped their allegiance* to other interested parties, namely: Philadelphia, Montreal, and Boston. It was during said performances, illustrating their apostasy -intended to inspire as much uncertainty as possible regarding Mohawk amity with the English at Albany, and *thereby extracting the highest price for the loyalty of these Indians*- that Mohawk spokesman Hendrick stated "Albany people...

have Cheated us out of our Land, Bribed our Chiefs to sign Deeds for them. They treated us as Slaves... We could see Albany burnt to the Ground..." (204) *The double dealing Iroquois* were quite shameless in their pursuit of the highest price attainable when it came to international diplomacy.

1750 Onondaga: Iroquois at a Treaty conference complain to the Euros about the dealings of the latter with the Ohio Indians; *complained that the Iroquois were receiving less of the Euros' allotment of Indian bribe money*. The Ohio, asserted the Iroquois, were cutting in on their extortion racket. (205) In 1753 a solicitation of bribes from the Euros, masquerading as pious dignity, occurred on the part of the Oneidas in Carlisle, Pennsylvania. At a treaty conference, *the Oneida refused to begin without the customary opening bribe* which was demanded of the Euros in exchange for the so-called "friendship" of the Oneida Indians. The Euros turned up ahead of the goods intended for said purpose, and offered the Oneida a list of the forthcoming cargo. This measure, combined with *many decades of prior success in extorting booty from the Europeans*, failed to prove sufficient assurance to the red men, as the European attempt to carry forth with business was rebuffed. (206) *No clearer example of pay to play, in practice, can be said to exist*. The basis of their "kinship" was purely remunerative.

A pair of meetings were held: one in Lancaster, PA, 1744, for those selling land in Maryland; and another in Albany, NY, 1754, for those selling land in the Susquehanna Valley to the Penn family. During each of these Treaty conferences, the *Indians demanded* of the Europeans *bribes, in addition to the customary bribes,* which accompanied the opening of any Treaty talk. This flagrant extortion occurred even during unofficial meetings which took place between official Treaty sessions, during which speeches were conducted formally while the other party sat silently. *These costs*, along with bribes at the opening of the Treaty talks, of course *increased the total compensation package paid for the land*. (207) For such Indians *to claim that no payment was received in exchange for the lands*, or for any others to assert such a claim, *is an unmitigated effrontery* and is incredibly disrespectful to their audience. Much like the "pay your fair share" crowd of communists alluded to elsewhere in this book (page# 80-81, 271), who seek an unspecified balance, which leaves the seekers eminently permitted to keep on taking, the Iroquois Indians were extortionists who were never satisfied with their payments. Europeans considered a sale completed after negotiation and payment in full. The Iroquois, on the other hand, considered land sold to Europeans as an opportunity for perpetual extortion; the bill was never paid in full, they kept coming back for more. (208)

A bribe to the Iroquois by the USA, persuading these red men to stay out of the war with the Ohio Indians in the West, called the Ohio War, is illuminative. 1794 in Canandaigua, NY, a Treaty read that $10,000 in riches was be spent to lavish gifts/bribes upon 1,600 Iroquois -mostly Senecas. A promise to increase the amount exacted annually from the USA, as a matter of routine bribery/extortion, from its present level of $1,500 to a robust $4,500, was also made. The following year, *the war ended with the Treaty of Greenville; thus stripping the Iroquois of their vitality in the conflict*, and drastically reducing their leverage in extorting the USA. Unsurprisingly, the booty forthcoming was promptly reduced. (209)

During the fall of 1846, West of Elko, near the south fork of the Humboldt, a party of American travelers crossed paths with some Digger Indians. A few Diggers struck the emigrants as nice people and were invited to stay with the whites. By morning the Diggers had fled -stealing 2 ox, 1 horse, and landing arrows in several of the oxen not stolen. (210) That same fall, in the Southwest, Digger Indians terrorize a group of traveling Americans: stealing the horses of Mary Graves on the first night of their encounter; stealing 18 ox and 1 cow from the group on the second night; shot some remaining oxen, non-lethally, the following night; and on the fourth consecutive evening of terror shot 21 oxen, incapacitating them all. (211)

RACIALLY MIXED COMBAT ALLIANCES

Of course, the various Europeans in the New World would combat the various Indian nations in North America. *The prevarication asserting that the white bullies came and plundered the red pacifists* is readily refuted by the ample instances of Indian attacks here, in addition to the preceding Indians vs. Indians section. Notice that the absurdly false image of Europeans fighting Indians, a rivalry and a hatred predicated solely upon skin color, *is quite readily disproven by a banal recitation of the historical record* which is rittled with instances of mixed alliances, a few excerpts of which follow here.

Indians attack Euros: Summer 1585, Cardinas: English travelers were desperately short of food. The local Indians, once alerted to the plight of the English, at once schemed to capitalize upon the situation. *The Indians stole from the English immediately, and were hatching plans for a wholesale slaughter.* English leader Ralph Lane was able to buy some time by killing off a handful of the savages, stalling long enough to escape 8 days hence when Sir Francis Drake arrived. Drake, having just eradicated a Spanish village in St. Augustine, and relieved them of a sizable amount of coin -a sum several times greater than most men labored an entire year for, or a decade- brought Lane and the other destitute English back to the mother country. (212)

Indians war against Indians, ally with Euros: 1610: Southern Ontario/Northern New York: The League of the Iroquois, then "the strongest and most formidable organization in North America", according to Edward Channing (213), were attacked by a coalition formed of the Indians living on the northern bank of the St. Lawrence river -*who were pre-existing enemies of the Iroquois*, no doubt eager for any alliance that would have them- and the French party of Samuel de Champlain. The Iroquois were defeated in this skirmish -small scale though it was, costing a mere 3 Indian lives.

To borrow a few phrases from the Race Industry, this act of aggression by the French colonists toward their *Red Supremacist, establishment oppressors, begat a series of systematic exclusion of the French* from a significant portion of the continent for some time. This, accompanied by a willful choice on the part of the Iroquois to have amicable relations with the English colonists, gave England a substantial advantage in gaining access to the land in that region. *The Iroquois were known to apprehend, murder, or torture, every frenchman that crossed their path thereafter* -including missionaries. (214)

Indians attack Euros: 1607 Virginia: Indian ruler Powhatan intercepted an English exploratory party. The English, quite hospitably, treated the Indian leader to beer, brandy, and wine. Concurrently, the Indians attacked the English back at their camp, wounding several Englishmen. (215)

Indians attack Euros: 1620: *Inhospitality towards immigrants on the part of the red men* was on full display, as those on the Mayflower ship had to fend off the attacks of the Indians -unprovoked- as they attempted to land along the inner shore of Cape Cod. (216)

Indians attack Euros: 1630s Massachusetts Bay Company: Voting had to be done by papers and submitted by proxy, as a matter of necessity for those living on the outskirts of the settlement or bordering Indian territory, as leaving to vote in person while leaving one's family and property undefended against Indian attacks was deemed a risk too imprudent to be taken. (217)

Indians attack Euros: 1630s: Narragansett Indians plotted to kill the people of Massachusetts; colluding with Samuel Gorton, who had been ejected by the authorities of the Massachusetts government. Gorton was later captured by the Massachusetts leaders; being deported to England, shortly thereafter. (218)

Foreign aid: The colonies of this era acted independently of one another in combat, just as the Indian nations acted independently of one another. Massachusetts was independent of Virgina, Pennsylvania independent of Georgia, and so forth. Sometimes colonies would ally together during times of combat, just as Indian nations as well as other nations around the globe have, sending aid to one another; such as during the Pequot War, as well as during the Narragansett War. (219)

Indians ally with Euros vs other Indians: First half 17th century: *Connecticut River Indians solicited English to inhabit some land within their territory*, hoping for an ally to defend against the vicious attacks of the powerful attacking Indians. The Mohegan and Narragansett tribes were the powerful tribes, and they performed the attacks upon whomever were their enemies or competitors; *particularly if they were weak or defenseless*. Many were taxed by these large Indian nations. The Narragansett teamed with the colonists of both Connecticut and of Massachusetts, to vanquish the Pequot nation of Indians. (220)

Indians vs Indians vs Euros: 1642, Manhattan: the *River Indians*, having been driven to Corlaer's Hook and Pavonia -opposite Manhattan- *in flight from the attacking Iroquois* Indians. *The Dutch*, owners of Manhattan land, *set upon these refugees in the dead of night and slaughtered 110 River Indians*. The River Indians found aid on the part of another tribe, and this group of red men subsequently attacked the Dutch, making great headway and backing the Dutch into a corner at Fort Amsterdam. In 1643, the desperate Dutchmen reached out to some hired-men to fight on their behalf. Captain John Underhill -of Pequot War renown- along with 150 fighting men, marched through the perilous winter terrain and positioned themselves to attack the Indians who were defeating the Dutchmen. Under the cover of darkness, Underhill and company invaded the Indian settlement and burned it to the ground. The reports are that 8 Indians fled, while 500 were burned or shot during the attack. *This military victory* on Strickland's Plains showed enough force to *subdue several Indian nations into a peace* with the Dutch, though the survivors of the defeated nation still bore a grudge. (221)

Indians attack Euros: 1643-44, Manhattan: Colonists erect a fence near today's Wall Street. Indians would trespass and murder Euros living in their huts, inhabiting the area adjacent to Fort Amsterdam. (222)

Indians attack Euros: 1644: Opechancanough brings forth another massacre of the English. The English captured the chief of the James River Indians during his raid upon them, and Opechancanough was shot dead while being held captive. (223)

Euros join Indians vs Euros: 1654, Manhattan: English and Dutch fight over commercial access to the New York trade -and conversely with Dutch access to outer colonial trade. The powers that be in England greenlit the attack upon the Dutch, however only forces from Newport undertook the cause; capturing Fort Good Hope. The other colonial bodies stalled in their decision to attack, with Massachusetts Bay chief among the procrastinators. The Netherlander, Peter Stuyvesant, openly negotiated with various local Indian nations, placing an emphasis upon quashing the English. Just as the English -excepting the Massachusetts Bay group- agreed to march on Manhattan, a peace was struck between the Netherlands and England. (224)

Indians defeat Euros: 1684, Iroquois territory (New York region): Count le Febvre de La Barre, chief among administrators of New France, sought revenge against the Iroquois, who had repeatedly attacked the French; this even after having been advised by Dongan of NY that the Iroquois were now under the protection of the English crown. The French were sent back to Montreal in disgrace, after having been made to treaty with the Senecas, on the terms of the latter. (225)

Indians and Euros vs Euros: 1688: Roman Catholic Indians in Canada join the French in attacking the English at various settlements, including Northfield in the Connecticut Valley on August 16, 1688. In November of that same year, Andros of the English anticipated Indian trouble on word that a French Baron was cross with the governor of NY colony, and with the knowledge that the French Canadians often hired

Indians to do their fighting -and so the English marched a procession on to the Penobscot River as a show of force to pre-emptively quell any Indian thoughts of attack. This was done on the part of Andros by plucking colonists from their homes against their will, subjecting them to Roman Catholic commanders. This act on the part of the governor helped to spark an uprising of popular distaste. (226)

Indians attack Euros: June 27, 1689: French Indians attacked a settlement at Coheco Valley, in New Hampshire; extracting several English as prisoners, and killing a few others. On the night of August fourth, 1,500 Iroquois attacked La Chine village in Montreal. 1,000 Canadians were slain, both French and Indian Canadians; *women and children were not spared by the Iroquois*. (227) The 25th of that month saw 1,500 Iroquois invade the La Chine portion of the Isle of Montreal. The Iroquois torched the village while its inhabitants slept, slaughtering the 200 who dared to resist being burnt alive in their homes. Having finished with this village, the Iroquois continued their trek towards the city of Montreal, collecting prisoners along the way. The Iroquois had run of Montreal until mid-October, having laid waste to all French settlements from Three Rivers to Mackinaw. (228)

Indians seek revenge on Euros: June 26, 1689: At Coheco -present day New Hampshire- the Penacook Indians sought to avenge the ambush of 350 unsuspecting Indians 13 years prior, an ambush which had *resulted in the sale of these captured men into foreign slavery at Boston*. In 1689 a pair of young squaws knocked upon the door of magistrate Richard Waldron, then in his eighties. Waldron invited the young Indians to sleep at his place for the night. While the magistrate slumbered, the squaw unhinged the gates fortifying the town, allowing their confederates entry into, and occupation of, the town. Waldron awoke before he could be murdered in his sleep, grabbed his sword, and prepared for defense. To no avail were his efforts, as *the red men made sport of torturing the aged man*. These particular Indians had honest debts with Waldron, which they referenced while slicing the magistrate's upper torso "Thus I cross out my account!". 23 in all were killed during the raid, while many homes were torched. (229)

Indians and Euros vs Euros: February 9, 1690: A band of 210 men -96 Indians, nearly half- from New France set about attacking the English in the village of Schenectady. Finding an unmanned, open gate, with two snowmen erected to replicate guards, this group took the unsuspecting villagers by surprise. 60 were slain, while 27 were taken captive by the Indians. The attack shook Albany into submission to the new colonial government of William and Mary, as they ascended to power during the Protestant Revolution. (230)

Indians extinguish Indians/Indians ally with Euros vs. Euros: 1685-1700, Iroquois/French/English: Iroquois wars on all fronts caused the French, to their north, to attack for diplomatic reasons -these stemming from the Iroquois warring with so many Indian nations. The Catholic Iroquois, *who had voluntarily out-migrated* to join the French, participated in the French raid on their former home in 1687. In 1690 Canadian Iroquois, with the French, attacked the Dutch at Schenectady. In 1693 the Canadian Iroquois joined the French in torching three towns in the Mohawk region of the Iroquois confederation, burning their food; *300 men surrendered* to them and returned with their captors, *many willingly, to join them and begin a new life*. During 1696 the French, and the Canadian Iroquois, join forces once more to eradicate the Oneidas and Onondagas. By 1700, the Iroquois numbered a mere 5,000. (231)

Euros and Indians vs Indians/Indian savagery: 1696: The French, along with Chippewas, Powtawatomies, and Ottawas, *came down to vanquish the Iroquois confederation*. Near Oswego, the invaders came to an Onondaga Indian village. The Onondagas bluffed their would-be combatants by means of an old Indian custom of hanging reeds; designed to signify that over 1,000 men awaited their invasion, ready to fight. The aggressors carried on undeterred, only to find an abandoned village set ablaze by the former residents. One old man was tortured, taunting his tormentors with his contentment during the process, refusing to yield the horrors and pained expressions that the perpetrators sought. (232)

Indians ally with Euros vs other Indians: 1745: French allied Indians sack Saratoga -then a small settlement of people. (233)

Indians with Euros vs Euros: 1753+1754: Iroquois leaders, Scanonady and Tanaghrisson, solicit the English for alliance against the French. Carlisle, PA, along with Winchester, VA, were unwilling to accept this offer. Weiser, and others in Pennsylvania, noted that the Senecas had formed a compact with them on an alliance of abstinence in Iroquois affairs. (234)

Indians with Euros vs Euros: French and Indian Wars, a.k.a. Seven Years War: 1757: 1,500 Indians join the French in attacks upon the English at Lake George and points north. (235)

Indians vs Indians and Euros: For a few years, beginning 1777, Mohawk Indians in the NY area would ambush the towns of other Indians, as well as of non-Indians. In so doing, they would burn all the homes, torch the cornfields, kill livestock, and occasionally loot the buildings prior to committing the inevitable arson. In October 1778, at Oquaga, NY, the patriots of the American Revolutionary War, in league with the Tuscarora and the Oneida red men, retaliated with an attack thereupon. These rebels, while setting fire to the cornfield of the locals, noticed a few children seeking cover. These children were murdered by the patriot faction; skewered with bayonets and spun around like pinwheels. While the Indians would generally abstain from killing or taking captive any Iroquois whose town was being raided, torched, and looted, they took an inverse policy towards Euros during the invasions. (236)

Indians and British vs Indians and Patriots: August 1777 Oriska, NY: Patriots raid the camp of those Iroquois who joined ranks against them, depriving the Indians of the loot they had secured from the British as payola for their loyalty. This raid having occurred during the battle, these Seneca Indians, of the Iroquois Confederation, were quite dismayed when they returned; doing so after deserting the British for the crime of actually having the Senecas participate in the battle, as opposed to merely extorting booty and remaining spectators. (237) Whether this turnabout by the Seneca Indians was due to their atrophy into professional extorters who had given up productive behavior, and their refusal to actually do the job which they had been hired and paid to execute; or it was a lingering revenge for previous English failure to provide troops to the Iroquois during battle, despite talk of having an alliance; is not clear.

Indians and Euros vs Euros: 1778, NY: Seneca Indians, with their chief, Cornplanter, at the helm, joined forces with the British as they dually attacked a settlement south of the Mohawk River, known as Cherry Valley. Seventy of the Cherry Valley inhabitants, patriots and loyalists alike, were taken prisoner. The British were appalled by the indiscriminate ferocity of the Senecas, as they slaughtered women and children as though they were equal to men as prey. (238)

Euros attack Indians: 1779, NY and PA regions: George Washington orders a decisive attack upon the Senecas and the Cayugas. The Patriots utilized three different brigades, each marching on these Indians from different sides. The Senecas and Cayugas took to their customary strategy of deserting their towns prior to the arrival of an oncoming attack. The patriots torched the more than 40 Indian towns; homes, crops, livestock, and all. This left the deserters homeless, and without provisions for the coming winter, which was said to be uncharacteristically brutal. *All told, the Iroquois population had decreased by one third by the episode's end; between expatriation to either the patriots or the British, and the fatalities of those who stayed on with the foundering Indians.* (239)

Indians attack Euros: March 8, 1780: A train of passenger boats, carrying many women and children, was attacked by Indians. While journeying westward from Virginia, an entire 28 person civilian crew intermittently experienced the fates of being taken captive, or killed, by Indians. When one of the convoy had their canoe capsize, the surrounding Indians rained arrows upon the travelers as they attempted to recover their property. (240)

Indians and Euros vs Euros: 1789, Nashville, TN: Creek Indians, in league with and under the direction of the Spanish in Louisiana, routinely terrorized residents and travelers alike. Attacks began in January and continued throughout the year -women and children were not spared. During 1789, the Creeks averaged 1 murder per 10 days in Nashville. September 1789, *the Spanish offered "protection" from the very Indian attacks that they had been ordering*, along with plots of land, to the Cumberland Mountain inhabitants. This was all arranged in an attempt to curry favor with, and draw them in from, the prostrated Atlantic Confederacy. (241)

Indians vs Euros vs USA: Whites, reds, and half-breeds: 1810 Tecumseh visits Red Eagle -born Alexander McGillivray- a ⅞ white man, selling his dream of a confederacy spanning all the territory from the Gulf of Mexico to the Great Lakes. This confederation's ambition would be to unite against the invaders who were defeating them. Having not forgotten the war two decades prior, Americans were furious that the British continually interfered with their foreign commerce, which spawned a battle for control of land and of the waterways during the years-long conflict known as the War of 1812. This conflict offered an opening to any enemies of the USA. During October of 1811, Tecumseh returned to the Creek Indians. Smelling an Indian attack, the settlers fled to fortified dwellings, the largest of which was owned by Samuel Mims, a Creek half-breed, who chose the European culture. On August 30, 1813, Red Eagle leads his army on an invasion of Mims' estate; slaughters the residents. Red Eagle had been first introduced to the culture of the Europeans, instead opting for the culture of the wigwam. (242)

Andrew Jackson, of the USA, authors a military campaign aimed at strengthening the nation. Objective 1: clear a path from the Gulf of Mexico, unimpeded by foreigners. Objective 2: invade Florida, take Pensacola; oust the Spanish allies of Britain, Creek Indians, and disruptors of the Cumberland region from Louisiana. Jackson hired woodsmen, whites and half-breeds, to act as spies upon his foes. November 3, 1813, John Coffee and an army of 1,000 troops descended upon the village of Tallushatchee -200 people- 13 miles from fort Strother, and Jackson. No warrior escaped the village, 84 women and children were taken captive. Coffee's brigade suffered 5 fatalities, with 41 wounded. Jackson saves a 3 year old Indian orphan, sending him to Huntsville on Jackson's dime. Talladega, a Creek Indian town, declares allegiance to Jackson. Weatherford - the opposing general- sent 1,000 braves to Talladega; the Talledaga people solicited Jackson for help. November 9th of 1813, Jackson's men face Weatherford again: 300 dead Indians, 15 whites. (243)

EUROS VS EUROS

Of course it wasn't always a mere matter of the old "Cowboys and Indians" game that children have played in the United States for centuries. Undoubtedly, Europeans fought with each other in the New World, just as they had in the Old World; and just as the American Indian nations had fought amongst each other. In 1565 Spanish forces, with Pedro Menedez de Aviles at the helm, attack the French forces captained by Laudonniere. The French are wiped out with few exceptions beyond women and children. (244)

1585, Porto Rico: English attempt to erect a structure; Spanish observe this and respond by refusing to sell the English settlers necessary supplies; English counter by setting the entire surrounding wooded area ablaze, as they vacated the premises. (245)

1588: England defeats the Spanish Armada, and take the reins as superpower of the seas. North America and the resulting trade, proved far more beneficial to the English henceforth. (246)

1613: Samuel Argall, up to the present New England region on a fishing cruise away from his Virginia home, attacks an attempted settlement led by four French Jesuit priests. Argall was able to capture a few of the colonists as they fled en masse, bringing the hostages back with him to Virginia. Argall returns in mere months and torches the village, as the inhabitants once again fled in fright. (247)

Some English individuals heard word of the French fur trade, and settlement in Newfoundland/Quebec. In 1629, the English assail the French, taking the St. Lawrence River to the trading post at Tadoussac, intercepting ships carrying supplies to the New World colonists in the exchange, and devastating the French traders who were entirely dependent upon supplies from the motherland. *The central planning* -assignment and revocation of monopoly "rights" to individuals at a moment's notice- *disincentivised the people from caring for the soil and making long term investment in the land* and in the settlement thereupon. This is similar to the communal land sharing noted in chapter [fallacy of lamp, or commerce uplifts? Page #] which held down production and advancement of everybody, in the name of "equality" or "fairness". The French are starved over the winter, and surrender the land to the returning English ships in 1629. England promptly returned the territory to France in exchange for $250,000 [1908 US dollar value]. (248)

Dutch and English clash over trading rights and control of land. Virginians -English- forbade the New Amsterdam faction -Dutch- from expanding into the Delaware territory. The English in Connecticut made it clear that they held the rights to trade on the Hudson River, as it passed through the Connecticut Valley. The Dutch wanted this trade, and so intercepted an English trading ship, seized its cargo of furs, and provided a chaperone for the ship's departure from the river. A separate instance occurred on the Connecticut River in 1633. Pilgrims sailed past an armed Dutch trading post. The Dutch threatened to fire on the English ship if it did not reverse course, but their threats proved empty. The English overtook all surrounding territory of Fort Good Hope and Manhattan Island. (249)

1683, Carolina: A band of Scotsmen erect a settlement near Port Royal, called Stewarts Town. Spanish attack the town, capturing and torturing those that they did not kill during the attack. (250)

INDIANS STEALING LAND/BREAKING TREATIES

The land transferred from the hands of the various American Indians, into the hands of various European entities and eventually the United States of America, was all either purchased outright, or won as the spoils of war. *This land changed hands amongst various Indians nations as spoils of war for centuries*, and this includes the several centuries of recorded European interactions with these nations. In addition to wresting territory through violent means, *many American Indian nations knowingly broke treaties; some even stole land from other Indian tribes* by acting as an illegitimate intermediary, selling the land of rival tribes to European interests, and pocketing the loot for themselves. The popular charges that the white man swindled the red man, "stealing his land", will be rejoindered by many instances of the red men behaving dishonestly, as *people are just people no matter how different their appearance may be*. Included also, will be instances of Europeans breaking treaties, both with red men as well as with white men, to illustrate how generic the entire matter is. Only captious parties, seeking to isolate a few examples of Americans, after having defeated the remaining Indian nations after centuries of warfare -which could very well have yielded anterior outcomes- during the 19th century, can possibly arrive at the conclusion that the white man has iniquitously deprived the honest red man of his lands.

European dishonesty towards Indians: Of course, the varied European groups who encountered the Indians were not free of sin, themselves. No group has a monopoly on dishonesty, and every nation has displayed some amount of it whether it be through policy, or in practice. Coronado and his band commandeered the city of Tiguex (Tiguesh) during the 1540s. These Spaniards literally took the clothes off of the backs of the entirety of the Indians residing in the city. After a miscommunication among Coronado's confederates, the Tiguex residents who had given up fighting based upon the promise that they may live, were ordered burned alive, with 200 stakes called for. Long before 200 could be torched, the captives resumed their fight and a lengthy battle ensued. (251)

Euro dishonesty towards Euros: Purveyors of the myth of "The White Supremacists Club" will again have some explaining to do, when confronted with the fact that during the 1560s the Spanish and the French engaged in ruthless battles over land in North and Central America. The Spanish, having uncovered the reality that the myth of the Seven Cities -rumored to possess endless wealth, and to be ripe for the taking for anyone who could locate these cities- was a hoax, withheld their intelligence on the matter when interacting with the French. The French continued to engage in a snipe hunt of sorts, as their European counterparts from Spain gleefully went about their own purposes while the French were distracted. Jean Ribault of Dieppe led one such expedition in 1562. On the banks of the St. Johns river, *the Indians received Ribaut's party well and with good favor, in stark contrast to the chicanery of the Spanish towards Ribaut.* (252)

English purchase land from Indians: 1620s, Virginia: Colonist William Claiborne -sometimes Cleburn- purchased land on Kent Island, located in the Chesapeake, from the Indian tribe that happened to presently own it. Claiborne was a fur trader and the land was valuable to him so that he might establish a post there and enjoy exclusive rights to hunt the area, without conflict from the neighboring Indians. (253)

Dutch buy land from Indians: Manhattan Island, 1620s: Peter Minuit struck a bargain with the local Indians for the title to Manhattan, trading them assorted goods said to be in the value of $24. (254)

Land not stolen: 1621: Pilgrims found abandoned Indian cornfields, purchased corn seed from the Indians, who offered sound advice to the immigrants regarding planting and cultivation. (255) This would be perhaps the least likely case in which "theft" could be applied as an honest label.

English purchase land from Indians: 1629, Massachusetts Bay Company: *The colonists set about unearthing every Indian claim to the land which had been granted them* -the colonists- from the crown. Deeds still exist which serve as evidence of a purchase from the Indian nations Webcomet and the Squaw Sachem, among others. The only land gotten by these colonists through use of force is thought to have been gotten from the Pequot nation. *The colonists sought to integrate the Indians into their ranks and erected school houses for them, including one known to be in connection with Harvard college.* Clergymen served as missionaries who, with some success, sought to convert the red man to their ways and to include them in their church. The Indians became alcoholic after their integration with the whites, so the whites passed laws forbidding the sale or barter of liquor to any Indian. (256) *The Massachusetts Bay Company took great pain to compensate the Indians for the land* upon which the colonists settled. (257)

Whites "steal land" from whites: 1630s: William Claiborne, who had purchased land from the Indians on Kent Island to carry on his fur trading business, had also in 1631 been issued legal paperwork from the king permitting himself to trade in furs along the coast of the Chesapeake. Claiborne was secretary of Virginia and a member of the Virginia council. When Lord Baltimore was issued the Maryland charter and his colonists arrived, Claiborne's legal rights to the land and the fur trade were nullified -in direct violation of not only the king, but also a Privy Council letter that expressly stated that VA colonists' private property rights would not be impacted by the Maryland charter- as Claiborne was jailed on flimsy, farcical, charges of inciting an Indian uprising; denied by the Indians, themselves. The Marylanders took Claiborne's trading boat. A battle was fought physically and the forces of Maryland overtook those defending Claiborne and his private property rights. (258)

Whites "steal land" from whites: 1635, Connecticut: Plymouth colony and Dutch fur traders built settlements and posts in today's Hartford and Wethersfield. These were unceremoniously overtaken without combat by Englishmen of Connecticut, who had been banished from the Plymouth colony; even impounding the livestock of the Dutch -on what was previously land belonging to the Dutchmen! - for trespassing onto the Englishmen's land. (259)

Euros buy land: 1638: Samuel Gorton made a purchase from a tribe at Shawomet, south of Providence on the western end of Narragansett Bay. (260)

Indian treaty breakers: "Purchase of land from Indian chiefs, fair trading, and the impartial administration of English law made no difference" in the attitude of the Indian towards the Europeans. Experiencing seller's remorse, the Indians simply wanted the land with which they had parted in exchange for just compensation, so that they might profit from its exploitation. The Indians cared little about the terms of the bargain struck, once they had received their payment. They simply wanted it all. By the 1640s in New England, *the rapacious Indians and their greed brought about a tremendous conflict*. (261)

Euros buy land: winter 1645-46: Roger Williams, having fled Massachusetts under threat of deportation to England, founded Providence by obtaining from the Indians a "small tract of land" for himself, where he opened a trading post. Williams made this bargain in defiance of the English law, and *in deference to the ownership claim of the Indians north of Narragansett Bay*. English law stated that only the king could grant patents for land in the area; and that once granted, land must be obtained via the Englishman who held rights through this chain of succession. (262)

Indians violate treaty; exterminate rival Indian nation: In 1647, 2 years after concluding a peace treaty, a father Jogues -French Jesuit missionary- arrived at Mohawk camp to offer a kinsman's amiability on behalf of the French. The Mohawks reacted favorably. Upon the return of Jogues to the French, it was decided that Jogues should head a permanent mission with the tribe, as he was competent in their dialect. Upon his return to the Mohawks, he was immediately taken captive. In short order he was murdered in a ritual killing, held in their "death-festival" cabin. Jogues' head was hung in the village, his body tossed into the Mohawk River. Though the others of the 5 nations of the Iroquois objected, the Mohawks fired off the declaration of war. (263)

In 1648, the Iroquois eradicate the ancient clans of the Wyandots, as the former mercilessly invaded the territory of the Huron nation; the French Jesuits made an unsuccessful plea to the New England colonies, imploring them to take up sides against the Iroquois. Iroquois forces invaded the village of St. Joseph on July 4, 1648, while the fighting men were away from their homes. The remaining women, children, and old men, discovered by the Mohawks, were ruthlessly assailed with tomahawks as their wigwams were incinerated. The priest, Father Anthony Daniel, emerged from the chapel to face the coming attackers, and blessed the Mohawks with the forgiveness of Christ as he faced a firing line of bows and arrows, prior to being bludgeoned out of existence. (264) By 1649, Channing describes the scattered remnants of the Hurons. (265)

March 16, 1649: As part of an ongoing conflict, 1,000 Mohawk Indians of the Iroquois Confederacy invaded the village of St. Ignatius. Torching the walls of the fortified city, the attackers went on to kill all inhabitants in their path while they slumbered. The nearby village of St. Louis readied an 80 man defense team to greet the invading Mohawk forces, but the effort proved futile as the invaders massacred those found to be in the Indian cabins within the village. The attacking Indians took the pair of Jesuit priests whom they came across, taking them captive prior to subjecting them to brutal torture. As Channing tells us:

> "Success was with the Mohawks: the Jesuit priests are now their prisoners, to endure all the tortures which the ruthless fury of a raging multitude could invent. Brebeuf was set apart on a scaffold, and, in the midst of every outrage, rebuked his persecutors, and encouraged his Huron converts. They cut his lower lip and nose; applied burning torches to his body; burned his gums, and thrust hot iron down his throat. Deprived of his voice, his assured countenance and confiding eye still bore witness to his firmness.

The delicate Lallemand was stripped naked, and enveloped from head to foot with bark full of rosin. Brought into the presence of Brebeuf, he exclaimed, "We are made a spectacle unto the world, and to angels, and to men." The pine bark was set on fire; and, when it was ablaze, boiling water was poured on the heads of both the missionaries. The voice of Lallemand was choked by the thick smoke; but, the fire having snapped his bonds, he lifted his hands to heaven, imploring the aid of Him who is an aid to the weak. What need of many words? Brebeuf was scalped while yet alive, and died after a torture of three hours; the sufferings of Lallemand were prolonged for seventeen hours. The lives of both had been a continual heroism; their deaths were the astonishment of their executioners." (266)

"Peaceful" Indians: *The Iroquois Confederation*, headed by the Mohawk tribe, *continued expanding their sphere of power* towards all sides. Victories gained at Sileri, Quebec, and at the Three Rivers in 1651, ensued *as the Iroquois sought sole domination of the region.* In 1654, a peace treaty was struck. (267) By 1657 the Iroquois were warring in the north of Ohio, wiping out the Erie nation during the proceedings. The Iroquois were also entangled with the Onondagas by 1657, and by 1659 had driven the French from the Oswego Valley of NY. (268) Oct 1665 a missionary finds a village of Chippewas, located at Bay of Che-goi-me-gon, as the Iroquois band was being dissuaded, by a grand council of 10 or more nations, from attacking the Sioux. (269)

Euros win land through war: Connecticut mid-17th century: The Pequot Indians, and the colonists interested in their territory, chose to settle it on the battlefield as the colonists defeated the Pequot in a war, *to verify their right to the land*. This same bunch, off of the boat from the Old World, also made a purchase agreement with the River Indians regarding the territory that the River people turned over to the immigrants. (270)

English violate English treaties/land claims of Euros: 1662: King Charles II grants John Winthrop, Jr., of Connecticut, a right of jurisdiction which infringed upon land held by Rhode Island colony. New Haven was absorbed into Connecticut by this process. (271)

Land/power succession: 1664 New World: English win the territory of the Dutch on and around Manhattan Island; conquering Fort Amsterdam without firing a shot. Some simple diplomacy and negotiation beforehand were the only forms of "combat" undertaken by either party. The English initially offered generous terms of surrender of the territory to the Dutch, which were not accepted. Troops were assembled and deployed. The Dutch -badly outmanned and unprepared to fight such a battle- saw their commander, Peter Stuyvesant, flee on the eve of the battle. (272)

English purchase land from Indians: Newly formed New Jersey, 1666: After purchase, land granted to willing settlers from New England -particularly New Haven and Connecticut- to entice productive population of the area; specifically in present day Newark, as well as the Oranges. (273)

Euros steal land from Euros; violate treaty: 1673: Dutch retake NY from the English, though Long Island towns on the eastern end retained their independence. These towns chose to join the colony of Connecticut, and were happy to continue under this arrangement when the English regained NY in 1674 -Treaty of Westminster. Edmund Andros, Governor of New York, told them to obey his authority or be declared rebels. Connecticut offered no help. The Long Island towns were returned to NY. John Burroughs, Newtown clerk, spends one hour at the whipping post with a confession of sedition pinned to his chest. (274)

Euros violate Euro treaty; aid Indians: November 16, 1686, French representatives, along with their English counterparts, agree to the Treaty of Neutrality, signed at Whitehall in London. This stated that each party was to stay out of each other's affairs, both at land and at sea, on the western side of the Atlantic.

Denonville in New France immediately attacked the Iroquois -English subjects- and took captive a group of English traders; all this, with the blessing of the French crown -Louis IV. Dongan, the NY Governor who had agreed to enter in league with the Iroquois, immediately sent arms and ammunition to the Iroquois, to aid in their fight against the French in the New World. During the following winter, Iroquois forces decimate the French settlements on the Montreal perimeter. England's new king, James II, rebuked the French king for his actions, as well as for his complaints about retaliation following attack upon his people -the Iroquois. (275)

Euros sign treaties with Euros, later not honored: 1670: England and Spain sign a pact assuring each other recognition of their respective possessions in the New World. (276)

Euros obtain land in Canada: June of 1671: Sault Ste. Marie, Canada: French send Daumont de Saint-Lusson and Nicholas Perrot "to take formal possession of the great inland basin for the king of France." This was begun with a formal meeting attended by reps of 14 Indian tribes. (277) The tribes assented to the French crown's symbolic possession of the land in exchange for promised protection from other nations, to be supplied by the king of France. (278)

Land/power succession: Holland re-acquires NY from the English for 15 months, this period culminating with the Treaty of Westminster in 1674. The Treaty gave ownership back to the English as one of the terms of peace between the two nations. (279)

Indians break treaty: July and August, 1684 Iroquois: "Since the time of the Courcelles, the Iroquois had risen to the height of their power; time and again they had attacked the French in the north and often successfully; they had also extended their sway to the south and through their tributary tribes had ravaged the frontiers of Maryland and Virginia." A conference held during July and August, at the urging of the governors of New York and Virginia, was held in Albany with the chiefs of the five nations of the Iroquois Confederation. During said conference, a bargain was struck which was to result in the Iroquois ceasing their attacks upon the back settlements of the Chesapeake colonies, along with accepting the protection of the English crown in return for their stated submission to said crown. Five ceremonial axes were buried, "one in Behalf of Virginia and their Indians, another on Behalf of Maryland and theirs, and three for the Onnondagas, Oneydoes, and Cayugas." The Iroquois consented to the hanging of the arms of the Duke of York upon their assorted forts, as a sign of this new agreement. (280) Fighting resumed in short order.

Beginning with the peace treaties of 1701, the *Iroquois ceased warring with and enslaving* their immediately geographically convenient potential prey; banded together to create an Iroquois Confederacy -absorbing the Tuscarora Indians, who had been losers in their tussle with North Carolina colonists, and fled to the Susquehanna Valley- took a policy of diplomatic neutrality with the French, as well as with the English. The Iroquois, warmongers still, fought the Catawba Indians, who were positioned well to their south in Virginia. Innocent farmers were *often collateral damage of these wars for war's sake*; their livestock and other property taken forcefully by war parties -sometimes their homes were torched. Virginia Governor, Alexander Spotswood, lavished the Iroquois with gifts and negotiated a peace treaty so that his area would cease to incur destruction. The *Iroquois and the Catawbas promptly broke the treaty*; warring for three decades more. (281)

Indians "steal land" from Indians/Indian slavers: 1701 treaty conference in Albany. Iroquois reluctantly grant permission to other nations, including the Huron and the Fox, to live, hunt, and trade, in the Upper Great Lakes territory; land which the Iroquois contended they had conquered by war during the century preceding. Western Algonquins and Iroquois dispute each other during the treaty over P.O.W.s taken captive and held -also known as enslaved. (282) Either the Iroquois conquered the land or they didn't. No matter which was true, *there was a minimum of one party engaging in land fraud*, which was the sole cause of the dispute.

Indians double-deal, swindling Euros and other Indians: 1701: Iroquois turn over rights to valuable hunting ground -which had been "won by the sword eighty years ago", according to the Iroquois- to the English. This *very same land had*, in Montreal, been promised to various Indian nations, as well as to the French, by the Iroquois. Land over which the Iroquois had spent the prior two decades engrossed in perpetual and *inconclusive warfare*, they pawned off on the English at Albany; this done to curry favor with the English. The land in question "stretched from the northwestern shore of Lake Ontario to Lake Huron, westward to encompass the lower Michigan peninsula, and then eastward again to Lake Erie." (283)

Indians "steal land" from Indians: Spring 1710: Four Indian leaders were invited to London and courted as foreign royalty -the toast of the city- one of whom was E Tow Oh Kaom "a war chief among the River Indians, who were mostly *Mahicans pushed east of the Hudson by the Mohawks* in the seventeenth century." Incidentally, the four leaders were invited, wined and dined, by the English in an attempt to cultivate a military alliance with the Indian armies as part of England's desire to begin a new campaign in pursuit of the French territory in Canada. The English respected the existing individual armies, and sought their allegiance -as opposed to swooping in and taking the strategically useful land. (284) *Notice how the English did not simply massacre the Indians, or hand them poisonous blankets, as some possessing a child's version of U.S. history have been known to assert.* What's more, note that the River Indians were in fact formerly the Mahican Indians, who had been driven from their former territory by Mohawk Indians. If it is "stealing land" for the white man to win a territory by force, then it is also "stealing land" when the red man does so; if we are sincerely utilizing *a true ethnic equality in the eyes of the evaluator*.

Indian fraud/Indians steal land from Indians: 1730s and 1740s: the *Iroquois sold land in Pennsylvania that was not their own*. (285) The episode in which the Iroquois fraudulently sold land which they did not possess, misrepresenting the true ownership of the land, *was repeated decades later*.

Euros honor treaty, Indians rejoice: Georgia 1730s: Governor Oglethorpe, having treated with the chiefs of the Creek Indian nation in 1733 concerning the ownership of territory, discovered private citizens of Georgia acting on their own and settling upon land belonging to the Uchee Indians. *The governor immediately rebuked the trespassers and recalled them to Georgia territory.* "They told me that my having done them justice before they asked it made them love me and not believe the stories that were told them against me and that Therefore instead of beginning War with the English they were come down to help me against the Spaniards..." said Gov. Oglethorpe. The Uchee offered soldiers for "an entire year". (286)

Indians defraud Indians: 1742: The Iroquois, along with the Pennsylvania immigrants, drum out the Delaware Indian tribal group by utilizing a quite dubious claim of purchase regarding the land once occupied by the Delawares. Iroquois leader, Canasatego, chastised the Delaware tribe during a formal Treaty conference in Philadelphia. Canasatego stated that the land had been sold, and that the Iroquois had command over the Delawares. Any such claim was merely due to the might of the Iroquois rendering any Delaware retaliation highly unlikely to be effective; *the Iroquois took the lunch money of the Delawares* simply because the latter seemed too weak to defend themselves. Canasatego chastised the Delaware for being what would later become known as Indian-givers, noting that the proceeds of the supposed sale of the land had been exhausted "...and now You want it again like Children as you are." (287)

Indian fraud/Indians steal land from Indians: 1744 Lancaster Pa: The Iroquois of New York and Pennsylvania locale, affect to possess claim on land in Maryland, which was in fact a fictitious assertion. Marylanders called the Indian swindler a liar, and made it clear that they were merely humoring the Iroquois. The Iroquois then extorted heavy sums from the Maryland and Virginia immigrants -who knew for certain that they owed the Iroquois nothing for said land- thereby "selling" land which the Iroquois most certainly did not own. *The land in question was inhabited and owned by weaker Indian nations*, who were not present at the Treaty. (288)

Indians "steal land" from Indians/defraud Euros: Albany June 1754: Mohawks, of the Iroquois Confederation, host a treaty attended by representatives of Maryland, New York, Pennsylvania, Rhode Island, Connecticut, New Hampshire, and Massachusetts. Conrad Weiser, in the employ of the Penn family, completes public purchase of lands in the Susquehanna Valley from the Iroquois; *land that the Iroquois did not own or rule over*, and land they did not inhabit or occupy. Simultaneously and knowingly, John Henry Lydius, working in the employ of the Susquehanna Company, made a backroom deal at his place -the Indians awarding him some of the same land sold to Weiser publicly. There go the *Iroquois, double dealing for land that wasn't even theirs*, again! The Iroquois left the treaty with 30 wagons filled with booty, including 400 guns. (289)

Indians duplicitous cheats and liars: 1756: Marquis De Vandreuil -Pierre Rigand de Vandreuil de Cavagnial- states to Oneidas and Onondagas: "You pretend to be friends of the French and of the English, in order to obtain what you want from both sides, which makes you invent lies that an upright man would never think of." (290)

Indians extort Euros/Indians sell land they do not own: 1768 Fort Stanwix: £10,000 worth of cash and other bounty was extracted from the English by the Iroquois. This was done as compensation for the "sale" of land to which these Indians held no claim, and exercised no authority. *Now becoming a familiar pattern, the Iroquois stole the land of the Shawnee Indians* in the Ohio Country, right out from under them. By 1774 war broke out as the Shawnee did not honor the treaty of Fort Stanwix, considering the English to be illegal invaders of land that the English owned via said treaty. (291)

Euros buy land from Indians: Writing in 1784, Jefferson tells us of the committee appointed to lay out a temporary plan of government for the Western territory, "the territory ceded or to be ceded by Individual States to the United States whensoever the same shall have been purchased of the Indian Inhabitants & offered for sale by the U.S...." (292)

Land cheats were not unique to the Indian nations. During the 1790s, land fraud was not uncommon in an embryonic USA, barely cohesive, as it rivaled other nations battling over the territory -Indian nations, French, Spanish, British. A visitor from Britain during this period describes an environment teeming with: "False titles, forged grants, fictitious patents, and... sale of land in the clouds were daily imposed on the unwary." (293)

USA violates treaty with Indians: Cherokee late 18th century: Cherokees sided with the British during the American Revolutionary War, and a separate peace was negotiated between the new country -USA- and the Cherokee nation. Though Philadelphia allotted territory for these Indians, in practice the citizens disregarded the boundary. *Treaty of 1791 negotiated, and violated the same day*, by the people in this territory in which mixed allegiance -USA, Spain, Cherokee- pervaded. The unhappy Cherokees found a ready ally in the Spanish, who supplied the Indians with firearms and ammo with which war was waged upon the residents of Nashville and Knoxville in 1793. The USA overcame the attack of this Cherokee-Spanish alliance. (294)

USA concern for Indian land rights: President Washington sent military Col. Butler to Tennessee for the purpose of removing settlers who were trespassing on Indian lands. The task was said to be executed with courage and courtesy. (295) This was a tough job. He didn't go there with an army, or with the backing of the juggernaut government of the 20th century USA. This guy -Butler- went into the wilderness with a musket and a knife to tell frontiersmen to get off of the land that they had settled. A rough job, necessitating immense courage.

Euro funny business with land: Florida: The closing years of Spanish rule, circa 1811, saw unscrupulous and inattentive land grants by Spaniards -directly conflicting with British policy regarding the Indians. Lands not surveyed, no interpreters, no check to see if others had claim to the same land. Governor O'reilly decreed that land grants -even those already made in larger amounts, or having been purchased from Indians- limited to one league square. Any differential between prior agreement -land size- and the new decree in Opelousas, Attacopus, or Natchitoches, to be property of the *crown*. (296)

USA violates treaty with Indians/Victors of war bully the defeated: 1828: The proposal of Indian removal from lands in the southeast was designed to expel the Creeks and the Cherokees from land guaranteed to them by treaty. (297) President Andrew Jackson, during June of 1830, began his journey to Tennessee so that he might treat with the chiefs of the Choctaws. Historian Marquis James, writing of Jackson: *"His [military] campaign of 1813 and '14 had broken forever the military power of the southern Indians.* On the lands left to them after that disaster, the Cherokees and the Creeks in Georgia, the Choctaws and Chickasaws in Mississippi and Alabama, had kept their word to bury the tomahawk." The Cherokees led the pack in their assimilation to, and application of, white culture: building roads, herding cattle, manufacturing cloth, running fair taverns, a court system, and living in houses. The other tribes were on the heels of these Cherokees, but following the same path.

After the election of Jackson to the presidency in 1828, but prior to his installation in 1829, the state of Georgia took it upon itself to nullify the federal treaties, annexing the Creek and Cherokee lands; Mississippi and Alabama did the same to the Chickasaws and the Choctaws. *The Indians hired a lawyer, and sued the USA for violating its own treaties.* It was Jackson's desire to buy these Indians off with silver and whiskey, persuading them to peaceably head westward. At this meeting in TN, the Chickasaws agreed to move west of the Mississippi River in 1832, and the Choctaws agreed to treat. (298)

Due to the violation of federal treaties by Georgia, Mississippi, and Alabama, the Indian removal issue became entangled with the tariff issue, in terms of states' rights and political parties (see page# 254). *In 1831 the Choctaws went back on their agreement to vacate their land.* The Cherokees and the Creeks were unwavering in their refusal to leave. The Supreme Court was roped into the matter of Removal during 1831 when one Indian killed another on the Cherokee land which had been "annexed" by Georgia. Georgia sentenced the killer to be hanged, and an appeal was made to the Court due to Georgia acting outside of its federally prescribed jurisdiction. The state of Georgia thumbed their nose at Washington, refusing to respond to their inquiries into the matter. Corn Tassel, the condemned Indian, was found dead.

This disrespect of federal authority called into question the strength of the union of states. Vice President Calhoun embraced secession, and championed the right of the states to nullify federal laws. Georgia would not join South Carolina in their threats to secede, as the former wished to steer clear of a civil war. Calhoun, and the S.C. legislature, declared Jackson a tyrant, and asserted secession to be neither treason nor insurrection. (299) More payola was offered to the Indian tribes involved, so that by the close of 1832, only the Cherokees held out from agreeing to move. (300)

Americans betray Indians: 1882: Arizona Territory: Apache Indians, who had dealt with a disreputable liaison to the Indian agency at San Carlos, had been denied a promised food delivery, and were facing the prospect of being ejected from the land promised them. The agent was selling off the government rations for his personal gain, leaving the Indians with a paltry proportion of the foodstuffs. While it is true that the Indians could have elected to be self-sustaining, as opposed to relying solely upon handouts from the government, *they were being cheated out of what had been promised them*. When an Apache, capable of speaking both Spanish and English, reported the wrongdoings and sought retribution, he was jailed for half of a year.

In addition to the insouciance regarding self-reliance and support typical in other failed Indian tribes we see in this book, alcoholism was a conspicuous deterrent to the sustaining of this nation. A General Crook -known also as Gray Fox, and as Three Stars, by the Apache and the Plains Indian tribes- lamented this during a correspondence with the Secretary of the Indian Rights Association. War with the Chiricahua Apaches broke out in 1883, involving the notorious fighter Geronimo, and lasted until US victory in 1886 sent the Apaches to Oklahoma. (301)

Unsubstantiated Claim #3: that the American Indians were a monolithic, united, people; a great nation who were somehow cheated, and uniquely so, of their greatness simply by crossing paths with Europeans. That the Indians were somehow free of all sins, and even that they were the only successful communist society in history who have ever experienced a half century or greater period of growth and prosperity; summarized as: *the peacefully living, while sustainably living off of the land, in harmony with nature, fallacy.*

Fact check: The myth that the Indians lived in harmony as they merely lived off of the land, prospered in comfort and perpetual brotherhood without any poverty or nobility, and lacked any desire for personal gain, is an absurd falsehood. The divided nations of the American Indians show an identical pattern in their own history as is found throughout that of the rest of the world, which is of course surprising only to one who is *so ignorant of the evidence that they would expect humans to behave differently simply because of the color of their skin.* Humans are just humans, and red people are no different from the other varieties of skin tone. The relative penury of the Indians, in comparison to the invaders from across the ocean, is evidenced by their ability to be so frequently bought off by the Europeans; the Indians' squandering of their payola, evidenced by their frequency in returning in search of additional sums; and in the ability of the Europeans to be extorted by various Indian nations, that is to say that the Euros could afford it while the Indians could not. *Those with the most self-destructive habits are the nations which have traditionally been overtaken by those with superior habits*; these habits sometimes referred to as cultures.

The coining of the term "Indians", as a label for those found to inhabit the lands, is said to have occurred during the late 15th century. Columbus' son, Ferdinand Columbus, says that his father decided to moniker the new lands discovered "India" prior to setting sight on the land or its inhabitants. This was done because the name suggested riches to the ear of the elder Columbus as he set sail on the voyage that would land him in the New World. Whether that is true, or whether the name came from the sought after distinction of being known to have the "reign of the Indies", and therefore any inhabitants found would be naturally called Indians, the name was not a derogatory term but rather a positive one. (302)

The Indians soon proved to be of varied character as different Europeans arrived at assorted points on the continent. Many of these people exemplified a hostile, murderous, and savage character. This may have been due to an expectation of being attacked, or invaded for the purpose of being conquered, by any incoming unfamiliar vessel. Many instances of such automatic response are known to have occurred both in South East Asia, and on the shores of Europe, during this several century period in history. Juan Ponce de Leon spent 1493-1513 on San Domingo and Porto Rico (Puerto Rico). The man divided his time between kidnapping or killing Indians, and gathering gold and silver. In 1513, on Easter Sunday, Leon anchored at what would be called later St. Augustine, Florida; sailed around the bottom of the peninsula and up the western end a ways –finding hostile Indians at every stop– before returning to Porto Rico. Leon claimed Florida for Spain, showing that any perception of threat to the Indians he encountered was quite valid. (303)

This unwelcoming demeanor towards invaders to their country, which contemporary readers will note are called *"immigrants"* by dishonest politicians and press members, *was again noted* on the coast of Florida in 1521 by Ponce de Leon. The sailor, along with a town's worth of colonists, cattle, horses, and sheep, found an attempt to immigrate and settle with his party on the Florida coast met with a violent onslaught from the Indians. The immigrating invaders were driven away by the Indians, with many in their ranks wounded or killed. Leon succumbed to wounds suffered during the attack, a few weeks thereafter. The previous commander, Cordova, was also killed as a result of wounds inflicted by the hands of the Indians. (304)

Indians vanquish Euros: In 1527, Panfilo de Narvaez heads an expedition comprised of 600 people on 5 ships -with a legal benediction from the Portuguese government called a *"Requerimento"*- intent on the conquest and colonization of the lands north of the Gulf of Mexico. After losing 2 ships and 60 men, along with 20 horses, to a hurricane in Cuba, an additional departure of 140 men due to desertion in San Domingo thinned their numbers further. Intent on converting those they found to Christianity, a document was recited to new company: "If you do this, you shall retain your women, children, and estates and shall not be required to become Christians except, when informed of the truth, you desire to be converted. If, however, you do not do this, I will subject you to obedience to the Church and their Majesties. And I will take the persons of yourselves, your wives, and your children to make slaves of, and your goods, doing you all the evil and injury that I may be able... And I declare to you that the deaths and damages that arise therefrom will be your fault and not that of his Majesty, nor mine, nor these vacaliers who accompany me." Within a decade this expedition was reduced to 4 men after being killed off by Indians -in both direct combat, and through poor advisement given by the Indians to the Spaniards which sent the recipients to their peril- being both beaten and starved by the Indians. Strangely, the remaining four were considered "medicine men" with hundreds of obedient followers. (305)

Divided nations of the American Indians vs the *United States* of America: The Iroquois in 1710 were a confederacy of 5 nations -Mohawks, Cayugas, Senecas, Oneidas, and Onondagas. During the American War of Independence, their confederacy fractured due to infighting, enabling the USA to defeat and disperse the divided nations. (306) Tuscarora brought the club up to 6 members during the early 1700s, having migrated from North Carolina (307)

INDIAN SELF DESTRUCTION/IMPLOSION

As was true of so many failed nations prior to the downfall of the various Indian nations, *self-defeating culture accompanied by voluntary defections, were of paramount import in their ruination.* It is important to point out the preponderance of voluntary defectors of nations which have fallen from existence, as to ignore this trend will inflate the perceived death toll, and the sense of tragedy, far beyond what the evidence calls for. A quasi-chronological listing of several instances of pertinent information follow here.

Indian culture inferior: written 1898 about 17th century European immigrants/invaders: "*But the tribes of Indians inhabiting this country were fierce savages, whose occupation was war, and whose subsistence was drawn chiefly from the forest. To leave them in possession of their country was to leave the country a wilderness*; to govern them as a distinct people was impossible, because they were as brave and as high spirited as they were fierce, and were ready to repel by arms every attempt on their independence." (308)

Europeans' better culture = better goods: 1624 English defense equipment superior to the Indians. Medieval chain mail, suit of armor, metal headpieces, and the like, rendered Indian attacks ineffective while in use. (309)

Indians self-destruct/Indian warmongers: Maryland colony 1639-44: The Indian nation who inhabited the St. Mary's area were weak and fading from existence when the English colonists entered the picture. *The moribound and nearly extinct nation rushed to ally with the colonists*, as they saw this as a pathway to escaping their Indian superiors in strength; the Susquehannas and the Indians of the middle Potomac. Those nations, strong and proud, along with being ambitious and eager to conquer, attacked the English as they had the weak Indians before. Each year from 1639-44, Maryland's accounting reflects at least one combative encounter with these Indians. In contrast to the hospitable relations that these very same English colonists had known with the friendly Indians of the St. Mary's region, it became necessary by the end of that time span to give orders instructing all to "shoot them whatsoever Indian they are." (310)

Indians self-destruct: "Spirituous liquors, the small-pox, war, and an abridgment of territory, to a people who lived principally on the spontaneous productions of nature, had committed terrible havoc among them... *That the lands of this country were taken from by conquest, is not so general a truth as is supposed.*" Jefferson also notes reduction in the approximate population of the Indians in Virginia during the 17th century. He relays that the varied Indians had fallen to a mere third of their 1607 numbers by 1669. The "repeated proofs of purchase", regarding the acquisition of territory, found in the historical record were also mentioned by the third president. (311)

Voluntary defections: (see out-migration of 1,000 by 1700; page# 298)

Indians welcome European takeover: 1682 Arkansas: La Salle, with a crew comprised of ⅝ Indians, ⅜ Frenchmen [31:22], come upon the village of the Arkansas Indians. The Arkansas greeted the La Salle group warmly, and reacted gleefully to the notion that La Salle formally take possession of the land for the king of France. La Salle, later in 1682, attempted to claim a great tract of land under the name Louisiana, for France. (312) This 2nd claim, interestingly, lacks any consultation with either the Spanish, or the Indians.

Indians self-destruct: late 1684: English [Dongan] and French [Denonville] leaders each note the excesses of the Iroquois when they would drink, Denonville: "...converts the Savages into Demons and their Cabins into counterparts and theatres of Hell." (313)

Indians show mercy; defy French order of brutality: 1693 January/February: Indians, allied with the French, attack Mohawks near Niagara. Montreal governor ordered no prisoners but women and children be taken, yet their allied Indians took mercy and made P.O.W.s of many Mohawk Indians. Incidentally, a party of 200 came from Albany and freed many of these captives. (314)

Indian defection: Indians defect from their nation for another nation; contributing to the ultimate demise of the former Indian nation: Late 17th century: French Jesuits converted many Mohawk Indians to their ways, and the defectors moved to the Montreal area. This voluntary defection "threatened the security and stability" of those faithful to their Mohawk nation. (315)

Indians self-destruct: Euros transfer bad habits to Indians?: 1701 Pennsylvania: Edward Channing: "Justus Falckner, writing from Germantown in 1701, declared that the Indians learned drunkardness and stealing and other vices from the whites and were not converted to Christianity." (316)

Indians self-destruct: 1720s to end of century: New York: Mohawk Indians in the town of Canajoharie found themselves on a well traveled path between the trading hubs of Oswego and Albany. This afforded many opportunities for the acquisition of rum, which likely *fueled their cycle of over-innebriation and poverty during the 18th century*. (317)

Indians self-destruct: 1750s Onondagas: One Euro estimate of the Onondaga nation's population -Conrad Weiser's- asserted that 50% had moved to Oswegatchie, while the remnants were *partaking in an alcoholism and poverty lifestyle*. (318)

Indians cause own demise: *Ben Franklin predicts alcoholism will cause the downfall of the Indians* with which he had become familiar in 1753, at the Carlisle Treaty: "And indeed if it be the Design of Providence to extirpate these Savages in order to make room for Cultivators of the Earth, it seems not improbable that Rum may be the appointed Means." (319)

Indians self-destruct: Declaration of Independence 1776: Jefferson engages in mere banality when he writes that the King of England "...has endeavored to bring on the inhabitants of our frontiers the merciless indian savages, whose known rule of warfare is an undistinguished destruction of all ages, sexes, and conditions." (320)

Indians self-destruct/Indians extort Euros: 3rd quarter 18th century: Tench Tilghman, of Philadelphia, *recorded the Indians in constant pursuit of more alcohol*; even granting someone a ceremonial Indian name, solely to expressly request "a bowl of punch or two" be paid back to them as a show of gratitude -an appalling display, which offended Tilghman for its transparency. (321)

Self-destruction is complete: 1784 Fort Stanwix. *The Iroquois face comeuppance for their years of sleazy diplomacy.* Decimated by their own inefficient and overtly self-obstructive, unproductive lifestyle/culture, the Iroquois that lingered on as a defeated nation found themselves in no position to do any dictating; Americans wore the pants now. Half a century of explicit extortion -as a sole profession- and fraudulent dealings -affecting a might and sway over other indians, which they did not in fact possess- while also selling the lands of other Indians out from under them -lands to which the Iroquois had no claim, only a counterfeit title to ruling over these distant Indians- caught up with them. *Their house of cards had collapsed.* (322) Indian power was castrated after the American Revolutionary War. The Iroquois could no longer extract ample sums from, nor exert any influence over, Americans. *The Iroquois were just another people who had lost a war.* (323)

Voluntary defections: Indians voluntarily defect to join with the better cultured Euros: 1788 Iroquois; in New York, south of Lake Erie: The Seneca nation had a population numbered at around 2,000 in this geographic area, living separately from another faction of theirs who had territory closer to the NY/Pennsylvania border. This northern group of Senecas were a mixed bag, *the remnants from various failed Indian nations cobbled together*, including those who represented the last of the born Senecas. *All of the others*, who had not been taken captive by other Indians during slave raids, or killed during warfare by Indians or Europeans, had *fled the nation and joined up with Europeans who lived a much better life* and utilized a better way of doing things. (324)

Indians self-destruct; leaders sell out the rank-and-file; land loss: 4th Quarter 18th century: Iroquois -NYS area: Between war's end (1783) and 1790, the Iroquois retained a mere 4% of their prewar territorial portfolio. The *pervasive voluntary defections of their former tribal members* from their former ways, in favor of the superior and more productive cultures and lifestyles of the various surrounding factions; deaths resulting from their own poor culture which featured subsistence living, *no manufacturing*, rampant alcoholism; and defeat in warfare; had coalesced to spell the undoing of the once mighty Iroquois Confederation. Their chiefs, whether out of sheer habit as professional leeches/extortionists, or because they could see that their failed culture was on its deathbed and therefore wanted to squeeze every ounce they could get out of it before it could pay out no more, *sold out their people and their remaining land rights in order to line the pockets of the chiefs*. Private pensions, personal land grants, promises of future pensions, for the chief alone, were exchanged for the lawful rights to the lion's share of their territory held prior to the war -though the Iroquois were truly in no position to defend it from attackers in their depleted state. (325)

Indians self-destruct: 1st half 19th century: Kentucky, Missousi, east of Rockies: "There was no problem in the Indian trade which firewater could not solve.", wrote Bernard DeVoto during the 1940s. (326)

Indians' failure their own doing: The Indians who did not assimilate with the European nations never learned to do the things that produced goods which could be useful to themselves or others, while also enduring an absence of engagement in self-sustaining, profitable production, failed. Bernard DeVoto, from his writing published during the 1940s, referring to the remnants of the Indians who remained Indians in the West during 1846: "He had to live in the wilderness. And that is the point. Woodcraft, forest craft, and river craft were his skill. To read the weather, the streams, the woods; to know the ways of animals and birds; to find food and shelter; to find the Indians when they were on the warpath and to know which caprice was on them; to take comfort in flood or blizzard; to move safely through the wilderness, to make the wilderness his bed, his table, and his tool - this was his vocation." (327)

COMITY

There have been several instances of recorded amity among people from different lands, *though these are the exception rather than the routine.* Some of them have even occurred in North America and involved American Indians.

Euro and Indian comity: 1524 Giovanni da Verrazano embarks for China, launching from France and heading westward, and reaches the proximate region of Cape Fear. There he meets Indians who seem as black as negroes to the Italian sailing for the French under the benediction of the French King Francis I. *They part ways without incident.* Verrazano ventured northward, eventually docking at Newport. Enjoying the company of the Indians he meets here, the explorer made a more lengthy stay. Again *departing after a period consisting of an amiable encounter with an Indian nation*, Verrazano finished his northward exploration of the continent prior to his return to France. (328)

Euro and Indian comity: 1584: Pamlico Sound, located in present day North Carolina: the English and the Indians get along splendidly during a two month stay of the English. The English described the Indians as "most gentle, loving, and faithful, void of all guile and treason, and such as live after the manner of the golden age." (329)

Euro and Indian comity: 1609: Slightly northward of today's Albany -via what is presently the Hudson River- Henry Hudson, ship at rest for a spell, invited the local Indians into his cabin to come and party together. The wine flowed freely, and a good time was had by all. The next day, these Iroquois Indians of the Mohawk tribe returned the favor by gifting Hudson and his men venison, tobacco, and wampum. This was contrasted by *Indians of the lower Hudson River, who incessantly engaged in unprovoked attacks on Hudson and on his ship.* Iroquois tradition and folklore carries tales of their amity with the whites at first sight -their being sources of booze and of munitions- that were told at the outbreak of the American Revolution. (330)

Indians die of infectious disease in absence of Europeans: 1621, Plymouth: Smallpox, or measles, were the specific ailments guessed at by historians that wiped out the entirety of the Indian nation living in the area, with the sole exception of Tisquantum -Squanto. Squanto was introduced to the English by an Indian who lived among the colonists named Samoset. Springtime brought a diplomat from the Wampanoags, a nation located well south of Plymouth. His name was Massasoit, and he was their war chief. A peace treaty was agreed upon which lasted over 50 years. Squanto aided the colonists in hauling and farming the land; help that may have been life saving to the English. *The two groups were in alliance against the unfriendly Indian nations in the adjacent areas.* (331)

Euros seek alliance with Indians: 1688: Edward Channing relays:

"Up to 1688 the Hudson Bay Company had not assumed formidable proportions; but the fact that Englishmen had made good a foothold on the southwestern shore of Hudson Bay was an important event in the history of the contest for the continent. Possibly its most important result was the making connections between the English and the Indians of the Great Lake system. At nearly the same time, Colonel Thomas Dongan brought the Indians of the Iroquois Confederation clearly within the scope of English policy.

The League of the Iroquois occupied the region which extends from the mountains of western New England to Lake Erie. In addition, from time to time they established their villages north of that lake and Lake Ontario. Their power extended westward of these limits and southward as far as the Ohio. Their hold on these western and southern tributary tribes was exposed to constant risk. When they were successful in war, the western tribes were submissive; but when the Five Nations suffered defeats, the westerners were prone to throw off the yoke. The easternmost tribe of the Iroquois was the Mohawk; next to them were the Oneidas, and then in order came the Onondagas, Cayugas, and Senecas. Their political organization was the most perfect of any Indian power in North America, and they were reputed to be the most bloodthirsty of Indian tribes" (332)

Author describes Iroquois as being the key nation in existence "north of the Potomac and the Ohio and east of the Mississippi." (333)

Euro and Indian comity: In 1698 a faction of the Shawnee nation relocated to Conestoga, Pennsylvania, disaffected with the French. 2 years later, William Penn welcomed them as Pennsylvanians, whereafter these Indians dispersed themselves along the Susquehannah and the Delaware rivers. In 1728 the Shawness headed to the Ohio river, seeking better hunting, where the adopted Seneca, named Joncaire, met them and persuaded the tribal chiefs to join him on a trek to Montreal in 1730. In 1731 the once *disaffected Shawnees reunited with the French, as Canadian funds were lavished upon the red men*. (334)

ANTAGONISM; MORE SLAVERY

"Peaceful" Indians: 1622 Massachusetts Bay -now Boston harbor: The desperate and failing colonists of present day Weymouth, Mass, were a major thorn in the side of the local Indians. *Begging and stealing were among the prominent traits of these English, and the Indians decided to eradicate the poor, starving, immigrants by force.* Those established at Plymouth caught wind of their plans and were able to evacuate the colonists of Weymouth to safe haven at Plymouth. Captain Miles Standish intervened with the attacking Indians to such effect that, for at least a decade thereafter, these red men deferred to the Governor of Plymouth whenever they encountered a white man in their vicinity, prior to acting upon him. (335)

Indians fight Euros: First quarter 17th century: Sir George Yeardley, and other English immigrants, would hire nearby Indians -providing them with guns and ammo for the purpose- to hunt food for them. This proved troublesome when the Virginia Company muscled in on the cornfields of the tribesmen as they cleared areas for their own planting. The James River Indians -led by Opechancanough- retaliated with an invasion, slaughtering at least 347 colonists; along with destroying some of their land. With approximately 25% of their people gone, the remainder of the English mostly fled to nearby towns. The colonists struck back in the fall, destroying the Indians' food supply and driving them from their village. (336)

"Peaceful" Indians: land succession: 1643: The New England Confederation was a formal and written alliance of the Massachusetts Bay, New Plymouth, Connecticut, and New Haven groups. Among the reasons for the deemed necessity of the alliance was the perceived likelihood of war with the Dutch to the West, the French to their North, and various Indians all around. This pact held together for four decades, *helping the colonists to ward off a possible extinction at the hands of the attacking Indian forces*. (337)

Just another people among the nations of the world: 1670 Carolina: English incomers to Carolina captured by Spaniards. However, the first settlement at Albemarle Point was selected with defense against Indian attacks in mind; as they were considered a more prominent threat. (338)

Indians vs Euros: 1675-76 New England: King Philip's War: "King Philip" was the Indian chief of the Wompanoags, named Metacom. The English called him Philip. (339) Early Indian victories were plentiful, as *they attacked the white men with the very firearms the whites had introduced to them and trained them to use*. The fates altered course after some months. At the onset of the conflict, the Narragansett Indians were the most mighty force in New England, east of the Connecticut River. December 19, 1675: Massachusetts, Connecticut, and New Plymouth, join forces to storm the base of the Narragansetts in present day Kingston, Rhode Island, breaking the Indian nation. August 12, 1676, King Philip is slain. *Colonists lost much in the victory*, spending £100,000 during the skirmish -*a sum greater than that of their combined assets at the time*. (340)

"Peaceful" Indians: In the midst of French infighting in Canada, enemies of La Salle (Robert Cavalier, Sieur de La Salle) spread rumor among Indians "that La Salle was striving to bring the dreaded Iroquois upon them." (350)

Indians Warlike/Strong National Defense: Summer 1846, Santa Fe Trail, Comanche Indians invaded Mexico, as well as Texas, with parties of raiders. The

Comanche assured the USA that they would be spared the wrath of the Indians, and went after the U.S. Quartermaster Corps immediately thereafter. (341)

Indians blackmail/menace: 1846 Santa Fe Trail: Pawnee Indians were known to deftly burgle from passersby; aggressive in the pursuit of blackmail victims; always demanding a price for having crossed paths with the other party -calling it a payment of tribute. *Stragglers* -those left alone or in small numbers- *hardly ever survived being discovered by the Kaw, the Shawnee, or by any Indian nation in the region.* Pawnee are known to have stolen 100 livestock from a single caravan of Americans. (342) Sioux Indians on the trail made a lot of noise, stating that they would kill all whites who entered their occupied territory; this was a bluff. They just wanted to use fear and intimidation to extract more loot when they extorted people. (343)

Indian Slavers: During 1539, Hernando de Soto and crew find Juan Ortiz, who had been captured and enslaved by Indians for 12 years. (344)

Indian slavers and terrorists: 1840s: Santa Fe Trail: Since the dawn of the 1700s, the Santa Fe Trail had been a treacherous territory. New Mexicans, Indians, Texans, Spanish, French, Mexicans, and Americans alike, *played the roles of predator and prey interchangeably from time to time.*

The southern portion of the trail was most heavily laden with murderous Indians; the Apache, Comanche, Arapaho, Cheyanne, and Pawnee, among them. Other plains Indian tribes included the Blackfeet and the Sioux. The Comanche organized loot and murder gangs. These gangs would venture hundreds of miles into Texan and Mexican territory; capturing all of their animals, subsequently selling them off as their own; also capturing the humans and selling them as slaves, or merely for ransom. *Their hobby was sadism*; unspeakable tortures were commonplace; *the Indians dismembered children for entertainment.* Comanche are also said to have kidnapped, tortured, and/or killed more whites than any Indians of the West. The Comanche teamed with the Kiowa Indians as allies. (345) *One wonders if the "legacy of slavery", asserted by Lyndon Johnson and others as being unique to black people in this land, will lose its luster. Or will it, perhaps, transfer to the white man; making whitey the new "victim" group?*

Euros enslave Indians: 1708: A man by the name of Doyle reports: "In Virginia and Maryland there are but few traces of any attempt to enslave the Indians." Commenting on the state of affairs in South Carolina: *"As late as 1708 the native population furnished a quarter of the whole body of slaves."* (346)

Indians enslaved by Mexicans: January 1846: Jim Clyman writes of Californians being more or less aimless drifters with minimal skill for hunting. They enslaved Indians to perform the hard labor. (347) The California territory was owned by Mexico at the time.

PART VI

The Beast Tightens/Loosens its Grip on the Windpipe of the Nation's Economy

"Once again, many Americans rate socialism as the generous philosophy. But the results of our socialism were not generous. May this book serve as a cautionary tale of the loveable people who, despite themselves, hurt those they loved. Nothing is new. It is just forgotten." –Amity Shlaes, referring to a work of her own in 2019 (1)

A recurring theme of history, which will be illustrated factually throughout this text, is the phenomenon of what could be described as the Beast tightening or loosening its grip on the windpipe of the populace. This tightening or loosening is a reflection of what we today call taxation and regulation. The tighter the Beast -the state- squeezes, the more that economic growth is restricted, and the less that money and prosperity make their way to the least-moneyed; the more relaxed the Beast's grip becomes, the more the economic activity flows freely, enabling growth and innovation, and providing the best outcomes to those who begin in the least-moneyed portion of the society.

The inferiority of tight regulation and rapacious taxation, when juxtaposed with the results of free trade and the opportunity to reap what one has sown, is unmistakable. During the 19th century, while England and the USA were industrializing, and producing products at a rate of rapidity never before achievable, including the introduction of new products to the marketplace, uber-regulated Japan was still at the technological level of late-Medieval Europe. "Of her 28 to 30 million people the overwhelming majority were unfree, poverty-stricken peasants. They lived mostly in self-sufficient rural villages." (2)

GRIP TIGHTENS, MASSES SUFFER MONOPOLY
(See also: part I, government makes monopoly in business;
along with: government makes monopoly in jobs)

Prevaricators will claim that, in absence of drastic interference via regulation and state redistribution, businesses will form ironclad monopolies which will unduly exploit the people and subject them to scarcity. ***Instances in which the grip of the Beast tightens, causing the masses to suffer monopoly, are plentiful.*** Only government makes and perpetuates monopolies; while free competition, which permits the tremendous accumulation of wealth by individuals, dissolves monopolies and staves them off. One episode exhibiting a condition of monopoly arising, due to the tightening of regulation by government, occurred in China during the 16th century. Portuguese ships sailed to Nagasaki, Japan, after 1571 for the purpose of executing trade. The central planning of the Chinese Ming Dynasty -known as the Great Withdrawal- prohibited Chinese merchants from trading with the Japanese; endowing the Europeans with a virtual monopoly in Chinese shipping. This not only kept the Chinese from the reduction in their own shipping costs which are brought about naturally by competition, but also cut their citizens off from the market, both importing from and exporting to, Japan. The Portuguese were the shippers of as much as half of all silk exported from China, according to estimates. The acquisition of silk took priority over gold for Japan by the 1630s. (3)

Peanut oil vendors were able to attain monopolies, through the exclusion of kerosene, thanks to the government of China during the 1880s: "In China the kerosene trade was burdened by competition from native vegetable oils, heavy taxes, irregular deliveries to the interior, and ***the control of retail trade by conservative*** *merchant guilds. In some cities regulations forbade the sale of kerosene*; this ban resulted from the pressure of vendors of peanut oil and the fires caused by the lack of safe, cheap lamps." (4)

During the later 16th century, in the New World Spanish colonies, Spain required that members of its colonies buy from Spain at prices fixed by the sellers, and also that the colonists must sell their goods to the Spanish homeland at prices fixed by those doing the purchasing. In other words, *there was a centrally planned dual cartel*, at whose mercy the colonists were left at all times. *Such outrageous requirements* of the central planners, of course, *made illegal trade attractive to all* but the Spanish crown. The English would "seize" booty from the colonists of Spain, as a cover for actually having purchased the cargo in secrecy; or at least that is a quite probable explanation for the proliferation of such reports, occurring during this period. (5) We see *the fallacy of the lamp* prevailing for the Spanish government, as their plan to increase revenue through this monopolization of shipping to and from these colonies, *turned out to not only deprive them of the shipping trade* of these clandestine sales, *but also deprived the Spanish people of the goods* which may have been received on these ships.

The use of *government regulation as the traditional implement for the creation of monopoly* is witnessed in the New World during the early 17th century. During 1611-1616, this incarnation of the Virginia Company -owned by shareholders who would reap any profits according to their number of shares owned- worked harder and with greater organization than before. The leaders -Sir Thomas Gates, Sir Thomas Dale, and George Yeardley- doled out stiff punishments, which were accepted by the body of the company, as the leaders worked the rest vigorously. The work of the company in this wilderness was made even more arduous by constant warfare with the local Indians, fending them off as best the company could. (6) These men were paid (7), though the company failed within two decades. (8)

In 1620, the Virginia Company records show that a rule was agreed upon that those in charge at each plantation -often the party who had money at stake- had free reign to direct the affairs of their plantation as they saw fit; including their servants on said plantation. The only stipulation was, of course, that these directives comply with, or at least not violate, the laws of England. This spurred John Smith of Nibley, along with other investors such as the Pilgrim Fathers, to attempt to profit in the potential development of the land in Virginia. Though his initial attempt in 1622 was ill-fated, Smith kept at it for another decade. Giving a glimpse into the realities of socialism in practice, as they existed in Monarchical England, the English presumed it necessary to bribe the Governor of Virginia. Sir George Yeardley, the man then holding the governorship, declined. (9)

The English system of monopolies, inherited from Elizabeth, as can be expected in the central planning of a monarchy, *led to an attempt to secure a monopoly in the tobacco area* for the Virginia Company by England. Its investors were many back in England, and some *were holders of political office in parliament*. This led to the company suffering a political death in 1624, though the entry was not placed on the books until 1632. This political death brought with it no change in the ownership of land for the colonists; respect for private property rights saw to that. This simply removed the government's tentacles from the land momentarily. (10) In 1625 Charles I took the throne, and by 1627 sought to exact taxation from the Virginia farmers. *The king proposed a monopoly* wherein production would be strictly limited by decree of the crown, to assure scarcity. *Colonists refused this*, along with other likewise attempts, occurring until 1635. During the period 1625-1635, the population of Virginia increased five-fold. This begat immigration from England to meet the demands for servants to work; *providing opportunity for advancement to some of the lowest citizens of England*. These workers included many vagabonds in their number, their lack of credential from the parish minister certifying religion -then a requirement for travel abroad- often being overlooked, as the crown's desire to rid the country of such people proved of primary import. (11)

In the years spanning 1675-1696, England placed oversight of colonial affairs in the hands of their own Privy Council -known also as the Lords of Trade and Plantations. The government went after the colonies, created and perpetuated by private businessmen, *as the bureaucrats attempted to stuff the royal coffers. A renewed attempt at monopolization of trade* in the New World colonies was undertaken. (12) *The colonies refused both compliance and assistance at every turn.* Legal challenges were made as to the charters of the colonies, particularly those in New England, with that of Massachusetts even being formally commandeered by the crown. (13) Though the Massachusetts Bay Company was formally dissolved and supplanted by a royal governor, this seizure of private property and *the attempted enforcement of monopoly by the government* officials delivered neither high tax revenues nor a monopoly in trade. The defiant colonies continued to do business with other European countries. (14)

Joseph Dudley, provisional governor of Massachusetts, along with Captain George of *the Rose*, would seize and condemn tradeships, splitting the loot amongst themselves without turning a penny over to the tax collector. (15) Sir Edmund Andros returned from England on December 20th, 1686, to act as governor of New England, having vacated his post as New York governor in 1681. (16) Andros was likely powerless in practice in both Rhode Island and Connecticut. (17) The king gave Andros formal authority over New York as well, and in practice Andros ran an "illegal despotism" according to historian Edward Channing. (18) All laws regarding the collection of money expired 1684, at which point Andros continued to impose the taxes; punishing those who resisted exaction. (19) Dudley referred to the colonists as slaves, differing only in that they were not bought and sold. (20)

Tight grip, and heavy regulation, are observed to enforce monopoly while simultaneously suppressing the masses during the 16th-17th centuries in Japan. William W. Lockwood tells us that: "Trade was predominantly a movement of rice from country to city, mostly in payment of feudal dues." Lockwood goes on: "Commerce remained crippled by manifold political restrictions and regulations,... through strict controls over travel and trade, as well as over freedom of occupation and enterprise, the Tokugawa regime sought to suppress the growth of any new forces which might threaten the feudal-agrarian foundations of the state." (21) In 1640, a ban on trade and foreign contacts was enacted. A single trading port remained in Nagasaki, and this operated within the most rigid of confinements. Punishment by execution awaited all who attempted to leave Japan, or were caught during re-entry. A ban was also placed on the construction of sea-faring vessels. (22)

The grip tightened, as special interest groups were catered to at the detriment of the general interest, exemplifying the plain truth that tariffs are a tax upon one's own people, in Germany during the 1850s. Under the oversight of Otto Von Bismarck, "The shareholder in railroads...the industrialist, the mineowner, the shipper, the viniculturist, etc., they all demand to be protected in their occupations by tariff laws *at the expense of their customers*." (23) Of course, *the cost to the customers goes far beyond* the mere higher prices that they must pay for said goods or services, but they also pay in terms of: the reduction in the amount of choices available to them, as innovation is less necessary for those domestic purveyors given an unearned advantage over their foreign competitors; the foreign competitors, employing many, whose products don't appear at all due to the prohibitive costs imposed by the tariffs.

During the early 17th century in Quebec/New France, the tight regulatory grip of central planning stifled the economy and depressed living conditions. The French government enjoyed the fur trade in Quebec, as private entrepreneurs had been eager to do. *The crown centrally planned the trade*, however, through the use of what today would be called *"licensing" or monopolies chosen by politicians and bureaucrats*. The exclusivity of the socialist monopoly to certain parties would change with the winds, and the legal benediction to do business in the region was replaced with a legal disbarment from doing so; as quickly as the license had been gotten, it was gone. *This centrally planned turmoil* resulting from shifts in political favor of certain parties, the uncertainty of length of access to the area, and the risk of being forbidden from accessing the area at any time, caused by the monopoly granted by government in the name of "economic efficiency" or "protections", *made for a dearth of long term capital investment*. As a result, not only did the people live a lower quality of life due to the perpetually scant accommodations and resources of the area, the fur acquisition was diminished, and France as a whole was hurt by the economic consequences of this foray into socialism. (24) Similar schemes, with their detrimental impacts upon the least-moneyed in the USA, are the TVA, and the 1933 AAA of the New Deal. (25)

In Russia during the final quarter of the 19th century, instances of both the tightening and the relaxing of the grip of the Beast are evidenced in the realm of petroleum. In 1873 the czar *disbanded a state created monopoly* -as if there were any other kind- in crude oil. *All* were now welcomed to take on the risk of the venture, if they dared. The *Russian share of world crude oil production, unsurprisingly, grew*. A level of 12.7% of the 35.7 million barrels world-wide was attained by 1882; by 1891, Russians accounted for 37.9% of the 91.1 million barrels in the world. In the year 1883, Russian kerosene broke into English and Austro-Hungarian markets, by 1885 into 9 countries, by 1887 into 17 countries -competing against products of the USA. During the 1870s, Russia abolished the excise tax on the refining of kerosene, though they also heavily taxed any imported kerosene. In 1886 the port of Batum had its freedom abolished, harming trade. In 1888 *a high excise tax on kerosene*, applicable only to illuminating oil sold *in* Russia, *directed the product away from Russia's own citizens*. (26)

The experience of Spain in the 1930s illustrates well *the crime spree that is expected when populist redistributors* -whether called communists, New Dealers, Jacobins, or wokers- *get their hands on concentrated governmental power*. The national elections of 1933 ejected from office those who had founded the Spanish Republic less than 3 years prior. A bloodless cession of power by the last of the Bourbons, who had been at the helm of Spain for half of a millennium, in spring 1931 led to a highly socialist, and nominally egalitarian, government run by "middle-class intellectuals, lawyers, doctors, professors and writers, backed by the Socialist party and the socialist trade unions." These people set in to the choosing of winners and losers, along with other central planning, full bore. *Nationalizing Church property*; disestablishing religion, as they separated Church and State -which was certainly a positive change-; restricting various religious orders, while also ordering the dissolution entirely, of the Jesuits. Primary education was paid for through general taxation, and made compulsory. Women's suffrage was instituted. While divorce had been forbidden, now it was made easy. *Minimum wages were instituted* -leaving on the outside looking in those whose abilities and aptitudes were then deemed to be worth a price below the dictated minimum price- while there was *official state regulation of its permissive attitude towards employee collusion and monopolization. Large estates were taken from the landowners in exchange for sums far less than their value*, and the stolen booty was then redistributed to the proletariat.

10,000 military officers. who would not swear an oath to the Republic, were removed from the military for life -but with *full pay* for life. Bill Shirer described the changes as being equivalent to those made "by Woodrow Wilson and Franklin D. Roosevelt over a period of a quarter of a century." Shirer described these measures of the "Republican regime" as being "impressive". Shirer described the newly voted in, as of 1933, "Rightist Coalition" as extracting these measures from use at once. Not only politicians, but "the Church, the wealthy landowners and capitalists, and the pensioned army generals", along with "the anarchists" who were popular among the "workers and peasants", *all revolted against the so-called help of the egalitarian central planners*. The wussy leaders of the Socialists "could not bring themselves to be drastic enough" to thwart their enemies, Shirer tells us. (27)

TIGHT GRIP HARMS THOSE LEAST-MONEYED

"If only everyone who said such things [denounce capitalist entrepreneurs in the city] was rounding up junk and turning it into usable consumer goods! All our problems would be solved!" -Late 1980s Magnitogorsk, Russia, city newspaper (28)

Income equality, or wealth equality, schemes have been shown to impact the lowest class of either category the most harshly. Instances of such are peppered throughout this volume. A handful of examples follow here.

Grip tightens; masses suffer: Stalin himself admits that commerce conducted for the personal gain of individuals involved in a transaction is more successful than central planning. During February of 1950, Stalin sends Mao advice, stating that postwar economic recovery will be hastened by an unmolested economy of the "rich peasants", known as "kulaks" in Russia. (29) *This is a confession that communism is, based upon experience, inferior to commerce motivated by the possibility of personal gain.*

The so-called worker's paradise, promised by central planners, was conspicuously absent in Russia during the late 1980s. A Russian steelworker, named Gurzhii, tells us: "How many decrees and proclamations? No goods, no equipment, no packaging, no containers for transporting goods." He continued "...Try to buy even the simplest machine. It's disgraceful. Seventy years we live like this." (30) Gurzhii again: "*There is no desire to do better, to produce more. We can't keep it, so why bother?* This nonsensical situation applies throughout the Russian republic." "...Maybe not this year, okay, we'll wait until next year. Not next year either. They offer us no prospects. It's hopeless." "The USSR Ministry of Trade, the Russian republic Ministry of Trade, the Cheliabinsk Regional Trade Management - they don't actually 'trade' anything. All they do is get in the way, hinder us, load us with insane regulations and contradictory orders. *They gave us independence in law, but in practice they take it away.*" (31)

The inhumane grip of Socialism upon the poor, and the working man, is illustrated in China during 1950. The grain confiscation rate -known alternatively as the income tax rate- in Guangdong province ranged from 15-60% of their current supply. Sichuan province farmers were tortured as a result of their refusal to comply with rapacious taxation. Southwest China, under Deng Xiaopeng's control, conducted gestapo style raids on residences. As a practice, they would loot all but a 3 day supply of food. *What had traditionally been a boone region, was reduced to bankruptcy* by Deng. Governmental spending was 4.3 million tonnes, while the region produced only 2.9 million. Rebellions against the tax collecting, and the general socialist tyranny, were rampant -some even succeeded in thwarting the communist cadres, sometimes killing their would-be oppressors; *refusing to offer themselves as lambs to be sacrificed upon the perverse altar of so-called "social justice".* An East China Bureau report stated that local officials "are completely unconcerned about the hardships of the masses, and even randomly beat, arrest and kill people in the course of their work, producing antagonisms with the masses." (32)

When the grip tightens, and power has been concentrated into the hands of bureaucrats and politicians, the Beast acts as its own master, and serves itself. In 17th century England, the opening portion of the century saw marked inflation, with wages for laborers suspiciously lagging behind pace with other costs. *The ability of government officials* -monikered as justices of the peace- *to set the prices of these wages was clearly the most obvious cause* of the disproportionate rate in growth. It happened that many justices of the peace were landowners, employing these very laborers, so that the special interest minority group -the landed- controlled the price through central planning. The landed rubbed the lamp and got their wish. If a laborer refused the government dictated wage, the justice of the peace could: arrest them; send them to the whipping post; bind them out to a master; or have them jailed. (33)

The battle to obtain the issuance of monopolist "rights", under conditions in which they are up for grabs, *impedes the greater good.* In Germany during 1848, in the midst of an overthrow of the government and attempted seizure of power by groups within Germany, the German Stock Exchange (Bourse) was down 8-10% during trading February 28th, 1848, after news of Louis Philippe's demise landed in Berlin. During mid-March, government bonds, which have a par value of 100, were down to 84, sliding further to 64 by April. The Bank of Prussia increased its discount by 25% -from a rate of 4% to the new rate of 5%- to counter the flight of 24 million marks worth of gold from their coffers during the preceding month. Prussian bonds went unsold at their customary rate of 3.5%, and now offered a 5% payout. Wurttemberg bonds fell from a price of 102 to 71 during a two month span. All this while private property rights were disregarded in practice, and *special interest groups were awarded monopolies through government as a reward for burning and looting* the property of the job providers and of the manufacturers of goods. (34) (see page# 188 for more about this episode)

During the first half of the 20th century, Africa was heavily dependent upon those colonizing their area -as the colonizers brought along with them a superior culture, yielding greater productivity- as well as on imports from the more advanced nations of the world. During the Second World War imports became more scarce, due to the diversion of energies on the part of both the exporting and the colonizing countries. *Price controls enacted by African governments at their ports*, done in the name of helping their people to receive lower priced goods, instead made those ports unattractive to potential importers, and *increased the scarcity of goods for their African constituents*. This state-induced increase in scarcity of course meant a state-induced increase in the prices of those goods, as *the retailers* -upon whom the state could not enforce price controls even if they wanted to, due to the spreading out of locales, and the hand-to-hand exchange occurring in absence of today's electronic transactions- within the various African nations *were free to charge prices commensurate with the scarcity of supply*. The natives found the prices to be too high, and turned up their noses at purchasing these necessities of food production -shotgun ammo, trapping wire- while also slowing their efforts to raise the money necessary to make purchases at these artificially elevated prices; these two factors acting concomitantly to diminish the production of cash crops on the part of these Africans, *thereby reducing the global supply of food*. Subsistence farming reigned for roughly one decade. (35) *When it comes to the supposed assistance of central planners*, who claim to be "protecting" their citizens from high prices by reducing competition, *their so-called help just hurts*.

"Consumer protection" hurts the consumer again, in East Africa during 1957. Legislation hindering non-Africans in the recovery of debts owed to them by Africans dissuades foreign capital from East African ventures. (36) The Africans pay the ultimate price of having fewer goods, services, and less new technology; along with the absence of the work that would have been involved with the existence of these additional elements.

Grip tightens; the aftermath: In China during the late 1980s, after the tightening of the grip at Liberation -a monicker wholly appropriate within the theme of comically misnomered political movements of the Proponents of Slavery (POS) variety, as it in fact delivered quite harsh and intense slavery- stifled the nation for so long, the gradual loosening of the grip in terms of both intense regulation on the masses, and the same intense regulation of, and monopoly on, the means of production, took place in the late 1970s. Deng Xiaopeng now stood at the center of the central planners, possessing total authority over the nation's businesses, judges, and police; while holding authority over the lot in life of each and every solitary citizen in the land. Socialism had hardly bestowed a bounty of liberty onto the masses, as we have seen. (see part II, page# 152). By 1980, the nation had become a land wherein the duration of the prior 3 decades saw only the highest party cadres with automobiles for personal use, while any other automobiles in the nation were property of the state, and therefore of the Party. Its factories were producing 1950s style Soviet Jeeps, and no other varieties, at a rate of two per factory worker per year. That is, an auto plant employing 10,000 workers produces 20,000 badly outdated jeeps per year. (195)

The New Dealers' desire to have as much tumult as they could muster upon the entry into presidential office of Franklin Roosevelt in the USA during March of 1933, so as to *capitalize politically on the crisis* and thereby enact as much of its control over the lives of Americans as possible, the "Bank Holiday" of that year was a welcome publicity stunt upon entering office. (37) Along with all Americans, newspaperman -and sympathizer of central planning- Bill Shirer was unable to transact any banking. Making matters worse for Shirer, he was hung up overseas in Europe. He was, at first, wholly unable to exchange his traveler's checks for foreign currency. Weeks later, once the USA had departed from the gold standard, Shirer was able to get just sixty cents on the dollar for his traveler's checks, in comparison to their value just a few weeks prior. (38)

LOOSE GRIP

"Let the motto of a free people be: 'The person is inviolable, property is sacred!'"
-A German, mid-19th century (39)

The relaxation of the grip of the Beast, around the windpipe of a nation, delivers a higher quality of life for the population as a whole. More food, more goods, more jobs, more social mobility, more of everything pertinent to the alleviation of hopeless poverty for the masses. *The most efficient exchange occurs between two parties*: each spending his own money, in an attempt to benefit himself. Any discrepancies between the bargain struck with his money, and with his desires, will be most readily identified and remediated. This exchange is preeminent in an environment free of cumbersome regulation on the part of government. *The least efficient exchange occurs between two parties*: the first party spending the money of the second party, in an attempt to benefit some distant third party who neither person knows. (40) This is the exchange taking place in tightly regulated, redistributive, centrally planned environments.

During the period in which more bounty was delivered, and more people of common birth were uplifted to lives of comfort or even opulence, the *loose hand* of the Beast is ever-present. Visiting the USA in 1831-32, Tocqueville noticed the strong state governments, along with the weak federal government. "We observe two completely separate and almost independent governments, one which answers the daily needs of society without clear limitations, the other which acts in exceptional circumstances to meet certain general concerns with very clear limitations." (41) America's third president, Thomas Jefferson, in a writing published 1821: "But it is not by the consolidation, or concentration of powers, but by their distribution, that good government is effected. Were not this country already divided into states, that division must be made, that each might do for itself what concerns itself directly, and what it can so much better do than a distant authority." He adds: "*Were we directed from Washington when to sow, & when to reap, we should soon want bread*. It is by this partition of cares, descending in gradation from general to particular, that the mass of human affairs may be best managed for the good and prosperity of all." (42) Cemented by the horrific New Deal period in the USA, each decade thereafter more and more people do in fact turn to Washington with expectations of bread. Jefferson's warning proved prophetic, as the two most cancerous legacies of the Great Failure of Socialism are: 1 the intentional creation of federally dependent special interest groups, and 2 the conversion of the Treasury into a perpetual campaign fund for politicians. (43)

Grip loosens: colonial USA 1688-Rev War: The colonial governors were mostly impotent, as the assemblies ran the show through its power over the purse. This was made possible through a combination of the strength of the colonists, and the general ineptitude of those placed into the positions of the various governorships by England during this period. Productivity was good. (44)

Grip loosens: USA October 12, 1781: The Virginia Legislature -with Thomas Jefferson among its number, having resigned his seat after being elected to the first Congress so that he could devote his attention to his state's legislature instead (45)- proposes successful legislation converting the system for inherited land within the family. The prior system, imported from England, was one in which: the state mandated that the "whole" of the land be divided into a number of parcels equivalent to the number of sons; *that the estate must be treated as a "whole" for purposes of sale or borrowing*, although it had in practice been divided two (or more) ways; and upon the death of these sons the land to be divided further for their heirs, should the sons outnumber the fathers, yet still retain the original "whole" for the purpose of buying or borrowing -thus crippling the individual in their quest to achieve sovereignty over their person, and not truly allowing the land to be private property as it was co-owned by state mandate, the business partners not of the individual's own choosing. This new legislation passed by the VA legislature nixed the aforementioned system, and *gave birth to a system* in which: the land was still divided among the heirs, in separate parcels, but this time *with each owning his own plot, personally.* Each could sell his land, leverage his land at his own risk, choose to combine with others, and it truly became private property. The new law did not *forbid* the prior practice, of course, it simply gave the individual the freedom to choose how he might behave with his own, private, property. (46)

Advocates of the loose grip approach can point out that ***the diffusion of power protects the masses, should one who desires tyranny get their hands on the levers of government***, as is illustrated by the Chinese experience of the 10th century AD. During the Five Dynasties Period: "...the existence of several Chinese states lessened the degree of terror wielded by the rulers compared to that wielded by rulers of dynasties that succeeded in unifying China." This terror pertained to ethnic minorities. (47) "It was thus not the Chinese elite but independent-minded merchants who spread Chinese culture in that direction when they established trading colonies in the littoral region from the South China Coast into Southeast Asia and the South Seas." (48)

The relaxation of regulatory grip facilitated much trade in later medieval Europe. Bazaars, or fairs, brought luxurious and rare items to the masses, while simultaneously providing the opportunity for wholesale transactions between merchants/traders. ***The prohibition on lending at interest was ignored*** at the fairs, as were any outstanding criminal matters in which attendees may have been entangled; ***these bazaars*** -like merchant owned and ruled towns which originated during this period- ***were self-governed by the merchants***. Commerce was benefited by their existence. Fairs ran from Italy to Belgium, and occurred year round. Some would attend fairs merely to engage in fiscal commerce; either borrowing anew, or repaying prior loans. During the 13th century, the financial and credit system had germinated and grown to the level of having established a crude clearing house amongst themselves. Wars on the lands, combined with the improvement in money trading which eliminated the necessity for in person exchanges between merchants, brought the demise of these bazaars. (49)

When presented with data pertaining to wealth, or income, we find that it is often split into various classes. When perusing such information, it is important to recognize that membership in each class is not necessarily static, and that *a lack of the predetermined outcomes* from above which are *doled out by tight regulation*, lead to the *greatest fluidity of movement*. Like tables of guests at a wedding, the number of tables may remain the same, but the name cards denoting the seating of the guests may be shuffled from one table to another. In Japan, beginning 1869, the throttling due to the clenched fist of regulators around the windpipe of the nation, began to be alleviated. *Equality of liberty took prominence over equality of outcome*. Although there were still many glaring instances of manipulation and interference by government, the relaxation of regulatory grip unleashed a copious prosperity, which lifted multitudes from penury over the forthcoming century. During the first decade, the proverbial deck was already being shuffled. The *removal of socialist "help"*, such as unions or guilds, regulatory bureaus, planning boards, and price fixing schemes, *aided the least-moneyed* in gaining the opportunity to improve their state; to sit at a better table, to continue with our analogy. Some, who had been living as royalty under the rigid controls of central planning, hadn't any skills or any mind for enterprise. Many of these were living in a niggardly state, barely staving off starvation, once they were left to succeed or to fail on their own merit. (50)

The iron grip of socialism loosened a bit in China after the death of Mao. In 1979, Deng Xiaopeng's changes included the allowance of private family farming in the countryside, *permitting some private enterprise*, thereby enabling the state to merely sit back and *allow the possibility of, though no guarantee of, personal gain and profit, to entice the citizens into productivity.* (51) In China during the years 1979-1988, Nicholas Lardy estimates a tripling of real per capita income, from a level of $400 at the onset of the period, to $1,200 by its culmination. Foreign trade quintupled to $102 billion by 1988. There were an estimated 3 million TV sets in the nation in 1979, which had swelled to 130 million by 1988. (52)

The grip of the Beast loosened, but only so much for POS China, as was epitomized by the 1989 Tiananmen Square demonstration/massacre. After 10 years of *loosening the regulatory grip slightly, which led to increased economic output*, the incident at the Square had revealed that the surface changes had not removed the roots of the nefarious socialist control. The "political study sessions", known alternatively as "brainwashing sessions", were back. "It's just like the Cultural Revolution again," said Tang -his only identification. "This Communist Party wants to control everything," continued Tang. "It's all they are good at. If they say the students are counterrevolutionaries, then you must say they are counterrevolutionaries. If they say no one was killed, then no one was killed." (53)

A relaxation of regulatory grip satisfied some customers in the USSR during the late 1980s. While centrally planned goods sat on shelves in the state stores, perpetually unsold -this while the citizens had enough currency on deposit to purchase about half of the stock at any time- two markets operated in which prices were permitted to fluctuate with supply and demand. While the undesired goods -which were badly outdated or obsolete- sat on shelves, the trade markets featured new and high quality products; but at higher prices than the state stores. *Soviet officials displayed anything but ignorance* of reality when they responded to complaints from the citizenry about the higher prices in these markets: "*If we tried to mandate lower prices, people would stop producing, and prices for the remaining goods would climb still higher.*" Curiously, goods that were not manufactured entirely by the seller were forbidden at the "free" market. "If you buy a t-shirt at a state store, affix a picture of Michael Jackson, and sell the shirt for five times what you paid, this is speculation. The product was not entirely self-produced." (54)

In Magnitogorsk during the late 1980s, the infirmity of property rights was glaring, perpetuating poverty during a gentle relaxation of the Beast's grip around the throat of the masses. A co-op (quasi-private enterprise) called Zhest reworked the inferior government produced metals so that they were suitable for use, catered meals to various workplaces, charged for transportation: "Where there's a need, we find and satisfy it." Leasing a shop, *they discharged the lion's share of the abundance of management brought on by the centrally planned bureaucracy*. "Everyone began working longer hours; now there's two shifts and work on weekends. We abolished the shopwide hour-long lunch break. Workers lunch in shifts so the shop stays in operation. *Wages went up, but productivity rose much faster*." This was done, continued Ivan Agalakov, despite unmistakable government hostility. "I know the boat idea will take off, but I still worry about sinking money into it. What kind of taxes can I anticipate? What kinds of rules and stipulations are they going to attach? *If you want to know, we have no faith in tomorrow. They might just take away your business*. What's to stop them?" (196)

Non-Egalitarian Government of 18th Century England Uplifts the Masses
(see also: page# 396, 401)

Loose grip of the Beast yields great improvement for the masses: 18th century England: "eighteenth-century society was emphatically not egalitarian." -T.S. Ashton. (55)

The assinine assertion espoused by many populist, redistributive, ringleaders, involves the supposed vitality of the so-called "safety net". *This "safety net" is nothing more than a rather ambiguous license to tax and spend indefinitely*, and with impunity, on the part of office seeking politicians. Private property rights and the desire for personal gain, of course, are the proven necessities which yield the best outcomes for those presently least-moneyed in a given area, and for those who are helpless. Examples are rittled throughout this book, yet a few examples from the notoriously non-egalitarian 18th century England will be presented here.

Commerce uplifts the masses; while populist movements demonize said uplifting commerce, in the name of uplifting the masses. Such a tactic is both sleazy and reprehensible, yet the tactic is frequently utilized because it is effective in the sense that the general public demand that they themselves be utilized as a tool in the hands of dishonest politicians; *a sort of key which opens the door to the vault containing a nation's treasure*, cast aside as soon as it has served its function.

Large enterprises are often illegitimately demonized, portrayed as imposing low wages, and causing unemployment in the aggregate by reducing the cumulative number of jobs. On the subject of the widespread myth of massive rural unemployment as large agricultural ventures increased in both scale and multitude, T.S. Ashton states plainly: "There is no evidence, however, of large-scale rural unemployment." New agricultural practices created new jobs engaged in said practices. Hedging and ditching created jobs for the lower end workers during the winter when they would have previously found no work on the farms during this period. "There was no mass eviction: the population of agricultural villages increased at a rate not much less than that of the industrial areas...". The poor were absolutely not driven from the countryside. (56) Other instances of big business, including the industrialization of business, positively impacting the workers as a class, and acting as magnets attracting and retaining members of the labor pool, can be found in (part VI, social mobility, page# 393; and also in part III, 19th century Germany, page# 188).

An example of the backwardness of the public's sense of right and wrong is exemplified when one describes a person who makes food, housing, or medicine, as a person who "became subject to the odium attached to all who made profit by dealing in the necessaries of life." (57) Of course we know that *the prospect of gain as a result of engagement in an activity*, particularly the prospect of immense gains, under conditions of free competition, as well as of low governmental impingement and involvement, *produce the greatest outcomes in terms of both long-term output and affordability*. We also know from our many examples in this volume that when we see the grip of governmental concentration of power tightened around the windpipe of a nation, that such behavior directly opposes and counteracts the environment necessary to produce the best outcomes as measured by the material quality of life for the masses. That is, *so long as we only consider cases that occur in real life, with real people, and real money*, as opposed to resorting to the religion and superstition of the socialists -or wokernists, or American Liberals, or whatever name you like to use to describe this element of society- *the only "odium" should be attached to those who demonize*, and seek to encumber, those who seek to make a *profit in dealing with the necessaries of life*.

During an era absent redistributive handouts for the healthy, as well as an era which frowned upon sloth and penury, new industries developed at the onset of the

1700s included: paper making, glass making, and silk throwing. (58) The new goods benefited all, while the new skills and jobs benefited the masses as well. Scholar T.S. Ashton tells us that: "Over the century as a whole, however, English manufactures were *offering increased opportunities to labour at rates of pay well above those of other countries.*" (59) Skilled English artisans were in demand, as countries such as Russia, and France, along with the New England settlement, desired replication of English techniques. (60) The desire of Englishmen to emigrate to France may have been mitigated by the decrease in social mobility, caused by central planners and their rigid assignment of place in the society: "English society was a class structure. But class never hardened into caste." This was distinctly different from the French arrangement in which the nobility were clearly and distinctly separate from the others. (61) (see part II, France 1789) In England, there was a mixture of the old feudal type -tightly controlled- municipalities and industries, and of free trade amongst individuals -absent the inhibiting encumbrances of trade guilds, unions, socialism, or any other affronts to their natural birthright to pursue their own objectives and to make of themselves what they might. "In the textile areas of Lancashire, Yorkshire, and the West Country, the unit of production was the individual who worked in his own way and determined his own hours of labor." (62)

Individual liberty was paramount among the English people during the 18th century, "Men and women were highly individual: the one characteristic they had in common was a refusal to conform." (63) "The territorial aristocrat wielded far more power over his neighbors than the sovereign state operating from London." The local justice of the peace held more sway than the civil servants in far off cities. Hospitals, roads, harbor construction, and entreats from new industries, *were all decided upon and funded locally as opposed to centrally.* (64) During this epoch, there were many "paupers who had, and often sought, no other designation [than poverty].", as "class gradations were rungs of a ladder which many climbed and descended." (65)

During the second half of the 19th century, England led the way as *individual gain spurred the industrial revolution, providing more goods and higher paying jobs than ever before.* The central authorities of other nations, into whose hands power had been concentrated, *were forced to relinquish their pretensions in regards to which method of economic arrangement yielded the most ample harvest*. As is alluded to in more detail later (part VII) such people were forced to admit that their plans were defective, or perish. In reference to 19th century Europe, Ivan T. Berend and Gyorgi Ranki tell us that: "Not even the Ottoman Empire, the least flexible of them all, could ignore the challenge the dual revolution posed to its military and political power. For a number of countries, however, it was a matter of a challenge to their very survival as independent nations. True, to the countries of the European periphery, it was a less explicit challenge than to Japan, where the example of neighbouring lands and repeated Western attempts on her autonomy left no doubt as to their alternatives of colonial status or national and economic revival; nevertheless, these alternatives were in the background for all underdeveloped nations." (66) *Their focus on survival motivated them to admit the inferiority of their own methods of control and organization*, and to adopt those of their betters. Nations outside of Western Europe often avoided social upheaval with an adoption of capitalistic ways "from above", with the old feudal lords retaining economic supremacy. (67)

During the 18th century in England, there were many industrial advancements. Technical advancements in agriculture increased the supplies of both cattle and grain, while new methods devised in transportation enabled food and other necessities to reach more people more quickly than before. Trade abroad ameliorated shortages at home by enabling the purchase of necessities, and improved storage of food increased the english supplies on hand in case of emergency. During 1773, Gilbert White noted: "Such a run of wet seasons as we have had the last ten or twelve years would have produced a famine a century or more ago." (68)

Smallpox inoculations made their way into England during the 18th century. Scotting led the way in medical advancements within England. Brothers William and John Hunter pioneered surgical advancements. The smallpox inoculation, first entering the country as early as 1718, eventually became available to the masses during the forthcoming decades. Hospitals are built in several large towns. (69)

COMMERCE UPLIFTS THE MASSES

Of the many benefits to mankind which are created by commerce, conducted by individuals pursuing their own ends, is that this *commerce unites distant peoples*. Beckwith tells us: "The European drive to discover sea routes to the Orient", uniting peoples of differing skin tones; culture; and geography, "was fueled completely by desire to trade with the producers of silks, spices, and other precious things." (70) The substantial difference between the low purchase price in the Orient, and the high sale prices realized in Europe, led to the Portuguese realizing 90% or greater profits on their trade. This, after all expenses -theft at the hands of pirates; construction of forts in Malabar towns; loss due to shipwrecks; costs of building ships and paying sailors- were taken into account. (71) *European military intervention occurred only during instances in which local governments*, wishing to deprive the people of this commerce due to a desire to protect their own socialized cartel of merchants, *interfered with the ability of the Europeans to trade*. Military intervention by Europeans was *not* imperialist, until the late 19th century. (72)

The Portuguese -motivated by commerce, as most Eurasian fights had been for 2,000 years prior- during a span of 50 years placed themselves squarely in command of the commercial waterways from Western Europe to Japan, establishing "forts and trading posts at the major stopping points along the way, all without controlling the interior or seriously threatening the major powers" of the territory adjacent to said sea routes. (73) During the period 1500-1600 AD gold and silver in Western Europe rose three fold. (74)

In Eurasia during the mid-8th century AD, there is evidence of communication occurring through the commerce chain. A rash of upheavals in Central Asia, from as far west as the city of Marw, and the Umayyad Dynasty of the Arab Empire, extending east to the Tang Dynasty in China, the Silk Road trade system during this period was largely comprised of Sogdians, who were the merchants that served as the sole link through which communications would most plausibly have been transmitted. (75) During the 12-14th centuries in Eurasia, the Mongol conquests, and the trade and commerce which drove and perpetuated all lasting civilisations, not only motivated Europeans to seek and eventually find a direct trade route to the Orient, but were responsible for the transmission of valuable knowledge from China to Western Europe pertaining to firearms and gunpowder. The famous accounts of Marco Polo are said to have served as a nexus of European interest in developing trade with the far off lands. (76)

In Greece, during the 7th century BC, in post Mycenaean Crete, Idaean shields were found. The placement of these shields in Crete illustrates contact made with the Orient, likely via one or several middlemen brokers. (77) Items available to Europeans due to Silk Road trade extending to Far East Asia included: silks and spices; brocades, drugs and indigo, cashmere shawls, amber, pearls, and diamonds.

This linking of distant peoples, achieved solely by the desire of dozens of individuals to each achieve a gain for themselves, *also spreads prosperity, and offers immense opportunities* to those presently least-moneyed. In approximately 500 BC, the Scythians developed a trade system linking Greece, Persia, and points eastward. Scythians were very wealthy and powerful as a result, with a strong comitatus. All parties benefited from international commerce, which was a creation born from nothing more than each party's desire for their own gain. The Scythians, as well as their many successors in power in Central Eurasia, traded with anyone they came into contact with. People living in territories separated by great distances, which had traditionally been known to live without any knowledge of each other, were now beginning to swell in terms of the material wealth of the inhabitants, but also in terms of *the clustering of population to areas of economic prosperity and opportunity*, which has been a recurring theme throughout the ages. The *material wealth* of those in these areas which ranged from Europe, to East Asia, South Asia, as well as to the Near East, *was enriched by a newfound diversity of goods* made possible by the trade with foreigners. This variety of enrichment is rarely reflected in the customary methods of evaluating the material condition of a given nation, and should be considered by the reader as one of immense import. This age without locomotives, automobiles, airplanes, electricity, and many more of the blessings of human innovation which have saved and improved so many lives since their advent by linking far away peoples with goods, through both commerce and charity. ***The network linking these distant lands in 500 BC, and making this all happen, was a network of traders.*** Middlemen and shippers, each out to make some gain for himself, linked buyers and sellers in distant lands who themselves each desired some gain, and improved the lives of so many. The life of the trader was not without its dangers, which of course is reflected in the price to be charged for performing the job. Traders were often challenged for both the lands to be traversed, as well as for their wealth or cargo -sometimes defeating their challengers, and other times being defeated by the challenger's hand- particularly in the east by the Chinese. (78)

Capitalism and trade are observed to spread prosperity during the 4th-6th centuries BC, in lands ranging from Greece, to India, and China, via the Silk Road. Nomads were the blood cells transporting and delivering nourishment all over Eurasia. Lao-tzu, Confucius, Panini, Plato, Gautama Buddha, Kautilya, and others, all began asking questions about the questions they normally asked; began to question the function of government; and began to employ logic. This occurring in lands of great distance, roughly simultaneously.

Their connection were the nomads -who themselves benefitted quite handsomely from their frequent engagement in trade, as well as from their direct interaction with many assorted peoples and thoughts- and the frequent and welcome ***interaction between these places and the nomads was motivated entirely by trade.*** It was trade that was responsible for the transmission of this tremendous advancement in thought and approach so far, and so fast. (79) The illustrious Tom Sowell points out the immense dearth of development caused by the disruption of trade throughout Europe by the Balkan Mountains, which caused a lagging of centuries in the transmission and adoption of superior and more productive habits of culture, beginning in the West, and slowly permeating into the East. (80)

The bountiful Silk Road would eventually meet its demise. Trade reached its apex during the 14th century. Channing credits the Fall of the Moguls of Cathay, followed by the Chinese isolationism in trade for centuries, culminating with the fall of Constantinople in 1453 at the hands of the Turks, as ending the Silk Road trade network. (81) (For more on the Silk Road network, see page# 279).

"A rising tide lifts all boats" effect was illustrated after for profit tertiary jobs were established, ferrying people to various places for a fee, "...peasant producers who had previously 'walked to Guatemala City and consumed a week to sell a load of onions' were able to ride to the city and spend only '2 or 3 days to sell a larger load of onions...The total result for the region was that more time could be spent on the production of wealth than previously, with less required for distribution of goods.' Similar effects of improvements in transport can be found in many parts of the world." (82)

During the 2nd half of the 19th century AD, interacting solely due to the desire for numismatic gain on the part of the white man, the West brought the wheel to Black Africa. (83) *This is another piece of evidence which dictates the conclusion that prosperity is not natural, and therefore "everybody's" for the taking.* In addition to the vital information transmitted during that purely financially motivated interaction in Africa, we see that European, and Portuguese, shipping during the Age of Exploration brought Eurasians into contact with the Europeans; commingling and transmitting knowledge in history, architecture, physical science, language, and other fields. (84)

Another observable fruit of commerce undertaken at the risk of the participants, and with the greatest ability for gain available to themselves, is the improvement in the goods available to people, as well as in their ability to rightfully obtain means by which to procure those goods. In the year 700 BC in Greece, commerce and manufacturing, artisans, along with for profit trading of food, *enable those who were not great farmers to be well fed*, and sometimes to be materially wealthy. Trading ports such as Corinth -Corinth is cited in the Iliad, and also in the year 378 BC, for its significance as a trade port- noted for the wealth of their citizenry as observed by traders and travelers, charged a fee for the use of their Isthmus. The trading ships were happy to pay the fee, as use of the port saved them from the treacherous waters of the high seas past Cape Malea. (85)

Farmers in Boeotia were known in 700 BC to farm exclusively for export. Around this time, evidence appears of a change in the lexicon to differentiate warships from trading ships. (86) *Those without land were able to attain political sway directly. This was unique at the time.* Those able to exercise influence and participate directly in the politics of their land, though they did not own land, were the traders. (87) *Commerce uplifted them, not handouts for the healthy.*

In Africa during the mid-20th century, the market economy was not long established. One man, who could not sign his own name, operated a large-scale cattle dealing operation in Accra on the Gold Coast. He began life as a migrant farm worker. During this present stage of his life, he imported cattle from distances as great as Duala in the French Cameroons, Lake Chad in French Equatorial Africa, and Timbuctoo on the Niger bend. The man concurrently operated a transportation business which reached as far as Khartoom, while also dealing in grain. The illiterate, former migrant worker, gave a deposit of £50,000 on a government contract, after the establishment of even a limited market economy. In Eastern Nigeria, approximately 1957, for several years an African had profitably operated a transport fleet of greater than 30 Lorries. 60 years prior, the wheel was foreign to the native population of that area. (88)

In reference to what many in the 20th and 21st centuries label as worker "oppression", it seems best to point out that low paid, menial work, is the key to upward social mobility. In poorer countries, services tend to be relatively cheaper than in more wealthy countries. People are usually willing to perform menial work such as bootblack or domestic servants because the money earned goes further than in more wealthy countries. The costs of living are relatively lower because the country as a whole is relatively poorer, of course. *The inability of such people to find regular work may be a result of* actual scarcity of opportunity for productive activity, caused by a surplus of job seekers relative to jobs in the area; or by *government actions such as minimum wage laws*, hiring quotas, or labor union monopolies. (89)

Luxury goods uplift the masses in S.E. Asia. Trade in "course cloth" -a luxury item of the day- used to pay for the spices of southeast Asia. This made new goods readily accessible to those without the means to go afar in pursuit of such. During the 16th century, the Portuguese and their Asian trading partners settled their transactions by utilizing the cloth as a medium of currency. (90)

Liberty was the currency -which is absent from numerical data regarding wealth- obtained by those who were their own men during the Western Han Dynasty (200 BC - 6 AD) in China. This regime was unable to fully control and dominate lands occupied by peoples who independently produced wealth and engaged in commerce with the nomadic Hsiung-nu, and sometimes with others, as the nomads could simply serve as middle men in a commerce chain. These nomadic middle man merchants were too strong, and difficult to subjugate. (91)

We see corporate innovation within the oil industry feed the masses during 1881 in Scotland. George T. Bielby and William Young invented a new way to get more use from decomposing shale. This caused extraction of sulphate of ammonia to double, in addition to upping the fuel gas extracted per gallon. The increase in sulphate of ammonia yield occurred just as the supply of Peruvian guano waned, *helping to feed the masses by replacing the guano for use in manufactured fertilizers*. Later, in 1884, the same duo invented a process which significantly reduced costs by distilling continuously, as opposed to in batches. (92)

In the New World, European trade improved the material condition of the Indians. Though some European metal wares fell into the hands of the Iroquois during the late 16th century via diplomatic trade with other Indian nations, reliable access to the superior goods of the Europeans was not had until they were buttressed by the Dutch to their south in fort Orange (Albany), along with the French to their north in the St. Lawrence River Valley of Quebec. The Iroquois Indians purchased as heavily as they could muster. Kettles, woven cloth, mouth harps, mirrors, liquor, and guns and ammo, were among the new goods introduced to these red men in a reliable supply. Copper and brass kettles replaced the old ceramic models. The stone implements of the Iroquois were displaced by the iron axes, knives, and scissors obtained from the Europeans. The industrious among the red men utilized this new metal to work into their traditional items such as arrowheads. Internal production of goods diminished greatly as *the Indians were able to obtain*, through trade of their furs, *superior goods at a cost less than that of manufacturing their inferior goods themselves*. (93)

Private energy prevails in absence of state organization: Pirenne on the success of international commerce in Europe during the 13th century:

"In view of all the difficulties which it had to conquer, deplorable conditions of circulation, inadequate means of transport, general insecurity and an insufficiently organised monetary system, it is impossible not to admire the magnitude of the results obtained. They are all the more remarkable because the governments contributed nothing to them, beyond protecting merchants for fiscal reasons. *The progress accomplished in the domain of international commerce is thus to be explained solely by the energy, the spirit of initiative and ingenuity of the merchants themselves.* The Italians, who, in this aspect, were the leaders of Europe, undoubtedly learned much from the Byzantines and the Moslems, whose more advanced civilisation exercised an influence over them analogous to that of Egypt and Persia over ancient Greece. But, like the Greeks, whom they also resembled in the violence of their internal struggles, they were quick to assimilate and develop what they borrowed. They founded commercial societies, created credit, and restored the currency, and the spread of their economic methods in Northern Europe is as striking as that of humanism in the fifteenth and sixteenth centuries." (94)

Though the desire for gain, capitalism, profiteering, and the formation of corporations to aid the commercial ventures of people, are all routinely demonized by charlatans purporting to have a desire to witness the advancement of the least-moneyed, these people demonize what they ought to be glorifying. ***In actuality, it is the disconnection of commerce/trade which harms the masses***. Take for an example Eurasia during the 5th-7th centuries. The 5th century Germanic invasion of Rome demonstrated no paralyzing impact upon commerce through the Mediterranean Sea from East to West. The Arab conquests of the 7th century delivered the anterior outcome, as their domination of the sea, including persistent piracy, closed Western Europe off from the flow of Silk Road commerce. During the 8th century, the old Roman cities lost their merchants and the urban life they provided. "An overall impoverishment was manifest." Carolingians were forced to substitute silver coins for gold, severing their ties with the Mediterranean economy. (95) Barbury, in England, from the time of the Islamic conquest through the duration of the Middle Ages, was like an extension of the Orient; wholly cut off from Western (Christian) Europe. (96)

Arab rule of the Mediterranean cut Christian Europe off from the Oriental trade. From the close of the 8th century AD, Western Europe was without transferable wealth as its commerce regressed back to a solely agrarian setup. Land, and its bounty, were the sole products and property of these nations. The feudal system was evidentiary of the disintegration of control from the crown into the hands of what today would be called bureaucrats (estate owners). (97) The former commerce -which brought a variety of goods and food to and from the region- atrophied to a level of subsistence production; even for large estate holders. (98)

"Sale and purchase were not the normal occupation of anyone; they were expedients to which people had recourse when obliged by necessity. Commerce had so completely ceased to be one of the branches of social activity that each estate aimed at supplying all its own needs", says Henri Pirenne, referring to feudal western Europe. (99) Jews were the only merchants evident in the Carolingian era, dealing in luxury items for a very limited clientele. Their impact on the whole of commerce was insignificant. They existed, but were not plentiful. (100)

MYTH OF COLONIAL "RAPE"
(see also: part I, False Alarms, page# 52)

As illustrated in part I, when those of a superior culture colonize those of an inferior culture, the colonized and their region routinely benefit immensely. The claims of prevaricators within the Victim Politics Industry, asserting a deleterious impact upon the colonized and the region itself, are counter to the reality expressed in the preceding sentence, and so several examples substantiating reality will follow here.

19th and 20th centuries: British colonies in Africa: Gold Coast children in schools: 1900-1909, 3,000; 1950, 150,000. Gold Coast travel and transportation: 1890s no rail or roads; 1930s rail and roads. Travel/*transportation required fewer hours than had previously taken days* (5 days in 1890 vs. 3 hours in 1930). British West Africa: *slavery and slave trading virtually eliminated during colonization*. By the 1930s, Nigerian trade hubs had switched from slave trading to groundnut trading. *Health and life expectancy for Africans soared, along with quality of life*. Exports from Sub-Saharan Africa rose, in its proportion of tropical trade, from 6.2% in 1913, climbing to 13.3% by 1937, and reaching 18.2% of all tropical trade by 1955. (101)

Grip loosens: 1948 Liberia: In an effort to attract shippers and commerce to itself, Liberia provided a free port near the port of Monrovia. No customs duties were charged there. An enterprising man set about providing a transportation service from Monrovia to Macenta in French Guinea. Though the Liberians had serviceable roads to the border of Guinea, the track thereafter was treacherous; with 125 miles of poor quality road to the Kankan rail which provided 400 miles of inefficient track to the port of Conakry. Beginning 1950, U.S. funds came pouring in by the tens of millions.

In addition to roads, a hydroelectric generator on the St. Paul river, and several harbors were constructed. A multinational caucus hypothesized during the 1930s that Liberian revenue might one day reach $650,000 in a year, and this projection was considered optimistic. In 1953 all Liberian floating debts had been squared, with revenue topping $10 million. Revenue grew to $25 million in 1959; then to $50 million in 1967, a year in which Liberia had a balanced budget. *All this was because a few Americans wanted to make money, and so uplifted the country by making it into something useful.* (102)

Writing in 1926, of the British colonies in Africa during the 19th-20th centuries, writer Allen Mcphee described it as "the superimposition of the twentieth century after Christ on[to] the twentieth century before Christ" in his tome *The Economic Revolution in British West Africa.* (103) During the period 1940-1970 occurred an explosion of the estimated population of West Africa in the amount of two and a half times, largely thanks to its colonizers. A peace established by the Europeans in their territories allowed for *security of private property* during travel across the region -currency, livestock, etc. *An immense increase in food production enabled and sustained the additional lives.* Communication between the regions, and with the outside world, was improved by the Europeans; thus bringing the tribesmen into the epoch of currency and trade, Europeans brought technological advancements such as: ploughs, irrigation, fertilizers, crop rotation, along with pest traps and poisons. Motor vehicles and communication alleviated famine, as the *Europeans* supplied grain to distressed colonies *in their automobiles.* (104)

As of 1980, transport beyond the rudimentary remained entirely dependent upon rails built and kept by foreigners. During colonization of British West Africa, all agricultural exports produced by West Africans were done on farms which were their own, more often than not. Similar patterns were noted in both Uganda and Tanganyika (Tanzania). (105)

The only "oppression" imposed by European colonization in Africa was the teaching of central planning: In Liberia, the True Whig Party dominated thoroughly, utilizing their position to contrive a system of patronage and licensing. Their tentacles reached out and clutched via judicial appointments, candidacies of politicians, foreign businesses seeking trade in the country, legal monopolies in domestic business (a la the 19th century ICC, or the New Deal's AAA, in the USA), civil service positions. Like the mafia, Works Progress Administration, and others, this group taxed those to whom it bestowed positions; in Liberia's case, one month's pay.

The True Whig Party outlawed a rival political party upon its formation, and also deported a challenger to the presidency for challenging the election results. These tyrants exploiting and ripping off the public, through government, also demanded a heavy stockholding position in the commercial ventures of foreigners in their country. (106) (see part III, page# 184, for more)

In a different part of the world, we see the myth of colonial rape further dispelled nearly 1,000 years prior to the African episode. After destroying a trade spot in the vicinity during the 9th century, during the later stages of the 10th century AD the *Northmen used force to establish their own trading hub* in the Rhine-Meuse-Scheldt delta, located in present day Amsterdam. The accompanying *trade brought new goods to and from the multitude* of lands located down each of these major rivers, along with those located along any branches which sprout from the main channels. The nearby area of Flanders, referring to the northern portion of Belgium, benefitted immensely from this trade during the coming centuries. Flemish coins struck during the period 965-1035 have turned up in Russia, Denmark, and Prussia. English records show Fleming among those who paid the trade tariff during the years 991-1002. Flanders became a pioneer of industry as a result of the trade brought in by the Northmens' trading hub, both in quantity of industries as well as in proficiency. The Celtic era saw the manufacture of wool in the lush meadows of the Lys, and the Scheldt valleys, on the part of both the Morini and the Menapii peoples. (107)

The Romans imported their techniques for the manufacture of cloth during their occupation of Flanders. The Flemish took to the task so competently that their cloth was sold as far away as Italy, by the 2nd century. *The Franks overtook the region* during the 5th century, who proceeded to *export the high quality Flemish cloth to the people throughout the Low Countries*, and the popularity of the product soared. This trade was halted by the Northmen's strategic destruction of the depot during the 9th century, to resume a century later when the Scandinavians sought use of it once again. By the end of the 10th century, wool had to be imported from England in order to meet the explosion in demand for the cloth. By the 12th century the trade had overtaken the nation; dozens of cities rose to existence and to prosperity as a result of creating shops in the city, which had migrated from the countryside, to engage in trade via land, while maritime trade continued without interruption. (108)

The 12th century saw gold from the south of the Alps brought in by Italians, in addition to their spices and silks, to trade with the Flemish for their cloth. The Flemish peddled at Novgorod. These men from the north of Belgium met heavy buyers at the fairs of Charlemagne, who went on to bring their newly acquired cloth to Genoa, from whence it sailed to ports as distant as the Levant. (109) Author Henri Pirenne asserts that the examples of Flanders, joined later by Brabant, were isolated within the history of Medieval Europe; attaining dual supremacy in luxury within the cloth market during the 13th century. (110) Belgium never developed their own trading ships, leaving the markup for other enterprising individuals. (111)

The *Romans also imported their ways in the metal working industry* to the peoples of the Meuse river valley *during their period of occupation*. This commerce waned with the loss of Mediterranean trade due to Arab supremacy during the 9th century –and the refusal of the Arabs to trade with them– but was revived with the later retaking of the lake by those who would trade with Western Europe. (112)

An alternative example refuting the myth of colonial rape was evident in 11th century Medieval Europe, as wanderers of the land would colonise undeveloped regions. The system, *prioritizing equality of wealth* (see page# 432, for more on this) for the passing on of land from one generation to the next led to many instances in which the land was to be divided up into so many portions that *the outcome was for each person to have a tiny sliver of unworkable land*, and as a result many of the children would flee the land as it was split up amongst a few of their siblings, leaving decent shares for those who did receive them. The manorial setup of the feudal system was such that if a serf was able to flee a great enough distance from their lord's manor, so that nobody in the new area recognized them, they would acquire the social status of guests, or *hotes*. *Hotes* congregated on lands undeveloped by the landowners. Permission to clear and to work the land was readily granted, as volunteers to develop one's land are difficult to refuse. The success of these *hote* colonists in working the unkempt territory on one estate persuaded other estates to make efforts to attract such *hotes* to colonize their own marshes, forests, and woodlands. Towns were erected without inhabitants, as recruiters boasting hefty promises of the conditions awaiting potential recruits, went about the business of matching opportunity with those seeking it. The lords who designed this system *were careful not to replicate the rigid controls of organization* in practice on their manors presently. The *hotes* remained free (113) though *hotes* still had to pay a tax to the lord for the use of his plot of land. The *hote* was exempt from many manorial taxes, and reaped what was sown on his plot. *For 200 years the land was improved through private means* and the desire for gain on the part of both parties. (114)

By the 12th and 13th centuries, the *hotes* -who again were comprised of both children born to large families without anything to offer them but privation, as well as of those who were once vagrants- not only found liberty for themselves in their legal status -*casting off the yoke of strict state regulation* holding back the serfs, along with the *rapacious taxation*, and the assignation of land- vastly improved the condition of previously neglected and undeveloped lands throughout the continent, but most significantly created -along with the cooperative lords- a *new European condition in which men were not bogged down by the odious system of tight regulation and debilitating taxation, in a no-profit environment*, which pervaded the feudal manors. The large landowners recognized that liberty, and the possibility of profit, for the people meant greater productivity, and so were careful *not* to replicate the central planning of the estates. The *new class of merchant hotes, creating and growing towns*, brought an increase in both the variety of goods available, jobs available, and the use of currency in Europe. Ordinary rank-and-file people began transacting in coin, as opposed to in kind. Through this process, the lowest classes were elevated, and it was during this period that the term "landlord" took on its modern meaning, becoming *rentiers* of the land. (115)

Colonization uplifting the colonized, the condition of the colonized area, as well as others located elsewhere, took place in North America/New World, when Europeans colonized the land of various American Indians. As we have seen occur so often in the other parts of the world, *many of the Indian nations were decimated by voluntary defection*, their whole number was not killed off. Those who defected to the Europeans (see page# 337) did so in order to enjoy the superior quality of life offered by their more productive culture. The superior culture of the Europeans, absent both strong central regulation and high taxation, with those former Indians absorbed into itself along with the rest of the hodgepodge of European nations, *went on to make much more productive use of the land and its resources during the forthcoming two centuries* than all of the peoples had cumulatively produced during the entirety of the time preceding.

An instance in which colonization improved trade, making more for everybody, took place in the 11th century AD, when Venice took over the Adriatic Sea, establishing colonies throughout the Constantinople Empire. Absent customs fees charged at Abydos, this exemption beginning 992, the Venetians established hegemony in transport amongst both Asian and European Empire possessions. By 1082 Venetians, both at home and in their various trading colonies, were exempted from commercial taxes of all varieties. (116)

Myth of "Pillaging for a Living"

Purveyors of the religion of redistributive Victim Politics put forth *the false impression that wealth and plenty are gained by the forceful removal of riches from the weak by the strong; that great nations are built and sustained through plunder*, and that therefore all you need is to put the preacher into a position to violate the rights and freedoms of those who you envy, and to do some stealing on your behalf -forfeiting your own rights and freedoms in the process. *Pillaging for a living has almost never been the course leading to the prosperity of nations throughout history.* Trading for a living, manufacturing goods and providing services which are of value to others, and at a price which the others willfully -even fervently- choose to pay, is the proven method of gaining and perpetuating the best conditions for all; and of uplifting those presently least-moneyed in any given land.

Some may observe the possession of a strong national defense, or military arm, along with the possession of splendor and succor, and mistakenly conclude that *sine qua non*, a military force is a prerequisite to wealth and therefore that wealth can only be obtained through forceful burglary. In Asia during ancient times, the comitatus -a sort of royal entourage, who ate well with the ruler and were otherwise well compensated, whose job it was to function as the military- which was ***vital to both the attainment of power, as well as preventing subjugation at the hands of foreign invaders***, was quite expensive. Only wealthy countries and peoples could ever afford to pay one. Noted scholar Christopher Beckwith, after commenting on the great material wealth such as gold and horses found buried with large groups of bodies, tells us that "Though some of this wealth was obtained by warfare or tribute, methods used by powerful states throughout Eurasia for the same purpose, ***the great bulk of it was accumulated by trade***, which was the most powerful driving force behind the internal economy of Central Eurasia, as noted by foreign commentators from Antiquity through the Middle Ages." (117) Written in ancient Greece, Aristotle relayed in politics IV that ***armed forces were necessary for defense, as opposed to pillaging and oppressing***. Aristotle notes that a defense force is necessary "...if a state is not to become a slave of invaders." (118)

An attempt to "pay" the people with the glory of conquest, as opposed to payment with material remuneration, was attempted in Sparta during the 4th century AD. Spartan ruler Lycurgus used the prospect of ruling other lands through military conquest as the incentive for personal gain, which replaced accumulation of and production of wealth. Authorities searched homes routinely, and punished those who lived there if gold or silver were discovered; enforced uniform rationing of food and clothing; persuaded subjects to pay each other with manual labor, as opposed to currency or goods. Xenophon tells us in his Constitution of the Lacedaimonians that Lycurgus told them that labor "was the work of the soul" as opposed to "the work of wealth". *Lycurgus could only get them to go along with this temporarily*, until they started conquering and ruling other lands. *Less than two decades later, the accumulation of wealth was in vogue*, and gold proudly possessed by Spartans. (119)

Invasions and international conflict were often a response to being barred from entering the commercial opportunities involving a nation -being denied a chance to set up their own stand at the market, as it were- as opposed to a one-time swipe at the wrongful acquisition of the treasure of another. During the late 14th century in Central Asia, especially Western and Southern Central Asia, Tamerlane was a very successful general who repeatedly got the better of his foes during battles in which he was significantly under-manned, overtaking a large territory consisting of many different peoples. Beckwith tells us that: "He was content with the submission of his enemies, especially if they submitted voluntarily, and nearly always left rulers on their thrones as long as they paid taxes and did not rebel against him." (120)

During the 17th century in North America, more particularly in what today is the southeastern Canada/Northeast US territory, the Algonquain Indians, warring with Iroquois Indians, sought to make a peace in order to facilitate their access to the fur trade of the English at Albany, formerly fort Orange. (121) In the year 1805 in the USA, control of the port at New Orleans was out of U.S. hands, and this sparked desire for secession from the USA, as the allegiances of those in the area were tied to whomever may control that port. In 1795, Spain elected to open the port to trade from U.S. boats and merchants. Where in 1792 twelve boats per year traveled to New Orleans, in 1802 five hundred U.S. boats made their way down river, and 2,000 by 1807. Land sales from federal offices swelled from 67,000 acres in the year 1800, to 581,000 acres by 1805. Cut off by the Spanish in 1802, president Jefferson was granted by the congress his requests: for James Monroe to be the authorized negotiator; along with an allowance of $2 million with which to acquire New Orleans, along with both east and west Florida, in a peaceful manner, from the Spanish and the French. Napoleon was an eager seller, parting with 828,000 square miles -later divided into 14 states- in exchange for $15 million in 1803 (equivalent to $600 million in 2012 dollars). This immense purchase was ratified by congress in October 1803. (122) (for more on the Louisiana Purchase, see page# 266)

Originating during the mid-1st millennium BC, and culminating in the 18th cent AD, *the Eurasian Silk Road commerce network exemplified the prevalence of trading over plundering*. From the Scythians to the Junghars, Central Eurasia was largely controlled by nomadic warrior civilizations. The nomadic lifestyle aided those states in war -as a result of their mobility, they were enabled to retreat when attacked, without deserting their property and homes. The nomadic groups provided a moving target for potential rivals, while their foes all had a "home base" which could be centered upon, scouted, and attacked. *The nomadic lifestyle*, in addition to providing elusivity in combat, also *necessitated that such a nation be competent in trade and commerce* in order to survive or thrive, because they did not tend the same fields for months and raise crops to be harvested therefrom. The various nomadic orders *lived longer lifespans, of greater leisure*, than those in anchored agricultural states. Chinese, Romans, and Greeks, all fled their homelands in numbers to join with the Central Eurasian nomad groups due to the greater wealth, better treatment, and overall superior quality of life, enjoyed by a member of a nomadic group. Beckwith tells us that: *"Central Eurasian peoples knew that it was far more profitable to trade and tax than it was to raid and destroy. Historical examples of the latter activity are the exception rather than the rule and are usually a consequence of open war."* Spending on what is called national defense today, then called the comitatus, was the lynchpin of all governments until the Middle Ages, for the societies of Central Eurasia. (123)

The European explorations which for centuries spread so much commerce, information, and sustenance, throughout India and Asia, were motivated by a desire for personal gain on the part of the sailors and their financial backers. In 1498, Vasco da Gama sailed from Portugal to the southwestern coast of India near Calicut -present day Kozhikode- establishing the first direct trade route between the Orient and Europe; eliminating all of the previous overland middlemen. Although he was robbed, and nearly killed, by the Muslim traders that he encountered, he returned to Portugal with a bounty 3,000 times as valuable as the amount invested. Over the next several decades the Portuguese repeatedly returned, and engaged in combat as a necessity with the hostile, and fiercely violent, Muslim traders along the coasts and in the port cities. The natives were eager to retain their positions of quasi-monopolistic status, and therefore were hostile to the new commerce, which is counterproductive for the people or nation as a whole. ***This near monopoly was, of course, only possible via collusion with the local government***. Religious persecution also played a role in the violence done unto the Europeans, "Yet force was generally unnecessary", Beckwith tells us. The European trade force "was led almost exclusively by private trading companies", though they did have some government backing. Almost *no* political or cultural impact was made on Asia as a result of this commerce. (124)

Turning now to Europe and Scandinavia: Though primarily trading for a living, for 50 years the Scandinavians would conduct annual excursions of plundering via both the Adriatic Sea and the northern river. The raids ceased after the Scandinavians took the northern ports of Quentovic and Duurstede during a Viking invasion in the 9th century. The professional traders had the trading ports, and this occupied their interest plentifully; leaving their hobby of plundering neglected. (125) The loss of these trading ports, and not any losses due to plundering, were to decimate economic life for the Europeans until their re-capture in the 12th century. (for more on this, see page# 240, and page# 398)

During the 10th century AD in Europe, ***castles built for defending*** themselves from Arab attackers became shelters for those in duress during inclement weather. Many shelter seekers were merchants, and others shippers of merchandise. While idling there as they waited out the weather, they naturally networked amongst each other, as well as with those at their eventual destinations. Soon, castles located in positions advantageous to trade -near important waterways- became trading hubs. This activity became so important that traders began living at the castles permanently. These castles became so overstuffed with merchants that ***the traders set up a small settlement for themselves***, adjacent to the castle. This settlement soon grew so large as to dwarf the castle which was once the looming presence, as ***the commerce conducted in pursuit of personal gain built homes, in addition to providing employment and providing goods for people near and far***. (126) From this, germinated the mechanism for the elevation of status on the social ladder, via trade, for many serfs and those displaced from serfdom into vagrancy due to overpopulation of a familial plot; that is, for those least advantaged and least-moneyed at birth.

Beginning in the 11th century, the new class of merchants/traders -which was being minted through their individual energy- later known as the bourgeoisie (see page# 393), took it upon themselves to provide for defense of the towns they had built; as the new wealth created by these traders, and transported with them to the area, attracted marauders. Protective walls were erected and maintained by the bourgeoisie, who took it upon themselves to impose a wealth tax -*a tax upon their own class, handled and spent by their own class*- as the device for implementing their group's choice to protect the people with fortification. From these beginnings, sprung formal organization and the necessary election of politicians who then continued taxing, while never ceasing to spend. The traders flourished and their blossoming municipalities provided ample funds, and what followed were not only bridges and churches, but also nefarious craft regulators, along with those meddling in food production. Marauders had to either go do something productive or starve; that is, if they couldn't split the difference by becoming politicians in the new towns built by the commerce of the former serfs now bourgeoisie! (127)

The traders took on a special legal status, which they shared with those in their towns. *These bourgeoisie carried their exemption from the rural stipulations of the lords over the serfs, and extended it to all within their city's ever swelling boundaries.* Life within the walls of the merchants' cities offered an unearned -because the others in the city were not themselves traders- legal liberty, in addition to allowing access to the ample array of goods afforded by the proximity of the merchants and their trading partners, while within the city's walls. *This respite from the harsh conditions of the rural feudal system*, backed rigidly by the Church, *was a godsend for those able to gain entry.* (128)

This new class of merchants, having uplifted themselves from serfdom in absence of centralized orchestration through the mechanism of the state, and who willfully uplifted and protected those around them in the towns that this merchant bourgeoisie had erected, *had by the 16th century propelled the European countries and their people on an upward trajectory which brought goods, sustenance, and wealth to millions.* Berend and Ranki:

> "Scholars investigating the issue of backwardness tend to pay special attention to the period between the sixteenth and nineteenth centuries, the time when modern capitalism began to take shape. It was at this time that the countries of Western Europe evolved the bourgeois class structure fitting them to become the core of a capitalist world economy, one in which Latin America and Eastern Europe, ossified in feudalism, were relegated to the role of foodstuff and raw material producers – were relegated in short, to the 'periphery' of this world economy. Some major colonial nations such as Spain and Portugal became 'semi-peripheral'. Most of Asia, Africa, and the Russian Empire remained totally outside the capitalist world-system during these centuries. Later on, when modern capitalism had not only spread geographically, but had also developed an international division of labour, Asia and Africa, too, became peripheral, even as the European periphery was becoming ever less so." (129)

When presented with an image of a "foreigner" stepping in to rule over a "native", some people infer that one party is wronging the other, and that the foreigner is oppressing the native for their own cruel and exacting gain. *As the the tables began to turn in regards to Asian supremacy over Europeans*, Beckwith summarizes for us thusly: "In short, *in order to be able to participate in international trade*, the Europeans needed to stabilize the trade routes and the port cities by *establishing their political dominance over them*, exactly as the Central Eurasians were forced to do over and over for the two millennia that the Central Eurasian economy flourished -the period of existence of the Silk Road. The result was European military defeat of the local Asian rulers, or pressure on them, and the growth of European political power in Asia. They established their right to maritime trade in the region, secured it with fortified trading posts, and took control of the open seas." The fall of several dynastic empires took place in Asia during the 19th century, at which juncture the Europeans took control of the rudderless locales. *Commerce, and the desire on the part of the Europeans not to be segregated out of it*, was what brought them there in the first place. (130) He continues: "It was only when the peripheral empires became feeble, or actually collapsed, that the Central Eurasians attempted to set up new governments or otherwise stepped in to attempt to stabilize things. This is just what the Europeans did in India and China in the nineteenth and early twentieth centuries. In both the Silk Road and the Littoral System cases, only gradually did the Central Eurasians and the Europeans, respectively, become involved in attempting to govern directly." (131)

This myth that foreign "rule" or "colonization" wrongs the ethnic majority is further disproven in (part I, Phantom Monsters), yet an example will follow here. Contacts with the West, motivated by the potential for profits to be made by individual Westerners, transformed Malaya. During the 1890s, Malaya was comprised of an assortment of fishing villages and hamlets. There were few inhabitants at this juncture. By the 1930s, this same area was an international powerhouse in the rubber and tin industries; millions now lived in the nations which at that time boasted several large metropolises; natives experienced vastly improved material conditions and life expectancy, while emigrants flocked in from India and China seeking to improve their lot in life. (132)

Capitalism is humane, benefiting the other party; wokernism is inhumane savagery, wronging the other party. Nature, absent all technology, dictates that 1st one must work in order to survive; and that 2nd one can work harder today in order to provide for an easier tomorrow, capturing dividend on their investments -building a simple dwelling or shelter in the woods today, provides an ease of life for months to come; planting and tending to the soil today make for a more bountiful harvest, or any harvest at all, tomorrow; and so forth. Capitalism advances from this stage, *which is dictated by nature and to which all beings are subjected*, going on to employ free exchange as a primary means of survival -particularly helpful to those who go through periods of ill health, or who advance to old age. Socialism regresses to the use of force. Indians in Iroquoia were a stark contrast to the European colonists of the

17th century; the Indians resorting exclusively to violence as a means of acquisition, while the Europeans by this time had become accustomed to a system of exchange and negotiation. (133)

IMMIGRANT ENTREPRENEURS ARE GOOD

For at least half of a century in the United States of America, once the cancerous seeds of the New Deal had metastasized into the invidious Great Society and War on Poverty redistributive horrors, debate has been conducted pertaining the desirability of immigrants into the USA. *The patently obvious fact is that ample availability of handouts for the healthy make it undoubtedly clear that newcomers can pose a significant cost unto the nation*, while such paid to fail handouts make it no longer clear that if these people are unable to engage in productive behaviors they will be flushed back out of the country, or least not act as a drain upon the rest. Questions as to which aspiring immigrants are desirable, and which, if any, ought to be systematically excluded, predate that era. *One fact that is evident throughout history is that immigrant entrepreneurs are, on the whole, a positive addition to any nation*. The instances of wanderers turned *hotes*, vagabonds turned bourgeoisie, have already been referenced elsewhere within this text. The nomadic conquerors of ancient Eurasia brought their superior methods to their subjugated regions, as did the Romans to Europe. A handful of other examples of such activity follow here.

SE Asia 1957: "The economic superiority they [the overseas Chinese] generally have over the indigenous Malays is due overwhelmingly to their greater industry, ingenuity, thrift, ambition and resourcefulness." A typical Chinese family might own and work 20 acres of rubber plants, along with active interests in a handful of other ventures, whereas a typical Malay might have 2 acres of rubber crops -with a hired hand to help them- and look after half an acre of padi. (134)

No access to handouts forces greater productivity, as evidenced in Greece during the 5th-4th centuries BC. *Metics* -who were not slaves, but also not citizens- were crucial to commerce. By the end of the 4th century BC, *metics* accounted for one half of the non-slave population -21,000 citizens, 10,000 *metics*. *Metics* were not, and never could become, citizens. As such, ***metics were disqualified from the receipt of handouts***, yet remained subject to taxation; this includes a tax peculiar to *metics* called the *metoikion*. Non-citizens could not own land, therefore *metics* were traders, shippers, merchants, artisans, and the like. ***Immigrants represented a possibility of gain to the state, without much likelihood of loss.*** (135) This is precisely the inverse of the conditions present in the United States of America from the onset of the 1960s, and as such the USA began rightly to oppose much immigration into their country, and justly so, yet still remained the most welcoming of incomers from other lands in all of the world.

Foreign investment is good, high corporate tax is bad: Huguenots develop British and German industry, post-WWII German refugees all over the world. (136) Overseas Chinese S.E. Asia, Indians in East Africa, Lebanese and Chinese in West Indies, Lebanese and other Levantines in West Africa. "They have accumulated capital, provided skills and aptitudes not present or developed among the local people, and have pioneered in the development of trade, transport and industries." Often, a small minority contributes heavily. In 1957, 2,000 Levantines among 30 million Nigerians raised "areas from subsistence production to a more advanced level of economic activity." (137)

SOCIAL MOBILITY:
FROM TIGHTLY REGULATED FEUDALISM, UNREGULATED FREE TRADE BIRTHED A NEW CLASS OF WEALTHY: THE BOURGEOISIE

The preachers of the religion known as Victim Politics frequently affix blame for the condition of the man with less upon the man with more -even one penny more- and *often advocate the prevention of an unequal accrual of gains*, claiming this method of reducing the chasm between the position of each man to be key to the uplifting of the man with less. Of course, *this does not elevate the lower man, but simply tears down the higher man*, leading to a condition in which not only has the man with less not gotten any better, but *the net impact upon society is to have reduced prosperity*. Only the preacher, whether a bureaucrat, or politician, or a media personality outside of those two functions, benefits from this process. A grand defalcation of both social elevation, and of riches, takes place which harms the sheep amongst the preacher's flock most of all.

Commerce uplifts the masses by creating a new class of wealthy people, thereby creating membership in and access to the more desirable status. Whereas Marxism demonizes the "bourgeoisie" as oppressive to those least-moneyed, this very class is in fact the vehicle to upward social mobility, and has been from the date of its reappearance in Europe. During the 11th-12th centuries AD in Europe, *a "Commercial Revolution" took place which yielded the creation of a new class*, this consisting of merchants/traders, *providing economic mobility to the masses*.

Serfs, who would flee their assigned plots at the risk of being re-captured and punished, along with the vagabonds; whether as a result of being born into a family with more mouths than food, or due to the resultant oversaturation of hereditary splits in the land amongst a plentitude of heirs, or those who relocated as a result of war -whether to fight as a hired man, or due to flight from vanquished territory- were able to carve out a niche and to re-introduce independent businessmen as a significant class.

Though many struck out during their time at bat, others elevated themselves and their families to better lives, and a few did exceptionally well. Those who achieved the greatest fortunes served as the examples which allured great numbers to try their hand at trading. One man, St. Godric of Finchale, stumbled upon cargo from a shipwreck which had washed up to shore and used it to begin as a trader. He shortly established himself, and partnered up, to bring trade to England, Flanders, Denmark, and Scotland. Buying what was plentiful and inexpensive in region "A", then transporting it to region "B", where the same good was scarce and commanded higher prices. *Profits soared while resources were distributed from those who had much to those who had little*.

This was true of food during "an age when local famines were continual". High profits to be made through buying low and selling high kept food growing, and kept people endeavoring to transport the food to the distressed areas. (138) If a serf escaped his assigned plot of land, and fled by a great enough distance from the rural estate to which they had ties to a lord, the search for the serf who fled would be called off. Escaping to a new town, and getting by, for a year and a day, *codified their liberty imbuing in them the right to contract*. (139)

An example of private funds building infrastructure occurred sometime 1114-1130. During this period, a man called Werimbold was hired by a merchant of means, married the man's daughter, and cultivated his own fortune in trade. Werimbold constructed a bridge with private funding, and upon his death left much of his property to the Church. (140) From the middle of the 12th through the late 13th century, the new class of *hotes* -particularly the merchants among them- spread commerce wherever they went, as they traded in pursuit of their own, personal, profit. *The lords extended the liberty* afforded to these land improving, and profiteering, *hotes, to those living within the walls of the towns built by these merchants*, which was a *condition demanded by the hotes*. Although the lords knew well that those populating the towns had escaped from their manors, *they were glad to escape the rigid system of commerce quashing controls required by the state* on the manors, by granting these liberties to the residents of the town. This was done because they had witnessed for centuries the irrefutably propitious impact it made upon the masses, and *they obeyed this evidence*.

These towns grew in size, and began displacing the seigneurial system. As per usual, the prosperity and better methods spread in a pattern which begins in the most frequented trading spots, often nearest the most frequented port at which goods arrive and depart, then are transmitted inward from the seas in a fashion which resembles sort of a bleed that thins as it proceeds; leaving a lessened impact as it travels inland, in addition to having a delayed date of arrival. Beginning mid-12th century, Flanders, the north of France, Tuscany, Lombardy; spreading to central Germany and England by the close of the 13th century. *Serfdom's demise was the gift of the bourgeoisie*. (141)

More than a thousand years prior to this epoch in Europe, there was an event containing many similarities in Greece circa 570-526 BC (142), a non-civic settlement was developed in the Egyptian Nile delta *by private traders from all over*. People from all over benefited from this avenue for exchange, as traders hailing from Aegina, from locales scattered about Asia minor, as well as from the islands adjacent the settlement, did business. This place was called Naukratis. *The only involvement of the state was merely their choice to stay out of it* and to not quash the trading post which benefited the members of the state, as well as the citizens. This does not mean that Naukratis was free of government rule via the Pharaoh, it means only that government did not conjure or facilitate its existence, creation, or perpetuation. The Pharaoh took note of all commerce which passed through and the conduct of the people. Intermarriage between Greeks and Egyptians was expressly forbidden. (143)

Several centuries later, commerce uplifted the masses by creating new classes of wealthy, thereby increasing membership in and access to the more desirable status. In Athens, during the 4th century BC, a wealthy class whose fortune was in workshops and workers (slaves), rather than in land, arose. (144) This broke the monopoly of landowners on the ability to be one's own man.

In addition to the towns, bridges, and trading hubs mentioned above in this section, more instances of privately built and funded infrastructure can be found with the railroads in Germany during the 19th century (page# 188-189), the case of the *hotes* clearing land in England during the 18th century (page# 380-382); and for the experience of the American transcontinental rails, which were mostly but not entirely, publicly funded lines, see a prior work. (145)

Upward social mobility through trading and profiteering, when it is not disallowed by government, is illustrated by goings on in 18th century England. The countryside was abundant in manorial estates complete with park, garden, manor house, and nearby acreage. Some were possessed by families who had responsibly and successfully preserved generational wealth, while others were owned by "men who had recently come to fortune by way of some trade or profession." *These last men increased their proportion of the estate owners during the 18th century.* (146)

An older landowner lamented to his son that "merchants had usurped the position of power and esteem that rightly belonged to men of pedigree and title." That is, that *merit was replacing heredity. This spurred the wealthy* -or those who wished to remain wealthy- *into the action of serving their fellow man* in a way in which only free trade and commerce can. The landed knew that the key to remaining wealthy was to be profitable, and that profit from their land depended largely upon their agrarian tenants and their productivity, which in turn caused the landed to be incentivized to teach their tenant farmers the best ways to cultivate their land and to experience the best crop yields. (147) During this period, there were many "paupers who had, and often sought, no other designation [than poverty]." T.S. Ashton continues, by pointing out that "class gradations were rungs of a ladder which many climbed and descended." (148)

"GREED"
– THE DESIRE TO GAIN MORE THAN ONE
NEEDS IN ORDER TO SURVIVE FOR THAT DAY–
IS GOOD

Many morally bankrupt, or feeble minded, people pretend that acquiring more than one foresees as necessary to achieve subsistence living for that day or week, is the contemptible embodiment of greed. Any perusal of the evidence dictates the conclusion that *the desire to attain immense riches, even enough for several lifetimes*, as the motivation to provide for one's children or grandchildren motivates their productivity, and also the lust for frivolous material objects, have inspired more productivity, and *lifted more people out of starvation and privation, than any demonization of one's superiors ever has*. Dissolute parties seek to prey upon the blinding envy, or the tremendous wealth of practical ignorance, of the ILC (see part IV), as these nefarious creatures pursue so-called populist, redistributive, socialism. While pursuit of riches via destructive means such as the establishment of monopolies through the mechanism of the state, theft of treasure through the mechanism of the state, or theft of treasure via the mechanism of petty burglary, are counterproductive towards the end of elevating the prosperity of the masses; when it comes to pursuit of treasure via legitimate trade, "greed", as they say in the movies, "is good". (149)

The desire for personal gain has always been evident throughout history: Medieval Europe, 12th century onwards: Pirenne, again, brings up Godric and the shipwreck (see page# 394 to learn more):

> "The case of Godric has already been quoted. The spirit which animated him was in every sense of the term the capitalistic spirit of all times. He reasoned, he calculated and his sole aim was the accumulation of profits. These are, after all, the essential characteristics of capitalism, of which a certain

school of historians makes so great a mystery, but which, nevertheless, is to be met with at all periods, fundamentally the same though in different degrees of development, because it corresponds with man's acquisitive instinct. Godric cannot have been in any way exceptional." (150)

In Medieval Europe, merchants from distant lands formed partnerships and traversed the rough terrain for lengthy periods of time -and at great risk of loss in terms of both their lives, and of their treasure- in order to provide for those in the markets of their ultimate destination. It is also true that some of the purchasers will in turn re-ship the loot to people of an even greater distance from the locale of the origin of the good's manufacture. All of this hardship was undertaken and endured due to nothing more than the merchants' desire for their own monetary profit; which was not always obtained, of course, due to piracy, damages to products en route, or to their own death. (151)

Capitalism and the desire for gain uplift the quality of life for the masses, even in the restrictive environment of India during the period 1900-1950. Construction of railroads and canals, for the purposes of profit and trade, greatly reduced famine for the masses. When a local harvest failed, those in the area could trade with others who were able to sell their cash crops to those in the poor harvest area, through these channels. The successful growers and harvesters, the middle men and transporters to and from the railway or waterway, and those shipping on the boats or rails, all got paid as *their desire for personal gain built those modes of conveyance in the first place* and fed the hungry people when their harvest failed. Much like the term "poverty" or "poor" in the USA continues to be applied to incrementally more wealthy groups -in an effort by those who are financially dependent upon the Victim Politics Industry to swindle the rubes into compliance with the ruse that "the work is never done"- the word "famine" in India has undergone similar treatment. In 100 years, the meaning of the word famine as used and understood in India, changed drastically. During the

1800s famine meant mass death from starvation, while by the mid-1900s the same word merely denoted large unemployment due to poor harvests. (152)

In the no-profit environment of Medieval Europe, particularly after the northern ports were lost to the Nordics in the 9th century, *the evil done by the systematically imposed inability to profit* is commented on by Pirenne:

> "Moreover, the whole idea of profit, and indeed the possibility of profit, was incompatible with the position occupied by the great medieval landowner. Unable to produce for sale *owing to the want of a market*, he had no need to tax his ingenuity in order to wring from his men and his land *a surplus which would merely be an encumbrance*, and as he was forced to consume his own produce, he was content to limit it to his needs. His means of existence was assured by the traditional functioning of an organisation which he did not try to improve. Before the middle of the twelfth century, *the greater part of the soil belonging to him was given over to heaths, forests and marshes*. Nowhere do we perceive the least effort to break with the age-old system of rotation, to suit the crops cultivated to the properties of the soil, or to improve agricultural implements. *Considering its potential capacity, the enormous landed capital at the disposal of the Church and the nobility produced in the main no more than an insignificant return.*" (153)

Given what we know about the detrimental impacts of the tightening of the Beast's grip around the windpipe of of a nation, through taxation, regulation, and redistribution, *an assessment regarding the return as paltry, in comparison with the potential capacity of the USA since the New Deal period, even with an ever-growing GPD, does not seem unlikely.* That the world's largest economy has been criminally under-performing for a century may seem anterior to one's conclusion at first glance, yet a familiarity with all of the factual, and incontrovertible, instances in which government interference has reduced plenty; coupled with the knowledge of examples in which an infusion of individual liberty has been interjected between the people and the state, sometimes with the very same people and territory as were present during conditions of harsh regulation and redistribution, that have yielded outcomes of greater output and social mobility; certainly lead one to conclude that it is so that America's economy is not providing nearly as much as it would have and should have, and that certain people are living worse than they ought to be, *due to this new tradition of voting against one's best interests by supporting handouts for the healthy and redistributionism.*

Exposure to toys motivated the poor to become productive in China during the late 20th century. In 1958 the first tv station was established in China, in 1979 fewer than 5 million tv sets were in the nation. In 1980 the Chinese government -still in control of programming and the information included in all forms of media- add 10 minutes of international news to their customary, dreary, flagrant propaganda, masquerading as "news". Images of Western Europe, the USA, and Japan - "The West"- and their vastly superior material wealth, as well as nourishment, were before the eyes of the previously isolated Chinese. During 1981 the Chinese government ups their production quota to 2.5 mil sets -half of the then-present supply of TVs in the nation- while importing another 1 mil sets from Japan. The Chinese masses wanted what they saw, and they wanted tv sets. Perhaps *the most popular program in China at that time was a tutorial on English, because English was one of the key tickets out of the "dictatorship of the proletariat"* and "worker's paradise" of Communist, Marxism loving, China and its horrible oppression and dictation from central planners. The teacher had been previously incarcerated during the Cultural Revolution because of a "crime" committed by their relatives. This "offense" was simply having a consensual romantic encounter with a person who would later become a high official in the Party. (154) Contemporary readers in the United States will notice an alarming similarity between this practice, and the present attempt at so-called "slave reparations" (see also: page# 270), which would in fact punish a person for an "offense" committed before the punished person was even born, and which therefore wrongly convicts the individual of the "crime".

The net impact of consumerism has been observed by Bauer and Yamey, who remark that: "In these circumstances consumption and investment are complimentary: the higher level of consumption induces additional and more productive effort, which serves to generate incomes, and which in turn renders possible both increased consumption and increased accumulation of capital." (155) Another instance in which exposure to the toys and tools of more affluent people motivated the poor to become productive, can be found in Africa during the mid-20th century, particularly in Rhodesia and Nyasaland in 1954. Wide advertisement of bicycles and accessories, toilet preparations, cosmetics, musical instruments, non-alcoholic drinks, records, along with cameras and film, all *stirred the poor into productivity as their desire to purchase the products provided goals that they sought to achieve*. Also, similar findings occurred in Bechuanaland in 1947. (156)

Many become "addicted to winning", as investing becomes more satisfying than consuming. Milton Friedman found this to be so in the early 20th century USA (157), and T.S. Ashton found the same in 18th century England. In England, *conspicuous investment prevailed over conspicuous consumption* as productivity and self propulsion of one's own -and by extension, one's family's own- advancement was a major priority for the overwhelming majority of the English during this time. *Saving and meticulous diligence* in watching over one's financial progress *were prevalent*, from the present aristocracy to those presently housewives of laborers and merchants. (158)

PAID TO FAIL:
YOU GET WHAT YOU PAY FOR
(see also: part III, page# 203)

"A blanket approval of Bolshevism in the abstract furnishes many a man an excuse for not supporting his family. You should be careful not to get in the frame of mind where a similar approval of all the effects of Vienna socialism justifies you in your own mind in not doing a real day's work." -Colonel Robert McCormick, Publisher, Chicago Tribune, 1932. *In response to a writer who wrote glowingly of socialism in Vienna. (159)*

Generous handouts quash initiative for work, productivity, and independence. This is exemplified by the experience of the Iroquois Indians during the mid-18th century, in the present day New York State region. The Iroquois, already living at a mere subsistence level, extorted the Europeans for loot as a matter of what they referred to as "diplomatic necessity". This extortion was conducted under a not so subtle threat of violence, either by an Iroquois attack or by an Iroquois desertion of alliance in the event that the Euros were attacked by others. A private citizen, William Johnson, eventually acted as a competing benefactor, and by 1763 had become their sole patron. *The Iroquois sat on the extorted booty, ceased their customary feeble efforts towards self-sufficient productivity, and became professional extortionists*. Their numbers, and *their independence, shriveled during this time*. (160)

A condition of dependency upon handouts can lead to violence upon their revocation -as opposed to a return to independence or productivity. We see this principle in practice with the Iroquois during what is known as Pontiac's War, which involved their assault upon Detroit, Fort Pitt, and parts of unfortified Pennsylvania and Virginia. (161)

During the 19th century, we find a nation switching from shaming the lazy and unproductive, in an effort to discourage such behavior and *to best utilize the nation's* resources, *both in terms of capital and of people*; to rewarding the very same behavior, incentivising counterproductive use of both capital and of people. England, in 1834, passed legislation which temporarily deprived handout recipients of their rights as citizens, which had been a consequence of dipping their hands into their neighbors' pockets through the mechanism of the state. Begging and loafing were contrary to the prevailing culture of the Victorian Era English, who lauded Puritan work ethic and self respect. In a world prior to the medical knowledge, cleaning chemicals, and medicine, of the 20th century, attention and funds were turned to means of reducing or eradicating contagious diseases, mostly through the construction and provision of hospitals and flop houses during the middle of the century. In what may have been the important difference in terms of incentives for the passing of legislation which sets the key variable to the setting which concentrates power into the hands of the few by decree, universal suffrage was enacted 1885. As of this writing, it's all been a downward progression from there in that country, as the tentacles of socialism have sprung from the Parliament and wrapped around an ever greater proportion of the jobs and rights of the people. (162)

"It ain't worth while to tell lies about a bit o' porridge." -The remark of one parent of a school aged child in Britain during the 20th century, but prior to the outbreak of the First World War, who confessed to previously cheating the charity via dishonesty when handouts were more generous. Changes had been implemented to disincentivize such behavior. (163)

From mid-century until the outbreak of the Great War, the proportion of those on the dole in England and Wales declined by roughly 50%, though *the proportion of those classified as able bodied increased by about 50%*:

Recipients of Handouts Through the Mechanism of the State in England and Wales

	Lowest Year	Highest Year
1850-59	4.4%	5.7%
1860-69	4.2%	5.3%
1870-79	2.9%	4.6%
1880-89	2.8%	3.1%
1890-99	2.4%	2.6%
1900-1914	2%	2.5%

ABLE BODIED PAUPERS   1850   0.29%   1906   0.46%

Source for chart: Bentley B. Gilbert, *The Evolution of National Insurance in Britain: The Origins of the Welfare State* (London: Michael Joseph Limited, 1966), p. 25

Paid to fail socialism, by 1869 in England, had led to a situation in which indiscriminate -in regard to the individual's personal conduct, or the reason for their state of penury- handouts produced a "professional welfare class". The Charity Organization Society -COS- formed in 1869 as an attempt to replace the variety of small private charities which had conducted their giving by rushing to give away all of their funds or food until their resources had been exhausted, and done so unconditionally. As a result, says Bentley B. Gilbert, professional charity workers noted that "*a sharp and seasoned clientele among the wastrels and loafers of the East End*" had developed. The COS wanted to aid the poor into generating their own rise above a state of want, by giving only on the condition that those doing the asking behave in ways conducive to improvement. Writing during the early 1890s, COS secretary Charles S. Loch: "want of employment, in nine cases out of ten in which the plea is used, is not the cause of distress. It is, as often as not, drink." (164)

KARL MARX STUFF
(see also: part III, "Worker's Paradise", page# 209)

"I studied Marxism-Leninism. You could read the book right side up or upside down. Whichever way suited you best at that moment. If you needed to justify something, no problem: the theory was at your service. Party-mindedness, they call it: the cleverest manipulation technique ever invented." -A middle-aged, skilled worker, at one of Magnitogorsk, Russia's, most sizeable factories. Quoted anonymously for reasons of safety. (165)

Although Marxism, and its failure to deliver upon its promises of splendor for those who wish to satisfy their enmity towards those who have more, via theft of their property, followed with misuse of these ill-gotten properties and mechanisms vital to the supply of necessities and of jobs, is disproven throughout the virtual totality of this volume, and is specifically addressed in several instances, a brief potpourri on the subject with follow here.

We begin with an introduction to Karl Marx, the doofus. ***The man concocts a bizarre contrivance, upon which the entirety of his failed religion is based***. To begin with, Marx claims that all commodities consist of two types of value: use value; and exchange value.

"The utility of a thing makes it a use value." "Exchange value,...the proportion in which values in use of one sort are exchanged for those of another sort." (166) But the change of commodities is evidently an act characterized by a total abstraction from use value. Then one use value is just as good as another, provided only it be present in sufficient quantity. Or, as old Barbon says, 'One sort of wares are as good as another, if the values be equal. There is no difference or distinction in things of equal value... An hundred pounds' worth of lead or iron, is of as great value as one hundred pounds' worth of silver or gold.'

As use values, commodities are, above all, of different quantities, but as exchange values they are merely different quantities, and consequently do not contain an atom of use value.

If we leave out of the consideration the use value of commodities, they have only one common property left, that of being products of labour." (167)

Have you ever heard of anything so asinine? Stating that an ounce of ground beef ought trade at equal value with an ounce of gold? Marx went on, as he compared the two supposedly equal -via this bizarre pathway- commodities, attempting to arrive at a way to determine their value:

> "The two things must therefore be equal to a third, which in itself is neither the one nor the other. Each of them, so far as it is exchange value, must therefore be reducible to this third." (168)

The answer, of course, is currency; though *Marx* goes through all of the aforementioned verbal gymnastics in order to *pretend* that labor is some sort of a kinetic energy, stored up inside of a coiled spring, unable to be accessed, and *that fully paid workers are therefore being cheated* because they are being paid in commodities which have utility for them to do many things -including graduating from their dependent wage slave status through investment and risk taking.

I found a U.S. textbook first published 1931, though the edition that I have was printed in 1944, and was used as a high school textbook. The book's author, Carl L. Becker, Professor Emeritus of History, Cornell University: "But the course of events has been very different from what Marx predicted." (169) (see page# 209 for complete quote) There has not been a mass uprising by the wage-earners, and those which have occurred have delivered the opposite of the paradise promised by Marx's writings. Could this, plainly accurate, banal statement, be printed in a textbook bought by a US high school today?

Marxist claims of industrial exploitation or oppression, or of the impact of business owners as being *a priori* parasitic, are contrary to what is actually best for each individual and particularly for the present day wage slaves. *Such a culture is one of self defeat and counterproductivity.* After all, providing for one's self or his progeny, a mechanism for providing income during and after incidences of illness, injury, bereavement, old age, along with other situations; and so doing by providing jobs to people, jobs which involve the creation and delivery of goods or services to other people; wholly negates the communist lifestyle of devoting all of one's energies to appropriating and destroying these existing machines of sustenance, while devoting absolutely no energy toward bettering one's self, and the community around them, through the creation and perpetuation of his own business.

During the 4th century BC in Athens, small shops never combined into larger enterprises through merger or sale. Wealth through workshop ownership, and through trading (merchants) were fashionable during this period, though real estate was not yet sold as a commodity -meaning that land was not sold for the highest price or greatest profit. (170) *The Greeks of this era emphasized a culture in which providing for one's own old age, and times of illness, was in vogue.* The societal definition of wealth was a life in which the necessity of work for survival was the standard by which one was measured. *The less that one must do, the more successful one was deemed to be.* (171) Living in conditions in which handouts for the healthy for the lazy and less industrious, from the coffers of those behaving in an anterior fashion, through the mechanism of the state was not yet commonplace, this culture meant that one was incentivised to aid his fellow man through the creation and delivery of goods and services, particularly food. *This is precisely the opposite of the culture of socialism which condemns self-sufficiency, and the production of goods and services*, through attack and theft.

While it is easy to complain about the boss, it's not so easy to be the boss. Wealth and prosperity are not mellifluous as a result of merely owning the means of production. Behaviors determine outcomes, leaving one person to have a different outcome than another person, even if they are utilizing the same implement towards a stated end, or are begun with an equal cache of supplies. We find this illustrated by events in Panama during the mid-20th century. In 1941, after resentment amongst an amount of the native Panamanian population had been brewing since at least 1928, President Arias is reported, by J. and M. Biesanz in *The People of Panama*, to have used "devious means" to "dispossess most Chinese owners of their shops and handed them to his henchmen or sold them for ridiculous amounts." The Panamanian constitution of 1946 restricted the entry of foreigners into the retail trade. By 1955, some of *the Panamanians who received the stolen booty had been forced, by their own inferiority* to the Chinese when it came to running the various businesses -illustrating that simply "owning a business" does not, in and of itself, equate to financial success or prosperity- *and ineptitude* at sustaining the enterprises, *to sell the stores back to their previous owners*, or to others. (172)

Disproving the Marxist claim of *a priori* worker exploitation or oppression: Germany 1st half 19th century: The hand of the Beast loosens: Freedom for the agricultural sector (de-regulation) led to privately funded research and experimentation, resulting in modernization and innovation which not only increased food output for the long term, but necessarily stirred demand for workers. Abolition of serfdom led the masses to pursue their own destiny with their new found liberty. The industrial centers of Germany expanded in population at a rate which exceeded the 38% national swelling of population between 1815-45. *The workers voluntarily sought the factories* in pursuit of the greater opportunity *for advancement, and higher wages*, that could be gotten. The proletariat fled to the cities and the factories in droves because it could make their lives better. This voluntary movement is evidenced, for example, in Berlin. Between 1834-44 the population of Berlin grew by 101,130 people, while the amount of births in the city exceeded deaths by only 15,453. During the time period 1840-44 the cities in Saxony grew in population by 8.48%, while its rural areas grew by a mere 4.25%. (173) *If it's so bad, why did they go there? And why did they remain there?* (see also: page# 195)

People flocked to the cities, and their factories, seeking and enjoying employment regularly. *These working class folks* were at liberty to move from one employer to another, as swiftly as they pleased, as they *exploited the risk taking factory owners for all of the remuneration that could be gotten*. Fleeing the villages and their lives as unlanded peasants, free from obligation and fidelity to the feudal style landlords, the workers enjoyed an increase in their quality of life and of their own fates. Men *steadily fled the restriction of monopoly imposed by the old guilds*, or associations (unions), willingly and freely, as *the chance to call their own shots* and to set the best prices and terms that they could for themselves, prevailed. Circa 1850: 33% of all non-agricultural workers in Germany worked in factories. (174)

During the Late 18th and early 19th centuries, the break up of the corporate guild's pervasive presence increased the liberty of the populace. The handicraft guild system was a state sanctioned monopoly in Germany -akin to the ICC in the USA- with much legal self-regulatory authority -like the NLRB of the New Deal in USA- engaged in an effort to manipulate and control: prices and wages, methods of production, acceptable standards of quality, and the terms for their industry's employees. The monopolies made *cries of social justice concerns*, but this nonsensical sophistry was *disregarded -as is proper to do* in all instances of the invocation of the slippery and mysterious phantom called "social justice"- and freedom to choose for one's self and to do one's own negotiating, won the day. (175)

Industrial workers, a new class of vocation that arose as a consequence of the creation of new industry, were "enjoying a period of full employment and rising income" during the period beginning 1815 and ranging until the mid 1840s, historian Theordore S. Hamerow tells us. German mill workers enjoyed an elevated quality of life, and of lifestyle standards, than those working in the handicraft shops or tending the fields. (176) The only "worker protection" type legislation during the first three quarters of the 19th century in Germany came in 1839-40, and that forbade the employment of children beneath the age of 9 by places engaged in manufacture, and limited those between 9 and 15 years of age to a working day no greater than 10 hours. (177)

During the middle of the 20th century, we find the same voluntary population clustering into the cities, and away from the countryside, in West Africa:

"In 1940 the number of people working for wages was small, but by 1960 it was estimated to be two million in the whole of West Africa. In the first dozen or fifteen years of the period the traditional scarcity of labour for wage employment was still a factor, but from the middle of the decade of the fifties the situation changed to one in which unemployment was a problem in nearly all the towns. The rise in wage levels of the period 1945 to 1955 had encouraged many young people to leave the country and flock to the towns in search of employment. This was most frequently the case with school-leavers who expected to be paid for being literate, but saw no prospect of earning a premium for literacy in farm work." (178)

Joseph A. Schumpeter -who shows himself to be quite Marxist or anti-capitalist, in another section of this book (part VII, Fictitious Play World, page # 439)- was named by Sebastian Haffner as one of "Two eminent modern economists", in Haffner's book originally published in 1987. (179) Schumpeter wrote of Marx in a book of his own, first published 1942. After noting that Karl Marx was accurate in his prediction that the size of the largest businesses in existence would grow larger as the years progressed, Schumpeter is honest when he tells us:

"But that is all. And against the achievement must be set the failure of the prediction of increasing misery, the joint result of wrong vision and faulty analysis, on which a great many Marxian speculations about the future course of social events had been based. He who places his trust in Marxian synthesis as a whole in order to understand present situations and problems is apt to be woefully wrong." (180)

Collectivism:
Outrageous Promises, Dreadful Results

In the USA during the years 1841-47, at Brook Farm in West Roxbury, Massachusetts, was *one of dozens of similar collectivist communities to fail* in the USA during the second quarter of the 19th century. People chose whatever work they wanted -irrespective of whether all necessary bases were covered- and all received equal compensation. Stated goals: "1. To indoctrinate the whole of the people of the United States with the principles of associative unity. 2. To prepare for the time when the nation, like one man, shall reorganize its townships on the basis of perfect justice." (181) *The repeated failures of such organizations leave your author perplexed regarding explanation of their continued popularity.* More bizarre claims regarding collectivism came from Charles Fourier. Fourier asserts that communism -or whatever synonym for "association" (their word)- results in: justice, unity, and harmony; regulation of the earth's temperature, fertilization of the deserts, moderation of the hot temperatures around the equator, and will bring forth an eternal springtime; increasing the lifespans of humans to three times their present length, and reducing diseases to a mere tenth of their present number; transformation of the seas into soda-pop; conversion of the lions into gentle humanitarians; and the end of wars for all time. Fourier was a leader at Brook Farm. (182)

Collectivism: If I don't directly benefit, why should I give a damn?: Amba tribe, eastern Uganda, 1955: A high rate of divorce, combined with the male receipt of all funds received from the sale of cash crops but not of food crops, resulted in women working harder on the food crops than the cash crops. The husbands tended to choose to buy some gifts for the family with a portion of these funds, though it was neither compulsory nor a fixed percentage; truly, an act of charity. Therefore when women did choose to expend effort on cash crops, they wanted work that would produce a return *this* year -while they were still married- and avoided crops that would pay out over many years; preferring cotton cultivation to that of coffee. (183)

In 1930, the first conveyor belt plant in the USSR produced its first tractor. A mere 43 were produced that summer -well beneath the centrally planned goal of 2,000- and these machines were only good for a paltry 70 hours of use once produced. (184) The state bank reported alarming inflation due to irresponsible spending, along with overprinting of currency. The bank heads recommended to Stalin a diminution of expense on vanity construction projects; as well as a reduction of domestic holding of animal products; along with a reduction of imports, which required payment in either gold or cash; in addition to advising a hike in prices domestically. (185) The general shortage of cash for the USSR was amplified by *their superstitious adherence to slogans and scripture*, conflicting with the rest of the world -who *were not obliged to humor them in their pretensions*. The wasteful and inefficient spending by central planners, combined with outlandishly ambitious timelines and a superstitious adherence to said timelines for fear of being outcast as sacreligious, left Russia short of hard currency. Theft of property in the name of benefitting and enriching their victims accounted for a massive diminution of the supply of livestock, as would-be victims slaughtered their own animals in waste. Good weather made for a grain surplus after the *de-regulation of a portion of the peasant farmers increased their productivity in planting*. Unhappily for Russia, the global demand for grain at that time was throttled by a wave of national hoarding around the world, cutting the price in 1930 to half of what it had been in 1929.

Under such self-made and imbecilic parameters, the USSR had little choice but to sell off grain for currency; no matter how much currency it might fetch today, they were in no position to wait out the buyers. 5 million tons of grain were exported, 15% of the global market for the year, in exchange for $80 million worth of rubles. (186) Heavy selling in a buyer's market: my, what tremendous planning by the central planners!

The most blatant refutation of the absurd claims of Marxist redistributors, comes from a bird's eye view of the conditions once private property rights were most respected, and regulation was the least in vogue, beginning the 18th century AD. Worldwide real GDP per capita in 2011 dollars: After patrolling a range no greater than $1,000 from year 0-1500, explodes from about $1,500 in 1700, to nearly $15,000 by year 2000. The extreme poverty class encompassed more than 80% in the early 1800s, and was only approximately 10% by 2022. *Expansion in private property rights*, and expansion/introduction of the element of *personal gain or loss into activities*, occur simultaneously with the beginning of this period of both increases in the wealthy, and of the shriveling of the proportion of the extremely impoverished. (187)

COLONIAL AMERICA

Under conditions in which there is *an infirmity of private property rights, a negative impact upon the masses* is a recurring consequence. Such can be observed in colonial America, specifically in the English colonies in America, during the first quarter of the 17th century. The loosening of the grip of the Beast, with an elimination of central planning, and a substitution of unregulated attempts at personal gain, brought life to the people emigrating from England, and gave birth to what would become the most formidable mechanism for the upliftment of the poor that the world has ever known. England's King James I issued what is known as the Virginia Charter. This document centrally planned land distribution in the New World, taking aim at land ranging from the 34th to the 45th parallels -Cape Fear to Halifax. The central planners denoted the space ranging from 34-38 degrees north latitude to one group of would-be settlers, and the tract spanning 41-45 degrees north latitude to another body of prospective migrants. The chasm between the two denoted areas, spanning from 38-41 degrees north latitude, *was marked by language ambiguous as the to present rights*. Understandably, future rights were also left mysterious. *This middle ground went undeveloped. Those in the area were not uplifted* by any increase in commerce, or in the supply of sustenance, which occurred in the other two regions, and would have yielded some greater amount had it been settled and developed to any degree. Because nobody could be assured of their rights to retain the land, it was not worthwhile for anyone to work that wilderness. This scarcity *may have been a factor in the failure of this attempt to settle in the New World, which involved much suffering and hunger.* (188)

The 1609 Virginia Charter issued by King James of England left the government of the expedition to the stakeholders, granting in 1612 the ability of the shareholders to form councils and hold general meetings to direct policy. This self governance was in direct opposition to the policy of the prior expeditions which were to be ruled from afar by the crown. Those who invested capital, but stayed home in England, could purchase shares for £12, 10 shillings apiece. All those who made the excursion overseas, being greater than ten years of age at the time, were to receive one share of stock each, even in absence of monetary payment for the single share; including the women. After 7 years, the cumulative assets of the company were to be divided up among the shareholders in proportion to their number of shares owned. It was from this expedition that the USA was germinated. (189) During the period 1804-1853, Virginia and North Carolina produce a combined $9.25 million in specie; in the year 1899 $42,000 worth of gold and silver. (190)

The cultivation and export of tobacco for profit provided the Virginia Company a cash crop, and source of financial sustenance. In 1613, 5,000 pounds sterling per year were offered in exchange for an exclusive license -known alternatively as a government created and protected monopoly- on the Virginia tobacco trade. In 1616 a batch of Virginia tobacco sold in London at a price which was deemed desirous, cementing interest in the company's continuance, and to the development of the region. (191) In an effort to encourage the population of the overwhelmingly desolate country, *50 acres of land were granted by the privately owned Virginia Company, in exchange for arranging the delivery of every one person delivered to the colony beginning 1618. This persisted through the colonial period.* (192)

From 1616 onward, the profitable growth and sale of tobacco created legitimate demand for labor, along with the legitimate possibility of money being procured via investment in the land. The demand for farm hands ramped up in 1624. Many of the poorest of England, often criminals with multiple offenses, were able to immigrate to Virginia not only for the purpose of providing a productive service to civilization by working a legitimate job, but also to perhaps better themselves and their station within their community; accruing earnings after working off their debt incurred due to the cost of their transport across the ocean, and possibly even owning a trading business or even land -which was a practical impossibility in England. (193) During 1629, the Massachusetts Bay Company saw its governance transferred legally and permanently to the inhabitants by England. Having departed the Isle of Wight on March 29th, 1630, eleven ships entered Salem harbor on the 12th of June. The group joined with those already in the vicinity, and migrated to Massachusetts Bay -known today as Boston Harbor- shortly thereafter. A 12 man body accounted for the entirety of the group emigrating who held the right to govern their fellow emigrants. Self governance in practice was once again granted. (194)

PART VII

Clinging to Blueprints of Airplanes that Don't Fly: Political "Experts" Oblivious to Evidence, and Their Fictitious Play World

"What is called 'planning' in political rhetoric is the government's suppression of other people's plans by superimposing on them a collective plan, created by third parties, armed with the power of government and **exempted from paying the costs that these collective plans impose on others.***"* –Tom Sowell (1)

A BRIEF INTRODUCTION
TO TERMS WITHOUT DEFINITION

While many people affect an expertise and an exactitude about themselves and their proclamations through the use of strict adherence to prefabricated definitions of the the various synonymous descriptors of central planning, occupying immense amounts of time splitting hairs over the perceived minute differences among terms such as fascism, socialism, communism, and others, as though the words imparted vastly differing consequences in real life, with real people, and real money, upon the implementation of central planning with their labor affixed to it; in fact, *what is presented as precise, is in practice inarticulate.*

Dictionary definitions of "the Left" in a political context include:

Macmillan describes "the Left", within the House of Commons, as pertaining to the "Opposition" of the regime presently in greater power. (2)

The Reader's Digest, Oxford, Complete Wordfinder describes "the Left" in a political context as favoring social reform; also as comprising the more advanced or innovative section of any group. (3)

Dictionary definitions of "the Right" in a political context include:

Roget's II defines "right", "rightist", and "right-winger" as favoring retention of the existing order. (4) The same volume hasn't any mention at all of "left", "leftist", or "left-winger", in any context.

Macmillan describes "the Right", in certain European legislative assemblies, as consisting of "Conservatives". (5) The same tome defines "Conservatives" as "one opposed to considerable changes in church or state for which the time does not seem ripe", and also "one who favors the maintaining of existing political policies, institutions, and forms of government." (6)

The Reader's Digest, Oxford, Complete Wordfinder describes "the Right" in a political context as a group or section favoring conservatism. (7) The same volume defines "conservatism" in a political context as belonging to a British political party promoting free enterprise and private ownership. (8)

Examples of "Leftist" as utilized by historians:

"...but many of the young leftist doctors and cadres promoted during the Cultural Revolution were still in key posts and they didn't want him." If leftist means to oppose the present authority, then how can they be in cahoots with the party that has been in authority for 15 years? (9)

Mignet refers to Jacobins and their cover groups -Mountain, Girondists- as being of the Left. This, even after Louis XVI had been executed, and the power had been in the hands of the Jacobins for years. (see part II, France 1789)

So-called Left hates the poor: German revolution of 1848-49: "The truth was that the industrial worker refused to play the role of downtrodden plebeian which socialist theory had chosen for him." "...he resented the insistence of the left that he was a proletarian." (10)

"Actors" of the "Left": Marx and his associates were unpopular in Germany during their day: Noted author Theodore S. Hamerow, speaking of Wilhelm Weitling, Stephan Born, Karl Grun, Friedrich Engels, and Karl Marx: "Their names have since become enshrined in the hagiography of the left, but in their own day they could find comfort only in the faith of a true believer." Says also that Marx and company preferred the "utopian socialist circles of Paris and London" as opposed to "stodgy...Biedermeier Germany." "The influence which they exerted on the world of their time was insignificant, and the proletariat...preferred to follow other prophets." None of the group of their followers were a part of the 1848 assemblies in Germany.

"Of all the political organizations in opposition to aristocratic monarchism theirs was the weakest." (11)

On the "Left" in Germany during 1848, written in 1958: Deplored a standing army, asserted that a worker must have "a share in the profits of labor", claimed to be against tyrannical bureaucracy; so said Gustav von Struve, member of a 7 man committee appointed independently of the framework of the government, as he proposed his agenda. Struve was described as a mountain-dweller "with a dash of socialism, the protagonist of egalitarian democracy and controlled economy." Hamerow also describes Struve as *a zealot interested in replacing a Monarch with a system of total control, enabling a bureaucrat possessing total control, masquerading as a man interested in liberating the masses* when he said: "Frankfurt was clearly no place for republican doctrinaires with visions of Jacobinism." After the rejection of Struve's plan, along with his subsequent conspicuous omission from the committee chosen to preside over the selection of delegates to the National Assembly, a few current politicians attempted to stoke the coals of the communist demands from the proletariat, designed to revive the flames of chaos, but those few dozen members of the preliminary parliament were unsuccessful. Author Hammerow describes this as "the call of the Left". (12)

Examples of "Rightist", as utilized by historians:

Bill Shirer, writing published in the middle 1980s of the early 1930s, describes "fascist authoritarianism of the Right in Germany and Italy", describing Russia as being of "the Left". While categorizing Britain and France as "decaying democracies" in "the West". (13)

Spain 1933: Bill Shirer describes "the Right" as being "hostile to the Republic", as being successful in their desire to oust the officials who had enacted the first

Constitution of the newly minted Spanish Republic less than 3 years prior. Shirer points out that some of his Spanish friends -he was living in Spain during the entirety of 1933- asserted that the initiation of women's suffrage aided "the Right" in the elections. (14)

Writing published 1987: Author Sebastian Haffner, referring to the early 19th century: "Prussia was 'rightist', a largely feudal agrarian state ruled by a rural nobility and a modern, absolutist bureaucracy. Both these would today be called 'rightist'." Haffner goes on to state that "The German National movement, on the other hand, was a "leftist" movement. From the very onset it modeled itself on revolutionary France, hence its original ties to libertarian, liberal-democratic movements." (15) The 1789 revolution in France was a period of absolutist tyranny, of laws changing by the hour, of a tyranny of the majority which would not wait for official votes to be cast prior to acting, of a play-money currency, and of mass penury. Of all of the things that this epoch was, "libertarian", it was not. (see part II, France 1789)

Germany 1850s: "The Left" in favor of freedom of contract between employee and employer. No regulations of wages or of hours, no age requirements, no monopolies or minimums. "The Right" favored precisely the opposite. (16) The utilization of these terms in 20th and 21st century America, would yield precisely anterior outcomes.

1933: Bill Shirer notes that he suspected Leon Trotsky gave a positive review to French novelist Ce'line because he "apparently believed that Ce'line was a communist". Shirer conjectures that Trotsky would have reacted to Ce'line's collaboration with Nazis during German occupation of France on the "Far Right" with shock and awe. (17) The NAZIS were central planners extraordinaire, utilizing the same methods of false promises and brutal dictation as the communists of the 20th century (see part II, Germany; also China).

CUTTING THROUGH THE BULL

A circle of professional "experts" engage in pretension as they assert that certain pre-fabricated theories -fascism, socialism, communism- with rigid definitions that have never been nearly as successful in real life as that of free trade, with limited governmental involvement in trade and commerce, beyond oversight, compilation of national statistics -income; production of x,y,z; imports; exports; and such- and the mediation of disputes. *Like inventors clinging to blueprints of flying machines that do nothing but crash and burn in real life, they just won't accept the truth, and continue to advocate for the continued subjection of people to crashes*; in addition to the waste of the materials used to construct the ineffective machine. Nonetheless, such people present themselves as experts. And these people are experts of a kind: they are experts at knowing very well the theory behind the failed blueprints. It is odd, however, that *this circle hardly ever seems to detail* the attempted flights and *the horrific damage* caused by the wreckage, *so that their students might be cautioned* against implementation of such a plan. Such people are members of a fraternity of fiction. A club in which college teachers and office-seeking politicians can attempt to supplement their incomes by treating closed questions as though they were not only open questions, but more egregiously, that they were perpetually unsolvable.

The lessons of history dictate the conclusion that government, while a grudging necessity, is a great and powerful Beast much more powerful than man and the general populace -particularly the least-moneyed- a Beast which must be restrained and limited in its ability to do harm. The most effective method for achieving this end has been to *reduce its size and scope so that, even if the Beast were to exercise its full capabilities, its damage would be insufficient toward the end of enslaving and brutally oppressing the masses*; simultaneously draining the nation and its people of the vital necessities of survival, as it induces an economic and industrial atrophy which leads to an ever shrinking pie being distributed in rations of ever decreasing slices, and with ever decreasing frequency.

It is alleged that there are two "sides", or adversarial parties, throughout history and current events. There are many names for these so-called "sides" such as: The Left, the Right, all of the "isms"... In reality, there are only two sides. ***The first, are those who would have the key variable set to the willful concentration of power into the hands of the few by decree***: those who demand monopoly in markets, both product and job; those who demand that a handful of people may steal from whomever they please, at any time, for any reason, but particularly to satiate their envy of a person or group; those who demand that prices, for both products and wages, be dictated by central planners and government bureaucrats; those who demand that the people be told where to live, how much healthcare they may have, and what food and clothing they may have, along with other goods and services. These are the Proponents of Slavery, or POS.

The second, are those who would have the key variable set to the willful diffusion of power into the hands of the people by decree, and by the same mechanism establish tremendous impediments to heavy central authority and planning: those who demand the freedom to choose which products they may buy or sell, along with the freedom to choose to enter any market as a business owner or employee at their own risk; those who demand strong private property rights, particularly the freedom to retain what they have earned from both investment and from direct employment or trade, and also that their posterity be free to retain any treasure passed along to them, as restraint, risk, and much labor were involved in the person's desire to make a better life for their posterity as well as for themselves; those who demand to be free to choose at which price they may buy or sell their labor or products, and to not be told by some party irrelevant to the exchange that they must either ask or accept a price that they feel will hinder themselves in their endeavors; nor that they must accept an enforced restriction on the necessities of human survival such as food, shelter, clothing, and medicine. These are the Advocates of Liberty, or AOL.

Proponents of Slavery	Advocates of Liberty
(POS)	(AOL)

Proponents of Slavery (POS)	Advocates of Liberty (AOL)
1. Concentrate power into the hands of the few by decree	1. Small central government with diffuse power
2. Dictates and attempts to micromanage outcomes for individuals	2. Unclenched grip of low tax and few regulations
3. Outlaws freedom of choice in all matters	3. Respect for individuals
4. Provides less for everybody	4. Obeys the evidence in its choice of this strategy to uplift the masses
5. Reduces total output	
6. Worst for the lowest economic class	5. Recognize that private property rights are the key difference between the free and the oppressed
7. Disregard the evidence as they implement strategies for the supposed advancement of the least-moneyed	

First degree murder, Second degree murder, Third degree murder; or Socialism, Communism, Democratic Fascism, National Socialism, Super-cala-fragil-istic-Wokernism, etc.. *These gradations of the same act are not of a character which is important to the victim, only important to the jury at the sentencing of the offending party*. As we have seen throughout this text, private property rights and individual responsibility for gain or loss, are the key differences between the free and the oppressed. There are those who waste words, time, and other valuable resources, affecting to be painstakingly and ardently seeking a solution that is best for the populace and that will lead to the best chance of prosperity for the masses, *yet do nothing but split hairs about the theoretical -as in pretend- differences between the various "isms"*. As we have seen, no attempt at writing the elusive "magic words" onto a piece of legislation or decree, and thereby controlling the masses through the establishment of a cabal into whose hands power is concentrated by said decree, and thusly *"seizing the means of production", has ever actually produced an outcome of plenty for the masses to match its promises. In fact, the precise opposite result is most reasonably expected*, as catastrophically negative outcomes occur nearly uniformly under the POS system of central planning. The reader will note the vast disparity in the presence of great *advancements* in the condition of the masses between the two possible settings of the key variable.

A conversation that goes like this:

[A small group, standing before a nation of people, attempt to construct a form of government that will provide the greatest opportunity for advancement to all of its citizens, and particularly to the least-moneyed at any given time.]

"The magic word is 'communism'!"

"NO! No, sir! The magic word is 'socialism!'"

"Now-now-now... here, here. My good fellows, if you don't see that the magic word is Neo-commu-social-fascism, then I'm afraid you're a [insert presently least favored group among their little circle]."

Is frankly, in terms of the impact that such a distinction makes upon the outcome of its invocation, no different than a conversation that goes like this:

[A small group of eight year olds, standing before a table, holding black wands and wearing matching top hats, attempting to transform a plain dinner spoon into a lion]

"The magic word is 'abra-ca-dabra'!"

"NO! No, sir! The magic word is 'Ala-ka-ZAM'!"

"You jokers don't know a darn thing! Everybody knows the magic word is 'Ta-DAAAA!'"

Such a discussion is really not worth taking seriously, if you're interested in actually achieving the stated aim. There are a grand total of zero important differences between the conversation described above, and a group of people debating the various terms affixed to central planning -socialism, wokernism, New Dealer-ism, communism, progressivism, and so forth- as though they were describing or advocating schemes which contain differences which have been proven to impact the outcome yielded, pertaining to the uplifting of the masses in the best material way possible. *How can the synonymous terms be "opposites" when they are in fact the same in practice?* The problem for those involved in the incredibly lucrative industry which keeps alive the bewildering falsehood that such discussions are in fact worth being taken seriously -along with stifling any plain observation that their assertions are blatant in their disregard for the mountain of evidence- is that *the system of large liberty and small government* with scant resources to attempt to extend beyond its legitimate three purposes (see page# 18) even if those operating it wanted to, *leaves the politicians with few opportunities for headlines*. The, by comparison, "set it and forget it" style of government, would then become attractive to the politicians *only* if serving in office were a transient experience, as opposed to the extended stays of multiple decades which have been customary in the United States of America.

Differences between such "systems", no matter which type of re-branding the same old product undergoes, *exist merely theoretically on paper in textbooks, but do not come to fruition in real life*. Even if one finds the pursuit noble, *the irresponsibility evident in the practice of ignoring the mountains of evidence in real life, with real people, and real money, is plain*. A prospective inventor must accept that the blueprint and diagrams they have drawn up, in pursuit of an imaginary theory, are incorrect and to be discarded when the weight of practical experimentation and experience prove said blueprints to not merely fail to achieve their stated ends of unleashing unlimited prosperity for all and the perpetual elimination of envy, want, and need, but that much worse than that, they in fact cause positive harm to the very people that the original designs intended to assist in the first place. A person attempting to invent a flying machine which can serve as a conveyance for man, faced with the repeated crashing and burning of their models, must admit that their promises of grandeur in fact result in calamity, and must also cease insistence that their blueprints are the pathway to a better life for the masses. *Such is the morally superior path, while repeated insistence that poison is medicine denotes one to be in a state of moral bankruptcy.*

There are certain terms which, while perhaps having a definition assigned them in a literal sense, in practice adopt new definitions as brand names of sorts. Words such as liberal, fascist, and leftist. By examining what contents are beyond the label, we can prevent ourselves from being sold a carton of eggplant which is labeled as containing chainsaws. In the USA, so-called progressives, or socialists, or liberals, or wokers, often attempt to *fearmonger the ignorant masses* when referring to proposed *legislation which would unshackle the people, and place those shackles onto the politicians in the government*, by utilizing the phrase "turn back the clock". Such a con-man will let the consumer infer whatever imaginary consequence to this that they will, while drawing upon their basis of few if any facts, whether that means concentration camps for Jews, chattel slavery for blacks (see page# 270), or any other specious inference one may draw from a law which, let's say, *disbands* bureaus whose very purpose it is to suppress entry into a particular field of business or of employment. However, these very accusers who, through increased regulation and centralized control, in fact intend to "turn back the clock" to the days of monarchy -the ultra concentration of power into the hands of the few by decree- and the very conditions of centralized control under which the German death camps were set up in Poland, and under which Mao made slaves of hundreds of millions of Chinese for decades. *Such an accuser is guilty of the very act which the accused party is expressly attempting to avoid!* Only an improvement in political literacy can remedy this situation, as the dishonest folks only utilize these methods because they are deemed and proven effective.

If "Left" denotes those seeking to overturn and displace an existing regime or structure of government, then such represents the challenger for the title -to use a boxing analogy. Unless "leftist" is a synonym for malcontent, then there truly can be no behaviors which are always leftist. If "left" means, as it often utilized conversationally, rapacious taxation under the guise of collectivisation, or redistribution, or the good of the masses; concentrating the fruits of productivity into the hands of the few by decree, who then dictate to the masses what they may or may not have, then you could say that Mao's communist, or Hitler's socialist, or Roosevelt's New Deal, regimes were leftist. However, if "left" is defined as being a challenger of present authority, then those regimes were only leftist until the moment that they gained power; from that moment forward, they became "right", although their policies and aims were wholly unaltered. One cannot be both the challenger, and the champ, simultaneously. To say that "throughout history, the right have always..." in reference to particular policies cannot be done reliably or accurately.

LEFT/RIGHT SYNONYMS; FLUID DEFINITIONS

The terms, Left and Right, as illustrated at the onset of this chapter, have such *fluid meanings in practice* that they are often used synonymously. In 1930, Stalin describes a centrally plotted massive increase in production of military equipment, as well as the training of soldiers, as both leftist and rightist; *utilizing each term as was convenient for him*, in an attempt to appeal to everybody. (18) Author Sebastian Haffner, writing nearly half of a century later, described the July 1932, Nazis on the right, Communists on the left. (19) He goes on to say that Nazis are both left and right. (20) "Three factors—misery, a resurgent nationalism, and Hitler himself—made the National Socialists into a mass movement that appropriated and nurtured and transformed the party into a political power. The German rightest establishment, the elitist right which had again come to power under Hindenburg, could not ignore it." (21) If "right" means in power, then how could the "rightists" have regained power? And what did the "right" displace when it took the reins, if "left" is always reserved for the challenger as opposed to the champion?

The practice of utilizing these words, and *altering their definition to fit whatever purpose that the user has in mind*, is hardly reserved to the above two terms. This particular volume has used many words as synonyms for the purpose of illustrating to the reader that there really are no important differences between them, in practice, when it comes to delivering prosperity and liberty to the masses; they all deliver the antithesis of these promises. The difficulty presented by words used conversationally, with ever-elusive definitions, in the political context, is lamented by Tocqueville during the 1830s: "Centralization is a word endlessly repeated nowadays whose meaning no one, in general, seeks to define." (22)

The terms, socialism and communism, being considered synonymous in practice is evidenced by former U.S. president Ronald "Dutch" Reagan during a press conference in January of 1981: "I know of no leader of the Soviet Union -since the revolution, including the present leadership- that has not, more than once, repeated in the various communist congresses they hold their determination that their goal must be the promotion of world revolution and a one would consider socialist or communist state; whichever you want to use." (23) Fidel Castro, Mao Zedong, and Joseph Stalin, have each been known to describe their own regimes with each of the two terms interchangeably.

The lack of any vital distinctions in the outcomes delivered by the words, after the decision has been made to concentrate the power into the hands of the few by decree -the key variable- is plain, yet the treatment of various "isms" as though they were vastly diverse, even opposites, is illustrated in a writing from the fall season of 1934. Bill Shirer says German Socialists and Communists would not become Nazis -National Socialists- as if there were an important difference beyond any minute deviations which each so-called faction may put forth in their campaign ads. Shirer notes, in the same paragraph, that the Nazis organized a massive union called the Labor Front, which included regulation of employers; all of which is overtly socialist or communist. (24) Can you name an important difference between that practice and those of Mao or Stalin? *All three regimes religiously engaged in central planning, to the detriment of the masses, and for the benefit alone of those holding power*.

Shirer would describe Stalin and Hitler as "opposites": "...the two dictatorships of opposing ideologies." (25) Fluidity of terms in practice is evidenced in England during the early 20th century, during which time the English feared that a lack of stout and able young men from the least-moneyed faction of their nation may hinder their ability to field a formidable fighting force, and turned to redistribution through the mechanism of the state as a supposed remedy. Politician T.J. Macnamara made clear that while his proposal for such may have seemed a vote in support of "rank socialism, in reality it is first-class imperialism." (26) By justifying the redistributive mechanism by claiming it would aid the military -which may, or may not, have been accurate- Macnamara may have been guilty of participating in a subterfuge in this instance; even if he did so unwittingly.

Sebastian Haffner denotes a 1918 German revolution as being a "left revolution", which seems superfluous if left simply denotes the challenger; yet it was deemed necessary, as in practice the term carries a variety of interpretations in the minds of those consuming the language: "That same evening the two had a critical, by now famous, telephone conversation. Ebert, even though not the legitimate chancellor (although he had dual legitimacy–through appointment by Prince Max von Baden and through his post with the revolutionary Berlin workers' and soldiers' councils) tried to resurrect the October agreement with the Supreme Command. He wanted to use the returning army units to suppress the revolution in the hope of winning the support of the Supreme Command for the new government and new constitution. Groener agreed, and to underscore his support he staged a counterrevolution in which he used the army to suppress the left revolution led by the Council of People's Delegates (headed, ironically, by Ebert himself)." (27)

A caution against use of the word "liberal" in a political context, and to be wary of its being its own antonym in practice, was already given (see page# 17). Writing in 1966, author Bentley B. Gilbert describes in England during the 20th century, prior to WWI, a New Liberalism. *This New Liberalism was the opposite of what liberalism had meant beforehand*: "...the departure was recognized for what it was, a breach in the wall of absolute personal responsibility for one's own fate. Here for the first time the State used its power on behalf of a particular segment of the population who were selected on the sole criterion that they were poor, who had rendered the State no service, who were afflicted by no contagious disease... and who finally were to suffer no penalty of disenfranchisement on account of the aids they received." (28)

Authors R.R. Palmer and Joel Colton list as characteristics of what might be termed a "classical liberal", as opposed to the "American Liberal" variety, liberal program: freedom from arbitrary arrest and confinement, guarantees of personal liberty for all". (29) This was not the outcome of the French revolution of 1789, and is counter to what so-called liberals in America today advocate when demanding slave reparations or heavy taxation and regulation; each of which infringe mightily upon the personal liberty of all, while the former arbitrarily punishes those who have not an iota of involvement in the enslavement of people 200 years ago.

Palmer and Colton also make clear that their use of the word "liberal" is one denoting individual liberty, and absence of control by central planners, when referring to the mid-19th century German episode (see page# 188). They refer to the "Question of a Liberal Germany", considering that a government "...should be liberal and constitutional, assuring civil rights to its citizens...", and referring to "The failure to produce a democratic Germany...". The authors clearly were not using the term in the same manner as a 20th or 21st century politician in the USA, who advocate the abrogation of choice by government. (30)

Some definitions provided by D.T. Armentano:

1- Pure Capitalism (laissez-Faire): all property to be private; no regulations on trade.

2- Mixed Capitalism: most property to be private; most trade free of regulation.

3- Corporatism or Fascism: all rights and property belong to the State, and the illusion of private property rights are temporarily bestowed to certain people only when it is deemed to benefit the interests of the minority in power (the State); heavy regulation on trade to serve the self interest of the minority group (politicians/bureaucrats).

4- Socialism: no private property. All trade regulated. (31)

Stephen Kotkin describes Stalin's "implanting socialism (noncapitalism) in the countryside", inferring the word socialism, in practice, to be defined as anything but capitalism, by the very man (Stalin) who was head of state. (96)

Socialism defined in practice: In Germany, during the 1848 uprising, the so-called artisanal congress proposed that the state guarantee a job for all, and provide for all injured or ill citizens. Author Ted Hamerow writes "...every man of means knew that this was socialism pure and simple, and that in France: that led from national workshop to subversion to class warfare." (32)

THE KEY VARIABLE

"...governments, like clocks, go from the motion men give them; and as governments are made and moved by men, so, by them they are ruined, too. Wherefore, governments rather depend on men than men upon governments." -Preamble to the Pennsylvania Constitution (33) 1680 or 1681 (34)

As has been alluded to earlier in this volume, the presently fashionable axiom "let no crisis go to waste" leads directly to "let no election go by without a 'crisis' ". As was done during the tyrannical New Deal period in the USA, the tyrannical Jacobin Revolution in 18th century France, in Germany during the tyrannical National Socialist period of the 1930s and 1940s, and others, a declaration of *a perpetual state of emergency is a common tactic utilized by oppressors to justify setting the key variable to the POS position*, and never allowing the AOL position to be realized. Power is concentrated into the hands of the few by decree, the individuals are shackled, and are told that this serves as their liberation. Palmer and Colton: "Totalitarianism, as it arose after the World War, was not merely a theory of government but a theory of life and of human nature. It claimed to be no expedient, but a permanent form of society and civilization, and so far as it *appealed to emergency for justification*, it regarded *life itself as an ever-lasting emergency*." (35)

The Important Variable: *Market freedom, and the individual ambition which is cultivated and incentivised by such freedom, are the important variables*; natural resources are non-essential, while public redistributive "generosity" is counterproductive. Peter Bauer notes Hong Kong, Japan, Switzerland, and Venice, as being prosperous but without natural resources; he also notes the unprosperous American Indians, who were on the very same land that Europeans utilized in a fashion which placed the USA among the countries considered most abundant in natural resources. (36)

"Natural Resources" an irrelevant factor: Natural resources are not necessarily determinative of economic prosperity, or a lack thereof. *Most of the world's natural resources lay dormant for most of the greater than 6 millenia of recorded human history.* Oil wasn't produced and refined on a large-scale basis until the mid-19th century AD. *World leadership in commerce and industry has transferred with tremendous fluidity* from region to region, or from nation to nation, *throughout history.* "Even in recent times countries which had once been in the forefront subsequently lost their economic supremacy and came to join the ranks of the present under-developed countries; parts of southern Europe and of the Mediterranean basin are examples." (37)

Important variable: disincentivization of gain: fallacy of "western European supremacists": In medieval Western Europe, beginning in the 9th century with the Arab takeover of the Mediterranean Sea which cut off commerce with the Orient for the Christian empire, resulted in an atrophy of commerce and of society as a whole for these Europeans. This left the Church as the greatest possessor of wealth, and therefore of authority or sway. Churchmen stood out for their literacy in a culture which was rife with both ignorance and illiteracy. The Church used its position to put forth a message discouraging advancement -or even the *desire* for advancement- perhaps simply because the message fit what their audience could possibly hope to attain, or perhaps because the Church enjoyed its position atop the heap and wanted to preserve this position. (38) Each of these tactics were employed by others ruling over oppressive regimes engaged in central planning and exorbitant taxation such as Mao, FDR, Castro, and Stalin.

The Church forbade lending at interest among the populace. Done *under the guise of protecting the borrower* from being wronged by the very payment of interest on a loan, *the practice removed* entirely any reward for lending out of money -or compensation for losses and delayed repayments of some borrowers, thereby rendering the overall return to not be worth the lender's trouble- which consequently removed *all options for the common man to attempt improve his position*, and frequently in a fashion which saves years or decades of waiting and saving in order to have the money to get started. Such an imposition from the top cemented the population precisely in the financial position in which the central planners permitted them to exist; movement between financial classes was nearly impossible unless placement by the authorities occurred. In what I hope will come to the surprise of absolutely none of the readers of this book, *poverty and the absence of legitimate hope of upward social mobility, pervaded.* (39)

Important variable: POS worship "equality" or "satiation of envy": Berend and Ranki find that the reason for the backwardness, or inferiority, of the countries outside of Western Europe during the 19th century, was the remnants of the Ottomans and their so-called "Asian System" of central planning, still lingering in these cultures after the fall of the Ottomans. This Asian mode of production, which existed in many places outside of Asia, has been described as "a social formation in which power was strongly centralized; private landholding was unknown, and as there were no private landlords, the majority of the population were slaves (or serfs) of the state. It was a system in which self-sufficient rural communities predominated. *The Asian mode of production* left no room for the development of any real class structure, and *made for static, immobile societies.*" (40) If the cultures of Western Europe, and of Eastern Europe, were each represented by a can of paint in their respective locations, which then spilled in the direction of the center of Europe -intersecting and overlapping clumsily at certain points, resembling a venn diagram- we find that *the remnants of the feudal Ottoman culture of "equality"* existing in the south and in the east, *was inferior in providing for the masses in comparison to the industrial and profiteering culture predominating in the west.* The financial and material superiority of the western countries was due to their superior culture -one that permitted much greater personal freedom, with far less regulation, and with far greater income and wealth inequality- as opposed to their having "wronged" the lesser nations in any way.

Income inequality: England was the first to have industrialization grow and displace the manorial system as the primary means for commerce, a process which began in approximately the year 1780. By 1860 the per capita GNP -Gross National Product- as an average for all of Europe, was 50% greater than it had been in the year

1800; similar gains were seen in Scandinavia. The leader in this category from beginning to end was Britain, who grew 63%. *Those who care about the least-moneyed are pleased* to see the average person earning $3 in 1860 for every $2 being earned in 1800, *while those who merely hate their betters disregard this improvement*; focusing solely on their envious stirrings at seeing England do better than another nation, and that the so-called income inequality gap had widened. Eastern European nations, on the "Asian" System of central planning, grew by a mere 10% during this time. *Hampered by their lust for income equality, everybody had less.* Those who sincerely wish to make a better existence for the masses, and particularly for those least-moneyed at any given point in time, have no trouble sanctioning the increased freedom to choose and absence of regulatory and redistributive controls which prevailed in England during this period. (41)

IT'S A RELIGION

"As such, it is a triumph of hope over experience to believe that more government spending will help the United States today." –Guy Sorman, 2009 (42)

The term "religion", is used pejoratively to distinguish a reliance upon superstitious chanting of favored slogans, from the scientific practice exemplified by learned peoples of humbling themselves before indubitable, evidence based, conclusions. A main theme of this chapter is the emphasis of *the pretension and make-believe* resorted to by many so-called experts in the pertinent fields, along with pointing out that such people are merely pushing a religion, *when evidence is readily available*. This seems a necessary step in bringing forth a societal solution to our woes.

It's a religion: ILC: 1929-30 USSR: While his deputies had resolved to permit some private ownership -of limited, but vital, components of successful agricultural production- among the peasant farmers in the countryside, Stalin forbade it all prior to the resolution's implementation. Stalin was quoted in Pravda in December of 1929, touting the new plan to obliterate the so-called "rich" peasants -kulaks- from existence; while secretly -within the closed ranks of his dictatorship within the dictatorship- recruiting a band to liquidate the "class enemy", *a productive and beneficial class* at that, in accordance with the pathway to heaven -worker's paradise- asserted in the sacred writings of Marxism. Labor camps were set up to accommodate this mission. (43) During 1930, Kagonovich was addressing the new soldiers, recruited under duress for the purpose of enforcing party policy in distant regions, heretofore beyond the reach of party headquarters: "...Either we destroy the kulaks as a class, or the kulaks will grow as a class of capitalists and liquidate the dictatorship of the proletariat." (44) *These so-called friends of the worker and of the poor*, imposed conditions in these remote villages which rewarded these government workers -and all others who partook- with *possession of all property of any kulak that was evicted; including the very clothes on their backs*. That such social workers were gre*eted by axe swings and shotgun blasts is encouraging to know.* (45) *Wouldn't possessing the property of one condemned as "rich*, and hoarding said property and capital", *make the thief*, once in possession of the same property and capital, *instantaneously just as guilty of the very same violation of their bizarre religion?* And equally as contemptible? Shouldn't a ceaseless succession of robberies ensue?

1830 Germany: "Magic Words": Adolph Hitler -properly so, though he likely stumbled into this accuracy by coincidence; that is, the statement happened to fit his prefabricated message and strategy, any truth contained therein was purely coincidental- placed communists, bolsheviks, marxists, and even socialists in the same basket. But in his next breath, espoused the virtues of socialism, *of his socialism.* The other people biting the wealthy and industrious hands which fed them, while these other people also concentrated the resources of the many into the hands of the few by decree, weren't doing it properly. *Once concentrated into his hands, it would somehow be different.* Hitler's financial backers foresaw themselves controlling all of the resources, once socialism concentrated these resources into one large pot, envisioning that the monopolies bestowed by such arrangements would exist for their own personal exploitation. (46)

If you give them an inch, they take a mile; and they'll use any excuse to do so. In England, the Education Act (Provision of Meals) 1906 paved the way for the ensuing political system of bribes and kickbacks enacted in the form of high taxation, campaign contributions and gifts, along with payouts from the Exchequer. As Bently B. Gilbert tells us, "Section IV of the Act marked the point of contest between the new radicalism and the old conservatism. This paragraph stipulated that notwithstanding any failure by any parent to pay for the meals provided for his child the parent should not suffer any losses of civil rights or privileges. In effect, meals, in the last analysis, were to be provided free. With this mild proposal the welfare state began." (47) Of course, the meals were not actually free of cost, they were merely free from out-of-pocket charge to the recipient on that day; the more subtle costs are made evident throughout the entirety of this volume. *It was around this time that the School Medical Service was snuck in under the cover of darkness, without the consent of the people*. (48) The demagogic phrase "national efficiency" may have first appeared as a political football in England in 1900, which would serve as phrases such as the "greater good", or "dictatorship of the proletariat", served in other countries. The Earl of Rosebery (Archibald Philip Primrose), who had been prime minister 1894-95, and was the son in law of Baron Meyer Amschel de Rothschild, headed the movement. (49)

Socialism, in practice, means whatever excuse to abrogate choices from the citizenry, and to steal, is desired by the preachers. Fritz Hayek, in a writing first published 1944:

"In their wishful belief that there is really no longer an economic problem people have been confirmed by irresponsible talk about "potential plenty"--which, if it were a fact, would indeed mean that there is no economic problem which makes the choice inevitable. But although this snare has served socialist propaganda under various names as long as socialism has existed, it is still as palpably untrue as it was when it was first used over a hundred years ago. In all this time not one of the many people who have used it has produced a workable plan of how production could be increased so as to abolish even in western Europe what we regard as poverty—not to speak of the world as a whole. ***The reader may take it that whoever talks about potential plenty is either dishonest or does not know what he is talking about. Yet it is this false hope as much as anything which drives us along the road to planning.***" (50)

20th century economic statistician, Colin Clark, who held government positions in Australia, England, and the USA, in his 1940 book *The Conditions of Economic Progress*, observes that:

"oft repeated phrases about poverty in the midst of plenty, and the problems of production having already been solved if only we understood the problems of distribution, ***turn out to be the most untruthful of all modern clichés.*** . . . The under-utilisation of productive capacity is a question of considerable importance only in the U.S.A., though in certain years also it has been of some importance in Great Britain, Germany and France, but for most of the world it is entirely subsidiary to the important fact that, with productive resources fully employed, they can produce so little. The age of plenty will still be a long while in coming. . . . If preventable unemployment were eliminated throughout the trade cycle, this would mean a distinct improvement in the standard of living of the population of the U.S.A., but from the standpoint of the world as a whole it would only make a small contribution towards the much greater problem of raising the real income of the bulk of the world population to anything like a civilised standard." (51)

FICTITIOUS PLAY WORLD

"Yet let not human arrogance assume to know intuitively, without observation, the tendency of the ages. Research must be unwearied, and must be conducted with indifference; as the student of natural history, examining even the humblest flower, seeks instruments that may unfold its wonderful structure, without color and without distortion. For the historic inquirer to swerve from exact observation, would be as absurd as for the astronomer to break his telescopes, and compute the path of a planet by conjecture."
-Edward Channing (52)

As an old television commercial once lamented, "where's the beef?". The substance verifying the claims of shysters, that their populist redistributive sermons will bring advancement to the masses and to society, is alarmingly absent from their materials. ***Who is hoarding and concealing all of the evidence*** that illustrates the outcome of improved material quality of life for the masses promised by the POS solutions during their sales pitches? Why isn't there an equivalent mountain of evidence offsetting the examples presented within the legitimate inquiries into important matters, which are themselves *teeming* with actual outcomes of improvement? ***Why are writings touting the POS schemes so bereft of evidence illustrating success in uplifting the condition of those presently lowest, while often comparatively rich in statistics designed to instigate and inflame envy within its readers?*** A fictitious play world is concocted by prevaricators, as they contrive half-truths and outright fallacies, in an effort to ride their wave of fiction into the land of power and riches for themselves, at the expense of both the masses, and of the human race in its entirety.

Those who speak only the language of tee-shirt slogans, and who repel absorption of the language of evidence and proof as oil repels water, are people who are disinterested in arriving at correct answers. ***The word disinterested is quite different from the word uninterested***, and that difference will be made plain for the reader. ***One who is uninterested*** in, let's say, a game of basketball, will not alter their gaze or their behavior in any way as a result of the playing of a game of basketball; this person *hasn't any interest, one way or another*. Conversely, *one who is disinterested* in a game of basketball, will flee from the scene at top speed, averting their gaze and covering their ears; this person *is decidedly antagonistic with regards to the subject matter*. Members of the ILC (see part IV), wishing to remain ensconced in the cocoon of their fictitious play world, evade the path of evidentiary consideration, and of soundly based conclusions, as though it would make their arms fall off. *Such people are disinterested in actually solving the problems which exist in this world*. Such people are truly evil to the very core of their souls, as they would rather billions of people live existences which are needlessly worse off than necessary, simply because this person will not permit their own advancement as a person; batting away evidence with their deflector shield words such "belief", "view", and "ideology", making certain that they go to sleep each night no better than they were when they awoke that day, and sentencing themselves to a lifetime of perpetual developmental stasis.

Joseph Schumpeter, writing mid-20th century: "The rigidity of prices has become, with some people, the outstanding defect of the capitalist engine and-almost-the fundamental factor in the explanation of depressions. But there is no wonder in this. Individuals and groups snatch at anything that will qualify as a discovery lending support to the political tendencies of the hour." (53) Roosevelt and Mao price fixed to the gills. Yet, they are central planners. Schumpeter himself, as is evidenced within this very book, is guilty of, to paraphrase his preceding quote, "snatching at anything that may lend support to his claims". (see page# 405; also the present section)

Schumpeter seems a Marxist in his writing first published 1942: "The atmosphere of hostility to capitalism which we shall have to explain presently makes it much more difficult than it otherwise would be to form a rational opinion about its economic and cultural performance. The public mind has by now so thoroughly grown out of humor with it as to make condemnation of capitalism and all its works a forgone conclusion——-almost a requirement of the etiquette of discussion...Any other attitude is voted not only foolish but anti-social and is looked upon as an indication of immoral servitude." (54) Schumpeter goes on to favorably compare

Christianity in the year 300 AD with socialism, or Marxism, or whatever label one assigns it. He then notes the impressive 3.7% average annual growth of the United States during the 1870-1930 period, before claiming that "from 1929 to 1939 capitalism had already failed to live up to that standard." (55) Of course, *it was the departure from the loose hand of government* on the windpipe of the citizenry -referred to by Schumpeter and many others as "capitalism"- *of Frank Roosevelt and the New Dealers*, accompanied by the failure of the central planners at the Fed which had been established 1913 but had not taken the helm in practice until after the Great War, *which yielded the horrific central planning of the 1929-1939 period*. (see page# 145, or consult the subject index, for more on New Deal tyranny) (For more on the Great Failure of Socialism, known commonly as the New Deal, see note 56) (56)

Instead of noting the massive intrusion into the affairs of the citizenry committed by the New Dealers, and their negative repercussions, the man chalks it up to growing pains: "The subnormal recovery to 1935, the subnormal prosperity to 1937 and the slump after that are easily accounted for by the difficulties incident to the adaptation to a new fiscal policy, new labor legislation and a general change in the attitude of government to private enterprise..." He continues, "I wish to emphasize that the last sentence does not in itself imply either an adverse criticism of the New Deal policies... All I now mean to imply is that so extensive and rapid a change of the social scene naturally affects productive performance for a time, and so much the most ardent New Dealer must *and also can* admit. I for one do not see how it would otherwise be possible to account for the fact that this country which had the best chance of recovering quickly was precisely the one to experience the most unsatisfactory recovery." (57)

The play world is evidenced whenever one treats the behavior of those who have hold of the reins once the authority has been centralized by design, as though their identities were important differences. Once the key variable has been set to the POS setting, the only vital decision has already been made; the people merely wait for someone to inevitably come along and abuse the unbridled authority. Palmer and

Colton discuss some differences in the behavior of tyrants, focusing on minute and inconsequential distinctions, while noting the tight grip of the unchained Beast:

"Totalitarianism, as distinct from mere dictatorship, though it appeared rather suddenly after the First World War, was no historic freak. It was an outgrowth of a good deal of development in the past. The state was an institution that had continuously acquired new powers ever since the Middle Ages; step by step since feudal times, it had assumed jurisdiction over law courts and men at arms, imposed taxes, regulated churches, guided economic policy, operated school systems, and devised schemes of public welfare. The First World War had continued and advanced the process. The twentieth-century totalitarian state, mammoth and monolithic, *claiming an absolute domination over every department of life*, now carried this old development of state sovereignty to a new extreme." (58) ... "In Marxism, the absolute subordination of the individual to his class came to much the same thing. The individual was a microscopic cell, meaningless outside the social body. He was a little particle within a monolithic slab. *He was but clay to be molded by the imprint of his group*." ... "Valid ideas were those of the group as a whole, or of the people or nation (or, in Marxism, the class) as a solid block. (59)... "Propaganda was monopolized by the state, and it demanded faith in a whole view of life and in every detail of this co-ordinated whole."... "The government manufactured thought. It manipulated opinion. *It re-wrote history*." (60)

In China, Wei Jingshen, born 1951, was 16 years old during the Cultural Revolution of 1966, during which he joined the Red Guards and later enlisted in the army: "The fate of Marxism is like that of many other schools of thought. ...Some of its ideals have been used by rulers as the *pretext for enslaving people*." (61)

The fictitious play world is again concocted by Joseph Schumpeter: "In the last resort, American agriculture, English coal mining, the English textile industry are costing consumers much more and are affecting *total* output much more injuriously than they would if controlled, each of them, by a dozen good brains." (62) Could any statement directly contradict the evidence more flagrantly than this one? The instances of the horrid outcomes yielded by central planning in agriculture by the New Dealers, Cubans, USSR, and the Chinese, are each noted in a prior work (63), and can also be found within this present volume. The present book is also a veritable treasure trove of instances chronicling the superiority of competition, and the diminution in returns caused by the monopoly which is only enacted by government interference in commerce. ***Please do take note that Schumpeter is advocating a monopoly, enforced by the state, which has been shown to result in nothing but inferior consequences*** to those yielded by unregulated free trade conducted by citizens, in the name of uplifting the masses and increasing productivity.

One example refuting the assertion that a state enforced monopoly will deliver greater outcomes for the masses; illustrating that commerce uplifts the masses, while competition both lowers prices, and yields efficiency; can be found in the oil trade involving Russia, Europe, and the USA, during the later 1880s. Competing firms, each seeking to enrich themselves, while personifying what some allege is "market inefficiency" simply by competing and providing choice to customers, ***reduced prices and increased the available products available for purchase to consumers***.

Russian oil wells and refineries were within a 5 sq/km region near Baku; while the USA had many spread all over. The average yield for Russia was 280 barrels/day; for the USA, a mere 4.5 barrels/day. For Russia 80% of crude was produced by 14 integrated companies; while the USA had hundreds of producers. Professor Mendleleeff estimated costs of producing crude in Russia to be ⅓ to ½ of costs in the USA. (64) Robert and Ludwig Nobel, from Sweden, set up a firm in Russia which manufactured approximately 33% of kerosene in 1888. (65) The Nobels, after the initial run of their venture, invested new capital before long –a not insignificant factor– and began shipping in tank cars, used the first bulk steamers on the Caspian Sea, and initiated the use of the continuous distillation process which reduced operating costs. (66) The Paris house of Rothschild also started a firm in Russia, theirs during the mid 1880s. "The very fact that such well-financed firms such as the Nobels and Rothschilds were attempting to develop foreign markets *in competition* both with each other and with outside exporters of Russian kerosene *reduced prices* to a level which made the products particularly acceptable." (67) Note that Standard Oil in the USA was still a juggernaut during this time, about which more can be learned in (part I, Rockefeller page# 25)

Membership in the fraternity of fiction, evading reality at any cost, is acknowledged by Schumpeter: "Economics is only an observational science which implies that in questions like ours the room for difference of opinion can be narrowed but not reduced to zero." (68) *Of course, the responsible mind concludes that we must obey the evidence which exists, in great quantities, and which dictates conclusions to the questions facing a person or a society. This, even though we may not understand fully the precise degree of impact* -as in being able to predict with confidence, in advance of a decrease in the production of corn in the amount of 0.0001% due to government interference, precisely the amount of increase in hunger/unemployment/reduction of GDP/and so forth; and to know precisely to whom these costs will be passed along- *that each cause contributes to the effects evident in the actual outcomes* -in real life, with real people, and real money- *the evidence of which we are so blessed to be in a time of plenty!*

For at least three centuries, as of this writing, data has been recorded more dutifully and in greater varieties of categories, and in a higher proportion of the lands on earth, than ever before. In addition, this information has been much more carefully *preserved and cataloged* than at any time known in history. And the topper to this bounty of evidence upon which present man can rely to have knowledge of the outcomes of many claims frequently asserted by con-men after your wallet, is that the *accessibility* of this information has expanded impressively with the advent of the internet for use in research, communication, and language translation.

We must also remember that, when some have much more than some others in a given set of outcomes in which the outcomes are not prescribed by some central planner -such as a bureaucrat or a monarch- this is not *a priori* (in and of itself) a crime to those who have less than their neighbor, simply because their neighbor has more. The evidence dictates the conclusion that when there is less for everybody, yet income and wealth disparities are comparatively minimal, a larger proportion of the population is both materially, and in terms of health, worse off and suffering. When everyone has more, and the gap between the lowest and the highest incomes and net worths is more vast, it is better for everybody; especially the least-moneyed, as their condition is better in the latter outcome than in the former.

The antithesis of Schumpeter, above: Alfred Marshall on responsible economists who deal with man as he is, as opposed to an abstract conception of an economic man:

"For in the first place, *they deal with facts which can be observed, and quantities which can be measured and recorded; so that when differences of opinion arise with regard to them, the differences can be brought to the test of public and well-established records*; and thus science obtains a solid basis on which to work. In the second place, the problems, which are grouped as economic, because they relate specially to man's conduct under the influence of motives that are measurable by a money price, are found to make a fairly homogeneous group. Of course they have a great deal of subject-matter in common: that is obvious from the nature of the case. But, though this is not so obvious a priori, it will also be found to be true that there is a fundamental unity of form underlying all the chief of them; and that in consequence, by studying them together, the same kind of economy is gained, as by sending a single postman to deliver all the letters in a certain street, instead of each one entrusting his letters to a separate messenger. For the analyses and organized processes of reasoning that are wanted for any one group of them, will be found generally useful for other groups.

The less then we trouble ourselves with scholastic inquiries as to whether a certain consideration comes within the scope of economics, the better. If the matter is important let us take account of it as far as we can. If it is one to which there exist divergent opinions, such as cannot be brought to the test of the exact and well-ascertained knowledge; if it is one on which the general machinery of economic analysis and reasoning cannot get any grip, then let us leave it aside in our purely economic studies. But let us do so simply because the attempt to include it would lessen the certainty and the exactness of our economic knowledge without any commensurate gain; and remembering always that some sort of account of it must be taken by our ethical instincts and our common sense; when they as ultimate arbiters come to apply to practical issues the knowledge obtained and arranged by economics and other sciences." (69)

WHICH CLASS BENEFITS?

"the art of taxation consists in plucking the largest amount of feathers with the least possible amount of hissing". -Jean-Baptiste Colbert (70)

As stated in the opening of this book, supposedly populist schemes purport to cater to one faction, representing themselves as trampling the private property rights of a second faction in favor of the first, then label this as a "favor" to that first faction. Each "favor" granted by the state often wrongs the party who themselves previously unjustly gained as a result of a prior "favor". None of said "favors" are government's to give in the first place. This cycle only benefits the class running the scheme, but only so long as the music doesn't stop on their game of musical chairs prior to the death of the schemer, as such tactics make for a world in which there is less for everyone.

The masses are dependent upon the whims of an individual under socialism. Tocqueville opined during the 1830s:

"But it is my opinion that administrative centralization only serves to weaken those nations who submit to it, because it has the constant effect of diminishing their sense of civic pride. It is true that administrative centralization succeeds in concentrating all the available resources of the nation at any given time and in a particular place but it militates against the increase of those resources. It brings victory on the day of battle but, in the long run, diminishes a nation's power. It can, therefore, contribute admirably to the passing greatness of one particular man while not at all the lasting prosperity of a nation." (71)

In ancient Greece, the "oikos", which was a term roughly synonymous with "family unit" -though membership therein was not necessarily due to blood or marriage- in which the material acquisitions of the group were funneled up to the sole head of the group. This individual, into whose hands all of the power over all of the material wealth within the group had been funneled by decree, then disbursed said materials -such as food, wine, buildings, livestock, land, equipment, etc..- as he wished. "Equality", whenever attempted legislatively, always creates and necessitates an environment containing distinctly separate classes of both *dependents* and *rulers*. (72)

Attacking what is good as though it were bad: Nevins: "Most great corporate aggregations in the United States did not compete with jobbers and retailers, and did not directly touch the consumer; the Standard did, and it paid the penalty in widespread popular dislike and fear." The author goes on to mention that by 1885, the Standard had acquired a bad name at home due to the resentment of its competitors and those envious of their betters. (73)

Milton Friedman, writing in 1981 of an occupational licensing scheme in New York City regarding taxicabs, illustrated the situation in which the amount of cabs are artificially suppressed via the process of occupational licensing through the sale of special medallions, which thereby raised prices and reduced supply of, taxicabs in the city.

"Why does the limitation of the number of cabs persist? This answer is obvious: the people who now own those medallions would lose and they know it. Although they are few, they would make a lot of noise at city hall. The people who would end up driving the additional cabs do not know that they would have new jobs or better jobs. *There is no New Yorker who would find it worth his or her time and effort to lobby city hall to remove the arbitrary limitation on medallions simply to get better cab service.* It does not pay the individual taxi riders to do so. They are right; it is rational ignorance on their part not to do so."

Going on to explain the reason that the desire for personal gain positively impacts private sector activity, while negatively impacting public sector business activity:

"One answer is that the incentive of profit is stronger than the incentive of public service. In one sense I believe that is right, but in another sense I believe it completely wrong. The people who run our private enterprises have the same incentive as the people who are involved in our government enterprises. In all cases the incentive is the same: to promote their own interest. My old friend Armen Alchian, who is a professor at the University of California at Los Angeles, put the point this way: There is one thing, he said, that you can trust everybody to do and that is to put his interest above yours. The people who run our private enterprises are people of the same kind as those who run our public enterprises, just as the Chinese in Hong Kong are the same as the Chinese in Mainland China; just as the West Germans and the East Germans were not different people, yet the results were vastly different.

The point is that self-interest is served by different actions in the private sphere than in the public sphere. The bottom line is different. An enterprise started by a group of people in the private sphere may succeed or fail. Most new enterprises fail (if the enterprise were clearly destined for success, it would probably already exist). If the enterprise fails, it loses money. The people who own it have a clear bottom line. To keep it going, they have to dig into their own pockets. They are reluctant to do that, so they have a strong incentive either to make the enterprise work or to shut it down."

Of course in the public sector a politician or bureaucrat, particularly one who is using the office as an implement to enrich their own pockets, looks to the vast pile of money at the Treasury -which is gotten from others by force through the legal mechanism of taxation, and which is not traceable directly to any particular citizen- and demands more of it for what they assert is an indispensable project, as they claim that under-funding was the reason for its failure; or they blame others for the mismanagement of the funds, while they are demanding more funds from the Treasury. Friedman sums it up this way *"If a private enterprise is a failure, it closes down—unless it can get a government subsidy to keep it going; if a government enterprise fails, it is expanded. I challenge you to find exceptions."* (74)

The incentives for bureaucrats are evident in China during 1989, as Fox Butterfield observed: "At its heart, China is still a vast network of *danweis*, or units, each like a feudal domain controlled by its Communist Party secretary. Although organizations such as the taxi company or a factory appeared to be business enterprises, they are organized more for social control over the populace and for the personal power of their leaders than for making a profit. *Any time a local official can expand his enterprise, adding more workers and more investment, it represents a gain in power for him.*" (97)

The counterproductivity of stigmatizing success, and of glamorizing poverty, that the ecclesiastical rulers bestowed unto medieval Europe has been illustrated (in page# 399). Another instance will be shown here, as only the ruling body gains when the people are prevented from advancing under the auspice of so-called morality.

Venice was founded 421 AD (75) on land which was not arable, its first members traded fish and salt with Europeans in exchange for corn, meat, and wine. From this foundation the Venetians, by the close of the 9th century AD, had command over the valley of the Po -enabling those from Venice to venture into Italy. By the close of the 10th century Venice had important contacts in Cesena, Vicenza, Pavia, Ancona, Treviso, Ravenna, along with a host of others.

"It is clear that the Venetians, taking the practice of trade with them, acclimatized it, so to speak, wherever they went. Their merchants gradually found imitators. It is impossible, in the absence of evidence, to trace the growth of the seeds sown by commerce in the midst of the agricultural population. That **growth was no doubt opposed by the Church, which was hostile to commerce**, and nowhere were bishoprics more numerous and more powerful than south of the Alps. A curious episode in the life of St. Gerald of Aurillac (d. 909) bears striking witness to the **incompatibility of the moral standards of the Church with the spirit of gain**, that is to say, the business spirit. As the pious lord was returning from a pilgrimage to Rome, he met in Pavia some Venetian merchants, who asked him to buy oriental stuffs and spices. Now, he had himself purchased in Rome a magnificent pallium which he took the opportunity of showing them, mentioning how much he had paid for it. But when they congratulated him on his good bargain, since according to them the pallium would have cost considerably more in Constantinople, Gerald, reproaching himself for having defrauded the vendor, hastened to forward him the difference, considering that he could not take advantage of it without falling into the sin of avarice." (76)

It is, of course, morally reprehensible to purposefully discourage and/or to punish behavior which is known to permit individuals license over their own fate, and to best uplift the least-moneyed as a class. In the USA we have seen this occur plentifully. From the banishment of tenement living -even though medical advances had occurred, which would stave off many of the contagious health issues which had been present during the prior period, in which so many were sustained and even uplifted- to the state enabling of monopolies under the guise of preventing monopoly -TVA, ICC, AAA, tv station licensure- and others. Nonetheless, the men of the established Church put forth moral codes which did just that. *Retaining their own position at the top of the pyramid* by keeping the tools of advancement out of the hands of outsiders *was of paramount importance to them*, just as has been the case for every "labor leader" of organized variety, Mao, Stalin, Roosevelt, and others like them.

Henri Perinne continued writing about this above incident with the purchase of the religious garment called a pallium, and the voluntary post-transactional overpayment on the part of Gerald:

> "This anecdote admirably illustrates the moral conflict which the revival of commerce was to provoke everywhere, and which indeed never ceased during the whole of the Middle Ages. From the beginning to the end the Church continued to regard commercial profits as a danger to salvation. Its ascetic ideal, which was perfectly suited to an agricultural civilisation, made it always suspicious of social changes, which it could not prevent and to which necessity even compelled it to submit, but to which it was never openly reconciled. Its prohibition of interest was to weigh heavily on the economic life of later centuries." (77)

"Violence was an indispensable feature of land distribution, implicating a majority in the murder of a carefully designated minority. Work teams were given quotas of people who had to be denounced, humiliated, beaten, dispossessed and then killed by the villagers, who were assembled in their hundreds in an atmosphere charged with hatred. In a pact sealed with blood between the party and the poor, close to 2 million so-called 'landlords', often hardly better off than their neighbors, were liquidated... Some children were slaughtered as little landlords." -Frank Dikottor, in regard to mid-20th century China (78)

When it comes to the battle between the special interests and the general interest, the general interest ought to prevail every time, or nearly every time, yet experience rarely illustrates that outcome. *Because the general interest includes everybody, it ought to be the most politically profitable group to please.* Yet, for centuries, special interest groups have prevailed in capturing gain for politicians. Why? Perhaps because the illusion of a free lunch can be more easily bestowed upon a few -it's less expensive to buy lunch for 300 people than for 300,000,000. Perhaps because enough people are sincerely ignorant of the farther-reaching consequences of such targeted bribes, and they do not realize that what they're doing is harmful. Perhaps these people simply do not give a damn about anybody else, or about the farther-reaching consequences of a bribe in terms of payola or of perceived privilege, and like non-sentient animals feeding at a trough simply and greedily want to sink their teeth into the payout today; consequences be damned. Perhaps other reasons offer valid explanations as well.

What seems clear is that elevating the standard for ordinary, in terms of historical literacy pertaining to proposals from politicians, is crucial to solving the problem. The *good people will change their ways once they are shown beyond any reasonable doubt, by the mountain of evidence available, what is best for everyone*; particularly when it is known that *their friends and neighbors* also possess this knowledge, and *will shun them for knowingly inflicting harm through selfishness masquerading as altruism.* Under such conditions, also, those doing wrong will be doing so without any legitimate claim to sincere ignorance. Dealing with them swiftly and decisively can be done legitimately and without any remorse, either through revocation of their opportunity to vote in elections -this author's most preferred method- through jailing, through deportation, or some other method.

Socialism is slavery: A man in the USA who had been enslaved for six decades, prior to purchasing his freedom in 1857, defined slavery in practice as one man's "receiving...the work of another man, and not by his consent." (79)

In later medieval Europe, whereas merchants had used profit, and their eventual accumulation thereof, along with involvement in a tremendous amount of risk-laden commerce, to live the lives of free men, those with feudal land in the country lived quite differently. Hereditary title to his land made the serf immune to any risk of its loss, though the lord had access to a share of each serf's estate upon the serf's demise, along with charge over their religion and marriages. Additionally, rapacious taxation by the state -in the form of the Church- was passed on to the lords, who passed it on to the serfs; the *tally* known to be the most arbitrary and burdensome. The landed serf was also subject to dictation of required use of the lord's means of production, at the lord's dictated rate for usage which included the lord's tax, and that he must use those means -perhaps a wine press, or a grain mill-exclusively; competition was forbidden for the customer. We see here a brand of communism bearing many similarities to that undertaken in 20th century China under Mao.

The villages pitched in together to farm and to perpetuate their meager survival, *initiative for improvement was absent, as was any reward for so doing*. Profit was absent in the countryside, and the resulting stagnation -with shortages perpetually looming, when not occurring- along with a lack of innovation, pervaded. (80)

Socialism is Treason: The evidence dictates the conclusion that the outcome of such legislation is harmful, to both the part (individual) and the whole (classes, and nation). Therefore, it is against the best interests of one's own nation, and in the interest of its enemies, to pass such legislation. To vote for, or to enact by decree, such measures which have been historically placed in the basket of that which is populist, redistributive, and seeking material equality of outcomes, is to act in direct support of the enemies of one's nation, by intentionally harming one's own nation. Each and every page of this present volume supplies veracity to this statement.

"Turn back the clock": Taking a macro, or bird's eye, view of history and trends, awash in as much evidence of prior experience as can possibly be gathered; as opposed to the myopic picture -which excludes as much evidence as possible- that is utilized by socialists, wokers, American liberals, and the rest of their kind; we find *the latter parties expressing a desire to create a long-history in which the 3 most recent centuries of relative plenty* -produced primarily as the result of here-to-fore unprecedented individual liberty in places such as the USA pre-1933, 19th century Britain, 20th century Hong Kong, and 20th century Japan- *will be reduced to a blip on the radar screen,* via the eradication of liberty so that it may be *supplanted by the abrogation-of-choice-ism* implemented through centrally planned redistributionism. The masses, in the above mentioned times and places, experienced an individual opportunity to prosper or to suffer; the immense prosperity of nations; the remarkable ascensions from poverty through the service of others, which communists would like to replace with a return to the prior pattern consisting of 4,000 steady years of consistent and firm control by rulers, with minor improvements brought about by relaxation or partial elimination of taxation and regulation. Such qualities as forcing the masses to work for the state, including forced entry into armed combat -many North American Indian tribes, along with the Ancient Eurasian nations utilizing the comitatus, come to mind; rapacious taxation; along with deplorable, when compared to the "free" age of the post Industrial Revolution West, living conditions. Fritz Hayek in a writing originally published 1944:

> "We should be seriously deceiving ourselves if for these apprehensions we sought comfort in consideration that the adoption of central planning would merely mean *a return, after a brief spell of a free economy, to the ties and regulations which have governed economic activity through most ages,* and that therefore the infringements of personal liberty need not be greater than they

were before the age of laissez faire. This is a dangerous illusion. Even during the periods of European history when the regimentation of economic life went furthest, it amounted to little more than the creation of a general and semipermanent framework of rules in which the individual preserved a wide free sphere." Hayek goes on to say: "The passion for the 'collective satisfaction of our needs', with which our socialists have so well prepared the way for totalitarianism, and which wants us to take our pleasures as well as our necessities at the appointed time and in the prescribed form is, of course, partly intended as a means of political education. But it is also the result of the exigencies of *planning, which consists essentially in depriving us of choice, in order to give us whatever fits best into the plan and that at a time determined by the plan.*" (81)

"Replace it with nothing" fallacy: American politicians in recent decades, when confronted with the proposal to remove redistributive handout programs which abrogate choices from the masses, often retort with a reply along the lines of "Remove this measure, and replace it with what? You don't even have a replacement for this eliminated program!". Such tactics falsely infer a condition of *sine qua non* –latin for without which, not– which spuriously imply the necessity of harmful, redistributive legislation. *Such a politician would just as well advise a cancer patient, whose treatment plan advises the removal of a cancerous tumor*, "but they're going to replace it with *nothing*! How can you let them remove this harmful element, without replacing it with another harmful element?". The proper evaluation, of course, yields the conclusion that to replace a life with a cancerous tumor, with a life absent such a nefarious element, is a case of addition by subtraction.

Steady and known rules cause the long term planning of private individuals to be less mysterious. In medieval Europe, although loans at interest were forbidden, they were made nonetheless through various methods. Just as the merchants led the way in obtaining liberation from the shackles of socialism and central planning, as those who owned the manors recognized the sensibility of encouraging the creators of plenty, in a land which knew much penury, the prohibition of lending at interest was lifted at the trading bazaars. This was done by adding interest into the initial loan. That is, that the borrower would actually receive goods or gold with an agreed upon value of 1,000 units, but would sign a bill of sale stating that they were in receipt of 1,200 units worth of goods or gold. The total interest was already baked into the price at the outset, thereby removing from the contract's language an initial sale of 1,000 units, an interest rate of 11.5%, and a statement that over time the amount to be repaid would grow to an amount of 1,200 units; the evidence of interest. Instead, the two parties would, at the outset, agree upon a price of repayment which was higher than the price borrowed. No evidence of interest was present in such an agreement.

Nonetheless, the Church's -*government's*- *official position against the practice hung like an executioner's blade over the heads of the general population.* This menacing prospect stood clearly in the way of long term loans, particularly in substantial quantities -one year was the customary term for repayment of loans made at the bazaars- hamstringing commercial activity and its resultant positive impact upon all of the people. (82) The concomitant elevation of outcomes for the masses in the areas of jobs, supply and quality of goods, upward professional mobility, food supply, housing, and so much more, was absent.

Private property rights uplift the poor, as was seen in the Virginia Company beginning in the 17th century in the New World. A privately owned business operation provided an opportunity for immense growth to the poor. Channing tells us: "Any freeman, with a reasonable amount of diligence and success, could accumulate hundreds of acres in a comparatively short space of time." These had often been *the lowest vagabonds, exiled to the colonies after being barbarically whipped and otherwise degraded, then made to travel on a ship in awful conditions*, who upon completion of their servitude owed to the man who paid their transit, were free themselves. *Landowners and proprietors in Virginia; dregs of society in England.* (83)

The lack of private property rights harmed the masses mightily in Germany during the late 1840s. *As rioting monopolists sought to acquire legal codification of unearned advantages* for their special interest groups -union monopolies; wage and hours mandates- through both the use of violence and threats of violence, *private property rights evaporated in practice for some time.* Incompetent statesmen and leaders failed to quash the rioting animals burning and looting the German Confederation of states; in fact, they hardly even stood up to them.

With no place for those who had achieved the acquisition of property -job providing and tax revenue generating enterprises- to turn for enforcement of their legitimate private property rights in the face of criminal mobs, the already stifled economic activity of the lands was further suppressed. *The lack of food and other necessities was exacerbated by this factor.* As a committee of the time noted of their investigation of the causes of their then-present economic woes "...we find that they lie above all in the fact that domestic commerce is lacking in confidence, that property appears to be threatened by constant agitation, and finally that concern about a disruption of foreign trade and of markets abroad has caused the extinction of almost all spirit of enterprise." (84)

"Let them beg"/"Make beggars of them": Socialism = Government confiscating the citizenry's property, and forcing the citizenry to beg for some of their own property back. Professor Sidney Hook, a teacher at New York University, during a debate with Bill Buckley on the latter's television show, *Firing Line*, cited this as an inducement to socialism; asserting that if one's private property was stolen from them by other individuals, through the mechanism of the state, that person could simply petition the thieves for a program which would fulfill the wants created by this theft! (85) As has been illustrated throughout this volume, experience has proven this claim, that wants will be quelled via this procedure, to be incontrovertibly false in practice.

A desirable alternative is to limit total government spending to 10-15% of GDP (Gross Domestic Product; sometimes referred to as the national income). Because prognostications regarding GDP can be made, but cannot be guaranteed to be accurate, it may be necessary to limit spending to a percentage of the prior year's GDP, because to overtax and overspend will be deemed treasonous, and carry with it the most ultimate and irreversible of punishments. Using data compiled by Christopher Chantrill, and published on his website (86), which lists total government spending for the federal, state, and local levels for each year of the existence of the USA, with national defense singled out each year, and with costs incurred by the judiciary singled out beginning in the mid-20th century, a chart showing costs of the three legitimate functions of the state -to establish and defend borders, issue and regulate currency, and provide courts for the mediation of disputes between citizens- shows that these costs are within the boundaries of the 10-15% limit of each current year's GDP; with the obvious exception of wartime, although not for each and every year of wartime. See appendix A (page# 468) for some specifics on this data.

A measure regarding a limitation upon taxation must also be included. It is true that the paying off of national debt, a persistent bugaboo familiar to contemporary readers, could allow some taxation beyond spending for the current year's 3 legitimate functions, an allowance for which can and should be made by those penning the actual legislation, in the event that this advice is heeded by citizens of this country. To make punishable as treasonous the passing of any and all budgets which either authorize spending outside of the 3 legitimate functions -particularly for the areas of so-called populist, redistributive, envy satiating, spending- is the only way to ensure that this law is respected. When I say all those who voted yes on such budgets, I do mean all of them, the congress, state legislatures, etc.. Let the government beg the citizenry for money to fund their projects.

Sell the people government bonds, if you want to raise money. Spend time in the legislatures garnering support for whatever it is that you want to spend other people's money on, but can't get a loan from any bank on earth for said purpose, and the citizens may buy bonds to help the cause if they so choose. *Instead of spending time inciting envy of some citizens so that they might empower politicians and bureaucrats to take from the People, these same employees in the government can spend time selling the citizens on proposals necessitating funds, and enticing the citizens to spend their own money on such, by writing a check from their own, personal, bank accounts.* Remember: the most efficient exchange is the one in which a person spends their own money in an attempt to benefit themselves. Frivolous spending and sham charities should see drastic reductions in both scale and plentitude. War bonds have been sold by many countries in the past, along with other special bond issues, so the idea is hardly radical. *The sham charities that are mere money laundering and voter bribing operations, will have been outlawed indirectly by the passing of these two new spending rules.*

Shysters and conmen will lose their iron grip on the People's money -as the populace is *forced* to pay under heavy penalties for non-payment- that it possesses presently, and instead leave them to attempt to swindle people into turning their money over voluntarily. This may be accomplished through alternative means of graft, but many will often turn to legitimate means of persuasion, as this is the most successful method for those without immense legal protection; and would obviously improve the greater good of the society as the time formerly spent grafting and operating a compulsory system of graft which has repeatedly statistically illustrated the most dire consequences for the least-moneyed, bringing people into a penurious condition who would not have been otherwise, in absence of this interference masquerading as assistance (that is, a 0.5% reduction in GDP means x fewer jobs, y more long term unemployed, z more impoverished, than otherwise).

One pervasive, historical, political reality: The least-moneyed, well spoken, or outwardly talented, of a society are palliated/bribed, by whoever seeks to achieve or retain political supremacy, with payola extracted from others, and dispensed by central authority, in return for the former's service as infantrymen in the military. From the comitatus of Ancient Eurasia, to Germany in the mid-19th century, to the USA after the Second World War; such tactics are often seen in use by the same group as a method to quell the occasional disruptive rioting by the least-moneyed class; in so doing, unwittingly rewarding them for engaging in the presumably unwanted behavior. "For he who serves the state with his life has also a claim on it for support." was Leopold Von Ranke's opening line of a proposal to offer welfare to ingratiate themselves with the proletariat, as an expense of military necessity, in order to stock the army with soldiers at all times; sent to Frederich William IV during the 1850s. (87) Ranke's preceding quotation is certainly true once the fighting has been done, but cannot be said prior to the fight.

TERM LIMITS SCHEME

It is easy to point out faults and to complain. While this is necessary during the process of persuading a reasonable, intelligent, audience that the evidence dictates the conclusion that central planning is harmful, dwelling on these realities only solves the problem of eliminating support for said measures. While there are those who dwell upon problems, better are those who focus on solutions. Suggesting what to do instead, and how to specifically implement the changes necessary, is the next step to a better world. As we have seen illustrated, particularly in part II, complaining about the way things are does not necessarily lead to making things better once the complainers get their hands on the levers of government. *How would you actually write the legislation advocating for whatever change you wish to see implemented?* How would you pen the rules of government, so that it would be free to achieve its three legitimate purposes (see page# 18), flexible enough to handle extreme duress such as natural disaster and military bombardment by a variety of sources, yet securely restrained and unable to infringe upon the liberties of the citizens who it exists to serve and to protect from tyranny? Doing so, while keeping an eye out for backdoor loopholes to be exploited by dissolute evildoers, without scruple as to speciousness and duplicity, may prove much more challenging than originally anticipated.

To successfully do so has proved to extend beyond the reach of this author, though I do have some suggestions and rationale, and I encourage others to utilize or improve upon these beginnings.

The elimination of a permanent political class has already been touched upon, and will be briefly revisited here. Serving the special interest group of power-brokers loses much appeal to those in a position to do so if membership in that class is *transient by design*, as opposed to one which has the possibility of permanency. To have a class of people who see themselves as permanently and professionally holding office, the success of which has little or nothing to do with producing goods or services in a fashion which is sustainable and which meets consumer demand; while passing through to the private sector and competing in the real economy in which they must be profitable, productive, and useful in order to thrive, only briefly if at all; seems to me the most obvious first hurdle in the elimination of the tyranny of the special interest groups over the general interest.

If instead, everyone considered the private sector to be their home base, and passed through the public sector briefly, if at all, then fetching for special interest groups would seem far less appealing to those in office, as *this person would consider their real life as existing out in the general population*, and be less likely to sell out for election to their office. Once in office, even a duplicitous and short-sighted scalawag who made it in, would be -hopefully- in the minority among the others in the government at that time; thereby standing in the way of legislative forays designed to gain favor of the special interest groups, to the detriment of the general interest of the people. *The banning of consecutive terms in office*, for all offices, seems an effective step towards this end. The temptation for politicians to seek headlines -and to sway the rubes into currying favor their way- by "solving" problems with "remedies" known for certain to cause maladies and calamities, should be removed because they're *not* running for re-election; at least not anytime soon. This was the practice utilized regarding the presidency of the republic of Texas, prior to its annexation to the United States. A limit of total government spending to 10-15% (see prior section, page# 456) of the year's GDP -Gross Domestic Product- would also *remediate the practice of using Treasury money as campaign funds*, as there would be very little to spare beyond those necessary to carry out the three legitimate functions of the state.

Support for banishment of re-election: Tocqueville, in 1831, commented about the advisability of presidential re-election specifically, concluding that the chief executive under such circumstances merely degenerates into an instrument of the whims of the general populace, cowering to any anticipated negative feedback -even if illegitimate- while obsequiously catering to their every perceived desire:

"Intrigue and corruption are natural weaknesses of elective governments. But when the head of state can be re-elected, these weaknesses stretch out endlessly and threaten the very existence of the country. When an ordinary candidate seeks success through intrigue, his maneuverings can only take place within a restricted sphere, but when the head of state puts himself forward he borrows the power of government for his private use.

In the first example, we see a man of modest resources; *in the second case, the state itself with its huge resources is involved in intrigue and corruption.*

The ordinary citizen who uses disreputable practices to gain power brings harm only indirectly to the prosperity of the public; but whenever the man who represents the executive power enters the fray, the cares of government move into a secondary place because his principal concern is his election. *For him, all negotiations, like laws, are only electoral schemings*; jobs become the reward for services rendered, not to the nation but to its head. Even if the action of the government is not always opposed to the interests of the country, at the very least it no longer serves it, even though it was created for that purpose.

The principle of re-election makes the corrupting influence of elective governments still more widespread and more dangerous, while leading to a decline in the political morality of the nation and the substitution of craft for patriotism." (88)

Thomas Jefferson, in a writing published 1821: "...insomuch that should a President consent to be a candidate for a 3d. election [after having served two, four year, terms], I trust he would be rejected on this demonstration of ambitious views." Jefferson having, in the same paragraph, cited the voluntary stepping aside of each of the first 4 presidents who had been elected to two terms -himself among their number- as having established a satisfactory precedent that the duty to serve is temporary, and limited to two full terms. (89) Unfortunately, the public did not behave as Jefferson had hoped during the New Deal period, and notorious tyrant Frank Roosevelt, with his relentless pursuit of the funneling of power into his hands, to the detriment of the general public -with persistent 15-20% unemployment for a decade, the slew of state enabled monopolies, increases in taxation exacerbating the government induced cash shortage caused by the Federal Reserve, Roosevelt fixing the price of gold at his whims, and so much more- as the New Dealers created a perpetual "emergency" by passing laws which spread poverty and monopoly in the name of preventing both, and in-so-doing bribed the citizens for votes with the citizens' own money; Frank Roosevelt utilized this scheme to bring himself four consecutive elections into the office of the president, and the horrors of the New Deal terrorized the public, and hold back the nation to this very day.

Forcing a citizen, who has been elected to government office, to *abstain from government service for a period of time which at a minimum is equal to the period of time in which that citizen had just engaged in holding office*, seems likely to result in a notable dissipation in the practice of *campaigning for one's next election during the time in which one is supposed to be serving the office* to which they were elected. Of course, an easily foreseeable consequence of such measures as have been suggested here, is for the branding of parties to become even more uniform, calculated, and strategic than it is presently, and so stunts may be pulled in an effort to gain election for those of one's political party. The efficacy of such a measure in the elimination of a person's estimation of themselves to be that of a professional politician, and so less incentivized to act against the general interest, does not seem marred by such possibilities.

By *prohibiting the holding of seats within the same body more than once*, simply by establishing residency in a different district, seems an obvious and practical measure towards diffusing the power of individuals, and of their consideration of themselves as permanent rulers, as opposed to permanent citizens in the private sector. One could foresee a family of 3 brothers, for instance, each of which holding a U.S. Senate seat in separate states, then changing states whereupon they are elected to the senate for the first time in that new state's federal seat, and thus remaining in the body for a period of 15-20 years between them. One might also foresee a similar scheme in a state legislature, with the swapping of districts creating a familial dynasty of sorts within the state.

Some concrete proposals:

I Total time served limited to 3 terms served, or 10 years total, whichever comes first
-should the person have served two terms in office,
which culminated either with a dismissal for cause; resignation; or completion of term,

the early termination of service in prior terms will not diminish the impact upon the 10 year limit, or the 3 term limit, the full value of the years of the terms to which the citizen had been elected will be applied in full, whether the citizen has actually served as many years or not,

and remain beneath the service limit of 10 years total, then be elected to a third term of service,

that term may be served until its culmination, however that may come about; although doing so will in fact cause the citizen to have exceeded the limit of 10 years upon the natural culmination of the office, whether that be via dismissal for cause, resignation, death, end of term, or any other means,

Thereupon the citizen will have fulfilled their service limit and be barred from serving in public office for life, upon penalty of conviction of Treason and execution if this banishment is violated.

II Citizen must sit out for at least as long as he or she just sat in.

That is, if one serves a 6 year term as a U.S. Senator, then one is forbidden from campaigning for or holding any public office, federal, state, or local, for a minimum of 6 years upon the culmination of the term to which one had been elected, even if said citizen has not exhausted their allotment of 3 terms elected, and 10 years of service. Had their term served been 2 years, then their banishment from office would be 2 years, and so forth.

III Citizen cannot hold the same office, or serve on the same body, twice.

One could serve one term on the Alabama State Legislature, and then serve a term on the Pennsylvania State Legislature, since these are separate legislative bodies. One could not, however, serve as U.S. Senator from Alabama, and then as U.S. Senator from Pennsylvania, since the U.S. Senate is a single body and this would involve merely changing seats within that same body.

One could never be mayor of the same city more than once, comptroller of the same country more than once, president of the United States more than once; the prohibition on multiple elections to the same office extends to all offices, at all levels of government, be they federal, state, or local.

IV Citizens must be barred from perpetual involvement, shuffled like a playing card throughout the deck, in government via characterization as a special assistant, or advisor, or receptionist, or window washer, or any other ruse under which the same people can be in the governmental bodies, pulling the strings from behind the throne. Practical application of this eludes the author as of this printing, and input is encouraged from the readership. The penalty of Treason, punishable by execution, must be applied to violation of whatever standard is set.

Constitutional amendment limiting total government spending to 10-15% of GDP, and limiting the spending of these funds to the 3 legitimate functions of the state (see above for GDP percentage information, as well as for the 3 legitimate functions).

-an intended consequence of this is to permanently disband present government owned and controlled bureaucracies, agencies, organizations, sham charities, of any variety outside of the three legitimate functions outlined in (page# 18), and outside of the spending limit denoted herein,

which will quell the obvious concern that political power might simply transfer, in the same persons, from elected positions to positions which had been appointed,

this permanent banishment of centrally planned sham charities and industries will liberate the mass of bodies who would otherwise have been devoting their efforts and industry to an entity which has proven detrimental to all nations and their peoples,

to now devote their energies to the private sector, whether charitable or industrious.

WHO SHOULD BE PERMITTED TO VOTE?
HOW SHOULD THIS BE DETERMINED OR ENFORCED?

This merely acts as a codicil. I don't have any answers to the two questions listed above, in bold print, yet know that they are of immense vitality, and so I encourage others to pursue evidence pertaining to their answers. Is it right to have a person serve for you in active combat, yet to deny them a vote in the elections of the officials in the very land for which they fought? Is it right to permit a person who is wholly ignorant of, and arrogant in regards to, public affairs, a vote merely because they fought in the armed forces? Does that best serve the nation for which this soldier fought? If we implement voter tests, who will decide which questions will be asked, and which answers will be deemed correct? Can these questions be decided at a federal level, without infringing upon the rights of the states and of the counties? Can they be decided on a national basis without begging for a rigged game, doctored by the party in power in the capital at any given time?

It seems sensible to me that the object ought to be to include as many people as can be deemed competent to vote responsibly, and from a position of some substance. Who fits that category, how to determine this, how to implement methods aimed at delivering the franchise to those best suited to make responsible decisions; while keeping out those who proceed from a position of ignorance, or awash in arrogance while drawing upon their ignorance, or who perceive themselves as voting to steal from their neighbors while avoiding incarceration; elude me. I merely list now a few tidbits that I have collected on the matter of suffrage, and encourage readers to seek more data elsewhere; or even better, to conduct your own research, and deliver it to the general public. With this, I thank you for taking time out of your day to read my book. I hope that it has been of some service to you, and that it has imparted new and useful information to you.

Germany mid-19th century revolution: suffrage: 4/12/1849 new law grants voting rights to all who were not pauperized, criminal, insane, or bankrupt -but such far reaching suffrage pertained solely to elections of delegates to the lower chamber of the legislature. (90) North German Confederation 1866 universal suffrage. (91)

Franchise: 1760 New World English colonies: "The suffrage was exercised according to general regulations, which usually conferred it upon those men who possessed a certain amount of property; landed property, — landed property in the South, and real and personal estate in the North." (92)

England: universal suffrage 1885 (93)

The possible odium of the wide expansion of the franchise was certainly reinforced in 1892 by Sidney Webb, a hardcore socialist and an influence in English politics during his days, as he so advised the Royal Commission on Labor in that year. Webb predicted that the poor, and other non-owners of businesses, would collude in an effort to use their votes to appropriate the fairly acquired private property of those people who were envied by this large voting block; while the politicians would eagerly exploit the minority group of job creators and producers of goods and food. "Collectivism is the economic obverse of democracy." Webb expanded upon this remark: "It appears to me that if you allow the tramway conductor to vote he will not forever be satisfied with exercising that vote over such matters as the appointment of the Ambassador to Paris, or even the position of the franchise. He will realize that the forces that keep him at work for sixteen hours a day for three shillings a day are not the forces of hostile kings, of nobles, of priests; but whatever forces they are will, it seems to me, seek so far as possible to control them by his vote. That is to say, he will more and more seek to convert his political democracy into what one may roughly term an industrial democracy, so that he may obtain some kind of control as a voter over the conditions under which he lives." (94)

Suffrage in France: In order to prevent the ignorant unwashed from having too much sway, the assembly restricted the right to vote to those who paid above a denoted amount of taxes; this to be an indicator of having some "skin in the game", or of having something to lose. While half of adult men met the initial criteria, electors made the only votes that counted in 1790, and 1791; these numbering 50,000. (95)

APPENDIX A

The official cost of the 3 legitimate functions of the state (to establish and defend borders, to coin and regulate currency, to provide courts for the mediation of disputes among citizens), as a percentage of that year's GDP, based upon information gathered by Christopher Chantrill, and published on his website usgovernmentspending.com, will follow here. Information for national defense, and for cumulative spending of all levels of government, for all purposes, are available for all years; information regarding the cost of the courts is available beginning in the mid-20th century; while information pertaining to the cost of operating the Federal Reserve, the U.S. Mint, or the Treasury, are not separated out.

2 or 3 years from each decade have been selected, more or less at random. Some wartime years have been included to provide some variety, as well as to see the fluctuation of cost regarding defense during such years. The percentages are approximate, as splitting hairs over decimal places, while extremely relevant to actual budgets, do not impact our interest in the business of the sufficiency of 10-15% of GDP to cover the necessaries of government. Notice how, even as spending as a proportion of income has grown since the advent of the New Deal period, defense and judiciary spending combine to fall within or beneath this 10-15% threshold.

YEAR	National Defense (% of present year's GDP)	Judiciary (% of GDP)	Total Spending: Federal, State, and Local	GDP
1792	0.5%		2.25%	$230 Mil
1795	0.75%		2%	$390 Mil
1799	1.2%		2.2%	$447 Mil
1804	0.4%		1.7%	$538 Mil
1807	0.52%		1.5%	$595 Mil
1811	0.53%		1.1%	$776 Mil
1817	1.5%		2.9%	$777 Mil

YEAR	National Defense (% of present year's GDP)	Judiciary (% of GDP)	Total Spending: Federal, State, and Local	GDP
1820	1.4%		3.82%	$718 Mil
1826	2.1%		3.6%	$876 Mil
1829	0.96%		3.4%	$940 Mil
1833	1.3%		4%	$1.172 Bil
1836	1.95%		4.12%	$1.497 Bil
1839	1.1%		4%	$1.685 Bil
1843	0.47%		3.52%	$1.595 Bil
1847	1.94%		4.2%	$2.476 Bil
1850	0.72%		3.4%	$2.656 Bil
1854	0.61%		3.4%	$3.789 Bil
1858	0.97%		4.1%	$4.151 Bil
1861	0.77%		4.1%	$4.673 Bil
1863	8.56%		11.15%	$7.745 Bil
1866	3.78%		8%	$9.098 Bil
1871	1.15%		7.78%	$7.751 Bil
1875	1.1%		7.3%	$8.331 Bil
1877	0.9%		6.7%	$8.7 Bil
1880	1%		5.9%	$10.592 Bil
1884	0.94%		5.71%	$12.107 Bil
1887	0.9%		5.9%	$13.56 Bil
1891	1.2%		6.5%	$15.94 Bil
1894	1.5%		7.9%	$14.606 Bil
1899	1.7%		6.3%	$20.119 Bil
1903	1.2%		6.6%	$26.647 Bil
1906	1.1%		6.6%	$31.794 Bil
1908	1.2%		7.7%	$30.797 Bil
1911	1.2%		8.2%	$34.675 Bil

YEAR	National Defense (% of present year's GDP)	Judiciary (% of GDP)	Total Spending: Federal, State, and Local	GDP
1915	1.1%		9.6%	$39.048 Bil
1919	21.8%		29%	$79.090 Bil
1922	1.8%		12.6%	$91.449 Bil
1925	1.4%		11.3%	$91.449 Bil
1928	1.3%		11.7%	$98.305 Bil
1931	2%		15.8%	$77.4 Bil
1934	1.6%		18.7%	$66.8 Bil
1938	1.9%		20.2%	$87.4 Bil
1940	2.1%		19.9%	$102.9 Bil
1943	34.7%	0.076%	45.6%	$203.1 Bil
1948	7.2%	0.062%	20%	$274.5 Bil
1952	14%	0.072%	27.3%	$367.3 Bil
1955	11%	0.06%	25.6%	$430.2 Bil
1959	10.2%	0.07%	27.7%	$525.5 Bil
1961	10%	0.071%	29%	$567.7 Bil
1964	9.5%	0.019%	27.4%	$692 Bil
1966	8.5%	0.019%	26.4%	$819.6 Bil
1970	8.7%	0.027%	29.6%	$1.086 Tril
1973	8.9%	0.07%	28.7%	$1.433 Tril
1976	6.1%	0.085%	32.9%	$1.886 Tril
1979	5.4%	0.069%	30.3%	$2.667 Tril
1983	6.7%	0.048%	34.8%	$3.689 Tril
1986	6.8%	0.051%	34.5%	$4.607 Tril
1988	6.2%	0.061%	33.5%	$5.282 Tril
1990	5.7%	0.067%	34.6%	$6.015 Tril
1993	5%	0.34%	32.6%	$6.882 Tril
1997	3.75%	0.34%	32.6%	$8.662 Tril

YEAR	National Defense (% of present year's GDP)	Judiciary (% of GDP)	Total Spending: Federal, State, and Local	GDP

YEAR	National Defense (% of present year's GDP)	Judiciary (% of GDP)	Total Spending: Federal, State, and Local	GDP
2001	3.5%	0.4%	32.4%	$10.598 Tril
2003	4.2%	0.4%	34.1%	$11.566 Tril
2009	5.5%	0.42%	41.3%	$14.448 Tril
2011	5.6%	0.4%	39.3%	$15.647 Tril
2014	4.5%	0.35%	34.9%	$17.804 Tril
2018	4.2%	0.34%	34.8%	$20.798 Tril
2022	4.3%	0.34%	37.8%	$25.994 Tril

NOTES

Whenever changes have been made by Paul Dayton, this will be denoted by the use of the abbreviation "PD". Efforts have been made to cite all sources as thoroughly and properly as possible. Any objections to the methods of citation should be brought to the attention of the author via the contact methods listed on the copyright page.

Introduction   Pages 12-18

1   Thomas Jefferson, *Writings* (New York, Literary Classics of the United States, Inc., 1984), p. 365

2   Paul Dayton, *Correcting Our Financial Miseducation: Raising the Bar for the Average* (USA: ISBN: 9798726908755, 2021), p. 207-208

Part I   Pages 19-88

1   Stephen Kotkin, *Steeltown, USSR* (Berkeley and Los Angeles: University of California Press, 1991), p. 26

2   Allan Nevins, *John D. Rockefeller: a One-Volume Abridgement* (New York: Charles Scriber's Sons, 1959), p. 350

3   Alexis de Tocqueville, *Democracy in America: and Two Essays on America* (New York: Penguin Books, 2003), p. 216-217

4   D.T. Armentano. Ph. D., *Myths of Antitrust: Economic Theory and Legal Cases* (New Rochelle: Arlington House, 1972), p. 61-62

5   Ibid, p. 56-58

6   Nevins, *Rockefeller*, p. 4-5

7   Burton W. Folsom, Jr., *The Myth of the Robber Barons: A New Look at the Rise of Big Business in America* (Herndon: Young America's Foundation, 2013), p. 83

8   Nevins, *Rockefeller*, p. 7-8

9   Ibid, p. 8

10   Ibid, p. 9

11   Ibid, p. 15

12   Ibid, p. 16-17

13   Folsom, Jr., *Robber Barons*, p. 85

14   Nevins, *Rockefeller*, p. 22

15   Folsom, Jr., *Robber Barons*, p. 85

16   Armentano, *Myths Antitrust*, p. 66-67

17   Ralph W. Hidy and Muriel E. Hidy, *Pioneering in Big Business 1882-1911* (New York: Harper & Brothers, 1955), p. 6

18   Ibid, p. 7

19   Ibid, p. 142

20   Folsom, Jr., *Robber Barons*, p. 87

21   Nevins, *Rockefeller*, p. 202

22   Ibid, p. 203

23   Ibid, p. 204

24   Ibid, p. 120

25   Ibid, p. 200-201

26   Ibid, p. 200

27   Ibid, p. 206

28   Hidy and Hidy, *Pioneering*, p. 5

29   Nevins, *Rockefeller*, p. 140-141

30   Harold F. Williamson, Ralph L. Andreano, Arnold R. Daum, Gilbert C. Klose, *The American Petroleum Industry: The age of energy 1899-1959* (Evanston: Northwest University Press, 1963), p. 8; bold and italics added by PD

31   Hidy and Hidy, *Pioneering*, p. 9

32   Nevins, *Rockefeller*, p. 133

33   Paul Dayton, *Correcting Our Financial Miseducation: Raising the Bar for the Average* (USA: ISBN: 9798726908755, 2021), p. 123-126

34   Nevins, *Rockefeller*, p. 121

35   Ibid, p. 74

36   Ibid, p. 125-126

37   Armentano, *Myths Antitrust*, p. 77

38   Joseph A. Schumpeter, *Capitalism, Socialism and Democracy* (New York: Harper & Row, 1950), p. 89

39   William L. Shirer, *20th Century Journey: A Memoir of a Life and the Times, Volume II: The Nightmare Years 1930-1940* (New York: Bantam Books, 1985), p. 45

40   Nevins, *Rockefeller*, p. 213-214

41   Ibid, p. 215

42   Ibid, p. 216-217

43   Ibid, p. 218

44   Ibid, p. 218-219

45   Ibid, p. 80-81

46   Hidy and Hidy, *Pioneering*, p. 139

47   Nevins, *Rockefeller*, p. 94

48   Hidy and Hidy, *Pioneering*, p. 261

49   Nevins, *Rockefeller*, p. 210-211

50   Armentano, *Myths Antitrust*, p. 72

51   Nevins, *Rockefeller*, p. 123-128

52   Hidy and Hidy, *Pioneering*, p. 12

53   Ibid, p. 10

54   Nevins, *Rockefeller*, p. 77-79

55   Ibid, p. 86-87

56   Ibid, p. 104-106

57   *American Petroleum Industry*, p.5

58   Ibid, p. 6 + p. 6, N. 6

59   Nevins, *Rockefeller*, p. 73

60   Ibid, p. 121

61   Ibid, p. 107-108

62   Hidy and Hidy, *Pioneering*, p. 131

63   Milton Friedman & Anna Jacobson Schwartz, *A Monetary History of the United States, 1867-1960* (Princeton: Princeton University Press, 1993), p. 94

64   Armentano, *Myths Antitrust*, p. 68-70

65   Nevins, *Rockefeller*, p. 143

66   Armentano, *Myths Antitrust*, p. 77-79

67   *American Petroleum Industry*, p. 237-238

68   Ibid, p. 231

69   Armentano, *Myths Antitrust*, p. 81-82; note: printed without the first author's emphasis

70   Dayton, *Correcting*, part two: p. 83-217

71   *American Petroleum Industry*, p. 319-320

72   Nevins, *Rockefeller*, p. 197

73   Ibid, p. 198

74   Ibid, p. 14

75   Ibid, p. 227-228

76   Ibid, p. 230

77   P.T. Bauer, *Equality, the Third World, and Economic Delusion* (Cambridge, Mass.: Harvard University Press, 1981), p. 14

78   Armentano, *Myths Antitrust*, p. 25-26

79   Bauer, *Economic Delusion*, p. 67

80   Ibid, p. 67-68

81   Ibid, p. 69

82   Ibid, p. 68

83   Ibid, p. 69-70

84   Ibid, p. 69

85   Armentano, *Myths Antitrust*, p. 56-58

86   Ibid, p. 99

87   Ibid, p. 103

88   Ibid, p. 103

89   Ibid, p. 88-89

90   Ibid, p. 91-92

91   Ibid, p. 93

92   Ibid, p. 95-97

93   Ibid, p. 97-99

94   Edward Channing, *A History of the United States, Volume I, The Planting of a Nation in the New World 1000-1660* (New York: The Macmillan Company, 1907), p. 523-524

95   Dayton, *Correcting*, p. 162-163

96   Amity Shlaes, *The Forgotten Man: A New History of the Great Depression* (New York: HarperCollins, 2008), chapter 7

97   Armentano, *Myths Antitrust*, p. 112

98   Dayton, *Correcting*, p. 177-179

99   Armentano, *Myths Antitrust*, p. 121

100   Ibid, p. 108-122

101   Theodore S. Hamerow, *Restoration, Revolution, Reaction: Economics and Politics in Germany, 1815-1871* (Princeton: Princeton University Press, 1972), p. 10-11

102   Frederick Pedler, *Main Currents of West African History 1940-1978* (London: The Macmillan Press LTD, 1979), p. 89; bold and italics added by PD

103   Ibid, p. 88-92

104   Ibid, p. 204

105   M.M. Austin & P. Vidal-Naquet, *Economic & Social History of Ancient Greece: An Introduction* (Berkeley/Los Angeles: University of California Press, 1980), p. 120-121

106   Channing, *History Volume I*, p. 193

107   Peter T. Bauer and Basil S. Yamey, *The Economics of Under-developed Countries* (Chicago: The University of Chicago Press, 1957), p. 256

108   Henri Pirenne, *Economic and Social History of Medieval Europe* (Monee, IL: Harcourt, Inc., 1937), p. 172-175

109   Ibid, p. 175-176

110   Kotkin, *Steeltown*, preface, p. xiv-xv

111   Ibid, p. 4

112   Ibid, preface, p. xiv-xv

113   Ibid, preface, p. xvi

114   Ibid, p. 17

115   Ibid, preface, p. xvi; Fox Butterfield, *China: Alive in a Bitter Sea, Revised and Updated* (New York: Times Books, 1990), contains many references to this secrecy throughout.

116   Hamerow, *Restoration, Revolution, Reaction*, p. 141–143

117   Ibid, p. 103

118   Ibid, p. 103–104

119   Ibid, p. 104–105

120   Ibid, p. 250–251

121   Ibid, p. 244–245

122   Dayton, *Correcting*, p. 151–159

123   Shirer, *Nightmare Years*, p. 201–202

124   Pirenne, *Medieval Europe*, p. 206–207

125   Ibid, p. 207

126   Ibid, p. 206–207

127   Ibid, p. 208

128   Ibid, p. 208–209

129   Ibid, p. 209

130   Ibid, p. 215

131   M.M. Austin & P. Vidal-Naquet, *Ancient Greece*, p. 121–122, 320, 321 n. 9

132   M.M. Austin & P. Vidal-Naquet, *Ancient Greece*, p. 123, regarding all taxes on metics

133   M.M. Austin & P. Vidal-Naquet, *Ancient Greece*, p. 307, regarding all taxes on citizens

134   Edward Channing, *A History of the United States Volume 3: History of the Colonization of the United States by George Bancroft. Vol. III. Seventeenth Edition* (Boston: Little, Brown, and Company, 1862), p. 112

135   Ivan T. Berend and Gyorgy Ranki, *The European Periphery & Industrialization 1780-1914* (Cambridge: Cambridge University Press, 1982), p. 69

136   William W. Lockwood, *The Economic Development of Japan: Growth and Structural Change 1868-1938* (Princeton: Princeton University Press, 1954), p. 4

137   Ibid, p. 528–529

138   Ibid, p. 528, N. 20

139   Ibid, p. 525

140   Ibid, p. 5-6

141   Pirenne, *Medieval Europe*, p. 86-87

142   Ibid, p. 87

143   Ibid, p. 88

144   Kevin Shillington, *History of Africa, Third Edition* (China: Palgrave Macmillan, 2012), p. 35-36

145   Ibid, p. 40

146   Bauer and Yamey, *Under-developed*, p. 98, N. 2

147   Kotkin, *Steeltown*, p. 11

148   Ibid, p. 2

149   Hamerow, *Restoration, Revolution, Reaction*, p. 10

150   T.S. Ashton, *An Economic HIstory of England: The 18th Century* (London: Methuen & CO LTD, 1969), p. 42

151   Ibid, p. 42

152   Ibid, p. 43

153   *American Petroleum Industry*, p. 302-303

154   Nevins, *Rockefeller*, p. 119

155   Nevins, *Rockefeller*, p. 82-84

Part II   P. 89-176

1   P.T. Bauer, *Equality, the Third World, and Economic Delusion* (Cambridge, Mass.: Harvard University Press, 1981), p. 1

2   Peter T. Bauer and Basil S. Yamey, *The Economics of Under-developed Countries* (Chicago: The University of Chicago Press, 1957), p. 52

3   Ibid, p. 52 FN1

4   Edward Channing, *A History of the United States, Volume I, The Planting of a Nation in the New World 1000-1660* (New York: The Macmillan Company, 1907), p. 259-260 + 264-268

5   Theodore S. Hamerow, *Restoration, Revolution, Reaction: Economics and Politics in Germany, 1815-1871* (Princeton: Princeton University Press, 1972), p. 5-6

6   Bauer, *Economic Delusion*, p. 189-190

7   Edmund Burke, *Reflections on the Revolution in France* (Monee, IL: Digireads.com Publishing, 2020), p. 38

8   William W. Lockwood, *The Economic Development of Japan: Growth and Structural Change 1868-1938* (Princeton: Princeton University Press, 1954), p. 11

9   R.R. Palmer and Joel Colton, *A History of the Modern World* (New York: Alfred A. Knopf, Inc., 1965), p. 334

10   Ibid, p. 335

11   Ibid, p. 335-336

12   Ibid, p. 336

13   Ibid, p. 339

14   Thomas Jefferson, *Writings* (New York, Literary Classics of the United States, Inc., 1984), p. 80-81

15   R.R. Palmer and Joel Colton, *A History of the Modern World* (New York: Alfred A. Knopf, Inc., 1965), p. 341

16   Ibid, p. 339

17   Ibid, p. 340

18   Jefferson, *Writings*, p. 85

19   R.R. Palmer and Joel Colton, *A History of the Modern World* (New York: Alfred A. Knopf, Inc., 1965), p. 343

20   F.A.M. Mignet, *History of the French Revolution from 1789 to 1814* (North Haven, CT: ISBN: 9781507614303, 2022), p. 47-48

21   Stephen D. Dillaye, *The Money and the Finances of the French Revolution of 1789. Assignats and Mandats: A True History. Including an Examination of Dr. Andrew D. White's "Paper Money Inflation in France", pp. 1-65* (New Haven, CT: Leopold Classic Library, 2022), p. 15

22   Dillaye, *Money and Finance*, p. 15-16

23   R.R. Palmer and Joel Colton, *History*, p. 347-348

24   Ibid, p. 343-344

25   Edmund Burke, *Reflections on the Revolution in France* (Monee, IL: Digireads.com Publishing, 2020), p. 54-55

26   Ibid, p. 7; bold and italics added by PD

27   Ibid, p. 29

28   Ibid, p. 30; bold and italics added by PD

29   Ibid, p. 30

30   Ibid, p. 32

31   Ibid, p. 33

32   Ibid, p. 35; bold and italics added by PD

33   Ibid, p. 35

34   Ibid, p. 44; bold and italics added by PD

35   Ibid, p. 45; bold and italics added by PD

36   Ibid, p. 44-45

37   Ibid, p. 45

38   Ibid, p. 46; bold and italics added by PD

39   Ibid, p. 46

40   Ibid, p. 47

41   Ibid, p. 52

42   Ibid, p. 61

43   Ibid, p. 82; bold and italics added by PD

44   Ibid, p. 88

45   Ibid, p. 89

46   R.R. Palmer and Joel Colton, *History*, p. 348

47   Ibid, p. 347

48   Mignet, *French Revolution*, p. 62

49   Ibid, p. 63

50   Ibid, p. 64

51   Dillaye, *Money and Finance*, p. 26

52   Mignet, *French Revolution*, p. 65

53   R.R. Palmer and Joel Colton, *History*, p. 353-354

54   Dillaye, *Money and Finance*, p. 27

55   Mignet, *French Revolution*, p. 68–69

56   R.R. Palmer and Joel Colton, *History*, p. 355

57   Mignet, *French Revolution*, p. 72–76

58   Ibid, p. 76–77

59   R.R. Palmer and Joel Colton, *History*, p. 355

60   Mignet, *French Revolution*, p. 77–78

61   Ibid, p. 80–81

62   Ibid, p. 80–81

63   Ibid, p. 82

64   Ibid, p. 83–84

65   Ibid, p. 84–85

66   R.R. Palmer and Joel Colton, *History*, p. 356

67   Mignet, *French Revolution*, p. 85–86

68   Ibid, p. 86–88

69   Ibid, p. 88; bold and italics, along with brackets, added by PD

70   Ibid, p. 89

71   Ibid, p. 89; bold and italics added by PD

72   Ibid, p. 90

73   Ibid, p. 91

74   Ibid, p. 92; bold and italics added by PD

75   Ibid, p. 93; paragraph spacing, bold and italics, added by PD

76   R.R. Palmer and Joel Colton, *History*, p. 357

77   Mignet, *French Revolution*, p. 96

78   Ibid, p. 96

79   Ibid, p. 97; bold and italics added by PD

80   Ibid, p. 97; bold and italics added by PD

81   Ibid, p. 98

82   Ibid, p. 99

83   Ibid, p. 98–102

84   R.R. Palmer and Joel Colton, *History*, p. 356

85   Mignet, *French Revolution*, p. 102

86   Ibid, p. 103

87   Ibid, p. 104

88   Ibid, p. 104-105

89   Ibid, p. 105

90   Ibid, p. 106-107

91   Ibid, p. 107

92   Dillaye, *Money and Finance*, p. 28-29

93   Mignet, *French Revolution*, p. 108-109; bold and italics added by PD

94   Ibid, p. 109

95   Ibid, p. 110

96   Ibid, p. 111

97   Ibid, p. 111

98   Ibid, p. 112-113

99   Ibid, p. 113

100   Ibid, p. 114-115

101   Ibid, p. 115-116

102   R.R. Palmer and Joel Colton, *History*, p. 358

103   Mignet, *French Revolution*, p. 116

104   Ibid, p. 117-118

105   Ibid, p. 118

106   Ibid, p. 120

107   Ibid, p. 120-122

108   Theodore S. Hamerow, *Restoration, Revolution, Reaction: Economics and Politics in Germany, 1815-1871* (Princeton: Princeton University Press, 1972), p. 160-161; brackets added by PD

109   Dillaye, *Money and Finance*, p. 29-30

110   Mignet, *French Revolution*, p. 123

111   Ibid, p. 123-124

112   Ibid, p. 124

113   Ibid, p. 125

114   Ibid, p. 125-126

115   Ibid, p. 125–126

116   Ibid, p. 128

117   Ibid, p. 129

118   Ibid, p. 129

119   Ibid, p. 131; bold and italics added by PD

120   Andrew Dickson White, *Fiat Money Inflation in France: How it Came, What it Brought, and How it Ended* (USA: Jefferson Publication, 2015), p. 40-42

121   Mignet, *French Revolution*, p. 130–131

122   Ibid, p. 131

123   Ibid, p. 132

124   Ibid, p. 132–133

125   Ibid, p. 134–135

126   Ibid, p. 135

127   Ibid, p. 136

128   Ibid, p. 136; bold and italics added by PD

129   Ibid, p. 137–138; bold and italics added by PD

130   Ibid, p. 139; bold and italics added by PD

131   Mignet, *French Revolution*, p. 141

132   Ibid, p. 142

133   Ibid, p. 143

134   Ibid, p. 143

135   Ibid, p. 144–145

136   Ibid, p. 145

137   Ibid, p. 145–147

138   Ibid, p. 147–148

139   Ibid, p. 148–150

140   Ibid, p. 150

141   Ibid, p. 150–151

142   Ibid, p. 151

143   Ibid, p. 152

144   Dillaye, *Money and Finance*, p. 38

145   Mignet, *French Revolution*, p. 154

146   Ibid, p. 156-157

147   R.R. Palmer and Joel Colton, *History*, p. 360

148   Ibid, p. 360-361

149   Mignet, *French Revolution*, p. 2

150   Dillaye, *Money and Finance*, p. 37-38

151   R.R. Palmer and Joel Colton, *History*, p. 360-361

152   Dillaye, *Money and Finance*, p. 38

153   R.R. Palmer and Joel Colton, *History*, p. 363

154   Mignet, *French Revolution*, p. 159-160; bold and italics added by PD

155   Ibid, p. 160-161

156   Ibid, p. 161

157   Dillaye, *Money and Finance*, p. 39-40

158   Mignet, *French Revolution*, p. 162-163

159   Ibid, p. 163

160   Dillaye, *Money and Finance*, p. 40

161   Mignet, *French Revolution*, p. 168-169

162   Ibid, p. 170-171

163   Dillaye, *Money and Finance*, p. 41

164   Mignet, *French Revolution*, p. 173

165   Ibid, p. 174

166   Ibid, p. 175

167   Ibid, p. 176

168   Ibid, p. 177; bracket added by PD

169   R.R. Palmer and Joel Colton, *History*, p. 365

170   Mignet, *French Revolution*, p. 179

171   Ibid, p. 180-181

172   Ibid, p. 186-187

173   Ibid, p.188-189

174   Ibid, p. 189

175   Sebastian Haffner, *The Ailing Empire: Germany from Bismark to Hitler* (New York: Fromm International Publishing Corporation, 1989), p. 14

176   Mignet, *French Revolution*, p. 192-194

177   Ibid, p. 195-196

178   Ibid, p. 196

179   Ibid, p. 197-198

180   Ibid, p. 197-199

181   Ibid, p. 202-203

182   Ibid, p. 208

183   Ibid, p. 207

184   Ibid, p. 207-208

185   Ibid, p. 209

186   Ibid, p. 210-211

187   Ibid, p. 214

188   Ibid, p. 225

189   Alexis de Tocqueville, *Democracy in America: and Two Essays on America* (New York: Penguin Books, 2003), p. 16+17

190   Ibid, p. 19

191   Ibid, p. 19+20; bracket added by PD

192   Ibid, p. 20

193   Ibid, p. 844

194   Ibid, p. 114-115

195   Bentley B. Gilbert, *The Evolution of National Insurance in Britain: The Origins of the Welfare State* (London: Michael Joseph Limited, 1966); unfortunately, the page number was lost from my notes, yet the information was important and useful, so the information has been included with reference to the work, but in absence of the page number. My apologies to Bentley B. Gilbert for this inexactitude.

196   Haffner, *Ailing Empire*, p. 35

197   Ibid, p. 144-145

198   William L. Shirer, *20th Century Journey: A Memoir of a Life and the Times, Volume II: The Nightmare Years 1930-1940* (New York: Bantam Books, 1985), p. 28-29

199 Haffner, *Ailing Empire*, p. 145

200 Ibid, p. 147

201 Ibid, p. 148

202 Paul Dayton, *Correcting Our Financial Miseducation: Raising the Bar for the Average* (USA: ISBN: 9798726908755, 2021), p. 140-148

203 Haffner, *Ailing Empire*, p. 152-153

204 Ibid, p. 154-155

205 Ibid, p. 165-167

206 Ibid, p. 168

207 Shirer, *Nightmare Years*, p. 29

208 Sarah Gordon, *Hitler, Germans, and the "Jewish Question"* (Princeton: Princeton University Press, 1984), p. 30-31

209 Ibid, p. 72

210 Haffner, *Ailing Empire*, p. 169

211 Ibid, p. 172

212 Shirer, *Nightmare Years*, p. 47-48

213 Haffner, *Ailing Empire*, p. 173

214 Shirer, *Nightmare Years*, p. 47-48

215 Haffner, *Ailing Empire*, p. 173-174

216 Ibid, p. 174-175

217 Ibid, p. 177

218 Shirer, *Nightmare Years*, p. 49

219 Haffner, *Ailing Empire*, p. 177-178

220 Ibid, p. 178-179

221 Ibid, p. 182

222 Ibid, p. 182-184

223 https://www.statista.com/statistics/1125024/us-presidents-executive-orders/

224 Dayton, *Correcting*, chapter 14

225 Shirer, *Nightmare Years*, p. 201-202

226 R.R. Palmer and Joel Colton, *History*, p. 810; bold and italics added by PD; bracket added by PD

227   Haffner, *Ailing Empire*, p. 191

228   Ibid, p. 193-196

229   Shirer, *Nightmare Years*, p. 115, note un-numbered at bottom of page 115

230   Ibid, p. 116

231   Ibid, p. 117

232   Ibid, p. 144, note un-numbered, but labeled as "right", at bottom of the page

233   Ibid, p. 148-149

234   Ibid, p. 118

235   Ibid, p. 122

236   Ibid, p. 137

237   Ibid, p. 147

238   Ibid, p. 135-36 + p. 136, note 2, denoted by a dagger

239   Ibid, p. 217+218

240   Gordon, "*Jewish Question*", p. 144

241   Shirer, *Nightmare Years*, p. 195

242   Dayton, *Correcting*, p. 150

243   Shirer, *Nightmare Years*, p. 193

244   Haffner, *Ailing Empire*, p. 202

245   Shirer, *Nightmare Years*, p. 163

246   Haffner, *Ailing Empire*, p. 207-208

247   Ibid, p. 214-215

248   Ibid, p. 215-216

249   Ibid, p. 233

250   Gordon, "*Jewish Question*", p. 144

251   Guy Sorman, *Economics Does Not Lie: A Defense of the Free Market in a Time of Crisis* (New York: Encounter Books, 2009), p. 30

252   Frank Dikotter, *The Tragedy of Liberation: A History of the Chinese Revolution 1945-1957* (London: Bloomsbury, 2017), p. 174-175; bold and italics added by PD

253   Fox Butterfield, *China: Alive in a Bitter Sea, Revised and Updated* (New York: Times Books, 1990), p. 370-375 for all regarding Bill Gao in the preceding pages

254   Dikotter, *Liberation*, p. 6-8

255 Ibid, p. 12

256 Ibid, p. 40

257 Ibid, p. 45-46

258 Ibid, p. 65-66

259 Ibid, p. 72-73

260 Ibid, p. 78

261 Ibid, p. 49-50

262 Ibid, p. 51

263 Ibid, p. 50

264 Ibid, p. 55

265 Ibid, p. 57

266 Ibid, p. 57

267 Ibid, p. 57-59

268 Ibid, p. 68-69

269 Ibid, p. 70-71

270 Ibid, p. 69-70

271 Ibid, p. 85; bold and italics added by PD

272 Ibid, p. 86-88

273 Ibid, p. 89-91

274 Ibid, p. 99-100

275 Ibid, p. 100

276 Ibid, p. 184; bold and italics added by PD

277 Ibid, p. 79-80

278 Ibid, p. 82

279 Ibid, p. 83

280 Butterfield, *China*, p. 376-377

281 Ibid, p. 377

282 Dikotter, *Liberation*, p. 236-237

283 Ibid, p. 327

284 William L. Parish and Martin King Whyte, *Village and Family in Contemporary China* (Chicago: The University of Chicago Press, 1978), p. 32

285   Dikotter, *Liberation*, p. 238

286   Ibid, p. 239

287   Ibid, p. 240; bold and italics added by PD

288   Butterfield, *China*, p. 378

289   William L. Parish and Martin King Whyte, *Village and Family in Contemporary China* (Chicago: The University of Chicago Press, 1978), p. 34; bold and italics added by PD

290   Ibid, p. 74-75

291   Ibid, p. 77

292   Ibid, p. 53-54

293   Ibid, p. 88

294   Murray Weidenbaum and Samuel Hughes, *The Bamboo Network: How Expatriate Chinese Entrepreneurs are Creating a New Economic Superpower in Asia* (New York: The Free Press, 1996), p. 14

295   Ibid, p. 15

296   Butterfield, *China*, p. 433

297   Ibid, p. 419-420

298   Ibid, p. 420

299   Ibid, p. 379

300   Ibid, p. 391

301   Ibid, p. 398-399

302   Ibid, p. 396-397

303   Ibid, p. 389-391

304   Murray Weidenbaum and Samuel Hughes, *The Bamboo Network*, p. 19; bold and italics added by PD

305   R.R. Palmer and Joel Colton, *History*, p. 344

306   Ibid, p. 345

Part III   P. 177-221

1   P.T. Bauer, *Equality, the Third World, and Economic Delusion* (Cambridge, Mass.: Harvard University Press, 1981), p. 8

2   Bradley R. Schiller, *The Economy* (Englewood Cliffs, NJ: Prentice-Hall Inc., 1975), p. 407

3   P.T. Bauer, *Equality, the Third World, and Economic Delusion* (Cambridge, Mass.: Harvard University Press, 1981), p. 37-38; bold and italics added by PD

4   T.S. Ashton, *An Economic HIstory of England: The 18th Century* (London: Methuen & CO LTD, 1969), p. 13

5   Henri Pirenne, *Economic and Social History of Medieval Europe* (Monee, IL: Harcourt, Inc., 1937), p. 179; bold and italics added by PD

6   Ibid, p. 180-181

7   For all, Ibid, p. 177-181

8   Ibid, p. 183-184; bold and italics added by PD

9   Ibid, p. 185; bold and italics added by PD

10   Ibid, p. 187-188

11   For all since note 4, Ibid, p. 176-188

12   Lee E. Ohanian, "The Effect of Economic Freedom on Labor Market Efficiency and Performance", Hoover Institution Prosperity Project, p. 10

www.hoover.org/research/effect-economic-freedom-labor-market-efficiency-and-performance

13   Ibid, p. 11

14   Frederick Pedler, *Main Currents of West African History 1940-1978* (London: The Macmillan Press LTD, 1979), p. 124

15   Ibid, p. 120

16   Ibid, p. 144-148

17   Lee E. Ohanian, "The Effect of Economic Freedom on Labor Market Efficiency and Performance", Hoover Institution Prosperity Project, p. 10

www.hoover.org/research/effect-economic-freedom-labor-market-efficiency-and-performance

18   Theodore S. Hamerow, *Restoration, Revolution, Reaction: Economics and Politics in Germany, 1815-1871* (Princeton: Princeton University Press, 1972), p. 23-37

19   Sebastian Haffner, *The Ailing Empire: Germany from Bismark to Hitler* (New York: Fromm International Publishing Corporation, 1989), p. 16-17

20   Ibid, p. 19

21   Theodore S. Hamerow, *Restoration, Revolution, Reaction: Economics and Politics in Germany, 1815-1871* (Princeton: Princeton University Press, 1972), p. 6

22   Ibid, p. 7-8

23   Ibid, p. 8-9

24   Ibid, p. 9

25   Ibid, p. 5

26   Ibid, p. 29

27   Ibid, p. 143-144; bold and italics added by PD

28   Ibid, p. 79

29   Ibid, p. 140

30   Ibid, p. 102-103

31   Ibid, p. 33

32   Ibid, p. 34

33   Ibid, p. 102

34   R.R. Palmer and Joel Colton, *A History of the Modern World* (New York: Alfred A. Knopf, Inc., 1965), p. 488

35   Theodore S. Hamerow, *Restoration, Revolution, Reaction: Economics and Politics in Germany, 1815-1871* (Princeton: Princeton University Press, 1972), p. 115-116

36   Ibid, p. 144-145; bold and italics added by PD

37   Ibid, p. 132-133

38   R.R. Palmer and Joel Colton, *A History of the Modern World* (New York: Alfred A. Knopf, Inc., 1965), p. 488

39   Hamerow, *Restoration*, p. 189

40   Ibid, p. 192

41   Ibid, p. 204

42   Ibid, p. 207-208; period of high inflation, ibid, p. 209-210

43   Ibid, p. 225-227

44   Sebastian Haffner, *The Ailing Empire: Germany from Bismark to Hitler* (New York: Fromm International Publishing Corporation, 1989), p. 38-39

45   Hamerow, *Restoration*, p. 246-248

46   Ibid, p. 252-253

47   Lee E. Ohanian, "The Effect of Economic Freedom on Labor Market Efficiency and Performance", Hoover Institution Prosperity Project, p. 5

www.hoover.org/research/effect-economic-freedom-labor-market-efficiency-and-performance

48   Ibid, p. 9

49   Ibid, p. 9

50   Ibid, p. 8-9

51   T.S. Ashton, *An Economic HIstory of England: The 18th Century* (London: Methuen & CO LTD, 1969), p. 56

52   Ibid, p. 57

53   Edward Channing, *A History of the United States, Volume I, The Planting of a Nation in the New World 1000-1660* (New York: The Macmillan Company, 1907), p. 148-149; 2024 value calculated by officialdata.org/us/inflation)

54   T.S. Ashton, *An Economic HIstory of England: The 18th Century* (London: Methuen & CO LTD, 1969), p. 27-29

55   Ibid, p. 27

56   Ibid, p. 29

57   Thomas Sowell, *Economic Facts and Fallacies* (New York: Basic Books, 2011), p. 4

58   Milton Friedman and Rose Friedman, *Free to Choose: A Personal Statement* (Orlando, FL: Harcourt, Inc., 1990), p. 109-110

59   Bentley B. Gilbert, *The Evolution of National Insurance in Britain: The Origins of the Welfare State* (London: Michael Joseph Limited, 1966), p. 28

60   Hamerow, *Restoration*, p. 64

61   M.M. Austin & P. Vidal-Naquet, *Economic & Social History of Ancient Greece: An Introduction* (Berkeley/Los Angeles: University of California Press, 1980), p. 342; bold and italics added by PD

62   Lee E. Ohanian, "The Effect of Economic Freedom on Labor Market Efficiency and Performance", Hoover Institution Prosperity Project, p. 8

www.hoover.org/research/effect-economic-freedom-labor-market-efficiency-and-performance

63   Ibid, p. 7

64   Ibid, p. 7+8

65   Gilbert, *Welfare State*, p. 113

66   T.S. Ashton, *An Economic HIstory of England: The 18th Century* (London: Methuen & CO LTD, 1969), p. 14 + p. 14, N. 2

67   Edward Channing, *A History of the United States, Volume I, The Planting of a Nation in the New World 1000-1660* (New York: The Macmillan Company, 1907), p. 210-212

68   Ibid, p. 423-425

69   T.S. Ashton, *An Economic HIstory of England: The 18th Century* (London: Methuen & CO LTD, 1969), p. 14

70   Ibid, p. 35

71   Gilbert, *Welfare State*, p. 105

72   Fox Butterfield, *China: Alive in a Bitter Sea, Revised and Updated* (New York: Times Books, 1990), p. 417

73   Carl L. Becker, *Modern History: The rise of a democratic, scientific, and industrialized civilization* (New York, Chicago, San Francisco: Silver Burdett Company, 1944), p. 535-536

74   Stephen Kotkin, *Stalin: Waiting for Hitler 1929-1941* (New York: Penguin Press, 2017), p. 24

75   Ibid, p. 9

76   Ibid, p. 10

77   Ibid, p. 14

78   Ibid, p. 15

79   Ibid, p. 16

80   Ibid, p. 16

81   Ibid, p. 27

82   Ibid, p. 29

83   Ibid, p. 29

84   Ibid, p. 38-39

85   Ibid, p. 46

86   Ibid, p. 41

87   Ibid, p. 41-43

88   Paul Dayton, *Correcting Our Financial Miseducation: Raising the Bar for the Average* (USA: ISBN: 9798726908755, 2021), p. 92

89   Frank Dikotter, *The Tragedy of Liberation: A History of the Chinese Revolution 1945-1957* (London: Bloomsbury, 2017), p. 227

90   William L. Shirer, *20th Century Journey: A Memoir of a Life and the Times, Volume II: The Nightmare Years 1930-1940* (New York: Bantam Books, 1985), p. 50

91   Ibid, p. 50

92   Sebastian Haffner, *The Ailing Empire: Germany from Bismark to Hitler* (New York: Fromm International Publishing Corporation, 1989), p. 242

93   Ibid, p. 244-245

94   Ibid, p. 248

95   Stephen Kotkin, *Steeltown, USSR* (Berkeley and Los Angeles: University of California Press, 1991), preface, p. xxii

96   William L. Shirer, *20th Century Journey: A Memoir of a Life and the Times, Volume II: The Nightmare Years 1930-1940* (New York: Bantam Books, 1985), p. 195-205

97   Peter T. Bauer and Basil S. Yamey, *The Economics of Under-developed Countries* (Chicago: The University of Chicago Press, 1957), p. 238-239

98   Fox Butterfield, *China: Alive in a Bitter Sea, Revised and Updated* (New York: Times Books, 1990), p. 332

99   Stephen Kotkin, *Steeltown, USSR* (Berkeley and Los Angeles: University of California Press, 1991), p. 5

100   Ibid, p. 30

101   Ibid, p. 33+34

102   Dayton, *Correcting*, chapter 14

103   Henri Pirenne, *Economic and Social History of Medieval Europe* (Monee, IL: Harcourt, Inc., 1937), p. 128

104   Edward Channing, *A History of the United States, Volume I, The Planting of a Nation in the New World 1000-1660* (New York: The Macmillan Company, 1907), p. 308-313

105   Fox Butterfield, *China: Alive in a Bitter Sea, Revised and Updated* (New York: Times Books, 1990), p. 408-409

106   Hamerow, *Restoration*, p. 113

107   Fox Butterfield, *China: Alive in a Bitter Sea, Revised and Updated* (New York: Times Books, 1990), p. 397

108   Paul Dayton, *Correcting Our Financial Miseducation: Raising the Bar for the Average* (USA: ISBN: 9798726908755, 2021), chapters 4 and 10

109   Henri Pirenne, *Economic and Social History of Medieval Europe* (Monee, IL: Harcourt, Inc., 1937), Part Two. The Towns, p. 39-56)

110   D.T. Armentano. Ph. D., *Myths of Antitrust: Economic Theory and Legal Cases* (New Rochelle: Arlington House, 1972), p. 16

Part IV   p. 222-234

1   Karen Horney, M.D., *Neurosis and Human Growth, The Struggle Toward Self-Realization* (W.W. Norton & Company, Inc., 1950), p. 30

2   Ibid, p. 39, n. 14

3   Ibid, p. 30; bold and italics of "indifferent to truth" added by PD

4   Fox Butterfield, *China: Alive in a Bitter Sea, Revised and Updated* (New York: Times Books, 1990), p. 402-403

5   Karen Horney, M.D., *Neurosis and Human Growth, The Struggle Toward Self-Realization* (W.W. Norton & Company, Inc., 1950), p. 36; bold and italics added by PD

6   Ibid, p. 35-37; bold and italics added by PD

7   Ibid, p. 42; bold and italics added by PD

8   William L. Shirer, *20th Century Journey: A Memoir of a Life and the Times, Volume II: The Nightmare Years 1930-1940* (New York: Bantam Books, 1985), p. 185

9   Karen Horney, M.D., *Neurosis and Human Growth, The Struggle Toward Self-Realization* (W.W. Norton & Company, Inc., 1950), p. 47; bold and italics added by PD

10   William L. Shirer, *20th Century Journey: A Memoir of a Life and the Times, Volume II: The Nightmare Years 1930-1940* (New York: Bantam Books, 1985), p. 183+184

11   Karen Horney, M.D., *Neurosis and Human Growth, The Struggle Toward Self-Realization* (W.W. Norton & Company, Inc., 1950), p. 48

12   Ibid, p. 48

13   Paul Dayton, *Correcting Our Financial Miseducation: Raising the Bar for the Average* (USA: ISBN: 9798726908755, 2021), p. 207-209

14   Karen Horney, M.D., *Neurosis and Human Growth, The Struggle Toward Self-Realization* (W.W. Norton & Company, Inc., 1950), p. 54; bold and italics on "assume responsibility for himself", and "it merely means that his own need to out claims on the basis of justice is generalized into a "philosophy", added by PD

15   Ibid, p. 55; bold and italics added by PD

16   Joseph A. Schumpeter, *Capitalism, Socialism and Democracy* (New York: Harper & Row, 1950), p. 89, n. 4

17   Peter T. Bauer and Basil S. Yamey, *The Economics of Under-developed Countries* (Chicago: The University of Chicago Press, 1957), p. 3

18   Frederick Pedler, *Main Currents of West African History 1940-1978* (London: The Macmillan Press LTD, 1979), p. 79-80

19   Henri Pirenne, *Economic and Social History of Medieval Europe* (Monee, IL: Harcourt, Inc., 1937), p. 18

20   Ibid, p. 18, n.3

21   Ibid, p. 18

22   Edmund Burke, *Reflections on the Revolution in France* (Monee, IL: Digireads.com Publishing, 2020), p. 9

23   *Reader's Digest Oxford Complete Wordfinder* (Pleasantville, NY: Oxford University Press, Inc., 1996) p. 1028

24   Ibid, p. 1450

Part V   p. 235-348

1   Theodore S. Hamerow, *Restoration, Revolution, Reaction: Economics and Politics in Germany, 1815-1871* (Princeton: Princeton University Press, 1972), p. 168-169

2   Bernard DeVoto, *The Year of Decision: 1846* (Boston: Little, Brown and Company, 1943), p. 7

3   Peter T. Bauer and Basil S. Yamey, *The Economics of Under-developed Countries* (Chicago: The University of Chicago Press, 1957), p. 58

4   Ibid, p. 105-106

5   Henri Pirenne, *Economic and Social History of Medieval Europe* (Monee, IL: Harcourt, Inc., 1937), p. 16-17; brackets, bold and italics, added by PD

6   Ibid, p. 80-81

7   P.T. Bauer, *Equality, the Third World, and Economic Delusion* (Cambridge, Mass.: Harvard University Press, 1981), p. 271, n. 12

8   Edward Channing, *A History of the United States, Volume I, The Planting of a Nation in the New World 1000-1660* (New York: The Macmillan Company, 1907), p. 214-215

9   Ibid, p. 208-214

10   Charles C. Royce and Cyrus Thomas, *Indian Land Cessions in the United States, 18th annual report 1899, part 2* (Library of Congress loc.gov/resource/llscdam.llss4015/?sp=114&st=image, LOC control number 13023487), p. 632; bold and italics added by PD)

11   Edward Channing, *A History of the United States, Volume II, A Century of Colonial History 1660-1760* (New York: The Macmillan Company, 1908), p. 38

12   Ibid, p. 39

13   Ibid, p. 137

14   Edmund Burke, *Reflections on the Revolution in France* (Monee, IL: Digireads.com Publishing, 2020), p. 42

15   Christopher I. Beckwith, *Empires of the Silk Road: A History of Central Eurasia from the Bronze Age to the Present* (Princeton: Princeton University Press, 2009), p. 227

16   Peter T. Bauer and Basil S. Yamey, *Under-developed*, p. 51

17   Eric Foner, *Reconstruction: America's Unfinished Revolution, 1863-1867* (New York: Harper & Row, 2014), p. 103-104

18   Walter E. Williams, *Race & Economics: How much can be blamed on discrimination?* (Stanford, CA: Hoover Institution Press, 2011), p.5-6

19   Edward Channing, *A History of the United States, Volume I, The Planting of a Nation in the New World 1000-1660* (New York: The Macmillan Company, 1907), p. 454

20 Ibid, p. 510

21 Edward Channing, *A History of the United States, Volume II, A Century of Colonial History 1660-1760* (New York: The Macmillan Company, 1908), p. 82-83

22 Ibid, p. 24-25

23 David O. Stewart, *American Emperor: Aaron Burr's Challenge to Jefferson's America* (New York: Simon & Schuster Paperbacks, 2012), p. 227

24 Ibid, p. 56+58

25 King John, *The Magna Carta* (Monee, IL: ISBN 9781500478568, 2021), p. 5

26 Edward Channing, *A History of the United States, Volume I, The Planting of a Nation in the New World 1000-1660* (New York: The Macmillan Company, 1907), p. 184-185

27 Ibid, p. 183-185

28 Ibid, p. 182-183

29 Ibid, p. 192

30 Ibid, p. 193

31 Ibid, p. 246-248

32 Thomas L. Purvis, *Revolutionary America, 1763 to 1800* (New York: Facts on File, Inc., 1995), p. 114

33 Edward Channing, *A History of the United States, Volume I, The Planting of a Nation in the New World 1000-1660* (New York: The Macmillan Company, 1907), preface, p. VI

34 Marquis James, *The Life of Andrew Jackson* (Camden, NJ: The Haddon Craftsmen, Inc., 1938), p. 58-59

35 David O. Stewart, *American Emperor*, p. 44-47

36 Alexis de Tocqueville, *Democracy in America: and Two Essays on America* (New York: Penguin Books, 2003), p. 206

37 Marquis James, *The Life of Andrew Jackson* (Camden, NJ: The Haddon Craftsmen, Inc., 1938), p. 523

38 Ibid, p. 538-541

39 Ibid, p. 580-582

40   Ibid, p. 603-604

41   Ibid, p. 607

42   Ibid, p. 610

43   Ibid, p. 610-619

44   Fox Butterfield, *China: Alive in a Bitter Sea, Revised and Updated* (New York: Times Books, 1990), p. 427

45   Ibid, p. 429

46   Ibid, p. 427-429

47   For more, see: Paul Dayton, *Correcting Our Financial Miseducation: Raising the Bar for the Average* (USA: ISBN: 9798726908755, 2021), chapter 5

48   Peter T. Bauer and Basil S. Yamey, *Under-developed*, p. 115, n. 3

49   Ibid, p. 116, n. 1

50   Edward Channing, *A History of the United States, Volume I*, p. 75-76

51   Henri Pirenne, *Economic and Social History of Medieval Europe* (Monee, IL: Harcourt, Inc., 1937), p. 17, n. 2

52   Thomas Sowell, *Black Rednecks and White Liberals* (New York: Encounter Books, 2005), p. 166

53   Ibid, p. 112

54   Christopher I. Beckwith, *Empires of the Silk Road*, p. 66

55   Bernard DeVoto, *The Year of Decision: 1846* (Boston: Little, Brown and Company, 1943), p. 41-42

56   Frederick Pedler, *Main Currents of West African History 1940-1978* (London: The Macmillan Press LTD, 1979), p. 37

57   M.M. Austin & P. Vidal-Naquet, *Economic & Social History of Ancient Greece: An Introduction* (Berkeley/Los Angeles: University of California Press, 1980), p. 19 + 180-181

58   Peter T. Bauer and Basil S. Yamey, *Under-developed*, p. 40, n. 1

59   Pirenne, *Medieval Europe*, p. 7

60   Christopher I. Beckwith, *Empires of the Silk Road*, p. 95

61   M.M. Austin & P. Vidal-Naquet, *Ancient Greece*, p. 65

62   P.T. Bauer, *Equality, the Third World, and Economic Delusion* (Cambridge, Mass.: Harvard University Press, 1981), p. 196

63   Henri Pirenne, *Economic and Social History of Medieval Europe* (Monee, IL: Harcourt, Inc., 1937), p. 22; brackets added by PD

64   Ibid, p. 131

65   Ibid, p. 28–30

66   Edward Channing, *A History of the United States, Volume I*, p. 118

67   P.T. Bauer, *Economic Delusion*, p. 195–196

68   Edward Channing, *A History of the United States, Volume II*, p. 143

69   Ibid, p. 20–23

70   Thomas L. Purvis, *Revolutionary America, 1763 to 1800* (New York: Facts on File, Inc., 1995), p. 113

71   Ibid, p. 122

72   Thomas Jefferson, *Writings* (New York, Literary Classics of the United States, Inc., 1984), p. 115–116

73   Ibid, p. 33–34

74   Thomas L. Purvis, *Revolutionary America, 1763 to 1800* (New York: Facts on File, Inc., 1995), p. 120

75   Marquis James, *The Life of Andrew Jackson* (Camden, NJ: The Haddon Craftsmen, Inc., 1938), p. 59

76   Thomas L. Purvis, *Revolutionary America, 1763 to 1800* (New York: Facts on File, Inc., 1995), p. 320

77   Edward Channing, *A History of the United States, Volume II*, p. 111

78   David O. Stewart, *American Emperor*, p. 97–98

79   Bernard DeVoto, *The Year of Decision*, p. 29–30

80   Eric Foner, *Reconstruction*, p. 103

81   Ibid, p. 103

82   David O. Stewart, *American Emperor*, p. 69–70

83   Ibid, p. 128

84   Thomas L. Purvis, *Revolutionary America, 1763 to 1800* (New York: Facts on File, Inc., 1995), p. 123

85   Ibid, p. 124

86   Ibid, p. 125

87   Ibid, p. 126

88   Ibid, p. 183

89   Eric Foner, *Reconstruction*, p. 45

90   Ibid, p. 47

91   Ibid, p. 48

92   Ibid, p. 39

93   Bernard DeVoto, *The Year of Decision*, p. 19-20

94   Thomas Jefferson, *Writings* (New York, Literary Classics of the United States, Inc., 1984), p. 43-44

95   Ibid, p. 377

96   Ibid, p. 4

97   Ibid, p. 18 + 22

98   Ibid, p. 47

99   Fox Butterfield, *China: Alive in a Bitter Sea, Revised and Updated* (New York: Times Books, 1990), p. 355

100   King John, *The Magna Carta* (Monee, IL: ISBN 9781500478568, 2021), p. 8

101   Ibid, p. 10

102   Carl L. Becker, *Modern History: The rise of a democratic, scientific, and industrialized civilization* (New York, Chicago, San Francisco: Silver Burdett Company, 1944), p. 71-72

103   Edward Channing, *A History of the United States, Volume II*, p. 156

104   Eric Foner, *Reconstruction*, p. 53

105   Ibid, p. 63

106   Ibid, p. 104-105

107   Ibid, p. 35-44

108   Ibid, p. 35-44

109   Christopher I. Beckwith, *Empires of the Silk Road*, p. 61-63

110   Ibid, p. 63-65

111   Ibid, p. 63-65

112   Ibid, p. 63, n. 21

113   Ibid, 84-85

114   Ibid, map in back of book

115   Kevin Shillington, *History of Africa, Third Edition* (China: Palgrave Macmillan, 2012), p. 40

116   Ibid, p. 41-42

117   Christopher I. Beckwith, *Empires of the Silk Road,* p. 86-89

118   Ibid, p. 107-108

119   Ibid, p. 79

120   Ibid, p. 94

121   Ibid, p. 100-101

122   Ibid, p. 101

123   Ibid, p. 94-99

124   Ibid, p. 103

125   Ibid, p. 118-123

126   Henri Pirenne, *Economic and Social History of Medieval Europe* (Monee, IL: Harcourt, Inc., 1937), p. 15

127   Ibid, p. 16

128   Christopher I. Beckwith, *Empires of the Silk Road,* p. 148-149

129   Ibid, p. 158-159

130   Timothy J. Shannon, *Iroquois Diplomacy on the Early American Frontier* (New York: Viking Penguin, 2008), p. 15

131   Henri Pirenne, *Medieval Europe,* p. 28-30

132   Ibid, p. 30

133   Ibid, p. 30-31

134   Ibid, p. 31

135   Ibid, p. 32

136   Ibid, p. 32-33

137   Ibid, p. 25

138   Christopher I. Beckwith, *Empires of the Silk Road,* p. 222

139   Ibid, p. 207-208

140 Ibid, p. 206-207

141 Edward Channing, *A History of the United States, Volume I*, p. 1

142 Ibid, p. 5

143 Ibid, p. 19

144 Ibid, p. 25; bracket added by PD

145 Timothy J. Shannon, *Iroquois Diplomacy on the Early American Frontier* (New York: Viking Penguin, 2008), p. 68-69

146 Christopher I. Beckwith, *Empires of the Silk Road*, p. 225-226

147 Ibid, p. 227-229

148 Edward Channing, *A History of the United States Volume 3: History of the Colonization of the United States by George Bancroft. Vol. III. Seventeenth Edition* (Boston: Little, Brown, and Company, 1862), p. 151

149 Ibid, p. 155

150 Ibid, p. 156

151 Ibid, p. 158

152 Ibid, p. 159

153 Ibid, p. 160

154 Ibid, p. 161

155 Ibid, p. 172

156 Ibid, p. 185

157 Ibid, p. 187

158 David O. Stewart, *American Emperor*, p. 184-185

159 James D. Horan, *The Great American West: A Pictorial History from Coronado to the Last Frontier* (New York: Crown Publishers, Inc., 1959), p. 252

160 Ibid, p. 252

161 Edward Channing, *A History of the United States, Volume I*, p. 322

162 Ibid, p. 61

163 Ibid, p. 84-85

164 Ibid, p. 78-79

165 Ibid, p. 68-70

166 Ibid, p. 85

167   Ibid, p. 90

168   Timothy J. Shannon, *Iroquois Diplomacy on the Early American Frontier* (New York: Viking Penguin, 2008), p. 25

169   Ibid, p. 22

170   Ibid, p. 22

171   Edward Channing, *A History of the United States, Volume I*, p. 96

172   Ibid, p. 106

173   Timothy J. Shannon, *Iroquois Diplomacy*, p. 35-36

174   Edward Channing, *A History of the United States, Volume II*, p. 60, n. 1

175   Timothy J. Shannon, *Iroquois Diplomacy*, p. 56

176   Ibid, p. 45-46

177   Thomas Jefferson, *Writings* (New York, Literary Classics of the United States, Inc., 1984), p. 221

178   Timothy J. Shannon, *Iroquois Diplomacy*, p. 36-38

179   Edward Channing, *A History of the United States Volume 3: History of the Colonization of the United States by George Bancroft. Vol. III. Seventeenth Edition* (Boston: Little, Brown, and Company, 1862), p. 165

180   Edward Channing, *A History of the United States, Volume I*, p. 93-94

181   Ibid, p. 440-441

182   Ibid, p. 216

183   Edward Channing, *A History of the United States, Volume II*, p. 79-80

184   Ibid, p. 84-90

185   Edward Channing, *A History of the United States, Volume I*, p. 117

186   Ibid, p. 71

187   Ibid, p. 156

188   Ibid, p. 164 + 165

189   Ibid, p. 169

190   Alexis de Tocqueville, *Democracy in America: and Two Essays on America* (New York: Penguin Books, 2003), p. 826-827

191   Edward Channing, *A History of the United States, Volume I*, p. 204-205

192   Timothy J. Shannon, *Iroquois Diplomacy*, p. 30

193   Ibid,p. 32-34

194   Edward Channing, *A History of the United States, Volume I*, p. 108-109

195   Timothy J. Shannon, *Iroquois Diplomacy*, p. 34

196   Ibid, p. 48

197   Edward Channing, *A History of the United States Volume 3: History of the Colonization of the United States by George Bancroft. Vol. III. Seventeenth Edition* (Boston: Little, Brown, and Company, 1862), p. 166-167

198   Marquis James, *The Life of Andrew Jackson* (Camden, NJ: The Haddon Craftsmen, Inc., 1938), p. 53

199   Bernard DeVoto, *The Year of Decision*, p. 58-59

200   Edward Channing, *A History of the United States, Volume I*, p. 188 + 189

201   Timothy J. Shannon, *Iroquois Diplomacy*, p. 23

202   Ibid, p. 121-124

203   Ibid, p. 163

204   Ibid, p. 119-121

205   Ibid, p. 131

206   Ibid, p. 88-89

207   Ibid, p. 96

208   Ibid, p. 102

209   Ibid, p. 207-208

210   Bernard DeVoto, *The Year of Decision*, p. 337-338

211   Ibid, p. 339

212   Edward Channing, *A History of the United States, Volume I*, p. 126-127

213   Ibid, p. 104

214   Ibid, p. 104-105

215   Ibid, p. 167

216   Ibid, p. 306

217   Ibid, p. 349

218   Ibid, p. 392-393

219   Ibid, p. 339-340

220   Ibid, p. 402-404

221 Ibid, p. 456-458

222 Ibid, p. 458

223 Ibid, p. 216

224 Ibid, p. 481-483

225 Edward Channing, *A History of the United States, Volume II*, p. 146-147

226 Ibid, p. 196-197

227 Ibid, p. 207

228 Edward Channing, *A History of the United States Volume 3*, p. 180

229 Edward Channing, *A History of the United States Volume 3*, p. 181-182

230 Edward Channing, *A History of the United States, Volume II*, p. 208-209

231 Timothy J. Shannon, *Iroquois Diplomacy*, p. 45-46

232 Edward Channing, *A History of the United States Volume 3: History of the Colonization of the United States by George Bancroft. Vol. III. Seventeenth Edition* (Boston: Little, Brown, and Company, 1862), p. 190-191

233 Timothy J. Shannon, *Iroquois Diplomacy*, p. 119

234 Ibid, p. 150

235 Ibid, p. 149

236 Ibid, p. 189-190

237 Ibid, p. 188-189

238 Ibid, p. 190

239 Ibid, p. 191-193

240 Marquis James, *The Life of Andrew Jackson* (Camden, NJ: The Haddon Craftsmen, Inc., 1938), p. 50

241 Ibid, p. 58-59

242 Ibid, p. 155-157

243 Ibid, p. 157-161

244 Edward Channing, *A History of the United States, Volume I*, p. 97-100

245 Ibid, p. 126

246 Ibid, p. 134-137

247 Ibid, p. 103

248 Ibid, p. 107 + 108

249   Ibid, p. 451-452

250   Edward Channing, *A History of the United States, Volume II*, p. 24

251   Edward Channing, *A History of the United States, Volume I*, p. 81-82

252   Ibid, p. 94-95

253   Ibid, p. 256

254   Ibid, p. 446-447

255   Ibid, p. 312

256   Ibid, p. 337-339

257   Ibid, p. 364

258   Ibid, p. 256-258

259   Ibid, p. 400 + p. 400, n. 1

260   Ibid, p. 391-392

261   Ibid, p. 454-455

262   Ibid, p. 382-385

263   Edward Channing, *A History of the United States Volume 3*, p. 137-138

264   Ibid, p. 138-139

265   Ibid, p. 141

266   Ibid, p. 138-141

267   Ibid, p. 141-142

268   Ibid, p. 144-145

269   Ibid, p. 150

270   Edward Channing, *A History of the United States, Volume I*, p. 402

271   Edward Channing, *A History of the United States, Volume II*, p. 70

272   Ibid, p. 33-37

273   Ibid, p. 47

274   Ibid, p. 54

275   Ibid, p. 149-152

276   Ibid, p. 14

277   Ibid, p. 132-133

278   Dictionary of Canadian Biography website, https://www.biographi.ca/en/bio/daumont_de_saint_lusson_simon_francois_1E.html

279   Edward Channing, *A History of the United States, Volume II*, p. 51

280   Ibid, p. 146

281   Timothy J. Shannon, *Iroquois Diplomacy*, p. 75-76

282   Ibid, p. 59-60

283   Ibid, p. 61-62

284   Ibid, p. 2-3

285   Ibid, p. 106

286   Charles C. Royce and Cyrus Thomas, *Indian Land Cessions in the United States, 18th annual report 1899, part 2* (Library of Congress loc.gov/resource/llscdam.llss4015/?sp=114&st=image, LOC control number 13023487), p. 635-636

287   Timothy J. Shannon, *Iroquois Diplomacy*, p. 109-111

288   Ibid, p. 111-115

289   Ibid, p. 138-142

290   Ibid, p. 149

291   Ibid, p. 167-169

292   Thomas Jefferson, *Writings*, p. 376

293   David O. Stewart, *American Emperor*, p. 51

294   Marquis James, *The Life of Andrew Jackson*, p. 69-70

295   Ibid, p. 95

296   Charles C. Royce and Cyrus Thomas, *Indian Land Cessions in the United States, 18th annual report 1899, part 1* (Library of Congress loc.gov/resource/llscdam.llss4015/?sp=114&st=image, LOC control number 13023487), p. 543-545

297   Marquis James, *The Life of Andrew Jackson*, p. 523

298   Ibid, p. 548-551; bracket, bold and italics, added to quote by PD

299   Ibid, p. 58-582

300   Ibid, p. 603-604

301   James D. Horan, *The Great American West: A Pictorial History from Coronado to the Last Frontier* (New York: Crown Publishers, Inc., 1959), p. 259-263

302   Edward Channing, *A History of the United States, Volume I*, p. 24

303   Ibid, p. 59-60

304   Ibid, p. 60-61

305   Ibid, p. 62-67

306   Timothy J. Shannon, *Iroquois Diplomacy*, p. 2 + 8

307   Ibid, p. 14

308   Charles C. Royce and Cyrus Thomas, *Indian Land Cessions in the United States, 18th annual report 1899, part 2* (Library of Congress loc.gov/resource/llscdam.llss4015/?sp=114&st=image, LOC control number 13023487), p. 532; bold and italics added by PD

309   Edward Channing, *A History of the United States, Volume I*, p. 207-208

310   Ibid, p. 258-259

311   Thomas Jefferson, *Writings* (New York, Literary Classics of the United States, Inc., 1984), p. 221; bold and italics added by PD

312   Edward Channing, *A History of the United States, Volume II*, p. 136

313   Ibid, p. 148-149

314   Edward Channing, *A History of the United States Volume 3: History of the Colonization of the United States by George Bancroft. Vol. III. Seventeenth Edition* (Boston: Little, Brown, and Company, 1862), p. 189

315   Timothy J. Shannon, *Iroquois Diplomacy*, p. 6

316   Edward Channing, *A History of the United States, Volume II*, p. 114

317   Timothy J. Shannon, *Iroquois Diplomacy*, p. 116

318   Ibid, p. 131

319   Ibid, p. 98

320   Thomas Jefferson, *Writings*, p. 21-22

321   Timothy J. Shannon, *Iroquois Diplomacy*, p. 181

322   Ibid, p. 194-196

323   Ibid, p. 202-203

324   Ibid, p. 200-201

325 Ibid, p. 197-198

326 Bernard DeVoto, *The Year of Decision*, p. 62

327 Ibid, p. 57

328 Edward Channing, *A History of the United States, Volume I*, p. 91

329 Ibid, p. 124-125

330 Ibid, p. 441-442

331 Ibid, p. 314-315

332 Edward Channing, *A History of the United States, Volume II*, p. 139

333 Ibid, p. 139-140

334 Edward Channing, *A History of the United States Volume 3*, p. 344

335 Edward Channing, *A History of the United States, Volume I*, p. 315-316

336 Ibid, p. 215-216

337 Ibid, p. 415-419

338 Edward Channing, *A History of the United States, Volume II*, p. 22-23 + p. 22, n. 2

339 Ibid, p. 78, n. 1

340 Ibid, p. 77-79

341 Bernard DeVoto, *The Year of Decision*, p. 153

342 Ibid, p. 152-153

343 Ibid, p. 154

344 Edward Channing, *A History of the United States, Volume I*, p. 67 + 68

345 Bernard DeVoto, *The Year of Decision*, p. 244-245

346 Charles C. Royce and Cyrus Thomas, *Indian Land Cessions in the United States, 18th annual report 1899, part 2* (Library of Congress loc.gov/resource/llscdam.llss4015/?sp=114&st=image, LOC control number 13023487), p. 632

347 Bernard DeVoto, *The Year of Decision*, p. 41-42

348 Fox Butterfield, *China: Alive in a Bitter Sea, Revised and Updated* (New York: Times Books, 1990), p. 428

349 Edward Channing, *A History of the United States, Volume I*, p. 60

350 Edward Channing, *A History of the United States, Volume II*, p. 133-134

Part VI   p. 349-415

1   Amity Shlaes, *Great Society: A New History* (New York: HarperCollins Publishers, 2019), p. 17

2   William W. Lockwood, *The Economic Development of Japan: Growth and Structural Change 1868-1938* (Princeton: Princeton University Press, 1954), p. 3

3   Christopher I. Beckwith, *Empires of the Silk Road: A History of Central Eurasia from the Bronze Age to the Present* (Princeton: Princeton University Press, 2009), p. 220

4   Ralph W. Hidy and Muriel E. Hidy, *Pioneering in Big Business 1882-1911* (New York: Harper & Brothers, 1955), p. 137; bold and italics added by PD

5   Edward Channing, *A History of the United States, Volume I, The Planting of a Nation in the New World 1000-1660* (New York: The Macmillan Company, 1907), p. 130-131

6   Ibid, p. 187

7   Ibid, p. 188

8   Ibid, p. 224-226

9   Ibid, p. 216-217

10   Ibid, p. 220-225

11   Ibid, p. 225-227

12   Edward Channing, *A History of the United States, Volume II, A Century of Colonial History 1660-1760* (New York: The Macmillan Company, 1908), p. 158-159

13   Ibid, p. 158+161-165

14   Ibid, p. 165

15   Ibid, p. 171

16   Ibid, p. 173

17   Ibid, p. 176, n.1

18   Ibid, p. 180

19   Ibid, p. 181

20   Ibid, p. 182; for more on the misdeeds of Andros during this period, see Ibid, p. 180-185; also p. 183, N3

21   William W. Lockwood, *The Economic Development of Japan*, p. 4-5

22   Ibid, p. 4, n.2

23   Theodore S. Hamerow, *Restoration, Revolution, Reaction: Economics and Politics in Germany, 1815-1871* (Princeton: Princeton University Press, 1972), p. 229; bold and italics added by PD

24   Edward Channing, *A History of the United States, Volume I*, p. 106+107

25   Paul Dayton, *Correcting Our Financial Miseducation: Raising the Bar for the Average* (USA: ISBN: 9798726908755, 2021), chapter 14. AAA p. 160-163. TVA p. 168-171

26   Ralph W. Hidy and Muriel E. Hidy, *Pioneering*, p. 131-132

27   William L. Shirer, *20th Century Journey: A Memoir of a Life and the Times, Volume II: The Nightmare Years 1930-1940* (New York: Bantam Books, 1985), p. 73-75

28   Stephen Kotkin, *Steeltown, USSR* (Berkeley and Los Angeles: University of California Press, 1991), p. 16

29   Frank Dikotter, *The Tragedy of Liberation: A History of the Chinese Revolution 1945-1957* (London: Bloomsbury, 2017), p. 75

30   Stephen Kotkin, *Steeltown, USSR* (Berkeley and Los Angeles: University of California Press, 1991), p. 8+9

31   Ibid, p. 9; bold and italics added by PD

32   Frank Dikotter, *The Tragedy of Liberation*, p. 76-77

33   Edward Channing, *A History of the United States, Volume I*, p. 143-147

34   Theodore S. Hamerow, *Restoration*, p. 111-112

35   Frederick Pedler, *Main Currents of West African History 1940-1978* (London: The Macmillan Press LTD, 1979), p. 85

36   Peter T. Bauer and Basil S. Yamey, *The Economics of Under-developed Countries* (Chicago: The University of Chicago Press, 1957), p. 114

37   Paul Dayton, *Correcting*, p. 146-147

38   William L. Shirer, *The Nightmare Years*, p. 64-65

39   Theodore S. Hamerow, *Restoration*, p. 194

40   Milton Friedman and Rose Friedman, *Free to Choose: A Personal Statement* (Orlando, FL: Harcourt, Inc., 1990), p 116

41   Alexis de Tocqueville, *Democracy in America: and Two Essays on America* (New York: Penguin Books, 2003), p. 71

42   Thomas Jefferson, *Writings* (New York, Literary Classics of the United States, Inc., 1984), p. 74-75; bold and italics added by PD

43   Paul Dayton, *Correcting*, chapter 14

44   Edward Channing, *A History of the United States, Volume II*, p. 247-249

45   Thomas Jefferson, *Writings* (New York, Literary Classics of the United States, Inc., 1984), p. 32

46   Ibid, p. 32-33

47   Christopher I. Beckwith, *Empires of the Silk Road*, p. 181

48   Ibid, p. 182

49   Henri Pirenne, *Economic and Social History of Medieval Europe* (Monee, IL: Harcourt, Inc., 1937), p. 98-102

50   William W. Lockwood, *The Economic Development of Japan*, p. 10 + p. 10, n. 9

51   Fox Butterfield, *China: Alive in a Bitter Sea, Revised and Updated* (New York: Times Books, 1990), p. 450

52   Ibid, p. 450

53   Ibid, p. 448-449

54   Stephen Kotkin, *Steeltown, USSR* (Berkeley and Los Angeles: University of California Press, 1991), p. 6+7

55   T.S. Ashton, *An Economic HIstory of England: The 18th Century* (London: Methuen & CO LTD, 1969), p. 21

56   Ibid, p. 47

57   Ibid, p. 56

58   Ibid, p. 10

59   Ibid, p. 11; bold and italics added by PD

60   Ibid, p. 11

61   Ibid, p. 20

62   Ibid, p. 17-18

63   Ibid, p. 17

64   Ibid, p. 18

65   Ibid, p. 21; brackets added by PD

66   Ivan T. Berend and Gyorgy Ranki, *The European Periphery & Industrialization 1780-1914* (Cambridge: Cambridge University Press, 1982), p. 26

67   Ibid, p. 28-29

68   T.S. Ashton, *An Economic HIstory of England: The 18th Century* (London: Methuen & CO LTD, 1969), p. 8

69   Ibid, p. 8

70   Christopher I. Beckwith, *Empires of the Silk Road*, p. 216

71   Ibid, p. 216, n. 33

72   Ibid, p. 216, n. 36

73   Ibid, p. 215

74   Edward Channing, *A History of the United States, Volume I*, p. 143

75   Christopher I. Beckwith, *Empires of the Silk Road*, p. 146

76   Ibid, p. 201-202

77   R.J. Hopper, *The Early Greeks* (New York: Harper & Row publishers Inc., 1977), p.103

78   Christopher I. Beckwith, *Empires of the Silk Road*, p. 58-60

79   Ibid, p. 73-75

80   Thomas Sowell, *Black Rednecks and White Liberals* (New York: Encounter Books, 2005), p. 172-174

81   Edward Channing, *A History of the United States, Volume I*, p. 10-11

82   Peter T. Bauer and Basil S. Yamey, *under-developed*, p. 42, n. 1

83   P.T. Bauer, *Equality, the Third World, and Economic Delusion* (Cambridge, Mass.: Harvard University Press, 1981), p. 72

84   Christopher I. Beckwith, *Empires of the Silk Road*, p. 220-221

85   M.M. Austin & P. Vidal-Naquet, *Economic & Social History of Ancient Greece: An Introduction* (Berkeley/Los Angeles: University of California Press, 1980), p. 223

86   Ibid, p. 54

87   Ibid, p. 55 + 207

88   Peter T. Bauer and Basil S. Yamey, *under-developed*, p. 104, n. 1

89   Ibid, p. 39 + 40

90   Christopher I. Beckwith, *Empires of the Silk Road*, p. 417, n. 87

91   Ibid, p. 87

92   Ralph W. Hidy and Muriel E. Hidy, *Pioneering*, p. 130

93   Timothy J. Shannon, *Iroquois Diplomacy on the Early American Frontier* (New York: Viking Penguin, 2008), p. 31

94   Henri Pirenne, *Medieval Europe*, p. 158; bold and italics added by PD

95   Ibid, p. 1-5

96   Ibid, p. 3, n. 3

97   Ibid, p. 7-8

98   Ibid, p. 8-12

99   Ibid, p. 10

100   Ibid, p. 11

101   P.T. Bauer, *Equality, the Third World, and Economic Delusion* (Cambridge, Mass.: Harvard University Press, 1981), p. 164-165

102   Frederick Pedler, *Main Currents of West African History 1940-1978* (London: The Macmillan Press LTD, 1979), p. 114-115

103   P.T. Bauer, *Equality, the Third World, and Economic Delusion* (Cambridge, Mass.: Harvard University Press, 1981), p. 167; bracket added by PD

104   Frederick Pedler, *Main Currents of West African History 1940-1978* (London: The Macmillan Press LTD, 1979), p. 81-82

105   P.T. Bauer, *Equality, the Third World, and Economic Delusion* (Cambridge, Mass.: Harvard University Press, 1981), p. 169

106   Frederick Pedler, *Main Currents of West African History 1940-1978* (London: The Macmillan Press LTD, 1979), p. 115-117

107   Henri Pirenne, *Medieval Europe*, p. 35

108   Ibid, p. 36

109   Ibid, p. 36-37

110   Ibid, p. 37

111   Ibid, p. 38

112   Ibid, p. 43

113   Ibid, p. 69-71

114   Ibid, p. 71-73

115   Ibid, p. 77-82

116   Ibid, p. 19-20

117   Christopher I. Beckwith, *Empires of the Silk Road*, p. 26; bold and italics added by PD

118   M.M. Austin & P. Vidal-Naquet, *Economic & Social History of Ancient Greece: An Introduction* (Berkeley/Los Angeles: University of California Press, 1980), p. 191

119   Ibid, p. 248-249 + 334-335

120   Christopher I. Beckwith, *Empires of the Silk Road*, p. 197-200

121   Timothy J. Shannon, *Iroquois Diplomacy on the Early American Frontier* (New York: Viking Penguin, 2008), p. 54

122   David O. Stewart, *American Emperor: Aaron Burr's Challenge to Jefferson's America* (New York: Simon & Schuster Paperbacks, 2012), p. 59-65

123   Christopher I. Beckwith, *Empires of the Silk Road*, p. 76; bold and italics added by PD

124   Ibid, p. 211-214

125   Henri Pirenne, *Medieval Europe*, p. 21

126   Ibid, p. 41-43

127   Ibid, p. 52-54

128   Ibid, p. 54-56

129   Ivan T. Berend and Gyorgy Ranki, *The European Periphery & Industrialization 1780-1914* (Cambridge: Cambridge University Press, 1982), p. 8-9

130   Christopher I. Beckwith, *Empires of the Silk Road*, p. 218; bold and italics added by PD

131   Ibid, p. 218

132   P.T. Bauer, *Equality, the Third World, and Economic Delusion* (Cambridge, Mass.: Harvard University Press, 1981), p. 71

133   Timothy J. Shannon, *Iroquois Diplomacy on the Early American Frontier* (New York: Viking Penguin, 2008), p. 34

134   Peter T. Bauer and Basil S. Yamey, *under-developed*, p. 107-108; brackets added by PD

135   M.M. Austin & P. Vidal-Naquet, *Economic & Social History of Ancient Greece: An Introduction* (Berkeley/Los Angeles: University of California Press, 1980), p. 99-101

136   Peter T. Bauer and Basil S. Yamey, *under-developed*, p. 106

137   Ibid, p. 107

138   Henri Pirenne, *Medieval Europe*, p. 44-46

139   Ibid, p. 50-51

140   Ibid, p. 48

141   Ibid, p. 82

142   M.M. Austin & P. Vidal-Naquet, *Economic & Social History of Ancient Greece: An Introduction* (Berkeley/Los Angeles: University of California Press, 1980), p. 236, n. 1

143   Ibid, p. 66-68

144   Ibid, p. 148

145   Paul Dayton, *Correcting*, chapter 11

146   T.S. Ashton, *An Economic HIstory of England: The 18th Century* (London: Methuen & CO LTD, 1969), p. 34

147   Ibid, p. 35

148   Ibid, p. 21; brackets added by PD

149   Oliver Stone, director. *Wall Street.* 20th Century Fox, 1987

150   Henri Pirenne, *Medieval Europe*, p. 161-162

151   Ibid, p. 92-95

152   Peter T. Bauer and Basil S. Yamey, *under-developed*, p. 62

153   Henri Pirenne, *Medieval Europe*, p. 63-64; bold and italics added by PD

154   Fox Butterfield, *China: Alive in a Bitter Sea, Revised and Updated* (New York: Times Books, 1990), p. 398-399

155   Peter T. Bauer and Basil S. Yamey, *under-developed*, p. 140

156   Ibid, p. 86, n. 1

157   Paul Dayton, *Correcting*, p. 24-25

158   T.S. Ashton, *An Economic HIstory of England: The 18th Century* (London: Methuen & CO LTD, 1969), p. 23

159   William L. Shirer, *The Nightmare Years*, p. 46

160   Timothy J. Shannon, *Iroquois Diplomacy on the Early American Frontier* (New York: Viking Penguin, 2008), p. 162-163

161   Ibid, p. 165

162   Bentley B. Gilbert, *The Evolution of National Insurance in Britain: The Origins of the Welfare State* (London: Michael Joseph Limited, 1966), p. 13-15

163   Ibid, p. 115

164   Ibid, p. 51-52; bold and italics added by PD

165   Stephen Kotkin, *Steeltown, USSR* (Berkeley and Los Angeles: University of California Press, 1991), p. 28

166   Karl Marx, *Das Kapital* (New Delhi: Prakash Books India Pvt. Ltd., 2023), p. 17

167   Ibid, p. 18

168   Ibid, p. 18

169   Carl L. Becker, *Modern History: The rise of a democratic, scientific, and industrialized civilization* (New York, Chicago, San Francisco: Silver Burdett Company, 1944), p. 535-536

170   M.M. Austin & P. Vidal-Naquet, *Economic & Social History of Ancient Greece: An Introduction* (Berkeley/Los Angeles: University of California Press, 1980), p. 150-151

171   Ibid, p. 16

172   Peter T. Bauer and Basil S. Yamey, *under-developed*, p. 110, n. 1

173   Theodore S. Hamerow, *Restoration*, p. 19-20

174   Ibid, p. 17-18

175   Ibid, p. 21-22

176   Ibid, p. 18

177   Ibid, p. 19

178   Frederick Pedler, *Main Currents of West African History 1940-1978* (London: The Macmillan Press LTD, 1979), p. 84

179   Sebastian Haffner, *The Ailing Empire: Germany from Bismark to Hitler* (New York: Fromm International Publishing Corporation, 1989), p. 64

180   Joseph A. Schumpeter, *Capitalism, Socialism and Democracy* (New York: Harper & Row, 1950), p. 48

181   Bernard DeVoto, *The Year of Decision: 1846* (Boston: Little, Brown and Company, 1943), p. 31-32

182   Ibid, p. 32-33

183   Peter T. Bauer and Basil S. Yamey, *under-developed*, p. 100-101

184   Stephen Kotkin, *Stalin: Waiting for Hitler 1929-1941* (New York: Penguin Press, 2017), p. 45

185   Ibid, p. 46

186   Ibid, p. 49-50

187   John F. Cogan and Kevin Warsh, "Reinvigorating Economic Governance: Advancing a New Framework for American Prosperity", Hoover Institution, (2022), p. 4-5, https://www.hoover.org/sites/default/files/research/docs/cogan-warsh_webreadypdf_220329.pdf

188   Edward Channing, *A History of the United States, Volume I*, p. 157-158

189   Ibid, p. 176-179

190   Ibid, p. 152

191   Ibid, p. 188

192   Ibid, p. 197

193   Ibid, p. 208-214

194   Ibid, p. 329-331

195   Fox Butterfield, *China: Alive in a Bitter Sea, Revised and Updated* (New York: Times Books, 1990), p. 447

196   Stephen Kotkin, *Steeltown, USSR* (Berkeley and Los Angeles: University of California Press, 1991), p. 20+21; bold and italics added by PD

Part VII   p. 416-467

1   Thomas Sowell, *Economic Facts and Fallacies* (New York: Basic Books, 2011), p. 35; bold and italics added by PD

2   *Macmillan's Modern Dictionary* (New York: The Macmillan Company, 1945), p. 622

3   *Reader's Digest Oxford Complete Wordfinder* (Pleasantville, NY: Oxford University Press, Inc., 1996) p. 854-855

4   *Roget's II: The New Thesaurus* (Boston: Houghton Mifflin Company, 1995), p. 842-843

5   *Macmillan's Modern Dictionary* (New York: The Macmillan Company, 1945), p. 992

6   Ibid, p. 201

7   *Reader's Digest Oxford Complete Wordfinder* (Pleasantville, NY: Oxford University Press, Inc., 1996) p.

8   Ibid, p. 298-299

9   Fox Butterfield, *China: Alive in a Bitter Sea, Revised and Updated* (New York: Times Books, 1990), p. 370-375

10   Theodore S. Hamerow, *Restoration, Revolution, Reaction: Economics and Politics in Germany, 1815-1871* (Princeton: Princeton University Press, 1972), p. 140

11   Ibid, p. 67

12   Ibid, p. 119-120

13   William L. Shirer, *20th Century Journey: A Memoir of a Life and the Times, Volume II: The Nightmare Years 1930-1940* (New York: Bantam Books, 1985), p. 79

14   Ibid, p. 73

15   Sebastian Haffner, *The Ailing Empire: Germany from Bismark to Hitler* (New York: Fromm International Publishing Corporation, 1989), p. 13

16   Theodore S. Hamerow, *Restoration*, p. 234-236

17   William L. Shirer, *Nightmare Years*, p. 66

18   Stephen Kotkin, *Stalin: Waiting for Hitler 1929-1941* (New York: Penguin Press, 2017), p. 51-52

19   Haffner, *Ailing Empire*, p. 173

20   Ibid, p. 176

21   Ibid, p. 171-172

22   Alexis de Tocqueville, *Democracy in America: and Two Essays on America* (New York: Penguin Books, 2003), p. 103

23 Ronald "Dutch" Reagan, 8:30-8:50, first press conference in room 450 of the OEOB, January 29, 1981. Reagan Library. Transposed from audio to text by PD.

24 William L. Shirer, *Nightmare Years*, p. 148-149

25 Ibid, p. 422

26 Bentley B. Gilbert, *The Evolution of National Insurance in Britain: The Origins of the Welfare State* (London: Michael Joseph Limited, 1966), p. 124

27 Haffner, *Ailing Empire*, p. 132

28 Bentley B. Gilbert, *The Evolution of National Insurance in Britain: The Origins of the Welfare State* (London: Michael Joseph Limited, 1966), p. 116

29 R.R. Palmer and Joel Colton, *A History of the Modern World* (New York: Alfred A. Knopf, Inc., 1965), p. 339

30 Ibid, p. 485

31 D.T. Armentano. Ph. D., *Myths of Antitrust: Economic Theory and Legal Cases* (New Rochelle: Arlington House, 1972), p. 19

32 Theodore S. Hamerow, *Restoration*, p. 146

33 Edward Channing, *A History of the United States, Volume II, A Century of Colonial History 1660-1760* (New York: The Macmillan Company, 1908), p. 118

34 Ibid, p. 116, n. 2

35 R.R. Palmer and Joel Colton, *A History of the Modern World* (New York: Alfred A. Knopf, Inc., 1965), p. 800; bold and italics added by PD

36 P.T. Bauer, *Equality, the Third World, and Economic Delusion* (Cambridge, Mass.: Harvard University Press, 1981), p. 189

37 Peter T. Bauer and Basil S. Yamey, *The Economics of Under-developed Countries* (Chicago: The University of Chicago Press, 1957), p. 46

38 Henri Pirenne, *Economic and Social History of Medieval Europe* (Monee, IL: Harcourt, Inc., 1937), p. 12-13

39 Ibid, p. 13

40 Ivan T. Berend and Gyorgy Ranki, *The European Periphery & Industrialization 1780-1914* (Cambridge: Cambridge University Press, 1982), p. 11; bold and italics added by PD

41   Ibid, p. 15-16

42   Guy Sorman, *Economics Does Not Lie: A Defense of the Free Market* (New York: Encounter Books, 2009), p. 28

43   Stephen Kotkin, *Stalin: Waiting for Hitler 1929-1941* (New York: Penguin Press, 2017), p. 34-36

44   Ibid, p. 36-37

45   Ibid, p. 37-38

46   R.R. Palmer and Joel Colton, *A History of the Modern World* (New York: Alfred A. Knopf, Inc., 1965), p. 808 + 809

47   Bentley B. Gilbert, *The Evolution of National Insurance in Britain: The Origins of the Welfare State* (London: Michael Joseph Limited, 1966), p. 111-112

48   Ibid, p. 117-118

49   Ibid, p. 72 + p.72, n. 26

50   F.A. Hayek, The Collected Works of F.A. Hayek, Volume II: *The Road to Serfdom, Text and Documents, The Definitive Edition* (London: The University of Chicago Press, 2007), p. 131; bold and italics added by PD

51   Ibid, p. 131, n. 5; bold and italics added by PD

52   Edward Channing, *A History of the United States Volume 3: History of the Colonization of the United States by George Bancroft. Vol. III. Seventeenth Edition* (Boston: Little, Brown, and Company, 1862), p. 397

53   Joseph A. Schumpeter, *Capitalism, Socialism and Democracy* (New York: Harper & Row, 1950), p. 95

54   Ibid, p. 63

55   Ibid, p. 64

56   Paul Dayton, *Correcting Our Financial Miseducation: Raising the Bar for the Average* (USA: ISBN: 9798726908755, 2021), chapter 14

57   Joseph A. Schumpeter, *Capitalism, Socialism and Democracy* (New York: Harper & Row, 1950), p. 64-65

58   R.R. Palmer and Joel Colton, *A History of the Modern World* (New York: Alfred A. Knopf, Inc., 1965), p. 811-812

59   Ibid, p. 812; bold and italics added by PD

60   Ibid, p. 813; bold and italics added by PD

61   Fox Butterfield, *China: Alive in a Bitter Sea*, p. 414; bold and italics added by PD

62   Joseph A. Schumpeter, *Capitalism, Socialism and Democracy* (New York: Harper & Row, 1950), p. 106

63   Paul Dayton, *Correcting Our Financial Miseducation: Raising the Bar for the Average* (USA: ISBN: 9798726908755, 2021), p. 90-96, 160-163, 182-183

64   Ralph W. Hidy and Muriel E. Hidy, *Pioneering in Big Business 1882-1911* (New York: Harper & Brothers, 1955), p. 132-133

65   Ibid, p. 133

66   Ibid, p. 133-134

67   Ibid, p. 135; bold and italics added by PD

68   Joseph A. Schumpeter, *Capitalism, Socialism and Democracy* (New York: Harper & Row, 1950), p. 107

69   Alfred Marshall, *Principles of Economics: An Introductory Volume* (USA: Digireads.com, 2012), p. 27-28; bold and italics added by PD

70   William W. Lockwood, *The Economic Development of Japan: Growth and Structural Change 1868-1938* (Princeton: Princeton University Press, 1954), p. 525

71   Alexis de Tocqueville, *Democracy in America: and Two Essays on America* (New York: Penguin Books, 2003), p. 104

72   M.M. Austin & P. Vidal-Naquet, *Economic & Social History of Ancient Greece: An Introduction* (Berkeley/Los Angeles: University of California Press, 1980), p. 41

73   Allan Nevins, *John D. Rockefeller: a One-Volume Abridgement* (New York: Charles Scriber's Sons, 1959), p. 207

74   Milton Friedman, "Why Government is the Problem", Hoover Institution (1993): p.7-9; bold and italics added by PD.
https://2305951.fs1.hubspotusercontent-na1.net/hubfs/2305951/2022%20Offers/Note%20from%20Greg%20PDF%20Updates/Why%20Government%20eBook.pdf?utm_campaign=Why%20Government%20Is%20the%20Problem&utm_medium=email&_hsmi=173347367&_hsenc=p2ANqtz-8Lkk4uMncBw3XfzYOIxm-l9CxNT8c-PgDht6QfWfB-WOAljFdbxE_mr8XRt2nzWozPXCXM_ArW-nOghszBmgOTyIvvFw&utm_content=173347367&utm_source=hs_automation

75   veniceinsiderguide.com

76   Henri Pirenne, *Economic and Social History of Medieval Europe* (Monee, IL: Harcourt, Inc., 1937), p. 26-27; bold and italics added by PD

77   Ibid, p. 27-28

78   Frank Dikotter, *The Tragedy of Liberation: A History of the Chinese Revolution 1945-1957* (London: Bloomsbury, 2017), preface, p. xii

79   Eric Foner, *Reconstruction: America's Unfinished Revolution, 1863-1867* (New York: Harper & Row, 2014), p. 70

80   Henri Pirenne, *Economic and Social History of Medieval Europe* (Monee, IL: Harcourt, Inc., 1937), p. 64-66

81   F.A. Hayek, *The Road to Serfdom*, p. 132; bold and italics added by PD

82   Henri Pirenne, *Economic and Social History of Medieval Europe* (Monee, IL: Harcourt, Inc., 1937), p. 116-139

83   Edward Channing, *A History of the United States, Volume I, The Planting of a Nation in the New World 1000-1660* (New York: The Macmillan Company, 1907), p. 524-525

84   Theodore S. Hamerow, *Restoration*, p. 111

85   *Firing Line with William F. Buckley.* Episode 52, Recorded on March 9, 1967. 6:10-6:30. https://www.youtube.com/watch?v=AWKRWgA7TVE&list=PLBD8B324842097EA2&index=25

86   usgovernmentspending.com

87   Theodore S. Hamerow, *Restoration*, p. 211-212

88   Alexis de Tocqueville, *Democracy in America: and Two Essays on America* (New York: Penguin Books, 2003), p. 158-161; bold and italics added by PD

89   Thomas Jefferson, *Writings* (New York, Literary Classics of the United States, Inc., 1984), p. 73; brackets added by PD

90   Theodore S. Hamerow, *Restoration*, p. 131

91   Haffner, *Ailing Empire*, p. 28

92   Edward Channing, *A History of the United States, Volume II, A*

Century of Colonial History 1660-1760 (New York: The Macmillan Company, 1908), p. 246

93   Bentley B. Gilbert, *The Evolution of National Insurance in Britain: The Origins of the Welfare State* (London: Michael Joseph Limited, 1966), p. 13-15

94   Ibid, p. 25-26

95   R.R. Palmer and Joel Colton, *A History of the Modern World* (New York: Alfred A. Knopf, Inc., 1965), p. 347

96   Stephen Kotkin, *Stalin: Waiting for Hitler 1929-1941* (New York: Penguin Press, 2017), p. 16

97   Fox Butterfield, *China: Alive in a Bitter Sea*, p. 470; bold and italics added by PD

SUBJECT INDEX

East Turkistan, 288

Egypt, 85, 202, 240, 259, 277, 279, 280, 294, 376, 395

England, 38, 53, 68, 79, 85, 87, 104, 122, 142, 181, 182, 198-200, 206, 207, 212, 219, 242, 247, 250, 251, 253, 257, 263, 267, 270, 271, 285, 286, 294, 296, 300, 301, 309, 311, 317, 318, 322, 323, 326, 328, 340, 349, 352, 352, 358, 362, 366-369, 377, 380, 394-396, 401, 403, 404, 413-415, 428, 429, 433, 434, 436, 437, 455, 466

Ericsson, Leif, 286

Europe, Medieval, 68, 78, 195, 350, 363, 381, 397-399, 448, 452, 454

Executive Directory, 131, 132

Fallacy of the Lamp, 15, 68, 99, 147, 177, 181, 197, 204, 206, 211, 214, 230, 351

First World War (see also: WWI, The Great War), 83, 88, 140-143, 289, 403, 429, 440, 441

Flagler, Henry, 44

Flanders, Belgium, 79, 380, 381, 394, 395

Foner, Eric, 272

Foreign Aid, 92, 310

France, 13, 30, 73, 74, 81, 84, 93-139, 142, 149, 151, 160, 187, 204, 205, 244, 286, 299, 318, 326, 338, 342, 354, 368, 395, 419, 420, 430, 431, 437, 467

Franklin, Benjamin, 269, 339

Franks, 281, 283, 380

Free Blacks, USA pre-1860, 27, 248, 263, 266, 267

Friedman, Milton, 202, 401, 446, 448

Gaul , 281

General Interest, The, 68, 76, 82, 163, 354, 451, 460, 462

Genoa, 232, 284, 381

Germany, 13, 73-75, 77, 81, 86, 92, 134, 139-151, 182, 187-196, 203, 205, 213, 214, 218, 220, 226, 227, 235, 246, 354, 358, 395, 396, 408, 409, 418-420, 430, 431, 435, 437, 455, 458, 466

Made in the USA
Monee, IL
31 December 2024

72545611R00299